PARK

The Global Information Society

Wiley Series in Information Systems

PREVIOUS VOLUMES IN THE SERIES

The Global Information Society

WENDY CURRIE

JOHN WILEY & SONS, LTD

Chichester · New York · Weinheim · Brisbane · Singapore · Toronto

Reprinted November 2000

Other Wiley Editorial Offices

John Wiley & Sons, Inc., 605 Third Avenue,
New York, NY 10158-0012, USA

WILEY-VCH Verlag GmbH, Pappelallee 3,
D-69469 Weinheim, Germany

Jacaranda Wiley Ltd, 33 Park Road, Milton,
Queensland 4064, Australia

John Wiley & Sons (Asia) Pte Ltd, 2 Clementi Loop #02-01,
Jin Xing Distripark, Singapore 129809

John Wiley & Sons (Canada) Ltd, 22 Worcester Road,
Rexdale, Ontario M9W 1L1, Canada

British Library Cataloguing in Publication Data

A catalogue record for this book is available from the British Library

ISBN 0-471-89507-5

Typeset in 10/12 pt Palatino by C.K.M. Typesetting, Salisbury, Wiltshire.
Printed and bound in Great Britain by Bookcraft (Bath) Ltd, Midsomer Norton, Somerset.
This book is printed on acid-free paper responsibly manufactured from sustainable forestry,
in which at least two trees are planted for each one used for paper production.

Wiley Series in Information Systems

To Christopher and William

Contents

Series Preface

The information systems community has grown considerably since 1984, when we began publishing the Wiley Series in Information Systems. We are pleased to be a part of the growth of the field, and believe that this series of books is playing an important role in the intellectual development of the discipline. The primary objective of the series is to publish scholarly works that reflect the best of the research in the information systems community. We are specifically interested in those works that are relevant to the practice of IS. To this end, Wendy Currie's text, *The Global Information Society*, is an excellent example.

The book offers a detailed treatment of the major issues confronting individuals, organisations and society as we move into the next millennium. In her book, Professor Currie addresses the key issues facing the emergence of the global information society. She explores the role of government, business and the individual in the global information society; Internet commerce; new opportunities for business and commerce; globalisation, standardisation and interoperability; organisation, management and control; strategic management, outsourcing and re-engineering; developing new competencies, capabilities and skills; and managing the corporation of the next millennium. These are extremely important issues for the success of our society in the future and we welcome Professor Currie's insights on them. There is no doubt that this book should be of interest to practitioners and academics alike.

Rudy Hirschheim

Preface

This book explores some of the major organisational, managerial and technical changes within industry and commerce in the last few decades. In conjunction with the rapid pace of technical change, a proliferation of management innovation and change panaceas have emerged from total quality management (TQM) to business process re-engineering (BPR) and, more recently, the knowledge worker. The practical worth of these panaceas to managers and technical specialists alike is the subject of much debate, particularly as each one seems to be superceded by another one within two to five years. In this book we look at the phenomenon of the global information society in the context of market, technology, management practice, capabilities and skills and the role of government. The primary objective is not to find definitive answers to complex business problems, but to raise key issues and concerns facing managers in coping with large-scale organisational change.

The book is intended for final year students on undergraduate and postgraduate courses in management and information systems, and specialist modules in these areas on MBA programmes and short courses. At Brunel University, the book is used on the Information Systems: Strategy and Management module for final year undergraduates on the BSc Information Systems course and on other joint honours degrees. Since these students undertake placements in industry, they are able to apply some of the theories and practices discussed. The nine chapters are divided into themes to include the growth and development of Internet commerce, management innovation and change panaceas, IT outsourcing and capabilities, and skills for the global information society. Case studies help to illustrate the issues and concerns raised in each chapter. An overview of the book is given below.

Chapter 1 begins with an overview of the emerging global information society. It explores the growing phenomenon of the Internet, World Wide Web (WWW) and electronic commerce. In particular, it examines definitions of e-commerce, some of the surveys on the growth and development of the Internet, and new models and frameworks for doing business in a virtual environment. Chapter 2 continues this theme by identifying 10 key challenges in the development of

Internet commerce. Whilst some of the literature tends to simplify the issues and concerns related to this topic, this discussion is intended to show that each of the 10 areas is complex and requires detailed strategies and plans. Chapter 3 covers the important subject of the role of government in defining a legal and regulatory framework for Internet commerce. Here we consider some cross-national comparisons on the diffusion of electronic commerce, noting in particular the relative advance of the United States compared with Europe. Chapter 4 continues to explore Internet commerce in the context of a market analysis. The chapter looks at popular examples of companies which are using the Internet to enhance their strategic position, namely the Dell Corporation, Cisco Systems and Federal Express. These examples provide useful insights for other companies wishing to maximise the market potential of the Internet. The theme of gaining competitive advantage from business-to-consumer Internet commerce is explored in Chapter 5. Some of the new theories and frameworks are considered, such as whether Internet commerce will generate a power shift from the supplier to the customer. In addition, the new economics of the Internet are examined. This hypothesis assumes that companies that exploit the potential of the Internet will reduce operating costs for the benefit of the customer.

Chapter 6 moves on to discuss the proliferation of management innovation and change panaceas that have emerged in the last few decades. The chapter attempts to show that new ideas in management thinking are largely developed from previous ones. Whilst they may offer a fresh analysis to current market, technical and managerial issues and concerns, they tend to be short lived and superceded by the next all-encompassing panacea. This has certainly been the case with TQM and BPR since both have now been eclipsed by the knowledge worker thesis. To some extent, the virtual organisation is yet another panacea, which may prove to be more of a theory than a reality over time. Chapter 7 raises the subject of IT outsourcing, which has proven to be a popular research area in recent years. Whilst the concept of outsourcing is not new, and is linked to ideas of make versus buy (i.e. whether companies should provide products and services in-house or source them from external suppliers), this discussion explores the different approaches adopted by companies towards outsourcing and insourcing. Detailed case studies are used which explore four types of sourcing arrangement: total outsourcing, multiple/selective sourcing, joint venture/project sourcing, and insourcing. It is therefore the task of companies to determine which arrangement suits their market, organisational, managerial and technical requirements. Chapter 8 continues the theme of IT outsourcing by examining the strategic positioning of companies in the software and computing services industry. Whilst outsourcing is often viewed from the point of view of client companies, it is equally important to understand the market strategies of service providers, particularly since this affects the client–supplier relationship. Chapter 9 concludes with a discussion of the capabilities and skills needed for the global information economy. A key issue is about determining the competencies required for managing the IT function, especially in a virtual organisation. This chapter considers the IS skills shortage crisis and looks at ways in which the culture gap between IT and business may be narrowed as we move into the twenty-first century.

GLOSSARY

APEC (Asia-Pacific Economic Cooperation)
APNIC (Asia-Pacific Network Information Centre)
APT (Asia-Pacific Telecommunity)
ARIN (American Registry for Internet Numbers)
ASEAN (Association of Southeast Asian Nations)
BIAC (Business and Industry Advisory Committee)
CITEL (Comisiœn Interamericana de Telecommunicaciones)
DVB (Digital Video Broadcasting Group)
EFF (Electronic Frontier Foundation)
ETSI (European Telecommunications Standardisation Institute)
FNC (Federal Networking Council)
GIP (Global Internet Project)
gTLD-MoU (Generic Top Level Domain Memorandum of Understanding)
IAB (Internet Architecture Board)
IANA (Internet Assigned Numbers Authority)
ICC (International Chamber of Commerce)
IESG (The Internet Engineering Steering Group)
IETF (Internet Engineering Task Force)
INTA (International Trademark Association)
InterNIC (Internet Network Information Centre)
ISO (International Organisation for Standardisation)
ISOC (Internet Society)
ITU (International Telecommunications Union)
MERCOSUR (Mercado Comun del Sur)
NAFTA (North American Free Trade Agreement)
NCC-RIPE (RIPE Network Coordination Centre)
NSF (National Science Foundation)
NSI (Network Solutions Incorporated)
OAS (Organisation of American States)
OECD (Organisation for Economic Cooperation and Development)
PANAFTEL (Pan-African Telecommunications Network)
PATU (Pan-African Telecommunications Union)
POC (Policy Oversight Committee)
RASCOM (Regional African Satellite Communications Organisation)
RIPE (Réseaux IP Européens)
TABD (Trans-Atlantic Business Dialogue)

UMTS—Forum (Univeral Mobile Telecommunications System—Forum)
UN (United Nations)
UN/ECA (United Nations Economic Commission for Africa)
UN/ECE (United Nations Economic Commission for Europe)
UNCITRAL (United Nations Commission on International Trade Law)
UNCTAD (United Nations Conference on Trade and Development)
UNDP (United Nations Development Programme)
UNESCO (United Nations Educational, Scientific and Cultural Organisation)
W^3C (World Wide Web Consortium)
WIPO (World Intellectual Property Organisation)
WRC (World Radiocommunications Conference)
WTO (World Trade Organisation)

1
The Emerging Global Information Society (GIS)

INTRODUCTION

The last 30 years have witnessed profound changes in strategy, structure, culture, management and technology in global private and public sector organisations. Pundits who witnessed the introduction of the personal computer (PC) in the early 1980s claimed this was the most significant change since the industrial revolution two centuries before. The introduction of the PC two decades ago generated new fears as some believed this would lead to the 'collapse of work' through massive job losses in the manufacturing and financial services sectors (Currie, 1995b). Coupled with this, new management methods and techniques were introduced.[1] The 1980s saw the emergence of total quality management (TQM) and just-in-time (JIT). Whilst the former had been developed in the United States after the post-war period (Rao *et al.*, 1996), it had been successfully transported to Japan (Schonberger, 1982). It was then *imported* back to the United States to tackle problems of economic and industrial decline in the manufacturing sector. It also became popular in Europe during this period. Similarly, JIT was seen as a useful way of resolving problems of poor performance and low productivity in manufacturing. So during the 1980s, several methods and techniques were used to assist management in their attempts to introduce the latest technologies such as computer-aided design (CAD), computer-aided manufacture (CAM), robotics and flexible manufacturing systems (FMS), etc. to compete internationally. The managerial focus during this decade was largely to downsize and de-layer companies combining methods and techniques with new technologies.

But although the technology at the time seemed revolutionary, many companies failed to exploit it fully (Currie, 1989). There were many examples of technical disasters, as some companies embarked upon ambitious management and technical change programmes without having a clearly defined strategy for meeting the business, operational and technical objectives. Technology was often seen as the panacea that would lead to competitive advantage, yet many companies experienced the technology–productivity paradox (David, 1999). In other words, the greater the expenditure on technology, the less productivity was achieved. During the 1990s, companies had gained more experience of evaluating the benefits from technology, and so were more cautious in making new capital investments. However, new pressures emerged during this decade in the form of increased global competition, de-regulation and more affordable and improved technology. The earlier emphasis upon downsizing and cost-cutting in the 1980s tended to shift towards performance measurement and customer service in the 1990s. Some companies had downsized and de-layered so much that they realised that some parts of their business had become fragmented, dysfunctional and inefficient. As a result, it became important to develop tools and techniques to measure performance. Activity based costing (ABC) was a cost management system developed to identify the real cost of all business activities, with the particular emphasis upon identifying variable costs. During the same decade, companies started to restructure or re-engineer their business processes. Traditional functional organisational structures had been replaced by product and matrix structures during the 1980s. But the 1990s demanded even more ambitious organisational structures in the form of the networked organisation.

Facilities management (FM)—where a company hands over the responsibility for the management and maintenance of a data centre or mainframe computer to a third party supplier, popular in the 1970s and 1980s—was replaced by the more ambitious IT outsourcing in the 1990s. During this decade, a number of mega deals were signed between client and supplier, often totalling more than US$1bn and lasting up to 10 years. So the management of technology has further undergone major changes. In recent years, the Internet, WWW and e-commerce have become the new panaceas for change in the business world. Today's pundits talk about another revolution in the form of the digital or information age (Gates, 1999). This view assumes that information flow will be the primary *differentiator* for business. The logic is that companies have hitherto focused upon restructuring, quality, productivity, supply chain management, culture and learning, and so now they should consider information as a strategic resource. This chapter is divided into four sections. First, we consider how the global information society (GIS)[2] has evolved in the last 30 years. In particular, we look at the emerging new technologies, which have enabled this change, such as the Internet and WWW. We explore some of the literature, which suggests that the Internet will change the shape of business as companies develop e-commerce. Second, we examine various definitions of e-commerce, which have emerged in recent years. Third, we consider some recent surveys on the development and growth of e-commerce. These surveys are speculative and all point to a massive growth in e-commerce in the short term. Fourth, we discuss some of the models and frameworks on e-commerce.

THE EMERGING GLOBAL INFORMATION SOCIETY

The last 30 years have witnessed unprecedented changes in the structure, management and technology of companies. According to Bill Gates, Chairman of

Microsoft, 'Business is going to change more in the next ten years than it has in the last fifty' (Gates, 1999).[1]

This thesis assumes that changes in the workplace will accelerate over the next two decades as a consequence of rapid progress with information and telecommunications technologies (Apgar, 1998).

An overview of the business drivers for change from the 1980s to the present suggests a shift in management thinking, enabling technologies, human resources practices, supply chain management and many more (Folt, 1996). Table 1.1 tracks some of these changes. For example, TQM and JIT, once very popular in the 1980s, have now become eclipsed by the concepts of knowledge management and the virtual organisation. Similarly, the technologies that enable corporate change have moved on. Two decades ago, CAD/CAM and robotics seemed to be the focus of much attention. Today, it is the Internet and WWW.

Other changes in emphasis involve human resources to organisational structure (Orlikowski, 1999). Human resources specialists tended to focus upon multitasking and flexibility during the 1980s. This has shifted to looking at the knowledge worker. The sourcing of IT has also changed from looking at facilities management (mainly of data centre and mainframe technologies) to business process outsourcing. The latter is a much more ambitious approach in that a third party supplier (or group of suppliers) takes control of a client's business processes. This may include payroll, help desk, recruitment, cheque processing services, or even IT strategy, planning and implementation. Customer–supplier relationships have also changed from being distant or non-integrated, to fully integrated in some cases. For example, in many cases of large-scale outsourcing, it is difficult to delineate responsibilities between client and supplier, particularly where the latter is involved in strategic elements of the client's business. The financial focus of companies has also tended to shift from one of cost-cutting and downsizing to one that aims to gain value. With the Internet and WWW, much of the focus is upon disintermediation—a process where obsolete levels of bureaucracy in the form of middlemen can be eliminated. This enables the customer to go direct to the supplier to purchase goods and services.

Hagel and Armstrong (1997, p. 84) have attempted to capture the evolving virtual community by identifying four stages: virtual villages, concentrated constellations, cosmic coalitions and integrated intermediaries (Table 1.2). They suggest that it is important for companies to understand how the virtual community will evolve, especially if profitability is going to be sustained. They claim that virtual communities will emerge from a highly fragmented group of businesses to a much more concentrated industry. During the initial stages, they claim that value creation and capture shifts from advertisers and vendors—where much of the value has resided prior to the advent of virtual communities—to the level of the community organiser. They stress that, 'at this level, the potential for value capture will be highest for organisers of "core" communities who mobilise and lock in broader constellations of more specialised communities'.

The authors claim that the stages of evolution in virtual communities will not be linear. They argue that organisers who perceive industry structure in a specific way may find that the 'virtual ground beneath them shifts in unanticipated ways'. They

Table 1.1 Business drivers in the emerging global information society

Business drivers for change	1980s	1990s	2000+
Key management concepts/ideas	Total quality management (TQM) Just-in-time (JIT)	Business process re-engineering Process innovation Organisational learning Activity based costing (ABC)	Knowledge management Virtual organisation
Enabling technology	Mainframe, personal computer (PC), CAD/CAM, robotics	Networked and distributed computing, decision support systems (DSS)	WWW, Internet, electronic commerce (e-commerce)
Human resources	Multi-tasking, flexibility	Core competencies, empowerment	Knowledge workers
Supplier chain management	Physical distribution	Semi-automated	Electronic distribution
IT sourcing	Facilities management	IT outsourcing	Business process outsourcing
Business goal	Competitive advantage	Customer care	Consumer choice
Management	IT directors/managers	Hybrid managers	Relationship management
Technical focus	Data capture/control	Information management	Intellectual property protection
Customer–supplier relationship	Non-integrated, distant	Semi-integrated	Fully integrated
Financial focus	Cost-cutting, downsizing	Performance measurement, process integration	Value added, disintermediation
Organisational structure	Functional, product, matrix organisations	De-layered, flat, networked organisations	Internet-enabled extended enterprise, virtual organisations

Table 1.2 *Four stages in the evolution of the virtual community*

Stage of evolution	Description	Key assumptions
Virtual villages	Communities are highly fragmented but profitable businesses, each containing multiple, small subcommunities	Low barriers to entry Many entrants Vendors participate across multiple communities Network users sample across multiple communities
Concentrated constellations	Concentration of core communities, and development of affiliate relationships with niche communities	Increasing returns lead to concentration within 'core' topics, such as travel Niche communities benefit from affiliating with core communities
Cosmic coalitions	Core communities aggregate across complementary core topic areas	Members find value in formation of coalitions, around common user interface and billing Coalition organisers realise economic value by integrating marketing programmes and member/vendor profiles across areas
Integrated infomediaries	Communities and coalitions evolve into agents for members, managing their integrated profiles to maximise value to members	Members themselves represent the most efficient location for capture of profiles Members assert ownership over their profiles Specialised infomediaries can organise and maximise value of member profiles

Adapted from: Hagel and Armstrong (1997).

suggest that, 'those who keep their eyes (and investments) focused on member acquisition, information capture, and emerging growth opportunities are likely to profit the most from the changes' (p. 82).

Despite claims of the emerging virtual community and how it will change the shape of industry structures and cultures, the digital or information revolution is still in its early stages. Growth is likely to accelerate in the near future in vertical markets, not least in the software and computing services industry, as the number of people connected to the Internet multiplies and as its commercial potential expands. According to a recent US government report, four types of economic activity will drive the growth:

1. *Building out the Internet.* In 1994, three million people, most of them in the United States, used the Internet. In 1998, 100 million people around the world used the Internet. Some experts believe that one billion people may be connected to the Internet by 2005. This expansion is driving dramatic increases in computer, software, services and communications investments.

2. *Electronic commerce among businesses.* Businesses began using the Internet for commercial transactions with their business partners about two years ago. Early users already report significant productivity improvements from using electronic networks to create, buy, distribute, sell, and service products and services. By 2002, the Internet may be used for more than US$300 billion worth of commerce between businesses.
3. *Digital delivery of goods and services.* Software programs, newspapers, and music CDs no longer need to be packaged and delivered to stores, homes or news kiosks. They can be delivered electronically over the Internet. Airline tickets and securities transactions over the Internet already occur in large numbers. Other industries such as consulting services, entertainment, banking and insurance, education and health care face some hurdles but are also beginning to use the Internet to change the way they do business. Over time, the sale and transmission of goods and services electronically is likely to be the largest and most visible driver of the new digital economy.
4. *Retail sale of tangible goods.* The Internet can also be used to order tangible goods and services that are produced, stored and physically delivered. Though Internet sales are less than 1% of total retail sales today, sales of certain products such as computers, software, cars, books and flowers are growing rapidly (US Department of Commerce, 1999, Forrester Research, 1997a,b).

Hagel and Armstrong (1997) identify four scenarios in the development of the virtual community. This offers a typology of the relationship between market dynamics and market structure in the virtual community. Market dynamics refers to change, flexibility, speed, companies and start-ups. Market structure refers to regulation, control, taxes and bureaucracy. The four scenarios are

*   customer driven,
*   supplier driven,
*   emerging markets, and
*   monopoly driven.

These authors describe the development of the virtual community as an 'evolving battle with enormous stakes' (Hagel and Armstrong, 1997, p. 109). They stress that, 'What is really at issue is who will own the customer, at least on networks and perhaps even more broadly.'

DEFINITIONS OF ELECTRONIC COMMERCE

The terms Internet, World Wide Web (WWW) and electronic commerce[3] are often used interchangeably in the existing academic and practitioner literature. The Internet first appeared as 'browser' software (the client of the system) in late 1993. This tool became the catalyst that launched the Internet into the commercial domain. The WWW and electronic mail (e-mail) are the most commercially used aspects of the entire network (Gray, M., 1996). A number of competing definitions of electronic commerce are found in the literature, with some suggesting that it encompasses all forms of electronic interaction between businesses. This definition tends to overlook the role of the consumer. Similarly, International Data Corporation (IDC) claim that, 'Electronic commerce is broadly defined as the exchange of business documents in an electronic format' (IDC, 1998a). Another definition is that electronic commerce is 'a broad term describing business activities with associated technical data that are conducted electronically'. A wider definition is that, 'the goal of electronic commerce is to mould the vast network of small businesses, government agencies, large corporations, and independent contractors into a single community with the ability to communicate with one another seamlessly across any computer platform' (Electronic Commerce Resource Centre, 1996). Other writers offer a more detailed definition. For example, Kalakota and Whinston (1997, p. 3) give four definitions of electronic commerce which encompass *communications, businesses processes, services* and from an *on-line* perspective. These authors claim that, in essence, electronic commerce 'emphasises the generation and exploitation of new business opportunities' and, to use popular phrases: 'generate business value' or 'do more with less'.

Companies also offer definitions of electronic commerce with British Telecom suggesting that it involves, 'the use of network computing and the Internet for commercial transactions' (Mike Lewis—marketing manager for BT). Another company, IBM, adopt the term e-business which is 'when you combine the broad reach of the Internet with the vast resources of traditional information technology systems'.[4]

Types of E-Commerce

Whilst there are many definitions of e-commerce in the literature, there are also different forms of e-commerce. For example, Kalakota and Whinston (1997, p. 18) give three types of e-commerce:

- inter-organisational—business to business
- intra-organisational (within business)
- customer to business

At the most basic level, e-commerce is about doing business electronically. It is based on the electronic processing and transmission of data, including text, sound and video. It includes activities such as electronic trading of goods and services, on-line delivery of digital content, electronic fund transfers, electronic share trading, electronic bills of lading, commercial auctions, collaborative design and engineering, on-line sourcing, public procurement, direct consumer marketing, and after-sales service. It involves both products (e.g. consumer goods, specialised medical equipment) and services (e.g. information services, financial and legal services); traditional activities (e.g. healthcare, education) and new activities (e.g. virtual malls). E-commerce is not a new phenomenon. For many years companies have exchanged business data over a variety of communication networks. But there is now accelerated expansion and radical changes, driven by the exponential growth of the Internet. Until recently no more than a business-to-business activity on closed proprietary networks, electronic commerce is now rapidly expanding into a complex Web of commercial activities transacted on a global scale between an ever-increasing number of participants, corporate and individual, known and unknown, on global open networks such as the Internet (Kalakota and Whinston, 1997).

Table 1.3 explores the change from traditional e-commerce to future e-commerce. In the former, companies have tended to deal mainly with their suppliers using closed proprietary networks. The scope has been industry or business sector specific. For example, a car manufacturer has procured goods from its suppliers in a relatively restricted market. In contrast, e-commerce of the future will be a fully global approach. In this scenario, more forms of e-commerce will emerge to include business-to-business, business-to-consumer and business-to-public administration. The latter development will involve central and local governments (and other public bodies) introducing systems to serve the public. For example, by 2002, 25% of UK government services will be accessible electronically. In addition, by March 2001, 90% by volume of routine procurement of goods by central government will be conducted electronically (HMSO, 1998). Through extending the global reach of markets, the network will enable companies to procure goods and services internationally. Consumers will also be able to do the same. Key issues will involve security and trust, particularly where goods and services are procured from companies without a strong market presence, such as virtual companies (DTI, 1999a).

There are two types of activities related to e-commerce.

- *Direct e-commerce*, e.g. the on-line ordering, payment and delivery of intangible goods and services such as computer software, entertainment content, or information services on a global scale.
- *Indirect e-commerce*, e.g. the electronic ordering of tangible goods, which are physically delivered using traditional channels, such as postal services or commercial couriers.

The same company may use direct and indirect e-commerce. For example, a company may sell software on-line as well as off the shelf. It is therefore possible to download software updates from a supplier. This saves time and money for both customer and supplier. Indirect e-commerce depends upon external factors, such as a well-developed infrastructure, e.g. a transportation system. Direct e-commerce, on the other hand, is a seamless approach, which enables end-to-end electronic transactions across geographical boundaries. So the global reach of direct e-commerce is international.

Clearly, there are many competing definitions of e-commerce—a factor that only serves to confuse those trying to make sense of the Internet and the WWW and their potential for developing new business and re-engineering, or even eliminating, traditional ways of doing business. Having offered some definitions of e-commerce, the following section gives an overview of some of the existing forecasts on the growth of Internet access, markets and revenue streams and companies currently doing business on the Internet. As we shall see, these forecasts are wide-ranging and often based more on pure speculation and hype than on a detailed and

Table 1.3 *From traditional e-commerce to future Internet commerce*

	Traditional e-commerce	**Future e-commerce**
Type	Business-to-business	Business-to-business Business-to-consumer Business-to-public administration User-to-user
Scope	Industry/sector specific	Open marketplace, global scale
Access	Limited number of partners	Unlimited number of partners
Technology	Closed proprietary networks	Open, unprotected networks
Relationship	Known and trusted partners	Known and unknown partners
Security	Part of network design	Security and authentication
Global reach	Restricted markets	Extended markets

thorough analysis of market, business and cultural factors. The one thing they all have in common, however, is the prediction that Internet access, markets and revenues will all follow an upwards trend.

FORECASTING THE GROWTH OF INTERNET ACCESS/USE, MARKETS AND REVENUE STREAMS

So far, the literature on e-commerce is characterised by much hype and speculation. This gives the impression that the global information society is fully operational. Terms such as the digital economy (David, 1999), the information economy (Gates, 1999), the knowledge-driven economy (HMSO, 1998) and virtual communities (Hagel and Armstrong, 1997) need to be evaluated in the context of four important factors. First, the scale of global Internet access and use.[5] Second, the potential to expand into vertical markets and to generate new revenue streams from e-commerce. Third, how technical developments from EDI to the Internet and WWW have enabled electronic trading (Kumar and Cooke, 1996). Fourth, a look at some of the key companies currently using the Internet and WWW to serve their customers, such as IBM, Amazon.com and Dell.

Internet Access and Use

Since 1995, which was labelled in the popular press as 'the year of the Internet', a wide range of forecasts have been generated about the potential growth in Internet access and use. Whilst many of these forecasts should be treated with some caution, there is some hard evidence about existing Internet access around the world. The following data have been provided by commercial and government sources, and show an upward trend in Internet access/use:

- Fewer than 40 million people around the world were connected to the Internet during 1996. By the end of 1997, more than 100 million people were using the Internet. By 1999, 171 million people across the globe had access to the Internet (Nua Internet Surveys, 1998).

- The breakdown of 171 million people who use the Internet is: Canada and the United States 56.6%, Europe 23.4%, Asia/Pacific 15.8%, Middle East 0.5%, Latin America 3.1% and Africa 0.6% (US Government, 1997).
- Approximately 100 countries now enjoy Internet access. There are around 20 million Internet hosts worldwide.
- Two hundred and fifty million people are expected to use the Internet in 2000 (European Union).
- Traffic on the Internet has been doubling every 100 days.

A cross-national comparison of Internet use produces some interesting findings, with Finland reported as having the highest percentage of its population using the Internet (35%). This is followed by the United States (29.8%) and Australia (17.8%). Singapore (14.7%) also has relatively high Internet access, as does the United Kingdom (12.2%). It is noteworthy that France (6.5%) and Germany (7.4%) fall somewhat behind the United Kingdom.

Another survey of *Internet users*[6] conducted by the OECD and measured between December 1997 and June 1998 found that the United States came first with 55.2%, Japan came second with 10%, Canada came third with 8% and the United Kingdom and Germany a close fourth with 5.5% and 5.3%, respectively (*Financial Times*, 8 October 1998, p. 20). These figures differ from those in Table 1.4 and would suggest that the US figure of 55.2% refers more to Internet access rather than to regular (daily) Internet use.

Hejndorf (1998) reinforces the above OECD study by claiming that Germany and the United Kingdom are

> rivals for the spot as the largest Internet market in Western Europe, each with a 1997 Web population of more than four million individuals ... Germany alone is expected to drive one-third of the WWW user growth in western Europe and dominate the market between 1998 and 2001 with more than 17 million Web users projected by the end 2001.

The IDC (1998b) claims that,

> Almost 4.3 per cent of all inhabitants in western Europe are now world wide Web users, with penetration rates by country varying from 0.8 per cent to 12.2 per cent. The Nordic countries take the clear lead but Switzerland, the United Kingdom, Netherlands and Germany are also all above the western European average.

The IDC (1998c) projects the number of devices accessing the Web in Western Europe will grow from 14.2 million in 1997 to almost 58 million by the end of 2001. The number of users associated with those devices will grow from 16.2 million in 1997 to 56 million by year end 2001.

Such impressive forecasts for growth in Internet access and use would suggest the expansion into new vertical markets to generate new revenue streams, particularly in the area of business-to-consumer e-commerce. The following section explores some recent surveys and forecasts on the growth of e-commerce worldwide.

Table 1.4   *An estimate of global Internet use*

Country	Population	Internet users	Percent of population using Internet
US	265m	79m	29.8
Finland	5.1m	1.79m	35
France	57.7m	3.8m	6.5
Germany	81.4m	6.1m	7.4
UK	58.6m	7.2m	12.2
Australia	18.4m	3.28m	17.8
Singapore	3.4m	500 000	14.7
Nigeria	108m	1000	0.0009
South Africa	43.8m	800 000	1.8
Israel	5.3m	300 000	5.6
China	1.2 billion	1.175m	0.097

Vertical Markets and Revenue Streams

A cursory glance at the popular press would suggest that *doing business electronically* is set to increase enormously. Whilst reliable figures on the revenue streams from e-commerce for particular markets are thin on the ground, the following examples from a variety of sources show that large increases are expected in vertical markets from financial services to retailing.

- E-business will double every year over a five-year period surging from US$43 billion in 1998 to US$1.3 trillion by 2003 (Forrester Research, 1999).
- Business-to-consumer e-commerce in the United States will increase from US$8 billion in 1998 to US$108 billion by 2003 (Forrester Research, 1999).
- E-commerce in Western Europe will grow from US$1 billion in 1997 to US$30 billion by 2001 (IDC, 1998a).
- Britain and Germany will move into 'hyper-growth' two years after the United States; Japan, France and Italy two years after Britain and Germany (Forrester Research, 1999).
- E-commerce will represent 1% of all world trade by 2001 (IDC, 1998a).
- Business-to-business commerce over the Internet will reach 7 billion ECU in 1997—a tenfold increase from 1996. In 2002, it is forecast that the value of goods and services traded between companies over the Internet will approach 300 billion ECU (EU).
- The four most advanced sectors to exploit on-line supply chains are: computing and electronics, aerospace and defence, utilities and motor vehicles. The slowest four are: industrial equipment, construction, food and agriculture and heavy industries (Forrester Research, 1999).
- Internet retail sales alone will grow from around US$9.7 billion in 1997 to US$96 billion by 1998 (Yankee Group, 1998).
- Retail sales on the Internet were £300 million in 1995. This is expected to rise to US$6 billion by the year 2000 (Forrester Research, 1999).
- Advertising revenue was US$74 million in 1996, and is estimated to increase to US$2.5 billion by the millennium (Forrester Research, 1999).

- In 1995, it was estimated that global non-Internet credit card transactions amounted to US$500 billion, whereas transactions via the Internet came to only US$500 million. In the year 2000, it is anticipated that the figure for Internet transactions could exceed US$100 billion.

Another study by Euromonitor noted that the global shopping market was approximately US$166 billion in 1994 (cited in the *Lansing State Journal*, 26 December 1995). Electronic shopping, including CD-ROMs, accounted for just US$300 million in sales, or less than 0.02%. In the United States in 1994, the 3.5 million people connected to on-line services spent an average of fewer than 60 cents each via their PCs, compared with US$94 through traditional mail ordering. This study was carried out in 1994 before the WWW had made significant inroads into the business community.

CAP Gemini Sogeti/Hoskyns suggest that, by 2006, 9.8% of sales will be direct to customers in their own homes or places of work. This figure excludes sales by traditional mail order. Almost half of the remote sales predicted are expected to be via the Internet. One estimate is that 30 million potential buyers will be on-line by the millennium (Meall, 1996). In 1996, the 30 million-plus business and individual users of the Internet were estimated to be growing by 10 million per month (TradeWave Corporation, 1996). Since 1995 there has been an exponential growth in the number of Internet users; the number of hosts connected to the WWW; and the number of companies establishing a Web presence.

The above figures suggest that a *gold rush* mentality has fuelled the growth of the Internet and WWW, with many businesses fearful of being left behind in this new technological race. Whilst Internet access and use around the world is large and growing every day, the scale and scope of e-commerce is yet to be fully developed. Many companies have been using electronic data interchange (EDI) for several years as a means of communicating and transacting with their suppliers. Yet EDI (which preceded business-to-business e-commerce) was often too expensive for many small and medium sized companies. Since the Internet and WWW offer a cheaper and faster means of capturing, storing, retrieving and processing data/information, this is likely to change. Financial savings in the form of reduced administrative costs (time and materials) will offer small and medium companies many cost advantages which were not available through EDI.

From EDI to E-Commerce

EDI was a technology introduced by the transportation industry in the late 1960s. It was deployed for years as a platform for e-commerce. The 1970s saw the adoption of the EDI concept by other industries and the formation of the American National Standards Institute X12 Committee to establish an EDI standard. Since the 1980s, EDI has been used to automate ordering, tracking, shipping, and billing of goods. Initially, the focus of EDI was to improve financial controls (e.g. payment, invoicing). More recently, the EDI standard has been expanded to cover automated payment. EDI is predominantly used for business-to-business transactions, rather than for consumer transactions. The technology does not specify what network should be used for communicating data or EDI forms, so some companies use modems. Others use value-added networks (VANs) which can store messages and forward them to the appropriate party. Yet many small and medium enterprises find the high cost of using VANs prohibitive. The Internet, however, offers lower-cost entry into the use of EDI and gives SMEs the opportunity to work with companies that have implemented EDI for order processing (Grant, 1996, p. 221). The US customs service uses EDI to process 94% of all customs declarations and collects 60% of all customs electronically, forcing down error rates from 17% to 1.7%, saving US$500 million in processing costs, and increasing productivity by 10% annually. Stone (1997, p. 28) claims that 'EDI is the fastest growing subset of e-commerce today ... It is the means by which standard business documents are exchanged electronically between companies according to industry standards.' Arunachalam (1995, pp. 60–61) claims that

> EDI is the electronic, computer to computer exchange of business information in a structured format between business trading partners or between various units within an organisation. Accordingly, EDI is a high-speed method of electronic communication that facilitates the exchange and processing of high volumes of business data from one computer to another.

He asserts that, in order to run EDI, five basic components are needed:

1. a body of EDI standards such as those developed by the American National Standards Institute (ANSI);
2. EDI software to generate, receive and interpret transactions with trading partners;
3. a capability to send and receive EDI transactions, a function often provided by VANs or by third party networks or point-to-point configurations;
4. enhancements to applications software required to accept or originate EDI transactions, and changes to traditional business procedures for strategic advantage;
5. hardware, including appropriate peripherals such as a printer, modem and storage devices.

The European market for EDI is relatively small even though it has existed for some 30 years. EDI services revenues were about £450 million in 1998. Mainly large organisations and industry sectors, such as manufacturing, use EDI. According to one study, this spread across Europe is broadly even with proportional expenditure on EDI matching IT expenditure in general. But there is low diffusion in Southern Europe due to poor infrastructure (*Computing*, 30 April 1998, p. 36). Limited use of EDI tends to be due to high set-up costs and complexity. Incompatibility of existing systems and standards often means that EDI cannot be implemented without a radical restructuring of business processes. In the short term, EDI, which is provided through a third party VAN services provider, is likely to flourish. However, the changing nature of business relationships and the nature of Web interfaces will drive major changes in the EDI services industry. The biggest impact will come from the realisation that the Web offers an alternative to the expensive, hand-crafted EDI systems of the past and this will drive the dynamic growth in the next five years (*Computing*, 30 April 1998, p. 36).

Lacovou *et al.* (1995) conducted research into EDI and small organisations focusing on adoption and impact issues. Two key questions were:

1. What are the major factors that influence the adoption and impact of EDI in the small business context?
2. How can EDI systems initiators assist in expediting the adoption process of their small partners?

The authors claim that EDIs are co-operative interorganisational systems (IOSs) that allow trading partners to exchange structured information electronically between separate computer applications (p. 466). Swatman and Swatman (1992) also hold this view. IOSs are telecommunication-based computer systems that are used by two or more organisations to support the sharing of data, and sometimes applications, among users in different organisations (p. 466). They claim that IOS may be classified as EDI if the former possesses four key characteristics:

1. It must have at least two organisations in a business relationship as users.
2. Data-processing tasks pertaining to a transaction at both (all) organisations must be supported by independent application systems. (This property is unique to EDI; other IOSs are based on a single application system that is used by multiple users.)
3. The integrity of the data exchange between application systems of trading partners must be guaranteed by agreements concerning data coding and formatting rules
4. Data exchange between the application systems must be accomplished via telecommunication links.

Lacovou *et al.* (1995) develop a model for small business EDI adoption which considers perceived benefits, organisational readiness, and external pressure. These factors were identified as the main reasons that could explain the EDI adoption behaviour of small firms and the expected impact of the technology (Figure 1.1).

The authors conducted a study on seven companies, all of which supplied the British Columbia government which was pursuing an EDI initiative. All companies contained fewer than 200 employees. The research found that a major reason that small firms become EDI-capable is due to external pressure, especially from trading partners. They found that small firms pressured into adopting EDI would only achieve benefits if they integrate the system within their operations. Therefore, both high organisational readiness and an awareness of the benefits (which induces the allocation of the available resources) are required for integrated, high impact EDI systems. Arunachalam (1995, p. 62) sent a survey to 900 registered EDI users. Some 180 responses were obtained with an average mean number of employees being 6728 and average revenues of US$40 million. The firms had an average of two outlets. The survey found that the most frequently cited barrier to EDI adoption was that of lack of awareness of EDI benefits. Thirty-seven per cent of all respondents indicated that this was a barrier. Only 9.9% said that there were no barriers to EDI adoption. A significant number of respondents (79.4%) said that

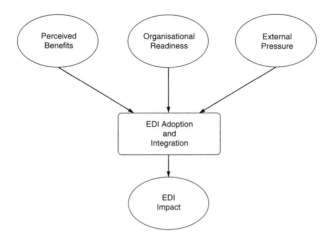

Figure 1.1   *Proposed small business EDI adoption model. Source: Lacovou et al. (1995)*

customers' request was instrumental in their EDI adoption. Other reasons for EDI adoption were given as: to remain competitive (51%); better customer service (48%); speed up/reduce paperwork (47%); accuracy (42%); cost efficiency (32%).

Kumar and Cooke (1996, p. 43) developed four case studies looking at EDI strategies. Their study looks at EDI in the context of total quality management (TQM) and business process re-engineering (BPR). The authors conclude that senior managers tend not to perceive EDI as a strategic resource. Rather, they see it as a 'facilitator of efficiencies in the low level processes of operational and tactical control'. They suggest that EDI will only be viewed strategically if its competitive strengths are fully understood by management. Lankford and Riggs (1996, p. 61) claim that the benefits from EDI can be categorised into three areas: direct, indirect and strategic. They claim that EDI offers more benefits than simply the electronic transmission of orders and invoices. EDI has the potential to link trading partners in a co-operative relationship to enhance profitability, higher levels of service and productivity improvements. Companies using EDI may link their computers through networks to exchange data electronically without the need for manual intervention in the data entry or manipulation process. Spinardi *et al.* (1996, p. 25) in a study on EDI which looks at the UK publishing industry (the book trade; the magazine and newspaper trade; and newsprint supply to newspapers) found that EDI has developed in a slow and incremental manner. This brings the authors to the conclusion that radical change programmes like BPR offer a somewhat misleading picture of EDI adoption and impact. The authors found that in the trading communities which they examined,

EDI has not been a catalyst for radical change; in fact, the nature of trading relationships and types of transactions have changed very little. These EDI communities have formed through agreement on the standardisation and harmonisation of information, with the agreed standards defining the limits of any particular electronic trading community.

Their three case studies found that EDI has been adopted as a means of replicating transactions within existing trading relationships. Thus,

> Although new technologies have been developed and promoted with apparently coherent and compelling visions of how these technologies should be implemented, in practice these have not been fulfilled … EDI looks likely to be no different (p. 25).

The implementation of EDI has been patchy across vertical markets, many writers are now claiming that the Internet and WWW will revolutionise business processes in the coming years. Whilst a substantial body of literature exists on the relationship between firm size and innovation, very little hard evidence exists at the current time on the development of e-commerce, particularly in the small and medium enterprise (SME) sector (Lerner, 1999). The following section looks at some of the companies currently developing e-commerce. Whilst our analysis concentrates on some of the high profile examples, it is likely that SMEs will follow suit in developing e-commerce strategies if the conditions discussed below are met.

Companies Doing Business on the Internet

The literature tends to highlight a few popular examples of companies that use the Internet and WWW as a core competence in serving their customer base. In fact, companies such as Cisco Systems and Amazon.com were built around the emerging Internet and WWW technologies and others, such as Dell Computer Corporation, have been able to transfer financial savings to their customers by receiving orders for their products electronically. The following figures show the recent financial performance of these companies:

- Cisco Systems ended 1996 having booked just over US$100 million in sales on the Internet. By the end of 1997, its Internet sales were running at a US$3.2 billion annual rate.
- In 1998 Cisco Systems generated profits of US$1.4 billion and had a market value of US$172 billion.
- Cisco's net sales for the first quarter of 1999 were US$3.88 billion compared with US$2.60 billion the previous year, which is an increase of 49%.
- Cisco Systems' chief executive predicts that in 2000, electronic trade will be a US$1.5 trillion industry. Cisco Systems sells 80% of the routers and other forms of networking technology that power the Internet (Larry Carter, CFO of Cisco Systems).
- 80% of Cisco Systems' sales come from the WWW.
- In 1996, Amazon.com, the first Internet bookstore, recorded sales of less than US$16 million. In 1997, it sold US$148 million worth of books to Internet customers. One of the nation's largest book retailers, Barnes and Noble, launched its own on-line bookstore in 1997 to compete with Amazon for this rapidly growing on-line market.
- In January 1997, Dell Computer Corporation was selling less than US$1 million worth of computers per day on the Internet. The company reported reaching

daily sales of US$6 million several times during the December 1997 holiday period.

- Dell sells US$18 million worth of computers from its Web site each day. This accounts for 30% of the company's US$5.5 billion first-quarter revenues. Dell expects this percentage to increase by 50% from 2000.
- IBM announced in 1999 that it would introduce direct selling over the Internet to compete with Dell.
- A banking transaction via the Internet cost one cent, compared with 27 cents at an ATM or 52 cents over the telephone (*Economist*, 1999).
- Processing an airline ticket on the Internet costs £1, compared with $11 through a travel agent.
- A quarter of IBM's revenues of £80 billion come from its e-business sales.
- GE has developed the Trading Process Network, a Web-based link to its suppliers that enables them easily and quickly to make bids. The system has cut procurement sales in half, processing costs by a third and the cost of goods purchased by 5%–50%. Now GE does over US$1 billion worth of Web-based business annually.
- Chrysler has generated more than 25 000 ideas for cost-cutting measures from its suppliers. It saved US$1.5 billion in 1998. This could reach US$3.7 billion at full implementation.

Many authors now see a radical redesign of companies brought about by the Internet and WWW. For example, Martin (1996, p. 17) claims that, 'Large companies are shifting from being geographically specific and product diversified to being product specific and geographically diversified.' He asserts that time and distance will not be a factor in determining how companies do business in future, since their global reach will depend on their strategic use of the Internet and WWW. For example, companies will not need to be located in one or more geographical areas to serve their customers. Rather, their customers will be able to acquire information about products and services over the Web from any location. Companies will become increasingly networked-based rather than functionally or product structured, and employees will work more and more from home as *teleworkers*. Vast cost savings will accrue to companies in moving towards a networked-based structure since they will reduce overhead costs associated with office space, furniture, heating, lighting, canteen services and many more facilities which are essential in traditional workplace environments.

If the above trends continue, e-commerce will drive economic growth and change the shape of industry structure. To realise this potential, private sector and governments will need to work together to create a seamless, market-driven and secure framework to facilitate e-commerce. A survey of 578 UK businesses published by the Institute of Directors (IoD) in April 1998 showed that just 4% of companies were using a Web site for sales, and 30% did not have a Web site at all. The retail sector reported that 9.3% of companies were using the Web to sell their goods. Utilities were the least interested, with just 2% of sales over the Web. Finance companies had the lowest take-up of corporate Web sites, with 41% still lacking a presence on the Internet. The IoD further found that a third of companies believed they did not use IT for competitive advantage. More than a third lacked board-level understanding of the business potential of IT (*Computing*, 23 April 1998, p. 18). Table 1.5 considers some statistics on the diffusion of information and communications technologies (ICTs) in the United Kingdom. As the data suggest, there is an upward trend to invest in ICTs by public sector organisations and UK citizens.

The Cambridge Information Network survey shows that IT departments greatly influence the e-commerce strategies of companies. But this finding calls into question the degree to which e-commerce strategies are integrated into the overall business strategies of companies. Whilst these findings are unsurprising, it is important to recognise that e-commerce is not simply confined to the IT department. Conversely, for e-commerce or e-business[7] to be fully exploited, it will require the involvement of the entire company. Cockburn and Wilson (1996 p. 86) conducted a survey over the Internet in 1995. First, the sample comprised 300 businesses with Web sites, across a range of industry types, using the *Yahoo!* Directory. The sites were investigated in relation to several areas—the purpose of the Web site, the use being made of electronic mail and the extent to which multimedia was being utilised. In addition, any other aspects of the site that were designed to make them more interesting to potential customers were also noted. Second, an electronic-mail questionnaire was sent to 222 of the 300 companies surveyed chosen largely because they provided an e-mail address. Fourteen were returned immediately due to unknown addresses or technical problems. Of the remaining 208, 102 replies were received, five of which were of no relevance, leaving 97 completed questionnaires to examine—a response rate of 47%. Some 22.5% and 13.9% of responses were from computer-related and Internet-related companies, respectively, which is unsurprising. The survey found that only 11.7% of companies surveyed currently engaged in on-line selling with credit card details being transmitted over the Internet and only a quarter of these having secure servers. The main problems facing electronic commerce were security (reported by 53.6% of companies) and payment issues (47.7%). Access was also high on the list at 43.3%.

Table 1.5   *Trends in public sector e-commerce*

50% of local authorities have their own Web sites

25% of government services, Labour promises, will be delivered electronically by 2000

80% of respondents to a Cabinet office survey said they would be willing to try new technology as a way of accessing government benefits and services

9% of the UK population accessed the Internet in a four-week period, according to a recent NOP survey

£20 million is earmarked to train the UK's 27 000 library staff in the use of network technology as part of the National Grid for Learning initiative

There has been an estimated 20% decrease in annual IT budgets across all UK local authorities since 1993

Adapted from: Cabinet Office; NOP Research Group; Kable; Ministry of Culture, Media and Sport; Socitm; *Computer Weekly*, 21 May 1998, p. 44.

E-commerce is not limited to the Internet. It includes a wide number of applications in the narrowband (videotex), broadcast (teleshopping), and off-line environment (catalogue sales on CD-ROM), as well as proprietary corporate networks (banking). The Internet, with its robust and network-independent protocols, is currently facilitating many different forms of e-commerce (see above). Corporate networks are becoming Intranets. The Internet is also generating many innovative hybrid forms of e-commerce in the form of digital television *infomercials* with Internet response mechanisms (for immediate ordering), CD-ROM catalogues with Internet connections (for content or price updates), and commercial Web sites with local CD-ROM extensions (for memory-intensive multimedia demonstrations). E-commerce is itself an emerging market. In such a fast-moving and dynamic environment a wide array of innovative virtual businesses, markets and trading communities are evolving. Companies are now routinely outsourcing over the Internet functions such as order fulfilment and shipping to distributors that specialise in these services. Distributors are also exploring the advantages of electronic trading by outsourcing the physical warehousing and movement of goods to logistics specialists such as commercial courier companies. Buyers, sellers and intermediaries are forming industry-specific Internet markets in such diverse fields as real estate, automobile parts and construction equipment. Similarly, global manufacturing industries, such as automobile, computers and aerospace, are actively integrating their supply chains through the Internet. New functions are now being created. Innovative virtual middlemen are providing value-added services—such as brokering, search and referral—to businesses and consumers. Catalogue aggregators offer buyers *one-stop shops* to select products at the best price from many niche merchants. Classified advertising supersites present single points of access to scores of other sites carrying advertisements. Government-sponsored gateways provide a single path to large numbers of selected companies trading on the Internet. Network operators, banks and computer companies are generating new revenues in their *hosting business*, offering turnkey virtual storefronts and virtual malls.

The era of the Web as a source of free information is giving way to one based on transactional (buying and selling) activities. New forms of individual-to-individual commerce are appearing, as users themselves may sell content they publish on the Web. Similarly, commercial publishers can now sell information on the Web, e.g. page by page, article by article, chapter by chapter and photograph by photograph. The very small payments for such services generate new revenue streams, maximise the use of archives, and encourage widespread content development. The possibilities for government, business and individuals in exploiting the Web for e-commerce seem endless. But as with many other new technologies, the Internet and WWW will evolve over time and perhaps not in the revolutionary way some pundits suggest. In the final section of this chapter we consider the issue of whether new models and frameworks need to be developed for the global information society.

MODELS AND FRAMEWORKS

Much of the literature on the global information society suggests that new models and frameworks will be needed to make sense of the changes taking place

(Haltiwanger and Jarmin, 1999). Past models and frameworks are seen to be obsolete, particularly if we accept the view that the 'Internet and WWW changes everything' (Gates, 1999). Angehrn (1997, p. 361), for example, argues that

> current strategies adopted by large and small companies worldwide have been generally based on a narrow, uni-dimensional interpretation of the Internet, as either an information, a communication, a distribution or transaction channel (ICDT) model. The model is then used as a systematic framework guiding (a) the analysis of how traditional products and services are redesigned in the light of the Internet, and (b) the identification of organisational adjustments companies need to undergo in order fully to exploit the business opportunities created by the Internet.

He suggests that companies entering a 'mature' phase in the application of new technology

1. require their Internet-related investments to result in measurable returns or cost reduction, and
2. develop a clear strategy—aligned with the specific business objectives and values—to guide in a systematic way the identification of the type and range of products and services to be developed and/or redesigned in the light of the Internet (p. 1).

The ICDT model illustrated in the next section enables the classification of Internet strategies adopted by companies in the 'maturity' phase by segmenting the space of business opportunities created by the extensive spread of the Internet and its related basic services, such as electronic mail and the WWW. The ICDT model provides the basis for identifying how, during this phase, existing products and services will be extended and redesigned, as well as the characteristics of completely new services whose conception and development has been made possible by the Internet. Angehrn's (1997) model of the four virtual spaces is given in Figure 1.2.

The virtual information space (VIS) consists of the new Internet-based channels through which economic agents can display information about themselves, and the products and services they offer. Functioning like a large billboard accessible flexibly, globally and at low cost, the WWW has opened up a new marketing channel for all the economic agents, from large companies displaying catalogues of their products and services to individuals seeking employment or business partners. *The virtual communication space* (VCS) is the extension of traditional spaces in which economic agents meet to exchange ideas and experiences, influence opinions, negotiate potential collaborations, lobby, engage in relationships and create different types of communities. *The virtual distribution space* (VDS) represents a new distribution channel suitable for a variety of products and services. A first category of products that can be efficiently distributed via the Internet are products that can be digitised and transmitted through computer networks. Electronic books, articles, pictures, digital music and video belong to this category, together with all the categories of software and electronic data (from computer games to database management systems). A second domain in which the Internet can be used as a distribution channel is the one of 'non-physical' services such as text: voice- or video-based consulting, and training. *The virtual transaction space* (VTS) consists of

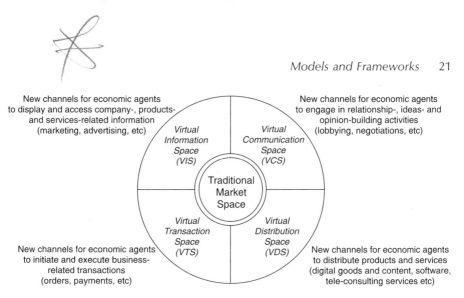

New channels for economic agents to display and access company-, products- and services-related information (marketing, advertising, etc)

New channels for economic agents to engage in relationship-, ideas- and opinion-building activities (lobbying, negotiations, etc)

Virtual Information Space (VIS)

Virtual Communication Space (VCS)

Traditional Market Space

Virtual Transaction Space (VTS)

Virtual Distribution Space (VDS)

New channels for economic agents to initiate and execute business-related transactions (orders, payments, etc)

New channels for economic agents to distribute products and services (digital goods and content, software, tele-consulting services etc)

Figure 1.2   *The four virtual spaces. Reproduced from European Management Journal, vol. 15, no. 4, August 1997 by permission of Elsevier Sciences*

the new Internet-based channels through which economic agents can exchange formal business transactions such as orders, invoices and payments. In the first phase of development, the Internet has not yet been extensively used as a transaction space, mainly because of its underdeveloped legal, security and reliability aspects. The identification of technically mature solutions and industry standards, together with the development of the necessary infrastructure of transaction processing services, in particular in the domain of electronic payments, are necessary preconditions for enabling companies to exploit the new virtual transaction space on a wider scale.

According to Angehrn (1997, p. 368) the ICDT model provides a framework for the analysis of business-related Internet strategies. It also provides a systematic approach for strategy formulation to companies intending to redesign or innovate their products and services. In addition, the model captures and extends the analysis of current trends such as the 'information-to-transaction' approach adopted by large companies aiming primarily at VIS and VCS presence, as well as the 'transaction-to-information' approach adopted by new entrants, whose strategy is oriented towards new products and services exploiting the Internet as an alternative distribution or transaction channel.

Another model on the e-commerce evolution gives four stages of growth (see Figure 1.3). The first stage is where an organisation may simply have a Web page or a 'window on the world'. Many SMEs are currently at this stage, and many more do not even have a Web site. The second stage is where an organisation sets up an Intranet. Employees may use e-mail to communicate (interact) with each other. Internal documents may be passed via the e-mail. The third stage is one where customers may transact with their suppliers and vice versa. Orders may be taken via the Internet. The fourth stage is a fully integrated approach. Companies such as Dell Computer Corporation have developed the 'Dell Direct' approach where customers can purchase goods and services over the Internet. IBM recently announced it would compete with Dell by also setting up an on-line service.

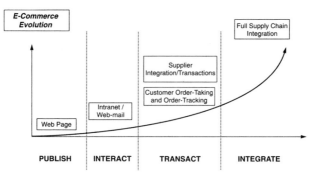

Figure 1.3   *The four stages of e-commerce evolution*

One of the current impediments of moving from stage one to four is the cost of setting up a Web site. Gartner Group (1999) recently announced that the cost of developing a Web site was about £1 million. This would rise by 25% annually by 2001. The labour costs were estimated to be 79% and hardware and software 11%, respectively. Gartner identifies three cost categories that will emerge based upon function. They are: US$300 000 to US$1 million to 'Get on Map'. This site is adequate but functionally behind the majority of participants; US$1 million to US$5 million to 'Run with the Pack'. This site is functionally equivalent to most industry participants; US$5 million to US$20 million to achieve 'Market Differentiator', which raises the industry competitive bar and changes the nature of on-line competition. Clearly, only large companies can afford the third cost category.

SUMMARY

So far, many companies continue to offer discrete products or services through physical distribution channels to a proprietary, undifferentiated customer base. This is likely to change as the Internet and WWW play a part in redefining the structures of markets and industries (Kehoe, 1995). The outcome may mean a power shift from a seller-driven to a buyer-driven model. But before this model becomes a reality, many impediments to e-commerce will need to be overcome. Rose *et al.* (1999) identify six main impediments. They are,

1. download delays,
2. limitations in the interface,
3. search problems,
4. inadequate measurement of Web application success,
5. security (real and perceived) weaknesses, and
6. a lack of Internet standards.

This chapter has intended to give an overview of the emerging global information society. Following chapters will explore many of the issues raised above in more detail. The next chapter looks at models and frameworks for Internet commerce[8] and asks whether it is a new paradigm for business.

2
Internet Commerce:
A New Paradigm for Business

INTRODUCTION

Prior to 1994 the Internet was a network of computers used by the academic and military communities. It was not exploited as a competitive nor commercial weapon by the business community as various barriers precluded this from occurring (Cockburn and Wilson, 1996). In recent years, many of these barriers to entry have been eliminated (Armstrong and Hagel, 1997). This has paved the way for the Internet to emerge as a tool to advance commercial and leisure activities. New terminology has entered the business and academic communities at a rapid rate. Terms such as, *Internet commerce, electronic commerce, cyberspace, cybermediaries, marketspace* and the *virtual organisation* are just a few that have been used in relation to the Internet in recent years. Whilst these terms seemingly offer new opportunities for business, in an era often referred to as the *information age* or *society*, they also engender much confusion, particularly for those people who are attempting to evaluate the potential benefits and pitfalls from Internet commerce.[9] At the present time, Internet commerce remains very much at the developmental or experimental stages, and business managers have very little experience from which to draw in distinguishing hype from practical reality (Lymer *et al.*, 1997).

In this chapter we consider whether Internet commerce is a new paradigm for business or simply just another expensive, high-tech fad created by the computer industry. As with every new technological artefact—from the mainframe computer to the personal computer (PC)—a great deal of optimism and hype surround the Internet and its potential to change the way businesses are managed, co-ordinated, costed and controlled. Prior to the development of the Internet, one of the most significant events was the introduction of the IBM PC in the United States in 1983 and the United Kingdom in 1984. Certainly, the widespread use of the PC in industrialised countries has revolutionised the world of work, as jobs have been simultaneously eliminated and created, thus contributing to the turbulent labour market in the last two decades. The same may be true of the Internet, following its launch in the business community from 1994 onwards (Kalakota and Whinston, 1996).

One observation of the rapid pace of development of the Internet is the need to develop new theories and models for understanding this phenomenon (Angehrn, 1997). Traditional models of corporate strategy, supply-chain management and logistics, management education and training, business economics and information flows, and many others, have lost much of their relevance. Notwithstanding the absence of relevant theoretical and conceptual models of the Internet, this chapter examines important themes and topics that are likely to emerge in both the academic and practitioner communities in the next few years.

KEY CHALLENGES IN THE DEVELOPMENT OF INTERNET COMMERCE

Interest in the Internet and its potential for developing business opportunities has grown considerably in the last few years. A great deal of speculative literature has been published in academic and practitioner circles on a whole range of topics. Internet commerce has tended to be linked with the 'automate or liquidate' scenario, which argues that unless companies jump on the bandwagon and invest large sums in technology, they will be left behind in the technological race. Such a view is over-simple and tends to overlook the complex issues that companies face in determining the advantages and pitfalls underpinning Internet commerce.

In this chapter we identify 10 areas that will comprise the key challenges to management in the development of Internet commerce. They relate to the market/ business sector; products/services; value chain; innovation and technology; customer focus; role of government; managerial issues; administrative/hierarchical structure; cost/performance; and risk/reward (Figure 2.1). These areas have been identified from reading the existing literature on the Internet, and are likely to become key research areas over time. Whilst these areas are not mutually exclusive, it is important to remember that the Internet is not simply a technological phenomenon. Indeed, the Internet will only emerge as a value-added artefact if management from a variety of market/business sectors develops effective strategies for its exploitation and competitive advantage. The following areas therefore give an overview of some of the emerging issues and concerns facing managers in their attempt to understand and develop Internet commerce.

The Market/Business Sector

The existing literature makes special reference to the market/business sectors most likely to exploit Internet commerce in the coming years (Cronin, 1996). The commercial potential of Internet commerce and its likely advantages and disadvantages will vary widely across the business community. Already, there are numerous examples of success stories related to the development of new business possibilities over the Internet, many of which stem from the United States. There are also many market/business contexts where Internet commerce is particularly inappropriate. It is therefore the responsibility of companies to carefully examine their market/

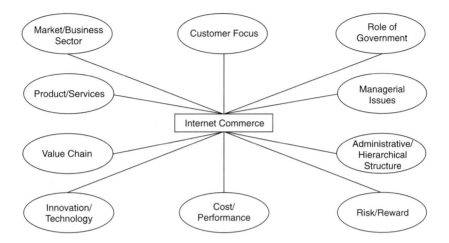

Figure 2.1   *Key issues in the development of Internet commerce*

business sector position to evaluate the potential for developing Internet commerce. This involves a much broader examination of not only their own position within the marketplace, but also their strategic partnerships with a whole range of suppliers (e.g. Internet Service Providers (ISPs) and many more).

Recent evidence shows that some companies have impulsively invested in Internet technology without having conducted a detailed analysis of the marketplace (*Information Week*, 1998). This has meant that the return on their investment (ROI) has been disappointing, with some companies simply abandoning their Internet commerce strategies altogether. One observation is that finding the right partner or supplier is the key to developing a successful Internet commerce facility. This is reminiscent of many outsourcing contracts, as poor partnerships between client and vendor rarely lead to successful outsourcing experiences. Table 2.1 gives a comparative overview of the reasons underpinning current and future Internet connections. As can be seen, many companies currently use the Internet for e-mail and WWW access only. This is relatively narrow in scope given that the forecast is for companies to take advantage of a wide range of Internet services from EDI across the Internet to developing virtual enterprises. In the case of EDI across the Internet, companies will be able to improve their market/business positioning by developing closer relationships with their staff, customers and suppliers.

The Internet enables people to work effectively in spite of being geographically remote. For example, computer programmers do not need to sit side-by-side to write code. Instead, they can communicate over the Internet and send programs and other documents to colleagues almost instantly. This offers many advantages to people engaged in business start-ups, since they can work from home yet communicate with their business partner/s just as effectively as if they were sharing an office. As technology advances and becomes more affordable, it will be

Table 2.1   *Current and future Internet connections*

Reasons for current Internet connection	Reasons for future Internet connections
E-mail	EDI across the Internet
Internet connectivity	Collaborative working
World Wide Web access	NetMeeting or team room
E-commerce	Virtual private networking
Newsgroup access	Voice over IP/video conferencing
Remote access	Virtual enterprises

Adapted from: Information Week (1998).

commonplace to hold meetings with colleagues aided by visual and sound capabilities. Currently, people are often reluctant to discuss sensitive issues over a telephone line without being able to see the other person's body language. With the latest technologies, a visual display of the other person can be seen on a computer screen and this will further develop remote collaborative working.

At the present time, the majority of companies use only a narrow range of Internet-related services and functions. There are numerous Web sites that outline the key commercial activities of companies, their contact addresses and current and forthcoming product/service launches, etc. Very few of these Web sites are interactive since they are used largely for informational (data/information gathering) reasons rather than for transactional (to purchase goods/services) purposes (Reynolds, 1997). Variations in the development of Internet commerce are wide both with market/business sectors and between countries. Current evidence confirms that Internet commerce is largely a US phenomenon, with the United Kingdom, Europe and rest of the world lagging behind (*Network News*, 1998). In the case of the financial services sector, many US banks are forging ahead with their plans to create the *virtual* bank. Whilst the rhetoric of virtual banking currently exceeds the practical reality, there are examples where certain banks are attempting to transform their business processes from traditional into virtual ones (Austin, 1996). For example, Citibank in the United States recently announced a worldwide licensing agreement based around Netscape's Internet commerce software. The bank has licensed Netscape's Xpert family of software to provide the infrastructure for its Internet commerce sites, and for constructing intranets and extranets. Citibank is the largest US bank with operations in 100 countries, and currently has a home banking service on the Internet. It plans to offer services based on Netscape products as an additional feature for business-to-business and business-to-consumer clients. The financial investment in this project has not been made public. According to the Executive Vice President of Citibank, 'Our goal of extending Citibank's global reach depends on launching global electronic commerce products and services ... This agreement with Netscape provides us with the tools to accelerate the development of these applications for corporations and consumers' (*Network News*, 1998).

Products/Services

One of the key challenges is in deciding which products/services should be sold over the Internet. This issue is currently being explored in numerous companies throughout the world, and there is little consensus about how the Internet will engender new product/service methods and techniques. Rayport and Sviokla (1995, p. 75) attempt to locate products/services within the context of marketplace and marketspace. The authors state that,

> When consumers use answering machines to store their phone messages, they are using objects made and sold in the physical world, but when they purchase electronic answering services from their local phone companies, they are utilising the marketspace—a virtual realm where products and services exist as digital information and can be delivered through information-based channels.

The central message from this work is twofold. First, it is important to distinguish between a marketplace and a marketspace (the physical world and the electronic world, respectively). Second, it is equally critical to understand how products/services are likely to change as a consequence of developing Internet commerce—or, the marketspace. It is therefore a misconception to assume that the same products/services will be sold over the Internet, given that the Internet offers possibilities for changing the nature of products/services and is not simply a new way of procuring and distributing them. As we shall see below, the Internet has to be conceptualised as a technology for product/service improvement and innovation and as a means through which they are procured and distributed.

Figure 2.2 is a heuristic device that considers the relationship between product/service types and their associated procurement/distribution channels in a variety of commercial settings. The matrix divides products/services into two distinct types—virtual (intangible) and physical (tangible). Procurement/distribution channels are divided into traditional (indirect) and virtual (direct).

Virtual

A virtual (intangible) product/service is one which is information based, e.g. books, newspapers and even music. Whilst they may continue to be delivered to people in a traditional (material) format, the Internet offers many possibilities for them to be procured and distributed electronically. It is therefore important to draw a distinction between the type of product/service and how it is procured and distributed. A common misconception in the literature is to confuse an informational product/service with a material-based one. For example, books are often treated as material (tangible) products because they are paper-based with a hard or soft jacket. However, a book is an informational (intangible) product. It is unlike a car or a stereo system, which are physical products since a book can be read or heard in more than one way (on paper, on a screen, from the radio, on a cassette/CD). With the further development of Internet technology, publishing companies may choose to transform their products/services from ones which are, in part, virtual, to being fully virtual. In other words, a book need not be sent to a person as a material (paper-based) product. Instead, it could be downloaded by the customer from the publisher's web site and read on a computer screen.[10] Similarly, music companies may also transform their products to enable their customers to download the work of their favourite artists in a digital format, and there are many other examples. According to Rayport and Sviokla (1995, p. 82), 'Companies that create value with

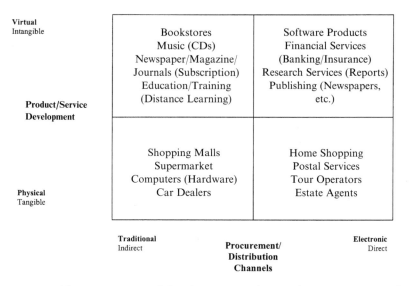

Figure 2.2   *The procurement and distribution of products and services in a virtual and physical environment*

digital assets may be able to reharvest them in an infinite number of transactions.' As such, only parts of books/journals could be sold as opposed to individuals having to purchase the entire publication. This would be advantageous to students and others in the academic sphere that may only be interested in a chapter or article.

Physical

A physical (tangible) product/service is the opposite of a virtual (intangible) product/service. The majority of goods purchased from shopping malls, supermarkets and car showrooms are essentially physical or material. Whilst they may be procured electronically, their actual delivery to the customer will be through traditional means. Clearly, it is not possible to download physical goods on the Internet. Nonetheless, the Internet offers many possibilities to procure physical goods electronically and in some cases, as with Federal Express, customers can track the delivery process of their parcels/packages at every stage. The retailing business is currently making good progress in developing Internet commerce. For example, Tesco supermarkets in the United Kingdom implemented an extranet, called Tesco Information Exchange (TIE), to improve product availability in stores and reduce waste. TIE has improved information-sharing by accurately predicting demand for products. Consequently, shelves are always full of what customers need and unsold goods are kept to a minimum. The company was also interested in gaining access to potential suppliers that were too small to join an EDI network. So far, it has improved cooperation between partners using traditional e-commerce techniques, thereby streamlining the supply chain. The company has also embarked on a number of pilot schemes to test the market for home shopping. These schemes have been targeted to only a few areas, and the initial response is promising. Basically, customers can either give their order over the Internet or by fax. They pay a relatively modest home delivery fee and receive their goods within a specified time scale. Such a scheme is of immense value to professional people working long hours, pensioners and disabled people without a car and many more. Recent evidence shows that the Internet clothing market is currently worth about US$100 million a year. Consumer Internet spending rose from US$1.5 billion to US$2.7 billion (£890 million to £1.6 billion) in the United State last year—and is forecast to double (*Financial Times*, 24 June 1998, p. 11). Successful Internet products share three essential characteristics: convenience, potential for lower prices, and consumer awareness. According to Craig Danuloff, chief executive of iCat, an Internet commerce software group, 'These are prerequisites for e-commerce success.'

The matrix considers two types of procurement/distribution channels, traditional and electronic.

Traditional

The traditional way of distributing goods and services has been via an indirect route. People visit shopping malls, supermarkets and car showrooms, etc. in order to purchase and, in many cases, collect their selected items. Common distribution channels are by air, rail and road. Postal services are also included under this category. The key issue is whether businesses and consumers will prefer to continue using traditional distribution channels or instead shift to electronic ones. The development of intranets and extranets will not be appropriate for all businesses, so it is unlikely that traditional distribution methods will be severely affected at least in the short term.

Electronic

With Internet commerce, virtual products/services will be procured and delivered electronically. People can already access software products/services, newspapers, share prices, etc. over the Internet and this is set to increase. In addition, physical products/services will be increasingly procured by electronic means. Recent figures on home shopping, for example, show that contrary to the belief that many people like to purchase clothes from department stores, they are now using Internet home shopping services, especially for standard items such as clothes, etc. (*Sunday Times*, 8 August 1999, pp. 12–13). Tour operators and estate agents are also exploring ways to offer their customers an electronic way of procuring goods and services. Transaction costs, especially for products/services, which can be downloaded by the customer on the Internet are continually falling (Cairncross, 1997; Rayport and Sviokla, 1995). This will have a large impact on the growth of electronic distribution channels as companies take advantage of this cheap and effective new medium.

The US's General Electric (GE) Lighting conducts its procurement process over an extranet and claims to have saved 20%–30% on the overall costs of materials and to have shortened the procurement cycle by 50%. Part of this saving came from a much cheaper Hungarian supplier that responded over the Internet to an invitation to bid. Similarly, Toshiba's Electronic Imaging Division says it has cut annual networking costs from US$1.3 million to US$600 000 since replacing a dial-up order entry method for its dealers with a Web-based one.

The Shift from Traditional to Electronic Product/Service Procurement and Distribution

The Internet is currently widely used for procuring/distributing many software products/services to users electronically. Software products/services can be downloaded and installed on office or home PCs simply by following a series of simple instructions. Examples being: upgrades to operating systems and programming languages, bug fixes, new features in software applications/packages, and sample programs. Software companies also offer their users a technical service via the Internet and provide a knowledge base which consists of frequently asked questions (FAQs) on their products/services. In this capacity, the Internet serves as an extremely important means of communicating and providing an excellent service to customers. Less advanced, at least at the current moment, is the provision of financial services to customers in a fully virtual capacity. Whilst many banks, for example, are exploring the possibilities of developing electronic cash, customers are not at the present time given a seamless banking service. So while they can use PC banking for some transactions, they must also employ more traditional methods should they require other services. However, the trend is that informational (intangible) products/services offered by bookstores, music stores, publishers, financial services companies and educational establishments will be procured and distributed increasingly by electronic means as the Internet infrastructure grows. This may be further aided by the relatively low cost of distribution of electronic data/information via the Internet.[11] Cairncross (1997, p. 89), in *The Death of Distance*, writes,

> ... the Internet is not dominated by a single large industry, forced to defend a pre-revolutionary cost structure or market. It therefore offers a glimpse of the communications future: a world where transmitting information costs almost nothing, where distance is irrelevant, and where any amount of content is instantly accessible.

Whilst the Internet offers great opportunities for transforming informational products/services from being traditionally procured/distributed to one where they are directly available to customers via the Internet, the procurement of physical products/services (if not their delivery) will also change. As we have seen, large supermarkets, for example, are currently experimenting with home shopping and it is only a matter of time before more and more customers take advantage of the benefits of this time-saving opportunity. Only two impediments seem to stand in the way of developing this service further. Firstly, peoples' habits will need to change—they are accustomed to purchasing their food shopping from supermarkets. As such, they will need to develop trust in using an electronically based medium like the Internet. Secondly, access to the Internet will need to grow—so far, the Internet is used largely by professional groups (academics, managers and technologists, etc.). Expansion is therefore critical if the general population is to take advantage of new services such as Internet shopping.

Other physical goods available on the Internet through home shopping services are cars, computers and clothes. In many cases, such as with cars, consumers will of course wish to test the product before making a purchase. In the United Kingdom, car magazines such as *Auto Trader* and *Exchange and Mart* offer customers a selection of cars for sale in their local area. Over time, it is likely that sales of these magazines will decline as more and more people use the Internet to search for a car instead of thumbing through numerous pages of largely irrelevant information. A key challenge for publishers selling goods over the Internet is to make the process as user friendly as possible. This will be achieved by designing the Web sites in such a way that customers are presented with simple and straightforward instructions to enable them to access the required information easily and quickly.[12]

In examining the relationship between products/services (virtual and physical) and procurement/distribution channels (traditional/electronic), the matrix shows that whilst some products/services may be ordered electronically, their distribution may continue to be via a traditional (indirect) route. Amazon.com, for example, which is a large US-based Internet bookstore, allows customers to purchase products electronically, but their distribution is through traditional methods (i.e. postal services). This is because, at the present time at least, books are sold predominantly as a paper-based (material) product even though their main purpose is to convey data, information and ideas. This situation may change over time, as books become available on the Internet. Publishers will of course need to develop a revised charging mechanism (revenue generation) if this is to occur.

The debate about whether people will continue to desire paper-based books is highly contentious. Clearly, books are purchased for a variety of reasons, from being read purely for entertainment to being used for academic purposes. In the case of the latter, it is not inconceivable that publishers could provide students with an effective Internet service whereby only part of a book could be downloaded instead of the entire book. Many publishers are currently exploring this avenue, but their main concern is cost and profit. One option is for students to pay for the content which has been downloaded—e.g. 10p (£) per page, and this money would go directly to the publisher. Another option would be to give individual students a personal account with the publisher so that any material they download from the Internet is charged for monthly or annually. These issues are critical to the development of Internet commerce in the publishing world, and their resolution will determine the future shape of this market sector.

Value Chain

As products/services are transformed through Internet commerce, so too will traditional value chains undergo marked changes. As we have noted in the previous section, Internet commerce is more than just a sophisticated electronic procurement/distribution channel. Rather, it has the capability to transform some products/ services from being physical (tangible) to fully virtual (intangible). This transformation will not take place overnight. It will be a gradual process and it is likely that many businesses will offer products/services which are both virtual and physical. This is depicted in Figure 2.3. For example, a bank will offer customers a range of

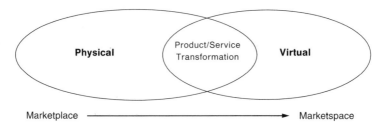

Figure 2.3   *Product and service transformation in the marketplace and marketspace*

products/services which can be obtained at a branch or via the Internet. Airline tickets are currently sold through travel agents, but can also be purchased through on-line services. In many cases, companies should aim to offer their customers flexibility rather than attempt to transform all their products/services into virtual offerings. A large proportion of the worldwide population is elderly people, many of whom are valued customers of banks and insurance companies. Evidence suggests that many people belonging to this group will be deterred from making purchases over the Internet, and companies must therefore keep this in mind when devising their Internet-related product/service strategies.

According to Rayport and Sviokla (1995, p. 75), senior managers should identify how to add value in both physical and virtual environments. They need to understand the 'value-adding processes' of each environment, although this poses new 'conceptual and tactical challenges'. These authors argue that creating value in any stage of a virtual value chain involves a sequence of five activities: gathering, organising, selecting, synthesising, and distributing information. The authors claim that the economic logic of both the physical and virtual value chains is different, and that a conventional understanding of the economies of scale and scope of the latter does not apply. They observe that companies adopt value-adding information processes in three stages: visibility, mirroring capability, and new customer relationships. *Visibility* is where companies acquire an ability to see physical operations more effectively through information. Information technology may be used to coordinate activities in the physical value chain and, by so doing, 'lay the foundation for a virtual value chain'. Information systems in the form of relational databases allow managers to see their physical value chains 'as an integrated system rather than as a set of discrete though related activities'.

Mirroring capability is where companies create a parallel value chain. This enables managers to determine which value-adding steps in the physical value chain can be shifted to mirror the virtual value chain. With the virtual value chain, employees can conduct their work without the need to be physically present with their project team. For example, designers can use computer-aided design (CAD) and send their drawings to their colleagues all over the world. Programmers working on a large-scale project can do the same, as can academics, artists, writers and numerous other professionals. Car manufacturers such as Ford have conducted many geographically disperse virtual projects where value-adding activities have accrued through using the best capabilities and skills worldwide.

Having developed visibility and parallel value chains, companies are then in a position to improve their relationships with customers. *New customer relationships* can be developed in the virtual value chain (VVC) by directly liaising with customers on a variety of issues: product design/improvement, customer service, pricing, etc. Many software manufacturers now distribute new products to customers directly over the Internet—a situation that allows them to 'get close to the customer' and receive almost instant feedback on their products and services. The authors claim that, 'As companies move into the information world to perform value-adding steps, the potential for topline growth increases. Each of the three stages represents considerable opportunity for managers' (p. 78).

Many companies continue to be at stage one (visibility) of the process and have yet to fully evaluate how they can enter stage two (developing parallel value chains). The final stage, new customer relationships, is presented by the authors as the most advanced position, held by only a selection of companies. However, it is likely that the progress from stages one to three will not be linear, but instead follow an iterative route. Many companies are likely to have developed strategies for each of the three stages, and it is equally likely that they may be inhibited not just by internal (organisational) factors, but also by external (market/environmental) conditions.

Intermediaries and the Value Chain

One of the most interesting debates in the literature is how intermediaries in the supply or value chain will be affected by Internet commerce. Like the global information infrastructure (GII), many companies will re-evaluate the economics of marketing channels and patterns of physical distribution (Pitt *et al.*, 1996). As we have already seen, traditional theories and models of product/service development, distribution channels and value chain economics are likely to become obsolete or in need of much revision as Internet commerce engenders changes to markets, businesses and organisations.

Benjamin and Wigand (1995, pp. 62–63) reinforce this point: one of the central issues facing managers today is the difficulty in identifying the boundaries of companies. IT has the potential to lower unit costs and radically alter supply chains and relationships with suppliers and customers. By so doing, the traditional links between company, supplier and customer are broken down. Important factors for managers to take into account are: electronic data integration, outsourcing, electronic hierarchies and markets, strategic alliances and joint ventures, networked organisations, among others. New organisational forms thus dictate an ongoing rethink of how to add value, and this may be achieved through IT-enabled transformation of business processes.

The debate surrounding the position of intermediaries in the virtual society is contentious. In essence, there are two competing arguments. The first assumes that, as the GII grows, companies will reduce their reliance upon specific intermediaries in the supply chain. Manufacturing companies, for example, will set up an elaborate web of intranets and extranets to procure goods and services and this will have a direct benefit to themselves and to their customers. Benjamin and Wigand (1995, p. 62) claim that:

1. all intermediaries between the manufacturer and the consumer may be threatened as the national information infrastructure (NII) reaches out to the consumer;
2. profit margins may be substantially lowered and redistributed;
3. the consumer will have access to a broad selection of lower priced goods; and
4. there will be many opportunities to restrict consumers' access to the potentially vast amount of commerce.

The other side to the debate about intermediaries assumes that, as the Internet expands, companies will outsource more of their information systems requirements to third parties (intermediaries). Many of these intermediaries will be high-tech suppliers offering a range of specialist *niche* services from Web site development, help desk services, software development and maintenance, data warehousing and many others. Figure 2.4. postulates a relationship between

1. the declining cost of computing;
2. the elimination of traditional intermediaries;
3. the growing use of the Internet; and
4. the growth in high-tech virtual intermediaries.

Whilst hard evidence, as opposed to speculative offerings are thin on the ground, Figure 2.4 captures the current trends in these four areas. Numerous statistics are available which show an increase in the use of the Internet worldwide. A recent estimate is that between 20 and 40 million people (four to six million in Europe) use

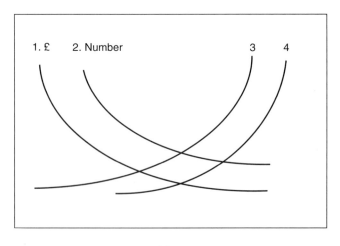

Time

Figure 2.4   *The relationship between the new economics of Internet commerce. 1. Cost of computing. 2. Traditional intermediaries. 3. Use of Internet. 4. High-tech virtual intermediaries*

the Internet from more than 50 countries, with a new computer being connected to it every 27 seconds (*Business and Technology*, December 1997, p. 55). International Data Corporation (IDC) claim that the European electronic commerce market will be worth about US$30 billion (£18.4 billion) by the year 2001. Part of this expansion is fuelled by the ever-declining costs of computing. Indeed, many companies and individual consumers find it frustrating that the cost of a PC they purchased six months ago has been reduced in price, sometimes by as much as 50%. Whilst *accelerated obsolescence* in the PC market dictates that companies and individuals purchase new equipment every couple of years, enhanced functionality at reduced cost seems to be a fair trade-off.

One interesting observation about the Internet is that, as more people become users, the content is likely to improve and this, in turn, will encourage more people to set up a network connection. The term 'network externalities' refers to '. . . the effect one person's decision to buy into a network has on others who are still thinking of buying-in—have been the Net's rocket fuel: the more people who connect, the more valuable a connection becomes (*Wired*, May 1998, p. 105).

Similarly, Cronin (1996, p. 10) writes,

> *Connectivity* is the cornerstone of the new electronic commerce; the more companies and consumers are linked up to computer networks, the more business will be transacted on-line. If growth trends on the Internet and other on-line services continue at their current pace, network connections will be as ubiquitous as telephone lines within the decade and computer interfaces will be the conduit of choice for the majority of commercial transactions . . . Today there is no simple, linear process for reaching a critical mass of networked buyers and sellers in either the business-to-business or the consumer marketplace. Connectivity is coming at different rates to different industries and consumer groups. It is possible, however, to map out highly connected sectors, to pinpoint areas of rapid growth, and to identify persistent connectivity gaps whose correction may require new infrastructure breakthroughs.

These factors will help to shape the future development and application of the Internet. In particular, the Internet will create (virtual) and eliminate (traditional) intermediaries. The process of eliminating intermediaries is termed *disintermediation* and the current evidence suggests that certain groups such as travel agents and insurance brokers may be affected as customers purchase holidays and insurance premiums directly (electronically) from the Internet. At the opposite end of the spectrum, new intermediaries will be generated by the demand for a range of support services. The growing trend for companies to outsource much of the in-house IT services will extend to their Internet facility. As a consequence, many companies will not possess the relevant in-house specialist IT skills to design, set up, implement and maintain a Web site. These companies will therefore go out to the marketplace for these services, and there has already been a mushrooming of small suppliers offering Internet support services. We will return to the subject of IT outsourcing in Chapter 7.

Innovation and Technology

The related subjects of innovation and technology are of critical importance to companies in deciding upon their Internet strategies. The concept of innovation is widely discussed in the literature, although there is little consensus about its definitive meaning (Vedin, 1994). In the context of the Internet, it is contended that innovation incorporates R&D strategies, technology assisted business development (new products and services), methods and techniques, capabilities and skills, support networks, organisational learning and continuous improvement. Drucker (1985) asserts,

> Innovation is a specific tool of entrepreneurs, the means by which they exploit change as an opportunity for a different business or a different service. It is capable of being presented as a discipline, capable of being learned and capable of being practised. Entrepreneurs need to search purposely for the sources of innovation, the changes and their symptoms that indicate opportunities for successful innovation. And they need to know and apply the principles of successful innovation.

Perhaps some of the tried and tested 'principles of successful innovation' do not apply in today's high-tech environment. For example, an important area which may enhance or inhibit innovation is the interoperability of services and interconnection of networks in the global information infrastructure (GII).[13] The Internet is a global matrix of interconnected computer networks using the Internet Protocol (IP) to communicate with each other. For simplicity, the term 'internet' encompasses all such data networks, even though some electronic commerce activities may take place on proprietary networks that are not technically part of the Internet. The term 'on-line service provider' is used to refer to both companies that provide access to the Internet and other on-line services, and companies that create content that is delivered over those networks.[14]

The responsibility for determining technical standards and other mechanisms for interoperability is generally within the domain of the private sector. Technology is moving rapidly and government attempts to establish technical standards to govern the Internet may inhibit technological innovation. Many governments, particularly in the United States, consider it unwise and unnecessary to mandate standards for Internet commerce. Rather, they urge industry to consider technical standards in this area.

To ensure the growth of global electronic commerce over the Internet, standards will be needed to assure reliability, interoperability, and ease of use and scalability in areas such as:

- electronic payments;
- security (confidentiality, authentication, data integrity, access control, non-repudiation);
- security services infrastructure (e.g. public key certificate authorities);
- electronic copyright management systems;
- video and data-conferencing;
- high-speed network technologies (e.g. asynchronous transfer mode, synchronous digital hierarchy); and
- digital object and data interchange.

As the itemised list shows, standards refer not only to technical issues but also extend to managerial and legal issues (payment and security) (Aldridge *et al.*, 1997).

There need not be one standard for every product or service associated with the GII, and technical standards need not be mandated. In some cases, multiple standards will compete for marketplace acceptance. In other cases, different standards will be used in different circumstances. These issues pose many challenges to companies wishing to develop or expand Internet commerce. So far, the Internet has been likened to a *wild west* scenario whereby companies, suppliers, customers, governments, pressure groups, etc. are all trying to make sense of Internet commerce from a market, business, organisational, technical and consumer perspective. Given the global nature of Internet commerce, it follows that laws and regulations governing corporate behaviour, intellectual property and consumer rights, etc. should be standardised, regulated, monitored and enforced worldwide. Failure to do so will create an uneven landscape where buyers and sellers choose not to do business in countries with few controls and concentrate only on those countries with established commercial practices.

Customer Focus

One of the central themes of Internet commerce relates to customer focus. The Internet will allow companies to develop closer relationships with their customers. As we have already seen, this may be achieved through the process of disintermediation. In the areas of retailing, financial services and publishing, companies are continuing to set up Web sites to enable their customers to deal directly with them. Key questions facing managers will be: How can our company develop closer links with our customers? How can we use the Internet to offer our customers a more focused and seamless service? In what ways can we use our customers to provide us with useful feedback to enable us to improve our products/services?

Kalakota and Whinston (1996, p. 254) claim there are a series of fundamental issues which must be addressed before consumer-orientated e-commerce can grow. They are:

- The establishment of standard business processes for buying and selling products and services in electronic markets.
- The development of widespread and easy-to-use implementations of mercantile protocols for order-taking, on-line payment, and service delivery similar to those found in retail/credit-card-based transactions.
- The development of transport and privacy methods that will allow parties that have no reason to trust one another to carry on secure commercial exchanges.

The authors contend that consumer-orientated Internet commerce will be more effective if a better understanding of the components of the business process from the initial search and discovery of the product/services via on-line catalogues to the management of the order-to-delivery cycle, including the all-important payment/settlement component, is achieved. They give four classifications for the consumer Internet commerce marketplace. They are

- entertainment,
- financial services and information,

- essential services, and
- education and training.

For consumer-orientated Internet commerce to succeed, the cost of providing a digital transmission as opposed to a physical transfer of information must be comparable or less. In addition, customers must find that its use must be more convenient or faster. The supportive rhetoric often overlooks some of the pitfalls in developing consumer-orientated Internet commerce. Clearly, companies will need to develop individual strategies in the four areas mentioned above, and offer customers an efficient and seamless service, which will be an improvement on traditional services.

Role of Government

As with other decisions taken by companies on product/service development, value and supply chain management, and innovation and technology, the role of government will be important in defining and shaping Internet commerce both nationally and internationally. What has emerged in the last decade is a growing concern from governments worldwide about the impact on society from the burgeoning Internet commerce marketplace. It would appear that critical issues about competition, security and intellectual property protection, among others, have seemingly raised more questions than answers. Moreover, concerns about the many serious aspects of the Internet, namely child pornography, credit card fraud and drug trafficking, have led many governments to develop a series of measures (laws, directives, reports, guidelines, etc.) to protect citizens (these will be discussed in greater detail in Chapter 3).

Whilst international governments believe that Internet commerce has tremendous possibilities for job creation, particularly for the small and medium enterprise (SME) sector, with the private sector taking the lead in developing and shaping the GII, the role of government is considered by many to be in the development of a legal and regulatory framework which will promote competitiveness in global markets. Coupled with this, governments will assist in developing 'awareness-raising measures' to ensure that as many people as possible worldwide are informed about the possibilities of Internet commerce.

Spar and Bussgang (1996, p. 128) claim that,

> The advent of electronic commerce does not eliminate business's basic need for an infrastructure to clarify ownership and allow owners to reap economic rewards. But at the moment, on-line property rights are imprecisely defined; the Net remains a virtual free-for-all where information is seen as a public good and ownership is up for grabs.

Such a situation will deter many companies from developing Internet commerce, particularly if their intellectual property rights vary from one country to the next. For example, a publishing house will need to address these issues very seriously, particularly if it decides to offer its material to customers over the Internet (Ives and Jarpenpaa, 1996). The same is true for educational establishments, especially where academics release unpublished working papers on the Internet. Indeed, one of the more disquieting factors surrounding student use of the Internet is the possibility that material can simply be downloaded and inserted into essays (plagiarism). Or even more worrying, complete essays can be obtained from what is essentially a black market for this type of academic material. Whilst this says little about the intellectual curiosity of some students and their concern about entering what should be a personal learning experience, these concerns must be dealt with by universities to ensure fair play and integrity of academic courses. At the present time, however, most universities have not thought through these issues in much detail.

A comparative analysis of the role of individual governments shows there has been a broad convergence between the United States, the European Union and Japan concerning issues of intellectual property protection (IPR), taxes, legal and harmful content on the Internet and liability issues. The main difference lies in the legislative approach, which is more directed towards self-regulation in the United States, and concerning data protection. The awareness issue is important in Europe and in Japan, but less so in the United States where Internet access is high. A European Commission Report (1998) from the Committee on Economic and Monetary Affairs and Industry Policy, p. 13). This report further considers other current problems associated with Internet commerce. It suggests that high tele-communications tariffs have long been a major impediment to the progress of Internet commerce throughout the European Union. The implementation of the telecommunications liberalisation measures is intended to create lower and more flexible pricing. Another organisation, The World Trade Organisation (WTO), with its report entitled *Agreement on Basic Telecommunications*, will make a contribution to the emergence of a global marketplace in e-commerce. Other international agree-ments to eliminate tariffs (ITAs) and non-tariff barriers (MRAs) will also lower the cost of IT products, reinforce EU competitiveness and encourage the further diffusion of e-commerce.

In the light of the above issues, many companies will await the outcome of proposed legislation before making any further commitments to developing their Internet sites. The dilemma is that whilst companies have traditionally argued that governments should not concern themselves with business and commerce, govern-ment failure to provide adequate protection for companies through the develop-ment of a legal and regulatory framework will only inhibit Internet commerce, particularly in situations where consumer trust breaks down.

Managerial Issues

One of the central themes in the literature concerns the management of technology and innovation. Many studies support the view that IS failures are directly related to poor management practice (Sauer, 1993; Currie, 1994, 1996a). The Internet is no exception. The key management issues which will determine the success or failure of Internet commerce relate to: senior management commitment; the development of core capabilities and skills; employment contracts and reward systems; training initiatives; and command and control structures. In a global business environment which is increasingly outsourcing more of the IT facility, management will be faced with new challenges. One of the key challenges will be in devising new and effective ways of managing an increasingly diverse organisation—one which is characterised by numerous contracts with suppliers and fewer permanent employees.

In a recent study on US and European outsourcing practices, Currie and Willcocks (1997) found that traditional management methods and techniques are becoming less relevant as outsourcing continues to flourish. For example, new capabilities and skills are needed in areas such as contracts management and negotiation skills. The authors identified a critical dilemma facing managers in that, as capabilities and skills are stripped out of the organisation with outsourcing, the supplier is expected to service the contract with its own personnel. However, the supplier is likely to experience serious skills shortages as the global IS labour market continues to show that chronic skills shortages are found in a variety of areas from management to technical personnel.

In the context of developing Internet commerce, evidence suggests that companies will hire the expertise from the labour market as they are unlikely to possess all the relevant managerial and technical capabilities and skills in-house. In the light of the above, they will need to ensure that their Internet strategies are not seriously inhibited through skills shortages over which they have little or no control. Indeed, the increasing tendency for companies to outsource or insource technical services shows that they must develop a greater understanding of the services and supplier marketplace to enable them to fully meet their strategic goals of developing Internet commerce. This will engender changes in the style and focus of management control, particularly as more people work remotely (e.g. from home or from other sites). The traditional command and control managerial approach will be increasingly phased out, as too will some of the key managerial activities of planning, organising, commanding, co-ordinating, and controlling (Fayol, 1949). In a virtual working environment, it is likely that there will be fewer hands-on managers and more portfolio or contract workers who are responsible for their own performance and work on a project rather than permanent basis. This is already largely the case in the IT contract labour market where people are hired on short- to medium-term contracts (commonly from three months to one year) and are re-hired according to their past performance.

Administrative/Hierarchical Structure

The structure of organisations will undergo major changes with the further development and implementation of new technology. Issues such as centralisation versus decentralisation and bureaucratic versus non-bureaucratic administrative/hierarchical structures will become more important as companies reconfigure their organisation structures. Internet commerce will have a major impact on these areas, as the customer will bypass traditional layers of administration and purchase goods and services direct. Information flows will change and it is likely that the trend of de-layering and downsizing which has been occurring since the 1980s will continue unabated.

The concepts of re-engineering (Hammer and Champy, 1993), process improvement and process innovation (Davenport, 1993a,b) which were popular in the early 1990s are relevant here. Whilst re-engineering and process innovation have proved to be more difficult to implement, despite all the supportive rhetoric these ideas have received from their advocates, the move towards Internet commerce will pose similar problems. As we have seen above, altering the supply chain from traditional (with many intermediaries) to virtual (with fewer or no intermediaries) will require significant changes to the administrative/hierarchical structure. Information management will become even more important, especially where customers purchase their goods/services direct from the Internet and do not discuss their purchases with a company contact such as a sales representative.

Cost/Performance

Changes to the administrative/hierarchical structure are inextricably linked to cost/performance issues. Understanding the economics of Internet commerce will pose an important challenge to managers. Key questions will be: What is the return on investment (ROI) from developing Internet commerce to our business? How can we reduce business processes to make further savings? Will accelerated obsolescence of information technology mean that our cost savings from Internet commerce will be offset by the regular purchase of new equipment? Will sourcing capabilities and skills from the marketplace to support Internet commerce become excessive over time?

The cost of developing and maintaining Internet commerce varies widely between companies and countries. Whilst the cost of computing has been falling sharply in recent years, the Internet has flourished mostly in countries where access is least expensive (Cairncross, 1997, p. 21). In the United States, local telephone calls are free. This means that companies and individuals can make great savings in their administration simply by using the e-mail facility. The Internet may also lower advertising and promotion costs and other services which can be electronically distributed. Notwithstanding the above, Maloff (1996, p. 165) cautions that 'Connection to the Internet, however, entails technical, security, and personnel requirements and costs, which may not make it a viable or an optimal solution for all companies.'

Companies attempting to measure the value of an Internet connection for business should first identify the costs of their existing business processes and administrative practices. Having done so, they will then be able to evaluate how Internet commerce will help reduce costs in these areas. It is likely that some companies may conclude that the Internet will be too expensive to develop and maintain and that anticipated benefits will not accrue. Maloff (1996, p. 167) points out that, 'The Internet is only one of the alternatives. If a company concludes that connection to the Internet is warranted, it needs to evaluate different kinds of Internet services, their anticipated benefits, and the corresponding requirements and costs.' Table 2.2 is adapted from Maloff (1996) and includes four performance areas where the Internet may produce value-added benefits for companies.

Table 2.2 shows that the Internet may reduce costs in external/internal communication expenses. In particular, the use of private line networks, internal telephone systems, voice mail, faxes, and messenger and overnight courier services which are commonplace in companies may all be reduced as companies rely more on Internet

Table 2.2   *Cost/performance benefits of Internet commerce*

External/internal communication expenses
- reduced private line network costs
- fewer fax transmissions
- fewer overnight courier services
- fewer paper-based transactions
- speed-up business/administrative processes
- reduction in administrative tasks

Revenues
- enhance company visibility (advertising, discussion groups, company literature, bulletin boards, samples, etc.)
- extend customer network
- extend supplier network
- find new international business partners (joint ventures)

Tangible benefits
- reduced office (floor) space
- reduced equipment/furniture costs
- flexible working practices
- seamless (focused) customer service

Intangible benefits
- improved employee morale
- enhanced customer satisfaction
- enhanced competitive position
- improved relations with customers (trust/confidence)

services. Internal communications include the transmission of organisational announcements, critical financial data for day-to-day operations, management reports, data/information for company use (e.g. reports, meetings, briefings), and so forth. External communications with customers, vendors, potential business partners, and others outside the organisation include sending and receiving purchase orders, invoices, delivery notices, press releases, marketing literature, and requests for proposals. By examining the costs of these activities, managers may be able to identify ways in which the Internet can reduce these costs at the same time as improving information flows.

The second area is concerned with company revenues. The Internet has great potential for generating revenue from current sources and new initiatives. By giving the company an Internet presence, new customers and suppliers may be gained, and even new international business partners through joint ventures. By offering customers additional information in a variety of areas from products, services, prices, contacts, frequently asked questions (FAQs), etc. a company may gain competitive advantage, particularly if its Web site is well designed, provides useful information and is easy to use.

Other tangible benefits may accrue from developing Internet commerce. These may include a reduction in the overall costs of administration, with fewer offices, and less furniture and equipment. Instead, staff may become teleworkers (home-working) with the company providing only a PC, modem, paid phone line and other office-related costs for their staff (e.g. some office furniture). The cost savings to the company will be immense.

Together with these tangible benefits, there may be many intangible benefits from Internet commerce. For example, teleworking will give people greater flexibility and freedom in when and how they undertake their work. People working on their own in private are likely to be more productive than those who work in open plan offices with noise and disruption. In addition, a well-designed and managed Internet site may improve the image of a company and, by so doing, its competitive position. Conversely, a poorly designed and mis-managed Internet site may do the company more damage than having no Internet site. Trust and confidence are immensely important issues surrounding the development of Internet commerce and companies must not undervalue their importance.

The Productivity Paradox

One of the problems with the relationship between technology and cost/performance is that the former is unpredictable, fast changing and difficult to manage. This is evident in discussions about the *productivity paradox*, which depicts the situation where large investment in technology is not always followed by increased productivity. Wealthy countries have invested large sums of money in their IT resource in the latter quarter of the twentieth century. In the United States, the increase was from 7% of corporate investment in 1970 to 40% today. IT expenditure now exceeds that of traditional machinery. Moreover, total spending on computers in 1996 comprised 3% of the GDP in the United States (Cairncross 1997, pp. 225–226).

The reasons for the productivity paradox are plentiful, yet need to be taken into consideration by companies thinking of investing in Internet technology. First, productivity is inherently difficult to measure. In a changing employment labour market, old jobs are eliminated and new ones created. A company implementing a database may eliminate some tasks/actions originally performed by an employee and add new ones. How this process is measured will of course determine productivity. However, in the case where a business process has been re-engineered, such as in the insurance industry, traditional methods and techniques for measuring productivity may be obsolete (Hammer and Champy, 1993). To this end, it becomes important to break down business processes into their component parts so that each stage in the process can be measured and costed accordingly.

Second, large investment in PCs to fulfil the goal of having 'a PC on every desk' does not equate with enhanced productivity. One observation, which has been made often, is that many employees do not exploit the full potential of the applications and packages they use to carry out their work. For example, many secretaries do not use their word processing packages fully and continue to perform some tasks manually. The same can be said of database software used by accountants and others. It is therefore reasonable to conclude that investment in hardware and software does not in itself enhance employee productivity. Similarly, at the corporate level, senior managers rarely have wide experience of information systems, and are often unaware of the benefits their companies can achieve by developing and implementing an effective information management strategy.

Clearly, before companies start to invest large sums of money in developing Internet commerce, they will need to consider the issues briefly discussed in this section so as to avoid fuelling an Internet-related productivity paradox. So far, many companies have set up a Web site, but have not thought through how this will be developed in the medium term.

Risk/Reward

The previous section on cost/performance is inextricably linked with the subject of risk/reward. Much of the hype surrounding Internet commerce underplays some of the more disquieting issues concerned with security and payment systems, privacy, criminal behaviour (e.g. fraud, drugs smuggling, child pornography) and others. Whilst intra-business (within business) and business-to-business (between business) forms of Internet commerce are making some progress, business-to-consumer Internet commerce is still in its early stages of development. As we have noted above, increasing consumer trust is critical if this type of Internet commerce is to grow. Yet many issues remain unclear. Evidence suggests that many consumers are reluctant to conduct financial transactions for the purchase of goods and services over the Internet. Whilst some commentators claim there is little difference in giving your credit card details to a waiter in a restaurant from typing them onto a computer screen on a vendor's Web site, the fact remains that many people are unconvinced that these two acts pose similar (low) risks.

Payment Systems

For payment systems to become effective on the Internet (measured by the growth in electronic purchases), the existing rules governing currency may be appropriate for electronic exchange. Spar and Bussgang (1996, p. 129) claim that

> Even in Cyberspace, customers can order goods priced in dollars, charge them to a credit card, and let banks intermediate the financial transaction. There is nothing intrinsic about the Internet that demands new means of exchange. There are no technical obstacles to routing and recording even non-traditional transactions through established routes, nor are there demands for new levels of financial oversight or regulation. Instead, the impetus for change stems from the instantaneous and intangible nature of electronic transactions. If electronic purchases become commonplace, they are likely to include such 'micro-transactions.'

This poses a problem for the small on-line entrepreneur since the cost of processing microtransactions would not be cost-effective. It could even be more expensive than the goods and services themselves! So measures would have to be put into place to ensure that payments could be instant with a corresponding reduction in the cost of transacting. Such moves would encourage the further use of the Internet. Whilst supermarkets, for example, are experimenting with home-shopping initiatives where the customer orders goods over the Internet (which are delivered to their home), a minimum purchase amount is necessary. Over time, supermarkets will develop more sophisticated payment and security systems so that customers will order and pay for their goods directly from the Internet.

Another important issue concerns privacy on the Internet. Many people are concerned about giving their personal details (name, home address, age, etc.) to companies operating on the Internet. The voluminous junk mail received by people has become a problem in recent years, and it is often difficult to determine its source. The same problem is now occurring on the Internet. The decision to join a discussion group (set up by a company, a government office, individuals, etc.) on the Internet can lead to an individual receiving a host of irrelevant and unwanted e-mails generated by people from all over the world. As a result, the initial interest in the discussion group can lead to immense frustration as some of the material received is from companies or individuals wishing to sell their products or services, or simply messages containing opinions of no significant interest.

A recent example is an Internet site set up by the EU to encourage discussion and learning about current and future developments in electronic commerce. Although English is used as the main language of communication, one message was sent in French. This generated a whole series of messages by people—some in support of receiving messages in French and others criticising the sender because they do not understand (written or spoken) French. What is interesting in this example is that the main purpose of the Internet site was lost in a heated debate (by numerous e-mail messages) about whether people living in Europe should use only English for communication or a whole variety of European (and perhaps other) languages.

Privacy and Security

The US Federal Trade Commission recently issued a report which focused upon the efforts of industry at privacy self-regulation of their Web sites, the disclosure of their information collection policies, and the safeguards in place for users. Some 1000 users were questioned. The report identified a complete disregard for privacy. Only 14% of Web sites in the sample disclosed their security policies.

There are clear differences between the privacy policy adopted/directives between the United States and Europe, the latter approach being more stringent. A European directive on privacy developed in 1995 aimed to harmonise the various national policies of all the European member states. Such a move poses problems for the United States since the directive reinforces liabilities. As such, the directive covers data identifying any individual gathered from any equipment in EU territory. To this end, US firms must comply or risk a lawsuit in Europe.

Countries in Asia (including Japan) may adopt the European directive, which gives strict protection of personal data (e.g. demographics, race, politics, finances, religion and health). For US companies wishing to trade within the EU, they are left with little alternative but to adopt privacy standards, which are different to those adopted at home. There are of course some voices of dissent in Europe that believe that the United States as opposed to the European privacy policies should be adopted. Notwithstanding this factor, the European directive seeks to accomplish a series of policy objectives on behalf of users' personal privacy protection. So companies with an international presence should ensure that personal data on the Internet is

- processed fairly and lawfully;
- collected and processed for a specified, explicit legitimate purpose;
- accurate and current; and
- kept no longer than deemed necessary to fulfil the stated purpose.

Users should also have rights to

- access;
- correction, erasure, or blocking of information;
- object to usage;
- oppose automated individual decision; and
- judicial remedy and compensation.

Before transferring information, companies must ensure an 'adequate' level of protection in the recipient country. The only exceptions are consent by the user; a contract with the user; information that is in the public interest; or legal claims. Consumers who use cash machines, telephones and home computers to do their banking may be vulnerable to criminal activity, especially if the banks fail to develop adequate security measures. An EC Report claims that European consumers have far less legal protection than their American counterparts when they become victims of fraud. In spite of the voluntary code that limits customers' losses to £50, banks refuse to compensate victims for their losses by claiming that 'remote' banking systems are infallible. By insisting that their remote banking security systems are infallible, some EU banks have passed on losses arising from criminal activity to individual customers. These findings are worrying and will do little to develop consumer trust and confidence in the Internet. The lack of harmonisation in consumer protection across national borders will need to be addressed by governments if Internet commerce is to develop into a global rather than regionally based phenomenon. Much of the rhetoric for developing business-to-consumer Internet commerce is to give people greater choice in the goods and services available to

Table 2.3   *Customer protection in purchasing goods and services on the Internet*

- Read the privacy policy of individual Web sites
- Check if it has an opt-out which allows you to prevent solicitation or sharing of personal information with third parties
- Guard your password and do not give it to anyone on-line who asks for it
- If performing credit card transactions via your browser, check for icons, such as unbroken keys or closed padlocks, which depict the secure transmission of data. If you do not see the icons, consider avoiding making the transaction
- Check software suppliers for any tools that will provide an additional layer of privacy protection. Examples include cookie cutters or anonymisers
- Use discretion in the data you give out. If you would not give out personal information to a stranger in the off-line world, adopt the same safeguards on-line

Adapted from: Computer Weekly, 18 June 1998, p. 39.

them. Yet problems in relation to payment systems, consumer privacy and protection need to be overcome. Table 2.3 gives some advice to customers in purchasing goods and services on the Internet (European Commission, 1998).

SUMMARY

This chapter has raised a variety of issues which are relevant to the further development and implementation of Internet commerce. Companies will need to address each one and formulate an all-embracing strategy to progress their plans for each of the three types of Internet commerce. Such a strategy will need to take into consideration external and internal factors. At the external level, companies will need to familiarise themselves with the latest government measures to develop a legal and regulatory framework for Internet commerce. Consumer associations and other pressure groups will be monitoring Internet commerce activities closely to determine whether appropriate measures are in place to protect consumers. At the internal level, companies will be faced with many challenges, as benefits from developing Internet commerce activities will not be immediate. On the contrary, a large investment in Internet technology and related support systems is unlikely to accrue financial benefits for some considerable time, if at all. Having given an overview of 10 key areas relating to the development of Internet commerce, the following chapter considers the role of government in developing a legal and regulatory framework.

3
Defining a Legal and Regulatory Framework for Internet Commerce: The Role of Government

INTRODUCTION

Any discussion about the growth and development of Internet commerce should not overlook the important role of government in defining a legal and regulatory framework. The potential of the Internet to create new businesses, new revenue streams, and new employment opportunities is immense. Traditional business sectors such as the travel industry and financial services are currently migrating substantial parts of their commercial activities on-line. So far, Internet commerce is most advanced in the United States, with Europe and the rest of the world lagging behind (*Network News*, 1998). In the United States, Internet commerce is building on a specific structural strength from a dense network of innovative SMEs (Ba *et al.*, 1999). Ideally suited to the Internet environment, and enjoying essentially the same access to world markets as multinational corporations, some of these start-ups claim impressive growth rates and profitability (Saxenian, 1999). One survey found that out of 1100 Internet-based firms, over 30% were profitable after a year, and that a further 30% expected to make a profit within two years. Reported profit margins of 20% and above are common (*Business Week*, 23 September 1996).

These companies were referred to in the previous chapter as high-tech inter-mediaries, and are likely to become significant players in providing services and support to Internet users. The infrastructure for Internet commerce in the United States is therefore well developed as witnessed by the more than 250 000 *cyber* companies that use the Internet commercially. For example, travel services and flower distribution companies operating in the United States are among the Internet success stories. Travel services currently amount to more than half of

Internet commerce. The current market leader, launched in October 1996, is already claiming to have more than a quarter of a million users. By the same token, there are nearly a thousand Internet flower distributors with Internet sites, with the market leader claiming to have achieved US$30 million in sales in 1996 alone.

A cross-national comparison shows that the United States has built a substantial lead over Europe. A similar lead is opening up in the strategic sector of Internet commerce tools, products and technologies. Japan and the Asia/Pacific region are also rapidly catching up and are positioned to become key players in the global Internet commerce marketplace. Spurred by industry and government initiatives, these countries are enjoying huge growth in Internet connectivity and commerce. Based on current growth rates and investments, they could soon rival Europe in terms of Internet commerce revenues.

In the light of severe international competition, the European Union (EU) is actively devising laws (directives) and policies to encourage the development of Internet commerce in a number of areas. Recent figures indicate that in some member states, Internet commerce usage has caught up with, and sometimes overtaken, the United States. Finland and the Netherlands are now among the most dynamic on-line markets in the world. Moreover, in what has become an intensely competitive environment, Europe must encourage and nurture its specific strengths if it is to retain its position as a key player. On a country-by-country analysis of European member states, the Internet commerce environment is variable. One of the leaders is the Netherlands, however, with a high PC penetration (38% of households) and high use of the Internet (22% of PC users have access to the Internet, against 16% in the United States, and 12% in the United Kingdom) (International Data Corporation).

Like the United States, Europe has a strong base in technology and infrastructure. It has powerful telecommunication operators (incumbents as well as new players), a highly reliable basic infrastructure, and early deployment of advanced digital networks (Kling and Lamb, 1999). Commitment to standardisation, exemplified by the success of industry-driven standards, is another crucial asset. So are Europe's commercial advances in key Internet commerce technologies such as smartcards and intelligent agents. Content development is another of Europe's greatest strengths. Content—computer software, business information, video entertainment—is the very essence of immaterial Internet commerce. European companies in the publishing and multimedia industries are harnessing their considerable resources and know-how in the global electronic information markets. Similarly, highly innovative SMEs are positioning themselves successfully in specialised markets such as multimedia production and multilingual content localisation. Europe also has a competitive retail sector, with adapted product ranges and an in-depth knowledge of the various consumer tastes around the continent, a strength that can also be leveraged to gain competitive advantage. Furthermore, the ability to trade electronically in a single currency—the euro—across the world's largest single market will give European businesses considerable competitive advantages. Cross-border price transparency resulting from the euro will stimulate the use of Internet commerce; conversely, Internet commerce will facilitate the transition to the euro.

Recently, the UK government published a report on 'promoting electronic commerce', which is a consultation on draft legislation and the government's response to the Trade and Industry Committee's Report (see DTI, 1999a). The Electronic Communications Bill is aimed at accelerating the adoption of e-commerce in the United Kingdom. It considers licensing a new radio spectrum for broadband wireless services; opening up British Telecom's (BT's) local network for broadband services; and introducing the third generation of mobile phones, giving mobile access to the Internet. It also intends to create a legal framework for the use of electronic signatures to give people confidence about the origin and integrity of communications. Another UK government report identifies three key priorities (Cabinet Office, 1999, p. 1). They are:

- to overcome business inertia—UK business is not yet fully switched on to e-commerce. The best UK companies are world class, but many are lagging behind. Small businesses especially need to wake up to the challenges;
- to ensure that government's own actions drive the take-up of e-commerce. Sustained progress must be made on electronic procurement; and
- to ensure better co-ordination between government and industry to gain maximum benefit from existing proposed programmes.

The above issues are central to current debates concerning the development of a global competitive Internet commerce infrastructure. But for Internet commerce to become global, it is essential for countries to develop laws, policies and practices covering many areas, e.g. developing a competitive telecommunications infrastructure, appropriate standards and interoperable solutions, focused R&D strategies, and business and consumer trust and confidence (notably privacy, security and the protection of intellectual properties). Initiatives to assist the business community will include the exchange of best practice, access and advice about venture capital to set up new businesses, and measures to encourage the development of capabilities and skills through targeted training programmes. In order to facilitate the above, governments worldwide are currently formulating their legal and regulatory frameworks for Internet commerce. In this chapter we consider the role of government by examining the policies and priorities of the United States and the European Union in their attempt to design a framework for Internet commerce. We also consider some of the cultural differences that influence governments' approach to formulating policies and frameworks on Internet commerce.

THE GLOBAL INFORMATION INFRASTRUCTURE

The global information infrastructure (GII)[15] which has emerged in the last decade is central to what is now referred to as the *information age* or *society*. Its potential for transforming the international business community is immense, and is likely to alter commercial relationships and the way people work. Over the next decade, companies, once separated by distance, time, language and culture, will be able to take advantage of the technological advances afforded by the GII. No single force embodies this trend more than the evolving medium known as the Internet, and its potential for business development and commerce. Once simply a tool used only by the military and academia, the Internet is used more and more by individuals in their everyday lives for leisure, health and work activities. Companies are also exploring ways to use the Internet for transactional (commercial) purposes rather than just for informational (data/information gathering) reasons (Reynolds, 1997).

In essence, the Internet has become the vehicle for a new, global digital economy that has significant implications for traditional theories of economics, politics and social relations. For example, the continuing growth and application of the Internet as a business tool will yield profound changes in the classic economic paradigm of buyer and seller (Quelch and Klein, 1996). New theories, models and methodologies of commercial behaviour will need to be developed as businesses and consumers participate in the electronic marketplace (Rayport and Sviokla, 1995). This is evident in the global trade in markets and services. It is unlikely that any business or commercial sector will be left out of the GII. Companies will undergo vast cultural, structural and processual changes as new Internet-based business solutions become available.

The GII, whilst still in the early stages of its development, is already transforming the commercial world. Over the next decade, advances in the GII will affect almost every aspect of daily life from education, health care, employment terms and conditions, and leisure activities. In the field of education, students are able to use the Internet to search for available degree/diploma courses worldwide. They can also download material to use in their studies as well as communicate with other students on similar study programmes. It is also likely that distance learning programmes will increase as universities and colleges become more adept at exploiting the Internet's commercial potential. Similarly, health care will undergo a transformation as medical personnel and even patients take advantage of the search facilities for a whole variety of reasons. The British government has tackled waiting lists in the NHS by investing in a system where patients can receive an initial diagnosis of their condition by nursing staff trained to use the Internet. Such off-site tele-medicine will save the time of medical staff in addition to reducing the time it takes for patients to receive diagnoses. Employment terms and conditions will change, as more people become *teleworkers* and work from home. There are two obvious advantages of telework. The first is the flexibility and freedom for individuals to combine homelife with work (which will be a major benefit to families), and the second is the reduction in traffic as fewer people take to the roads and railways to commute to the office.

The Internet will also boost leisure activities, as more information about clubs and activities becomes available. The availability of entertainment products and services will also increase, particularly with the advent of digital television. According to current figures, world trade involving computer software, entertainment products (motion pictures, videos, games, sound recordings), information services (databases, on-line newspapers), technical information, product licenses, financial services, and professional services (businesses and technical consulting, accounting, architectural design, legal advice, travel services, etc.) now accounts for well over US$40 billion of US exports alone. An increasing share of these transactions occurs on-line. To this end, the GII has the potential to revolutionise the business community by significantly reducing transaction costs as well as facilitating new types of commercial transactions (Pitt et al., 1996).

Since Internet commerce is likely to total tens of billions of dollars by the turn of the century, governments worldwide must develop a legal and regulatory framework which supports rather than inhibits global Internet commerce. Whereas some commentators call for a non-regulatory, market-orientated approach, one that facilitates the emergence of a transparent and predictable legal environment to support Internet commerce, others call for tighter regulation to protect businesses and consumers. Many businesses and consumers have expressed concern about conducting extensive business over the Internet because of the lack of a predictable legal and regulatory framework governing financial transactions (Consumers' Association, 1997). This issues continue to dominate. For example, there have been instances where a bogus company has imitated a legitimate company on the Internet. The latter has set up an almost identical Web site that serves to confuse the customer. The scam is designed so that the unsuspecting customer pays for their chosen goods over the Internet by giving their credit card details. Needless to say, money is deducted from their bank account and the goods are never received. This type of fraud is causing governments worldwide to urgently seek ways to eliminate Internet crime. But as Internet commerce expands, many companies and individuals are concerned that some governments will impose extensive regulations on Internet commerce. Controversial areas, which may be regulated, include taxes and duties, restrictions on the type of information transmitted, control over standards development, licensing requirements and regulation of service providers.

Governments are likely to have a profound effect on the nature and scope of Internet commerce. By their actions they can facilitate electronic trade or inhibit it. The following section examines the US government's vision for the emergence of the GII as a vibrant global marketplace. It suggests a set of principles, presents a series of policies, and establishes a road map for international discussions and agreements to facilitate the growth of Internet commerce.

The National Telecommunications and Infrastructure Administration

In the United States, the National Telecommunications and Infrastructure Administration (NTIA) contends that electronic commerce can mean any use of electronic technology in any aspect of commercial activity. Their task force on electronic commerce more narrowly uses the term to mean the use of a National Information Infrastructure (NII) to perform any of the following functions:

- to bring products to market (e.g. R&D via telecommunications);
- to match buyers with sellers (e.g. electronic malls, electronic funds transfer);
- to communicate with government in pursuit of commerce (e.g. electronic tax filings); and
- to deliver electronic goods (e.g. information).

Many technologies can be used in support of electronic commerce, demonstrating that it is more than just an Internet-based phenomenon. For example, the following list of key technologies and procedures may be used in undertaking electronic commerce: streamlining processes, interconnectivity, Internet, electronic data interchange (EDI), electronic funds transfer, e-mail, security, electronic document management, workflow processing, middleware, bar coding, imaging, smart cards, voice response, and networking.

US PRINCIPLES AND ISSUES GOVERNING INTERNET COMMERCE

The United States is often cited as one of the least regulated market economies in the world. Ideas like the *Amercian Dream* and the *free market* epitomise a society with few restrictions and many opportunities for commercial and economic advancement. In the context of the GII, the US government has developed a framework document that outlines the key principles and issues that govern Internet commerce. The policy document gives five principles and nine key issues. The five principles are given below.

1. The private sector should lead.
2. Governments should avoid undue restrictions on electronic commerce.
3. Where governmental involvement is needed, its aim should be to support and enforce a predictable, minimalist, consistent and simple legal environment for commerce.
4. Governments should recognise the unique qualities of the Internet.
5. Electronic commerce over the Internet should be facilitated on a global basis.

First, the framework document claims that although the US government has played an important role in financing the initial development of the Internet, its expansion has been driven primarily by the private sector. It contends that Internet commerce will only flourish in an environment where the private sector continues to lead. The US government is against excessive regulation and instead prefers self-regulation where companies develop, implement and monitor their own Internet sites. The US administration holds the view that innovation, expanded services, broader participation, and lower prices will arise in a market-driven arena, rather than in an environment that operates as a regulated industry. In important policy areas regarding standardisation and interoperability, the private sector rather than government should spearhead privacy and security. However, government action or intergovernmental agreements will be necessary in areas such as taxation, crime and pornography.

Second, the framework document claims that government should avoid undue restrictions on Internet commerce. Stakeholders should be allowed to enter into legitimate commercial agreements (buying and selling) across the Internet with minimal government involvement or intervention. Too much regulation of commercial activities is likely to inhibit the further development of Internet commerce, which will result in higher costs of products and services, and less choice. Another relevant issue is that, given the rapid pace of technological and business change, many imposed government models for regulation are likely to be out of date at the point of implementation. The US government is therefore against excessive regulation, bureaucracy, taxes and tariffs if the outcome is to deter people from developing Internet commerce strategies.

Third, the role of government should be to support and enforce a predictable, minimalist, consistent and simple legal environment for commerce. The US government is aware of the importance of protecting businesses and consumers from illegal practices across the Internet, yet it believes that limited regulation based upon a decentralised, contractual model of law rather than one based on top-down regulation is the way forward. In the United States, this may involve the 50 plus states and the national government. Currently, the US government believes its role should be to encourage 'competition, protect intellectual property and privacy, prevent fraud, foster transparency, support commercial transactions, and facilitate dispute resolution'.

Fourth, the US government contends that the unique qualities of the Internet should be recognised and exploited to enhance competition. Currently, the Internet has operated as a decentralised and unregulated technology in a tradition of bottom-up governance. To this end, there are many people who wish to retain this approach and yet are aware of the problems associated with lack of regulation. However, existing regulatory schemes in the telecommunications, radio and television sectors may be inappropriate for the Internet. It may therefore be the case that existing laws and regulatory frameworks may need to be tailored to govern Internet commerce, and not completely changed.

Fifth, Internet commerce should be facilitated on a global basis. The emergence of Internet commerce offers businesses and individuals the opportunity to operate within a global rather than a local marketplace. As Internet sites become more sophisticated and easier to use, coupled with greater access to the Internet, people will be able to procure goods and services across states, and across national and international borders. But this will only be facilitated by the harmonisation of a legal and regulatory framework—one that leads to predictable results regardless of the jurisdiction in which a particular buyer or seller resides. At the present time, a simple purchase of, say, a suit by a buyer in one country from a seller in another may lead to insurmountable problems associated with the transaction (payment), security (customer details), customs duty (tariffs/taxes), delivery (of goods), quality (of product), and complaints procedure (if the goods are substandard and need to be returned). One bad experience may therefore deter a person from making further purchases over the Internet.

The five principles cited by the US government are simple in themselves although their implementation may be problematic. The following section considers the nine key issues discussed in the US framework document. Whilst it highlights more questions than answers, companies wishing to develop Internet commerce will need to take into consideration each one if they are to avoid experiencing serious problems.

KEY FINANCIAL, LEGAL AND MARKET ISSUES GOVERNING INTERNET COMMERCE

The US framework document highlights nine key issues where international agreements are necessary to develop global Internet commerce. They are sub-divided

Table 3.1   *Key issues governing Internet commerce*

Financial issues	Customs and taxation
	Electronic payments
Legal issues	'Uniform Commercial Code' for electronic commerce
	Intellectual property protection
	Privacy
	Security
Market access issues	Telecommunications infrastructure and information technology
	Content
	Technical standards

Adapted from: US government framework document
`http://www.ecommerce.gov/framewrk.htm`

into three areas as shown in Table 3.1: financial issues, legal issues, and market access issues. These areas are not mutually exclusive, and it is evident that government progress in developing laws (directives), policies and guidelines for each one is uneven across state, national and international borders.

Financial Issues

Customs and Taxation

The issue of taxes and tariffs on goods and services delivered over the Internet is highly contentious. The US government, which prides itself on supporting free trade and commerce, has, for over 50 years, negotiated tariff reductions with other countries largely on the basis of reciprocal agreements. Since the Internet is a global phenomenon, the imposition of taxes and tariffs on goods and services bought and sold over the Internet is likely to create an immense amount of bureaucracy without producing any benefits to governments, businesses or consumers.

One of the problems in imposing taxes and tariffs is that, historically, goods and services have been procured and delivered by traditional (physical) means. With the advent of Internet commerce, physical goods may be procured electronically and delivered via surface or air transport, and virtual goods and services may be both procured and delivered via the Internet. In the latter case, it will become increasingly difficult to police electronically based commercial exchanges between buyers and sellers. However, governments continuously seek out new sources of revenue generation, and it is likely that some new forms of taxes and tariffs will be levied on global Internet commerce.

The US government recognises these difficulties and intends to advocate in the World Trade Organisation (WTO) and other appropriate international fora that the Internet is declared a *tariff-free environment* in the delivery of products or services. Other countries will, of course, have to agree to this principle as it is likely that some may impose their own tariffs, which would go against the desire for fiscal harmonisation. Similarly, the US government is against the imposition of new taxes on Internet commerce. It calls for greater consistency in the taxation of Internet commerce, relying on the established principles of international taxation. Problems will arise where there is inconsistency across state and national tax jurisdictions leading to double taxation. This would lead to the overpricing of certain goods and services and make them less competitive in the marketplace. Excessive administration and bureaucracy would also damage sales. The framework document contends that any taxation of Internet sales should follow these principles:

- It should neither distort nor hinder commerce. No tax system should discriminate among types of commerce, nor should it create incentives that will change the nature or location of transactions.
- The system should be simple and transparent. It should be capable of capturing the overwhelming majority of appropriate revenues, be easy to implement, and minimise burdensome record-keeping and costs for all parties.
- The system should be able to accommodate tax systems used by the United States and its international partners today. Wherever feasible, we should look to existing taxation concepts and principles to achieve these goals.

The above goals will need to be achieved in the context of the differences between Internet commerce and traditional (physically based) commerce. For example, on the Internet, buyers and sellers can retain greater anonymity, especially where encryption is used. With goods and services procured and delivered over the Internet, such as computer software, it will be difficult for any external body to identify and monitor electronically based commercial transactions. This will become even more pronounced in the case of multiple small transactions where any tax levy could prove to be chaotic (e.g. difficult to administer and collect). In order to achieve an agreement on the international taxation of Internet commerce, the Treasury Department of the US government is liaising with the Organisation for Economic Cooperation and Development (OECD). Notwithstanding the difficulties in obtaining an international agreement, the situation becomes even more complex in that variations exist in state and local taxes across the United States. Whilst the US government does not wish to inhibit the further development of Internet commerce, it is aware that no new taxes should be applied to Internet commerce, and states should co-ordinate their allocation of income derived from Internet commerce. However, it recognises that the implementation of these principles may vary at the sub-federal level where indirect taxation plays a more significant role. Customs and taxation will therefore need to be agreed across states and by local governments to ensure harmonisation and, where possible, the US government hopes that existing principles of taxation will be adopted.

Electronic Payment Systems

An area that has received widespread attention in recent years is electronic payment systems. Financial services companies, notably banks, are currently developing information technology which will facilitate electronic banking and payment systems, including credit and debit card networks, with retail interfaces via the Internet to provide customers with a 'seamless' as opposed to a disjointed service. Electronic money (e-cash) based on a system of stored-value, smartcard technologies and other developments are also underway. One problem facing the US government is that rapid technical change precludes the development and implementation of regulations targeted at payment systems. The preferred approach is for the private sector to develop electronic payment systems in a marketplace that relies upon industry self-regulation. However, this may not be enough to safeguard the interests of business and private citizens. In the case of unscrupulous Internet traders, there will be a role for government to ensure the safety of electronic payment systems. Appropriate law enforcement measures will therefore need to be put into place to achieve this objective. As with customs and taxes (see above), the Treasury Department of the US government is working with other international governments to examine the worldwide implications of emerging electronic payment systems. Whilst the private sector will develop the technologies to facilitate electronic payment systems, there will need to be close co-operation with government and other interested parties (e.g. consumer groups, trade associations, chambers of commerce), to inform future policy development and safeguard the interests of citizens, whether they are using the Internet for business or private purposes.

Legal Issues

'Uniform Commercial Code' for Internet Commerce

The Uniform Commercial Code (UCC) is a codification of substantial portions of commercial law. In the United States, every state government has adopted it. The National Conference of Commissioners of Uniform State Law (NCCUSL) and the American Law Institute, domestic sponsors of the UCC, are already working to adapt the UCC to cyberspace. Other interested parties, such as the American Bar Association (ABA), are also supporting this initiative. There is also a proposed electronic contracting and records act for transactions not covered by the UCC. The US government is hoping that all states adopt uniform legislation, which will enhance the development of Internet commerce.

The above initiatives have arisen from a perceived need to update current legislation governing commercial transactions in an Internet environment. Whilst the US government and the business community in general adopts the view that parties should be able to do business with each other on the Internet under whatever terms and conditions they agree upon, they recognise that Internet commerce should not become a vehicle for illegal and dishonest business practice. Whilst much media attention has focused upon some of the disquieting aspects of the Internet, notably drugs trafficking, pornography and prostitution, there are many more avenues that are open to crime, particularly where individuals have set up bogus businesses. By supporting the development of a domestic and global uniform commercial legal framework that recognises, facilitates, and enforces electronic transactions worldwide, the US government hopes to win the trust and confidence of people, which in turn will enhance global Internet commerce. Fully informed buyers and sellers could voluntarily agree to form a contract subject to this uniform legal framework, in the same way that parties choose the body of law to interpret their commercial contracts. Internationally, the United Nations Commission on International Trade Law (UNCITRAL) has completed work on a model law that supports the commercial use of international contracts in electronic commerce. This model law:

- establishes rules and norms that validate and recognise contracts formed through electronic means;
- sets default rules for contract formation and governance of electronic contract performance;
- defines the characteristics of a valid electronic writing and an original document;
- provides for the acceptability of electronic signatures for legal and commercial purposes; and
- supports the admission of computer evidence in courts and arbitration proceedings.

The US government supports the adoption of principles along these lines by all nations as a start to defining an international set of uniform commercial principles for Internet commerce. It hopes that UNCITRAL, other appropriate international bodies, bar associations, and other private sector groups will continue working in this field. The following principles should, to the extent possible, guide the drafting of rules governing global electronic commerce.

- Parties should be free to order the contractual relationship between themselves as they see fit.
- Rules should be technology-neutral (i.e. the rules should neither require nor assume a particular technology) and forward-looking (i.e. the rules should not hinder the use or development of technologies in the future).
- Existing rules should be modified and new rules should be adopted only as necessary or substantially desirable to support the use of electronic technologies.
- The process should involve the high-tech commercial sector as well as businesses that have not yet moved on-line.

With these principles in mind, UNCITRAL, UNIDROIT, the International Chamber of Commerce (ICC), and others should develop additional model provisions and uniform fundamental principles designed to eliminate administrative and regulatory barriers and to facilitate Internet commerce by:

- encouraging governmental recognition, acceptance and facilitation of electronic communications (i.e. contracts, notarised documents, etc.);
- encouraging consistent international rules to support the acceptance of electronic signatures and other authentication procedures; and
- promoting the development of adequate, efficient, and effective alternative dispute resolution mechanisms for global commercial transactions.

As Internet commerce expands, citizens should be protected from being exposed to liability for any damage or injury that might result from their actions. Inconsistent local tort laws, coupled with uncertainties regarding jurisdiction, could substantially increase litigation. This may, in turn, expose consumers to unnecessary financial costs. By working with other nations, the US government hopes to clarify applicable jurisdictional rules and to generally favour and enforce contract provisions that allow parties to select substantive rules governing liability.

Intellectual Property Protection

Intellectual property protection has become an important issue, not just for Internet commerce but for any business operating on a global scale. Areas such as copyright, patent, and trademark protection are critical and a global legal framework will need to be developed and enforced to prevent piracy and fraud. Internet commerce will involve the sale and licensing of intellectual property, and businesses will need guarantees that their *intangible assets* will not be stolen and misused by dishonest individuals. This is a key challenge to government and one that is not only a problem for Internet users. However, in the context of Internet commerce, technology, such as encryption, can help defeat piracy; a global legal framework will help to ensure that businesses and individuals will have some redress if they find their intellectual property the subject of fraudulent acts by others. The four critical areas of intellectual property protection in relation to Internet commerce that are highlighted in the US framework document are copyrights, *sui generis* protection of databases, patents, and trademark and domain names.

An overview of the US government's policy objectives *vis-à-vis* the four areas of intellectual property protection is given in Table 3.2. First, in the case of copyrights, there are currently several ongoing treaties that establish international norms for the protection of copyrights. The World Intellectual Property Organisation (WIPO) recently adopted two new treaties: the WIPO Copyright Treaty and the WIPO Performances and Phonograms Treaty. These will facilitate the commercial applications of on-line digital communications over the GII. Both treaties include provisions relating to technological protection, copyright management information, and the right of communication to the public, all of which are indispensable for an efficient exercise of rights in the digital environment. The US government recognises private sector efforts to develop international and domestic standards in these areas. It understands the surrounding issues relating to copyright management information and technological protection measures, and is working to implement legislation. The two new WIPO treaties do not address issues of on-line service provider liability. They will be determined by domestic legislation. The US government will work with Congress as these issues are addressed and supports efforts to achieve an equitable and balanced solution that is agreeable to interested parties and consistent with international copyright obligations. It will pursue these international objectives through bilateral discussions and multilateral discussions at WIPO and other appropriate fora and will encourage private sector participation in these discussions.

Second, the US government is currently taking advice from the scientific, academic and information communities on the *sui generis* protection of databases. It believes that there is a need for such protection, although a recent WIPO con-

Table 3.2 *Four aspects of intellectual property protection*

Copyrights	The US government's copyright-related objectives will include: (1) encouraging countries to fully and immediately implement the obligations contained in the Agreement on Trade-Related Aspects of Intellectual Property (TRIPS); (2) seeking immediate US ratification and deposit of the instruments of accession to the two new WIPO treaties and implementation of the obligations in these treaties in a balanced and appropriate way as soon as possible; (3) encouraging other countries to join the two new WIPO treaties and to implement fully the treaty obligations as soon as possible; and (4) ensuring that US trading partners establish laws and regulations that provide adequate and effective protection for copyrighted works, including motion pictures, computer software, and sound recordings, disseminated via the GII, and that these laws and regulations are fully implemented and actively enforced.
***Sui generis* protection of databases**	A proposal to protect the non-original elements of databases was rejected by WIPO. The US government will seek to develop policy with the help of the scientific, academic and library communities and the private sector.
Patents	The US Patent and Trademark Office (PTO) will (1) significantly enhance its collaboration with the private sector to assemble a larger, more complete collection of prior art (both patent and non-patent publications), and provide its patent examiners with better access to prior art in GII-related technologies; (2) train its patent examiners in GII-related technologies to raise and maintain their level of technical expertise; and (3) support legislative proposals for the early publication of pending patent applications, particularly in areas involving fast moving technology.
Trademark and domain names	The US government (1) supports efforts already underway to create domestic and international fora for discussion of Internet-related trademark issues; (2) plans to seek public input on the resolution of trademark disputes in the context of domain names; and (3) supports private efforts to address Internet governance issues including those related to domain names and has formed an inter-agency working group under the leadership of the Department of Commerce to study domain name system issues.

ference rejected a proposed treaty to protect the non-original elements of databases.

Third, the US government believes that patent agreements should seek to achieve three key objectives:

1. to prohibit member countries from authorising parties to exploit patented inventions related to the GII without the patent owner's authority (i.e. disapproval of compulsory licensing of GII-related technology except to remedy

a practice determined after judicial or administrative process to be anti-competitive);

2. to require member countries to provide adequate and effective protection for patentable subject-matter important to the development and success of the GII; and

3. to establish international standards for determining the validity of a patent claim.

The US government will pursue these objectives internationally. Officials of the European, Japanese and US Patent Offices meet, for example each year, to foster co-operation on patent-related issues. The United States will recommend at the next meeting that a special committee be established to make recommendations on GII-related patent issues. At a separate venue, 100 countries and international inter-governmental organisations will participate as members of WIPO's permanent committee on industrial property information (PCIPI). The United States will attempt to establish a working group of this organisation to address GII-related patent issues.

Fourth, in the area of trademark rights, which are national in scope, various conflicts may arise where different parties in different countries own the same or similar trademarks for similar goods or services. Countries may also apply different standards for determining infringement. Conflicts have arisen on the GII where third parties have registered Internet domain names that are the same as, or similar to, registered or common law trademarks. An Internet domain name functions as a source identifier on the Internet. Ordinarily, source identifiers like addresses are not protected intellectual property (i.e. a trademark) *per se*. The use of domain names as source identifiers has burgeoned. As such, the courts have begun to attribute intellectual property rights to them, while recognising that misuse of a domain name could significantly infringe, dilute, and weaken valuable trademark rights. To date, conflicts between trademark rights and domain names have been resolved through negotiations and/or litigation. It may be possible to create a contractually based self-regulatory regime that deals with potential conflicts between domain name usage and trademark laws on a global basis without the need to litigate. This could create a more stable business environment on the Internet. Governance of the domain name system (DNS) raises other important issues unrelated to intellectual property.

Privacy

An important issue involving Internet commerce is that of privacy. A Privacy Working Group of the US government Information Infrastructure Task Force (IITF) issued a report which recommends a set of principles (the 'Privacy Principles') to govern the collection, processing, storage, and re-use of personal data in the information age (US Government, 1997). These Privacy Principles, which are based on the OECD's guidelines that govern the protection of privacy and transborder data flow of personal data, together with incorporating the principles of fair information practices, rest on the following fundamental precepts of awareness and choice.

- Data-gatherers should inform consumers what information they are collecting, and how they intend to use such data.
- Data-gatherers should provide consumers with a meaningful way to limit the use and re-use of personal information.

Disclosure by data-gatherers is designed to stimulate market resolution of privacy concerns by empowering individuals to obtain relevant knowledge about why information is being collected, what the information will be used for, what steps will be taken to protect that information, the consequences of providing or with-holding information, and any rights of redress that they may have. Such disclosure will enable consumers to make better judgements about the levels of privacy available and their willingness to participate.

Three values are identified in the Privacy Principles which govern the way in which personal information is obtained, disclosed and used on-line. They are (i) information privacy; (ii) information integrity; and (iii) information quality. First, an individual's reasonable expectation of privacy regarding access to and use of his or her personal information should be assured. Second, personal information should not be improperly altered or destroyed. And third, personal information should be accurate, timely, complete, and relevant for the purposes for which it is provided and used. Under these principles, consumers are entitled to redress if improper use or disclosure of personal information harms them or if decisions are based on inaccurate, outdated, incomplete, or irrelevant personal information.

In April 1997 the Information Policy Committee of the IITF issued a draft paper entitled 'Options for Promoting Privacy on the National Information Infrastructure'. The paper surveys information practices in the United States and solicits public comment on the best way to implement the Privacy Principles. The IITF goal is to find a way to balance the competing values of personal privacy and the free flow of information in a digital democratic society. Meanwhile, other federal agencies have studied privacy issues in the context of specific industry sectors. In October 1995, for example, the National Telecommunications and Information Administration (NTIA) issued a report which explores the application of the Privacy Principles in the context of telecommunications and on-line services and advocates a voluntary framework based on notice and consent (NTIA, 1995). On 6 January 1997 the Federal Trade Commission (FTC) also issued a staff report which focuses on the direct marketing and advertising industries (FTC, 1997). The report concludes that notice, choice, security, and access are recognised as necessary elements of fair information practices on-line. In June 1997 the FTC held four days of hearings on technology tools and industry self-regulation regimes designed to enhance personal privacy on the Internet.

The US government supports private sector efforts now underway to implement meaningful, consumer-friendly, self-regulatory privacy regimes. These include mechanisms for facilitating awareness and the exercise of choice on-line, evaluating private sector adoption of and adherence to fair information practices, and dispute resolution. It also anticipates that technology will offer solutions to many privacy concerns in the on-line environment, including the appropriate use of anonymity. If privacy concerns are not addressed by industry through self-regulation and technology, the Administration will face increasing pressure to play a more direct role in safeguarding consumer choice regarding privacy on-line. The US government is particularly concerned about the use of information gathered from children, who may lack the cognitive ability to recognise and appreciate privacy concerns. Parents should be able to choose whether or not personally identifiable information can be collected from or about their children. Industry, consumers, and child-advocacy groups are encouraged to use technology, self-regulation, and education to provide solutions to the particular dangers arising in this area and to facilitate parental choice. This problem warrants prompt attention. Failure to do so will mean that government action may be needed.

Privacy concerns are being raised in many countries around the world, and some countries have enacted laws, implemented industry self-regulation, or instituted administrative solutions designed to safeguard their citizens' privacy. Disparate policies could emerge that might disrupt transborder data flows. For example, the European Union (EU) has adopted a directive that prohibits the transfer of personal data to countries that, in its view, do not extend adequate privacy protection to EU citizens. To ensure that differing privacy policies around the world do not impede the flow of data on the Internet, the US government will engage its key trading partners in discussions to build support for industry-developed solutions to privacy problems and for market-driven mechanisms to ensure customer satisfaction about how private data are handled. The United States will continue policy discussions with the European Union to increase understanding about the US approach to privacy and to ensure that the criteria they use for evaluating adequacy are sufficiently flexible to accommodate its approach. These discussions are led by the Department of Commerce, through NTIA, and the State Department, and include the Executive Office of the President, the Treasury Department, the FTC and other relevant federal agencies. NTIA is also working with the private sector to assess the impact that the implementation of the EU directive could have on the United States. The United States will also enter into a dialogue with trading partners on these issues through existing bilateral fora as well as through regional fora such as the Asia Pacific Economic Cooperation (APEC) forum, the Summit of the Americas, the North American Free Trade Agreement (NAFTA), and the Inter-American Telecommunications Commission (CITEL) of the Organisation of American States, and broader multilateral organisations.

Notwithstanding the above, the US government considers data protection critically important and that the efforts of industry working in co-operation with consumer groups are preferable to government regulation. However, it recognises that if effective privacy protection cannot be provided in this way, it will be forced to reconsider the policy.

Security

The US government believes that the GII must offer businesses and consumers security and reliability. Insecure data and unauthorised access or modification of data will result in a loss of trust and confidence and a decline in the use of the Internet for commerce. The US government believes that a secure GII has four key characteristics:

1. secure and reliable telecommunications networks;
2. effective means for protecting the information systems attached to those networks;
3. effective means for authenticating and ensuring confidentiality of electronic information to protect data from unauthorised use; and
4. well-trained GII users who understand how to protect their systems and their data.

To achieve the goal of enhanced security on the Internet, a range of technologies, e.g. encryption, authentication, password controls, firewalls, will need to be put into place. They will need to be supported internationally by trustworthy key and security management infrastructures. Of particular importance is the development of trusted certification services that support the digital signatures that will permit users to know with whom they are communicating on the Internet. Both signatures and confidentiality rely on the use of cryptographic keys. To promote the growth of a trusted Internet commerce environment, the US government is encouraging the development of a voluntary, market-driven key management infrastructure that will support authentication, integrity, and confidentiality.

Encryption products protect the confidentiality of stored data and electronic communications by making them unreadable without a decryption key. But strong encryption is a double-edged sword. Law-abiding citizens can use strong encryption to protect their trade secrets and personal records, but those trade secrets and personal records could be lost forever if the decrypt key is lost. Depending upon the value of the information, the loss could be quite substantial. Criminals and terrorists can also use encryption to reduce law enforcement capabilities to read their communications. Key recovery-based encryption can help address some of these issues.

In promoting the robust security needed for Internet commerce, the US government has already taken steps that will enable trust in encryption and provide the safeguards that users and society will need. Working in partnership with industry, the US government is taking steps to promote the development of market-driven standards, public–key management infrastructure services and key recoverable encryption products. Additionally, it has liberalised export controls for commercial encryption products while protecting public safety and national security interests. The US government is also working with Congress to ensure legislation is enacted that would facilitate the development of voluntary key management infrastructures and would govern the release of recovery information to law enforcement officials pursuant to lawful authority. It will work internationally to promote the development of market-driven key management infrastructure with key recovery. Specifically, the United States has worked closely within the OECD to develop international guidelines for encryption policies and will continue to promote the development of policies to provide a predictable and secure environment for global Internet commerce.

Market Access Issues

Telecommunications Infrastructure and Information Technology

Global Internet commerce depends upon a modern, seamless, global telecommunications network and upon the computers and information appliances that connect to it. Unfortunately, in too many countries telecommunications policies are hindering the development of advanced digital networks. Customers find that telecommunications services often are too expensive, bandwidth is too limited, and services are unavailable or unreliable. Likewise, many countries maintain trade barriers to imported information technology, making it difficult for both merchants and customers to purchase the computers and information systems they need to participate in electronic commerce. In order to spur the removal of barriers, in March 1994, Vice President Gore spoke to the World Telecommunications Development Conference in Buenos Aires. He articulated several principles that the United States believes should be the foundation for government policy, including:

- encouraging private sector investment by privatising government-controlled telecommunications companies;
- promoting and preserving competition by introducing competition to monopoly phone markets, ensuring interconnection at fair prices, opening markets to foreign investment, and enforcing anti-trust safeguards;
- guaranteeing open access to networks on a non-discriminatory basis, so that GII users have access to the broadest range of information and services; and
- implementing, by an independent regulator, pro-competitive and flexible regulation that keeps pace with technological development.

Domestically, the US government recognises that there are various constraints in the present network that may impede the evolution of services requiring higher bandwidth. Initiatives include Internet II, or Next Generation Internet. In addition, the FCC has undertaken several initiatives designed to stimulate bandwidth expansion, especially to residential and small/home office customers. The goal of the United States will be to ensure that on-line service providers can reach end-users on reasonable and non-discriminatory terms and conditions. Genuine market opening will lead to increased competition, improved telecommunications infrastructures, more customer choice, lower prices, and increased and improved services.

Areas of concern include:

- *Leased lines.* Data networks of most on-line service providers are constructed with leased lines that must be obtained from national telephone companies, often monopolies or governmental entities. In the absence of effective competition, telephone companies may impose artificially inflated leased line prices and usage restrictions that impede the provision of service by on-line service providers.
- *Local loops pricing.* To reach their subscribers, on-line service providers often have no choice but to purchase local exchange services from monopoly or government-owned telephone companies. These services also are often priced at excessive rates, inflating the cost of data services to customers.

- *Interconnection and unbundling.* On-line service providers must be able to interconnect with the networks of incumbent telecommunication companies so that information can pass seamlessly between all users of the network. Monopolies or dominant telephone companies often price interconnection well above cost, and refuse to interconnect because of alleged concerns about network compatibility or absence of need for other providers.
- *Attaching equipment to the network.* Over the years, some telecommunication providers have used their monopoly power to restrict the connection of communication or technology devices to the network. Even when the monopoly has been broken, a host of unnecessary burdensome 'type acceptance' practices have been used to retard competition and make it difficult for consumers to connect.
- *Internet voice and multimedia.* Officials of some nations claim that 'real time' services provided over the Internet are 'like services' to traditionally regulated voice telephony and broadcasting, and therefore should be subject to the same regulatory restrictions that apply to those traditional services. In some countries these providers must be licensed as a way to control both the carriage and content offered. Such an approach could hinder the development of new technologies and new services.

In addition, countries have different levels of telecommunications infrastructure development, which may hinder the global provision and use of some Internet-based services. The NTIA believes that the introduction of policies promoting foreign investment, competition, regulatory flexibility and open access will support infrastructure development and the creation of more data-friendly networks. To address these issues, the US government successfully concluded the WTO Basic Telecommunications negotiations, which will ensure global competition in the provision of basic telecommunication services and will address the many underlying issues affecting on-line service providers. During those negotiations, the United States succeeded in ensuring that new regulatory burdens would not be imposed upon on-line service providers that would stifle the deployment of new technologies and services. As the WTO Agreement is implemented, the US government will seek to ensure that new rules of competition in the global communications marketplace will be technology neutral and will not hinder the development of Internet commerce. In particular, rules for licensing new technologies and new services must be sufficiently flexible to accommodate the changing needs of consumers while allowing governments to protect important public interest objectives like universal service. In this context, rules to promote such public interest objectives should not fall disproportionately on any one segment of the telecommunications industry or on new entrants.

The US government is also seeking effective implementation of the Information Technology Agreement (ITA) concluded by the members of the WTO in March 1997, which is designed to remove tariffs on almost all types of information technology. Building on this success, and with the encouragement of US companies, the Administration is developing plans for ITA II, in which it will to seek to remove remaining tariffs on, and existing non-tariff barriers to, information technology goods and services. In addition, it is committed to finding other ways to streamline requirements to demonstrate product conformity, including through Mutual Recognition Agreements (MRAs) that can eliminate the need for a single product to be certified by different standards laboratories across national borders. Bilateral exchanges with individual foreign governments, regional fora such as APEC and CITEL, and multilateral fora such as the OECD and ITU, and various other fora (i.e. international alliances of private businesses, the International Organisation of Standardisation [ISO], the International Electrotechnical Commission [IEC]), also will be used for international discussions on telecommunication-related Internet issues and removing trade barriers that inhibit the export of information technology. These issues include the terms and conditions governing the exchange of on-line traffic, addressing, and reliability. In all fora, US government positions that might influence Internet pricing, service delivery options or technical standards will reflect the principles established by the US government, and US government representatives will survey the work of their study groups to ensure that this is the case. In addition, many Internet governance issues will best be dealt with by means of private, open standards processes and contracts involving participants from both government and the private sector.

Content

The US government supports the broadest possible free flow of information across international borders. This includes most informational material now accessible and transmitted through the Internet, including through World Wide Web pages, news and other information services, virtual shopping malls, and entertainment features, such as audio and video products, and the arts. This principle extends to information created by commercial enterprises as well as by schools, libraries, governments and other non-profit entities. In contrast to traditional broadcast media, the Internet promises users greater opportunity to shield themselves and their children from content they deem offensive or inappropriate. New technology, for example, may enable parents to block their children's access to sensitive information or confine their children to pre-approved Web sites. To the extent, then, that effective filtering technology becomes available, content regulations traditionally imposed on radio and television would not need to be applied to the Internet. In fact, unnecessary regulation could cripple the growth and diversity of the Internet. The US government therefore supports industry self-regulation, adoption of competing ratings systems, and development of easy-to-use technical solutions (e.g. filtering technologies and age verification systems) to assist in screening information on-line.

There are four priority areas of concern.

1. *Regulation of content.* Companies wishing to do business over the Internet, and to provide access to the Internet (including US on-line service providers with foreign affiliates or joint ventures), are concerned about liability based on the different policies of every country through which their information may travel. Countries that are considering or have adopted laws to restrict access to certain types of content through the Internet emphasise different concerns

as a result of cultural, social, and political differences. These different laws can impede electronic commerce in the global environment.

The US government is concerned about Internet regulation of this sort, and will develop an informal dialogue with key trading partners on public policy issues such as hate speech, violence, sedition, pornography and other content to ensure that differences in national regulation, especially those undertaken to foster cultural identity, do not serve as disguised trade barriers.

2. *Foreign content quotas.* Some countries currently require that a specific proportion of traditional broadcast transmission time be devoted to 'domestically produced' content. Problems could arise on the Internet if the definition of 'broadcasting' is changed to extend these current regulations to 'new services'. Countries also might decide to regulate Internet content and establish restrictions under administrative authority, rather than under broadcast regulatory structures.

    The US government will pursue a dialogue with other nations on how to promote content diversity, including cultural and linguistic diversity, without limiting content. These discussions could consider the promotion of cultural identity through subsidy programmes that rely solely on general tax revenues and that are implemented in a non-discriminatory manner.

3. *Regulation of advertising.* Advertising will allow the new interactive media to offer more affordable products and services to a wider, global audience. Some countries stringently restrict the language, amount, frequency, duration, and type of tele-shopping and advertising spots used by advertisers. In principle, the United States does not favour such regulations. While recognising legitimate cultural and social concerns, these concerns should not be invoked to justify unnecessarily burdensome regulation of the Internet.

    There are laws in many countries around the world that require support for advertising claims. Advertising industry self-regulation also exists in many countries around the globe. Truthful and accurate advertising should be the cornerstone of advertising on all media, including the Internet.

    A strong body of cognitive and behavioural research demonstrates that children are particularly vulnerable to advertising. As a result, the United States has well-established rules (self-regulatory and otherwise) for protecting children from certain harmful advertising practices. The Administration will work with industry and children's advocates to ensure that these protections are translated to, and implemented appropriately in, the on-line media environment.

    The rules of the 'country-of-origin' should serve as the basis for controlling Internet advertising to alleviate national legislative roadblocks and trade barriers.

4. *Regulation to prevent fraud.* Recently, there have been a number of cases where fraudulent information on companies and their stocks, and phony investment schemes, have been broadcast on the Internet. The appropriate federal agencies (i.e. Federal Trade Commission and the Securities and Exchange Commission) are determining whether new regulations are needed to prevent fraud over the Internet.

In order to realise the commercial and cultural potential of the Internet, consumers must have confidence that the goods and services offered are fairly represented, that they will get what they pay for, and that recourse or redress will be available if they do not. This is an area where government action is appropriate.

The US government will explore opportunities for international co-operation to protect consumers and to prosecute false, deceptive, and fraudulent commercial practices in cyberspace.

Federal agencies such as the Department of State, United States Trade Representative (USTR), the Commerce Department (NTIA), the FTC, the Office of Consumer Affairs and others have already engaged in efforts to promote such positions, through both bilateral and multilateral channels, including through the OECD, the G-7 Information Society and Development Conference, the Latin American Telecommunications Summits, and the Summit of the Americas, as well as APEC Telecommunications Ministerials. All participating agencies will focus on pragmatic solutions to issues related to content control.

Technical Standards

Standards are critical to the long-term commercial success of the Internet as they can allow products and services from different vendors to work together. They also encourage competition and reduce uncertainty in the global marketplace. Premature standardisation, however, can 'lock in' outdated technology. Standards also can be employed as *de facto* non-tariff trade barriers, to 'lock out' non-indigenous businesses from a particular national market. The US government believes that the marketplace, not governments, should determine technical standards and other mechanisms for interoperability. Technology is moving rapidly and government attempts to establish technical standards to govern the Internet would only risk inhibiting technological innovation. It considers it unwise and unnecessary for governments to mandate standards for electronic commerce. Rather, industry-driven multilateral fora are urged to consider technical standards in this area. To ensure the growth of global Internet commerce, standards will be needed to ensure reliability, interoperability, and ease of use and scalability in areas such as:

- electronic payments;
- security (confidentiality, authentication, data integrity, access control, non-repudiation);
- security services infrastructure (e.g. public key certificate authorities);
- electronic copyright management systems;
- video and data-conferencing;
- high-speed network technologies (e.g. asynchronous transfer mode, synchronous digital hierarchy); and
- digital object and data interchange.

There need not be one standard for every product or service associated with the GII, and technical standards need not be mandated. In some cases, multiple standards will compete for marketplace acceptance. In other cases, different standards will be used in different circumstances.

The prevalence of voluntary standards on the Internet, and the medium's consensus-based process of standards development and acceptance, are stimulating its rapid growth. These standards flourish because of a non-bureaucratic system of development managed by technical practitioners working through various organisations. These organisations require demonstrated deployment of systems incorporating a given standard prior to formal acceptance, but the process facilitates rapid deployment of standards and can accommodate evolving standards as well. Only a handful of countries allow private sector standards development; most rely on government-mandated solutions, causing these nations to fall behind the technological cutting edge and creating non-tariff trade barriers. Numerous private sector bodies have contributed to the process of developing voluntary standards that promote interoperability. The United States has encouraged the development of voluntary standards through private standards organisations, consortia, testbeds and R&D activities. The US government also has adopted a set of principles to promote acceptance of domestic and international voluntary standards.

While no formal government-sponsored negotiations are called for at this time, the United States will use various fora (i.e. international alliances of private businesses, the International Organisation for Standardisation [ISO], the International Electrotechnical Commission [IEC], the International Telecommunications Union [ITU], etc.) to discourage the use of standards to erect barriers to free trade on the developing GII. The private sector should assert global leadership to address standards-setting needs. The United States will work through intergovernmental organisations as needed to monitor and support private sector leadership.

EUROPEAN UNION PRINCIPLES AND ISSUES GOVERNING INTERNET COMMERCE

Like the US government, the European Union is keen to formulate laws (directives), policies and frameworks to promote Internet commerce. The European Union believes that Internet commerce will offer significant opportunities for Europe, with estimated revenues (direct and indirect) to increase to over 2 billion ECU worldwide by the year 2000 (EITO, 1997). This revolutionary growth will lead to profound structural changes. Sectors such as retail and distribution with 20 million employed, and tourism with six million employed, will need to adapt to exploit these opportunities, expand existing businesses and launch new ones. New businesses will replace some existing services. Significant efficiency gains will be realised. As a result, Internet commerce will have considerable impact on the structure and operations of the labour market. Further analysis is needed fully to assess these changes. Already at this stage it is apparent that new employment potential will principally be in information-based, high-value services. Training and education for these new skills will be needed. Faced with intense, global competition in a borderless digital environment, the European Union hopes to ensure that these new jobs are created and maintained in the European Single Market. In Europe, Internet commerce already offers considerable incentives for both established and new players. SMEs are capitalising on the unprecedented opportunities to access global markets which the WWW offers. Similarly, large economic sectors, such as the distance selling industry in Europe, are actively integrating the Internet into their marketing and order-fulfilment strategies. Internet commerce offers improved transaction management and enhances business efficiency. It brings increased responsiveness and accountability—as well as cost reductions. It lowers barriers to entry, enlarges existing markets and creates whole new business areas for knowledge-based intangible products—potentially one of Europe's greatest strengths. Consumers also stand to gain significantly. Internet commerce revolutionises the relationship between consumer and provider. The consumer benefits from increased choice by being able to compare and choose instantly from a wide range of offers. Specialised products are increasingly available. Lower prices are possible as overheads and 'bricks and mortar' costs fall and efficiency improves. A personalised, one-to-one relationship is replacing traditional mass-marketing and mass-distribution techniques, bringing more responsive service.

By its very nature, Internet commerce is transnational and encourages cross-border ordering and delivery of goods and services. It directly stimulates competition in the Single Market. The Single Market, in turn, offers Internet commerce the prospect of a critical mass of businesses and customers across national borders. In addition, Internet commerce gives peripheral regions new opportunities for accessing main markets. It is therefore a potentially vital factor for cohesion and integration in Europe.

The development of a legal and regulatory framework to govern Internet commerce in the European Union poses many difficulties which are not dissimilar from those facing the US government. Whilst there is a lack of harmonisation across EU member states, similar problems face the US administration in its attempt to impose uniformity across all the states. A recent commentary on the European Union claims that

> EU states have so far tried to shape the growth of global data networks through national legislation, though the Internet—with its lack of central control and indifference to national borders—is already proving a slippery eel for such regulation. Compounding matters is the rapid growth of the Internet, and what is widely expected to be a parallel explosion in ecommerce, whether as a medium for exchanging data between business communities or selling goods and services directly to the public (*Computing*, 30 April 1998, p. 52).

We will now examine some of these issues in more detail.

Policy Challenges Facing the European Union

The European Union has made substantial progress in putting in place the necessary framework conditions for Internet commerce. One of its key objectives is to develop the information society with a view to creating new employment opportunities across the region to offset the high unemployment in some EU member states. Like the US government, the European Union believes that the private sector will play a major part in developing Internet commerce and the legal and regulatory framework that underpins it. Recently, the European Union has launched a broad consultation to explore the nature and regulatory implications of convergence between the telecommunications, media and information technology sectors. It hopes to strengthen international co-ordination to formulate a framework for the global electronic marketplace, or on-line economy, which it perceives is fundamental to the development of the global information society (GIS).

The European Union has begun to formulate several policy lines on Internet commerce by stimulating the development of an internal market for those services whilst safeguarding public interests. In parallel, the European Union is contributing to the development of favourable conditions at the international level for electronic communications and commerce, namely the WTO agreement on basic telecommunication services, the ITA agreement on tariffs for information technology products, and the WIPO agreement on the protection of intellectual property. This policy is based on the conviction that the Information Society can only be a global one with the wide participation of the international community, including developing countries. The European Union recognises that international initiatives to regulate Internet commerce lack harmonisation and therefore need to be better co-ordinated to be effective in a global economy. It believes that divergent regulation will inhibit the development of Internet commerce. Decision-makers in the public and private sectors are becoming aware of the fact that greater consistency in these national and regional approaches is required.

Against this background the European Union is examining its policies with a view to adapting or clarifying traditional regulation to the requirements of the on-line economy or, more narrowly, Internet commerce. This does not mean delaying legislative activities at member states or Union level until global rules are settled in the respective fields. Equally it does not mean surrendering national or regional traditions and cultures. The European Union hopes to engage in an open debate and awareness-raising exercise about the implications of the global electronic marketplace and its particular characteristics on certain rules and their application. Progress should be made in parallel on technology changes, national and European regulatory actions, and co-operation at the international level on regulatory principles. The European Union hopes to be a major player in shaping Internet commerce, and believes its rich scientific, cultural and social background will qualify it for such a role. The European Union hopes to signal to the international community that it is determined to contribute its experience and vision to building a legal and regulatory framework based on fair competition, private sector investments, open markets, and social inclusion, accompanied by appropriate safeguards covering both the wider public interest and the interests of the individual. In conjunction with the aims of the US government, the European Union hopes to play a large part in defining and shaping the future of Internet commerce. This will be achieved through communication with a variety of international organisations to create a deeper understanding of the relevant issues.

Internet Commerce and the Need for Interoperable Solutions

One of the key challenges of Internet commerce is to oversee agreements on technical issues, including the connection and interoperability of national networks, standards and frequencies. The European Union cites three areas where a need exists for interoperable solutions. They are: international interconnection, a global system for mobile communication (GSM), and a domain name system (DNS).

Initially, telegraph lines were installed within countries, and each country used its own system and telegraph code. Messages destined for overseas were received at national borders and then re-transmitted over the telegraph network of the neighbouring country. Agreements were then made between countries to interconnect national networks. The ability to offer users access to personal communications facilities wherever they travel in the world would not have been possible had it not been for the conclusion of international accords on standards and frequencies.

The introduction of a global system for mobile communication (GSM) allowed for trans-border mobility or 'roaming' between networks, irrespective of their geographical location. This had not been possible before. Developments in new technology are giving way to new needs. These are linked to issues such as the development of Internet architecture, the frequency and technical requirements of the next generation of mobile wireless communications, and new satellite and navigational systems, including reconciliation of requirements posed by commercial and public interest applications, as well as the legal protection of user interfaces for multimedia services. The speed of technological developments combined with the changing role of the actors concerned mean that standardisation is beginning to follow a different mechanism to that which has operated historically in telecommunications (public bodies) and in the IT sector (agreements between 'big' players, proprietary systems leading sometimes to *de facto* monopolies); namely, a more open and flexible consensus-building process. A particularly striking illustration is the Internet community. Unlike the international switched telephone network, which has largely been built up within a formal and institutionalised framework agreed by governments, the Internet has developed according to its own unique user-driven model into a loose federation of interconnected computer networks worldwide. It is made up of groups that are open and follow a more spontaneous organisational model, but are therefore more difficult to define.

In an increasingly commercialised Internet, the most coveted domain is '.com', intended for commercial organisations. But '.com' is a non-country-specific generic top level domain that can be used by anyone in the world. The availability of useful names is quickly running out and registering under the narrow confines of '.com' cannot work for much longer. In 1996 there were around 40 000 registrations. In 1999, there are over four million. In the future, questions such as who should be responsible for managing the funding, administration, and assigning of domain names in generic Top Level Domains, and how to introduce more competition into the management of the DNS system, will have to be answered. The Internet community is trying to build on open standards that allow both interoperability and competition. Open standards are particularly important with regard to hardware and software tools for Internet use and access. Items such as browser software are in a way the 'entry ramps' to the information superhighway, and it is important that they be based on open standards so that all users have equal access to the Internet. Otherwise proprietary standards and their attendant licensing schemes will control access to content and Internet commerce transactions, and will adversely influence licensing and other market behaviour. Because of an open and flexible model, Internet standardisation up to now has been quick and agile. Measures to facilitate the continued growth of the Internet as an important feature in global communications will need to take this open, user-led approach into account.

The European Union's Role in Promoting Market Access and Competition

The electronic marketplace will reinforce the ongoing trend towards globalisation, which, as trade figures show, is gathering speed. As a share of world output, trade has more than tripled since 1950—from 7% to over 22%. Investment, too, has become a powerful force for economic integration with cumulative assets of foreign investment having trebled since 1987 to over 2.5 trillion ECU. A significant proportion of trade in money markets takes place on-line. The daily volume of foreign exchange deals worldwide exceeds 1000 billion ECU. A number of agreements have given an added impetus to these trends, notably within the WTO, through the GATT, GATS and TRIPS agreements, which will continue to play an important role in promoting trade liberalisation, including the recent agreement on telecommunication services.

One of the major obstacles to the development of advanced communication services which are the basis of the on-line economy are high telecommunications costs. Dramatic reductions in the cost of computing power together with competition are pushing tariffs and giving rise to a global infrastructure where distance becomes meaningless. A transatlantic telephone call now costs just 1.5% of what it cost 60 years ago. And the World Bank predicts that by 2010 the cost will have fallen by another two-thirds, making transatlantic telecommunications, for instance, increasingly affordable to all. This will allow small businesses and individuals to establish remote presence, beyond the geo-political borders of their physical location. Doing global business is already no longer limited to big multinational companies but within the reach of everyone who, for instance by using the Internet, is able to set up a global business at low costs. Falling tariffs will create further dynamism in the electronic marketplace, notably when broadband communications become more affordable. The current limitations of Internet access and also mobile communications to relatively narrow bandwidths needs to be overcome as quickly as possible. In most cases, market demand and competition will provide the necessary incentives. Therefore effective implementation of agreed WTO rules is crucial.

Defining a Legal and Regulatory Framework for Internet Commerce

One of the interesting observations about the EU member states is the variation in legal and administrative systems. In the context of Internet commerce, the

Table 3.3 *Requirements for an international legal and regulatory framework*

Value Added Tax (VAT)	Harmonise VAT rates across the EU
Jurisdiction	Define legal rules governing trans-national commerce
Labour law	Establish rights of teleworkers throughout the EU
Copyright	Harmonise copyright laws across the EU
Data protection	Harmonise data protection regulations
Trade marks	Enhance legal security and trust of trade marks
Authentication	Establish one Certification Authority (CA)
Consumer protection	Establish a Uniform Commercial Code (UCC) for consumers
Terms and conditions of contract	Simplify or harmonise terms and conditions
Harmful and illegal content	Develop measures to remove harmful and illegal content

European Union hopes to harmonise the legal system to ensure that the interests of citizens are safeguarded throughout the region. Whilst the European Union hopes to extend the legal frameworks of the off-line business community to the on-line world, it recognises the inherent difficulties of doing so. In some cases, the specific character of the borderless electronic marketplace and the transmissions that circulate within it, may require clarification or adaptation of existing legal frameworks and enforcement mechanisms. Table 3.3 outlines 10 areas that illustrate the diversity of these issues.

ELECTRONIC COMMERCE AND THE LAW IN THE UNITED KINGDOM

Much attention has been focused upon whether governments internationally should develop a regulatory and legal framework to monitor and control electronic commerce on the Internet. Trust and confidence will only develop once buyers and sellers believe that undertaking commercial transactions on the Internet is safe. EURIM (1997) reminds us that most international law, including the United Kingdom, perceives commerce to be manual. For the virtual society to progress, it will be important for UK law to achieve global parity in Statute in both manual and electronic commerce. The priority is in consumer protection law. By and large, business-to-business e-commerce requires less urgency than business-to-consumer e-commerce. This is because businesses tend to have tightly defined legal contracts with their suppliers and customers. The exception may be SMEs since they may not spend large sums of money on legal advice. Along with individuals, SMEs may find their interests less protected when dealing with highly resourced larger corporations. As such, the advent of e-commerce which allows people to procure goods and services via the Internet, the TV screen, or even the kiosk, poses new risks for SMEs and consumers. Measures will need to be put into place to protect vulnerable consumers through the law, education and advice. The reports claim that the concept of *caveat emptor* is relevant. Statute reform is required in trading disciplines associated with the Internet and the protection of citizen interests. Reforming the law in the areas of privacy, security, rights and across border payment are also important.

EURIM has found that

- existing legislation is ill suited to respond appropriately to electronic commerce;
- because technology will always outdistance law, relevant law needs routine periodic review;
- new electronic commerce technologies have already led to Regulatory involvement;
- the distinction between a very small company and a consumer is becoming blurred.

According to one writer, 'Internet-relevant laws exist on a hand-to-mouth basis, squeezed alongside what is now an inadequate centuries-old legal framework, with lawyers struggling to come to terms with the possibilities offered by the worldwide network' (David Bicknell, *Computer Weekly*, 15 January 1998, p. 28). The global electronic marketplace requires an appropriate international framework covering legal, commercial and technical considerations. This should clearly foster a defined legal and regulatory framework, business methods and practices that promote competition, and interoperable technical solutions. There are several key challenges facing international governments if a harmonised legal and regulatory framework is to be achieved. For example, the cultural, economic and technical diversity within and across national and international borders may preclude a full agreement from being reached on a variety of legal, financial and market issues concerning the governance of electronic commerce. Some countries may retain their flexible and liberal approach to the free flow of data and information while others regulate content much more strictly.

Because of the fast-moving environment that characterises electronic communications and commerce, some of the issues may be resolved relatively soon, others may prove to be significant bottlenecks, whilst others are yet to emerge. The development of an international framework must therefore be based on a forward-looking and flexible approach. The above analysis makes it clear that increasingly issues touch upon legal and regulatory frameworks. It is increasingly necessary to examine them at a global level as uncertainty surrounding different national and regional responses to these challenges will hamper the further development of the electronic marketplace. Therefore, a broad dialogue on the key issues amongst public authorities, industry, consumers and international organisations should be envisaged.

What is required is an urgent and detailed examination of the problems and the priorities in order to allow the international community to address them in a substantive and co-ordinated manner. There is growing experience amongst industry, consumer groups, governments, and international organisations of the key problems needing solutions in order to foster the development of the global electronic marketplace. The difficulty lies in obtaining a consistent approach in view of the number of different groups engaged in parallel activities, which are not always co-ordinated. One can however observe in many areas an emerging convergence of views on the definition of problems. These include, for instance, requirements from industry for proportionate and technology-neutral regulations, from consumer groups seeking adequate data protection, as well as consistent implementation of competition rules. Opportunities to exchange information can help to identify and solve problems that arise from a lack of sufficient knowledge on applicable frameworks and help to distinguish them from those problems that will require the clarification or adaptation of binding or non-binding regulations.

The success of Internet commerce will require an effective partnership between the private and public sectors, with the private sector in the lead. Government participation must be coherent and cautious, avoiding the contradictions and confusions that can sometimes arise when different governmental agencies individually assert authority too vigorously and operate without co-ordination. The variety of issues being raised, the interaction among them, and the diverse environments in which they are being addressed will necessitate a co-ordinated, targeted governmental approach to avoid inefficiencies and duplication in developing and reviewing policy. An interagency team will continue to meet in order to monitor progress and update this strategy as events unfold. Sufficient resources will be committed to allow rapid and effective policy implementation. The process of further developing and implementing the strategy is as important as the content itself. The US Government will consult openly and often with groups representing industry, consumers and Internet users, Congress, state and local governments, foreign governments, and international organisations as updating and implementation is sought in the coming years.

According to the US government, private sector leadership accounts for the growth of the Internet, and the success of electronic commerce will depend on private sector leadership. Accordingly, the US government will encourage the creation of private fora to take the lead in areas requiring self-regulation such as privacy, content ratings, and consumer protection and in areas such as standards development, commercial code, and fostering interoperability. The strategy above will be updated and new releases will be issued as changes in technology and the marketplace help electronic commerce to flourish. There is a great opportunity for commercial activity on the Internet and the private sector and governments will need to work together.

CASE STUDY—THE ROLE OF GOVERNMENT IN BUSINESS

Microsoft vs. US Department of Justice (DoJ)

The Microsoft Corporation (Microsoft) was founded in 1975 when the software and computing services industry was entering a dynamic period of intense growth and competition. Today, Microsoft's annual revenues exceed US$11.4 billion, and it is worth US$220 billion. The company is now the ninth largest within the industry, employing over 20 000 people in 48 countries. In recent years, Microsoft has come under intense criticism in some quarters for allegedly using unfair business practices to fight competition. This has resulted in a lengthy investigation of the company by the US Department of Justice (DoJ) dating back to 1990. In this case study we examine the case in favour of and against Microsoft. The main purpose is to consider the role of government in regulating the business practices of companies through anti-trust laws. The main issue is whether Microsoft should be allowed to dominate the Internet and WWW in the same way as it does with PC operating systems. At the present time, Microsoft still operates as a large company, though some would like to see it broken up into distinct business units to destroy its monopoly powers. The US government has rarely attempted to split up monopolies. But Standard Oil in 1911 through to IBM and AT&T in recent years are examples of companies targeted by the US anti-trust policy against monopolies. The US government spent 13 years (unsuccessfully) trying to break up IBM. One solution that has been mooted is to divide Microsoft into an operating systems company and an applications company.

Attitudes Towards Microsoft

Attitudes towards Microsoft among the media, business leaders, academics and the public are polarised. Some claim that the company is an example of unparalleled success in corporate America, while others suggest it devours its competitors using unsavoury, anti-competitive business practices. The latter attitudes have led to Microsoft being embroiled in various anti-trust disputes with the United States since 1990 and more recently with the European Union as well. So far, the case against Microsoft continues to rumble on on both sides of the Atlantic, with attitudes both for and against the company more polarised than ever. Table 3.4 gives an example of some of the attitudes expressed about Microsoft from people in a variety of private and public sector roles.

Implicit in the comments and views outlined in Table 3.4 is that the software and computing services industry is new, dynamic and fast changing. Products and services offered by the various companies within this industry have changed significantly over the past 15 years, and continue to change at a rapid pace. For example, the emergence of the PC in the United States in 1983, and in Europe in 1984, was seen by many as a revolution in itself. This was eclipsed in the 1990s when the Internet became a commercial possibility for many businesses and even individuals. To this end, the US government has experienced many difficulties in defining, writing and enforcing anti-trust laws simply because it is dealing with an industry that is complex, unique and unpredictable. Nevertheless, Microsoft, like IBM before it, has experienced a decade of negotiations and conflict with the DoJ since a policy of free enterprise is paradoxically one which also attempts to identify and correct anti-competitive business practices. Table 3.5 tracks some of the major events affecting Microsoft's relationship with the US government from 1990 to the present.

Whilst it is outside the scope of this case study to discuss all these events in detail, we concentrate on the two major disputes between Microsoft and the DoJ. We first consider the anti-trust case concerning Microsoft's hegemony in the operating systems market during the first half of the 1990s. Here we look at Microsoft's dealings with manufacturers and introduce some theories which are useful for understanding a company's market position. The second anti-trust case considers the more recent dispute of the Internet (Web) browser. Microsoft's

Table 3.4   *Arguments in favour of and against in the anti-trust case between Microsoft and the Department of Justice (DoJ)*

The case in favour of Microsoft	The case against Microsoft
'The Microsoft case is reminiscent of the Justice Department's persecution of an earlier monopolist, the United Shoe Machinery Corp. As late as the 1950s, United Shoe possessed 75 per cent or 85 per cent of the domestic shoe-machinery market, at a time when shoemaking was dominated by American firms. In that case too, the Justice Department attached a set of leading practices that it did not well understand. And with no greater understanding, the courts struck those practices down, leading United Shoe to decline and ultimately to drop out of the market. The results: The price of shoe machinery went up, and foreign firms began to enter the market. Foreign companies now dominate the market both for shoe machinery and shoemaking itself. There was no clear benefit to consumers whatsoever. Those are the stakes in the attack against Microsoft.'	'Microsoft is using strong-arm tactics to force PC manufacturers to licence its Web browser and application software. This is unacceptable, given the unique position Microsoft has in the PC industry. To deny PC manufacturers access to vital operating system technology is a death sentence to any new PC. It is also unacceptable that Microsoft is forcing PC manufacturers to set up its Web browser so that the first Web page it goes to is Microsoft's home page. Microsoft says this is in the best interest of users—but this is not the case. For most people when they switch on their new PC for the first time, it would be more useful if the start-up Web page loaded the home page for the maker of their PC. The government should not try delaying Windows 98, as any delay would adversely affect PC manufacturers, not Microsoft. A more suitable action would be to split the operating systems group from the rest of Microsoft.'
Source: G.L. Priest, 'US vs. Microsoft: A case built on wide speculation, dubious theories', *Wall Street Journal*, 19 May 1998.	*Source*: 'Comment', *Computer Weekly*, 23 May 1998, p. 6.
'A company develops a new product. A product consumers want. But now the government steps in and is in effect attempting to dictate the terms on which that product can be marketed and sold … Pinch me, but I thought we were still in America.' *Source*: Senate Majority Leader Bob Dole (Former Presidential Candidate), 30 June 1997.	'Microsoft used its monopoly power to develop a chokehold on the browser market needed to access the Internet.' Janet Reno, US attorney-general.
'There is no anti-trust case against Microsoft. What is happening is that Sun Microsystems, Netscape Communications, and Novell are trying to achieve through anti-trust politics what they could not achieve in the marketplace. Economists have known for decades that anti-trust is what losers do to winners.' *Source*: Paul Craig, 'Microsoft is the victim of a legal mugging', *Business Week*, 13 April 1998.	'According to the survey, by a margin of 68 per cent to 13 per cent, respondents said they consider it a bad use of taxpayer dollars for state attorneys general to bring a lawsuit blocking Microsoft from releasing Windows 98. By the same margin, respondents said state attorneys general should not try to force Microsoft to remove Internet capabilities from Windows 98.' *Source*: D. Taft, 'Microsoft Poll: Americans oppose blocking windows 98', *Computer Reseller News*, 6 May 1998.

(Continues)

Table 3.4　*Continued*

The case in favour of Microsoft	The case against Microsoft
'If you asked customers who they would rather have deciding what innovations go into their computer—the government or software companies—the answer would be clear. They'd want the decision left to the marketplace, with competition driving improvements. This is the question at the center of the Justice Department's recent action aimed at forcing Microsoft to remove Internet Explorer from Windows. In this instance, consumer benefits seem to be less important than the complaints of a handful of our competitors who want the government to help them complete— by preventing Microsoft from enhancing its products.' Bill Gates, 1998.	'Microsoft has misappropriated the use of technology that was licensed to them. That is not the kind of thing we are going to leave to the market.' Alan Baratz, president of Sun's JavaSoft Division.

business tactics in attempting to compete with a much smaller supplier, Netscape, are observed.

The Microsoft Anti-Trust Case

1990–95

The Federal Trade Commission (FTC) began investigating Microsoft in 1990. During this time there was criticism that Microsoft's pricing policies violated the Sherman and Clayton Anti-trust Acts, which are designed to stop monopolists restricting the trade of other businesses (notably their competitors). By August 1993 the FTC had made little progress. As a result, the case was given to the Department of Justice (DoJ). Anne K. Bingaman, the head of the Anti-trust Division of the DoJ, continued to pursue Microsoft. The DoJ believed that Microsoft had a monopoly in the field of operating systems (OSs) which was strengthened through unlawful uses of monopoly power. Competitors of Microsoft were also adding weight to the charges of anti-competitive behaviour. In July 1994 a settlement was signed between Microsoft and the DoJ. The consent decree addressed Microsoft's illegal pricing policies and overly restrictive non-disclosure agreements (NDAs). There were distinct advantages for Microsoft settling out of court. First, it would not have to publicly accept charges that it had engaged in unfair business practices. Second, it could avoid a potentially damaging court battle which, if it lost, would instigate prima-facie cases from private litigants who would then be awarded treble damages. So, by signing the consent decree, Microsoft agreed to terms and conditions and avoided a public relations disaster.

Table 3.5   *Microsoft vs. the US Department of Justice (DoJ): the key milestones*

June 1990	Federal Trade Commission launches an anti-trust investigation into Microsoft.
August 1993	US Justice Department gets involved in the investigation, as Commission is unable to decide whether to bring charges.
September 1993	European Union Competition authorises launch of anti-trust investigation.
July 1994	Microsoft and Department of Justice sign a consent decree regulating the software company's marketing practices and Microsoft agrees to modify contracts with PC manufacturers. The company is not prohibited from developing 'integrated products'.
August 1995	Consent decree approved and entered by US District Court. Microsoft launches Windows 95.
November 1995	Microsoft releases Internet Explorer for Windows 95, and gives it away to users in challenge to Netscape's Navigator.
1996	Netscape files complaint with the Justice Department, alleging that Microsoft used unfair and anti-competitive practices in promoting Internet Explorer. Department starts investigation into Microsoft's licensing practices and requests documents on browser agreements with PC manufacturers.
1997	State of Texas launches formal anti-trust investigation of Microsoft's business practices on the Internet. State of Massachusetts begins an anti-trust investigation.
October 1997	Justice Department sues Microsoft, alleging violation of 1994 consent decree by forcing PC manufacturers to use Internet Explorer as a condition of selling Windows.
December 1997	US District Judge Thomas Penfield Jackson issues preliminary injunction forcing Microsoft to stop requiring manufacturers which sell Windows to install Internet Explorer on PCs. Microsoft appeals against court order but says it will sell modified versions of Windows to comply with the preliminary injunction.
January 1998	Microsoft's efforts to remove Harvard University Law Professor Lawrence Lessig as court appointed 'special master' to review technical issues in the dispute overruled by the judge. The company claim the professor is biased and appeals the ruling.
March 1998	Gates testifies before the Senate Judiciary Committee along with other top technology executives.
May 1998	US government and 20 states file anti-trust suits against Microsoft prohibiting it from requiring PC makers to install Internet Explorer on new machines.

Adapted from: Computer Weekly, 21 May 1998, p. 4.

The Case Against Microsoft

The events leading up to the signing of the consent decree began in early 1990. At this time there were serious allegations against Microsoft based on its contracts with computer manufacturers for the supply of its operating system (OS), MS-DOS. OSs form a link between computer hardware and applications software, such as word processors and spreadsheets. The OS is an integral part of the PC. As a consequence of its arrangement with IBM, Microsoft became the industry leader installing over three million copies of MS-DOS per month. As Microsoft's monopoly of the PC OS market expanded, so too did its power and control in the marketplace.

One of Microsoft's competitors, Novell, decided to make a case under Article 86. In June 1993 Novell filed a complaint with the Competition Directorate of the European Commission. Novell had recently acquired Digital Research, which produces DR-DOS, an OS interchangeable with Microsoft's MS-DOS, and hence in direct competition with it. The stalled United States investigations were taken over by the DoJ and were soon running at a scale not seen since the 1984 break-up of AT&T. In February 1994, with simultaneous enquiries underway on two continents, the United States and the European Union took the unprecedented step of collaborating. From then on events moved rapidly, concluding with Microsoft being offered a tight deadline to agree a settlement. In pursuing this case, three areas need to be considered. They are identified in Table 3.6.

As Table 3.6 suggests, any anti-trust case should define three areas. Market demarcation is very important since it is concerned to locate a company within a specific industry or business sector, in addition to defining the products and services of the company in question. It appears that Microsoft spans a number of business sectors given its wide product and service offerings. This creates difficulties for those pursuing an anti-trust agenda since companies in some industry sectors are constantly re-inventing themselves. Microsoft is no exception. Market domination is perhaps easier to identify since it is possible to use market share as one indicator. Microsoft is the market leader in the PC OS system market. Market strategy, on the other hand, is not easy to elicit for two reasons. First, companies do not make explicit their market strategy if this means giving a competitor an unfair advantage. Second, market strategy is not *cast in stone*, and is therefore an evolving process. In the mid-1990s, Microsoft was seen by some as entering the Internet and e-commerce marketplace as a late starter. Yet once Microsoft realised the potential business opportunities of this emerging market, it quickly made serious inroads to compete with more established competitors like Netscape (see below). However, the question of whether a company is pursuing a competitive business strategy or an unfair business practice is open to much debate.

The market position of Microsoft is both complex and changing. Defining the PC OS market is not easy. At the time of this dispute, the market was divided into two types:

1. DOSs (disk operating systems), which included Microsoft's MS-DOS, Novell's DR-DOS and IBM's PC-DOS.

Table 3.6 *Factors in understanding the market position of Microsoft*

Market demarcation	The relevant market needs to be demarcated
Market domination	The firm must be shown to have a dominant position within that market
Market strategy	The firm must be shown to be abusing this dominant position

2. non-DOS operating systems (such as OS/2, UNIX, Nextstep, and Windows NT).

Microsoft's MS-DOS emerged as the major OS. If it was assumed that the market included both DOSs for PCs and non-DOS operating systems, then Microsoft's market share would be reduced. It was therefore important to ascertain whether the two OSs belonged to the same market. This would determine the extent of consumer choice. Three key factors of the market for OSs affected consumers' demand and their ability to choose between the two OSs. They were *network externalities*, *consumer switching costs* and *barriers to entry*. These concepts are discussed in the strategy literature (cf. Porter, 1980).

Theories and Concepts

Network externalities means that, as the total number of users of an OS grows, so too will the benefit to the individuals who use it. A user will be able to exchange data and programs with a larger group of other users. There is also likely to be an increased range of applications software available for an OS with a larger user base. Consumer switching costs take into account the cost of switching between OSs. In terms of consumer behaviour, it is important to recognise the learning curve in training to use an OS and deciding to adopt another one. So, externalities and switching costs are important factors in understanding the consumer's ability to replace a non-DOS OS for a DOS one. Barriers to entry may be erected by a company to damage a competitor's market position or they may be intrinsic to the market.

Since Microsoft had become the market leader in PC OSs, a potential new entrant would have to offer an OS that was compatible with MS-DOS. This would be very difficult since consumers would have to trust that a new OS was compatible with MS-DOS and existing hardware and applications software. Operating systems are *experience products* since vendor claims can only be verified by using the product. Since to purchase the product is expensive and risky, consumers would face switching costs between DOS and non-DOS OSs. Network externalities also act as a barrier to entry. Consumers therefore benefit from using the most prevalent DOS, since this reflects the technical standards which determine the development of other new products and services.

Leading Up to the Settlement

In the mid-1990s, questions were posed about Microsoft contracts (terms and conditions) with equipment manufacturers. Many claimed that such contracts posed serious barriers to entry into the DOS market. The supply of new PCs is a dynamic and competitive market. An OS is usually installed in most new PCs. Given that manufacturers procure OSs at a much lower price compared with retail customers, there is a strong incentive to *bundle* the sale of PCs and OSs. Microsoft offered contracts to manufacturers where payments were conditional on the total number of PCs shipped, irrespective of whether MS-DOS or a competitor's OS was installed. Contracts of this nature have an added advantage of controlling the copying of intellectual property (piracy). But they have the disadvantage of increasing the costs to manufacturers should they wish to offer a variety of OSs. Assuming manufacturers wanted to ship PCs with another DOS, this would only be cost-effective if all their PCs were installed with the rival DOS. This posed many risks, not least because consumers would fear incompatibility with two manufacturers' products.

Microsoft's contracts further stipulated a minimum quantity clause for manufacturers. This created an exclusive dealing arrangement, though it was not formalised. While it was clearly not in the collective interests of manufacturers to have a near-monopoly supplier of OSs, such as Microsoft, defining terms and conditions, other competitive pressures were in force. This helped to influence the decisions taken by manufacturers in accepting Microsoft's terms and conditions even though they came with advantages (per system licences, which are cheaper than per copy licences) and disadvantages. Long running contracts would enable Microsoft to prevent entrants from building up demand for their products quickly. New OSs would need to gain markets sufficiently quickly to be able to benefit from network externalities and to convince customers of the product's quality. Long-term contracts prevent this from happening.

A more serious issue was whether Microsoft could use its dominance in other markets to gain leverage on the DOS market where it faced competition. Microsoft's Windows, a graphical extension to DOS, had little direct competition in the mid-1990s (though this is currently changing). Microsoft offered discounts to manufacturers if they procured both MS-DOS and Windows. One allegation was that Microsoft threatened not to supply Windows to manufacturers who did not purchase MS-DOS. This would enable Microsoft to use its dominance in the Windows market to severely damage Novell and IBM so that they were unable to compete in the DOS market. Clearly, allegations of this nature were very damaging to Microsoft and have been fiercely defended.

In July 1994, Microsoft signed an agreement covering the following six and a half years. It would prohibit the company from:

- charging for its OS on the basis of computers shipped rather than on copies of MS-DOS shipped;
- imposing minimum quantity commitments on original equipment manufacturers (OEMs);
- entering into contracts lasting longer than one year;
- tying the sale of MS-DOS to the sale of other Microsoft products, especially Windows.

The settlement was designed to significantly alter Microsoft's business practices. Yet the reaction to the settlement was mixed, with some believing that it went too far, and others thinking it did not go far enough. One complaint was that Microsoft defines technical standards for DOS and Windows and also writes applications software to run under these systems. This would enable the company to build into the design compatibility problems between Windows and the applications software of its competitors. Such a situation would secure Microsoft's dominant position over the short to medium term. Whilst the settlement was a clear indication that US and EU anti-trust authorities were tackling anti-competitive business practices, it is difficult to predict the effects of such behaviour on the company's existing or potential competitors. Network externalities and switching costs have the effect that, once a particular OS becomes the standard, it can be hard for competitors enter the market.

1995–

Since the mid-1990s, Microsoft has been embroiled in another anti-trust dispute with the DoJ, which is to some extent a continuation of its previous problems with the authorities. This dispute involves Microsoft's attempt to compete in the Internet (Web) browser market. In 1995, Netscape, a small company by comparison, had 80% of the Internet browser market share. Microsoft in contrast had been slow to enter this market. But in recognising the growing importance of the browser market, Gates claimed in 1995, 'The Internet is the most important single development to come along since the IBM PC was introduced in 1981. It has enough users that it is benefiting from the positive feedback loop of the more users it gets, the more content it gets; and the more content it gets, the more users it gets.'

When Netscape was listed on the stock market in August 1995, its shares sold widely. Prior to the company making a net profit, it was valued at US$2.7 billion (£1.7 billion). Observing the growth of Netscape led Microsoft to mobilise its vast R&D resource base to develop a competing Internet browser. This resulted in the development of the Microsoft Internet Explorer which was given to customers free with Windows 95. According to one report, a Microsoft Executive claimed that, 'We are going to cut off their (Netscape's) air supply. Everything they are selling, we're going to give away for free' (*The Sunday Times*, 24 May 1998, p. 3). Microsoft's share of the browser market increased from 2.9% at the end of 1995 to more than 40% by 1997. Netscape's share has fallen to 54%. In January 1998, Netscape said it would lose between US$85 million and US$89 million in the first quarter of the financial year. It announced it would take a US$35 million charge to cover redundancies and other restructuring moves. However, Netscape has claimed that losing the browser was not catastrophic since about 80% of its business comes from developing 'enterprise software' for its corporate clients.

Observing the growth in Microsoft's share of the browser market in conjunction with Netscape's declining market share, led the DoJ once again to level fresh anti-trust charges against Microsoft. To give relief to Netscape and other companies, the DoJ wanted Microsoft to terminate the practice of forcing PC manufacturers to install its Web browser and other software as a condition of licensing its OS (which is now used by 91% of PCs). It also wanted Microsoft to provide a version of Windows 98 that manufacturers can customise so the start-up screen did not display icons for its own Web browser as well as other services, sites and partners. It also wanted Microsoft to include Netscape's browser if its own one (the Internet Explorer) was bundled with Windows 98. This led Bill Gates to comment, 'It's like asking us to include three cans of Pepsi with every six pack of Coke.' He believed the DoJ did not understand the economics of the software and computing services industry. He claimed that it was important that Microsoft built extra functionality into new versions of Windows. Moreover, this is what consumers wanted, according to Microsoft.

In 1998 Judge Thomas Jackson issued a preliminary injunction to force Microsoft to make available two versions of Windows to PC manufacturers, one including the browser and one without. The DoJ also wanted Microsoft to remove the Explorer icon that automatically appears on the computer screen when a user starts the Windows programme.

An Issue of Product Integration

One of the key questions relating to the Internet browser dispute between Microsoft and the DoJ is: Should product integration be treated as an anti-competitive business practice? Alternatively, the question may be posed in a different way: Why should companies not integrate (bundle) their products and services if they think this would benefit their consumers?

There are many examples throughout history of companies attempting to lock customers into using their products and services against those of a competitor, e.g. ice cream or soft drink manufacturers giving away freezers and refrigerators to retailers that exclusively stock their products. Or mortgage companies who force their customers to take out their own insurance policies. To a large extent, Microsoft is no different in 'bundling' one product with another to offer the consumer an integrated or seamless solution. Microsoft believes it should not be penalised for offering its customers a free Internet browser with its Windows operating system. This is its strongest defense. In the light of the dispute with the DoJ, Microsoft argued:

> The Justice Department's position is equivalent to the government telling personal computer manufacturers that they can't include word processing, spreadsheet or email functionality in PCs because it would be unfair to typewriter, calculator and courier companies. Microsoft and the DoJ anticipated this very issue three years ago when we signed a consent decree that specifically allowed Microsoft to develop 'integrated software products'. At the time, the DoJ was fully aware that we were planning to integrate Internet capabilities into the forthcoming Windows 95 operating system. Microsoft has a long history of improving its operating system products and building in a new functionality, just as Apple, IBM, Sun, Novell and other have. These features have included such things as a graphical user interface (GUI), memory management, type fonts, disc compression and networking. Every one of these was available first as a separate offering but eventually was integrated to meet customer demand for greater functionality in Windows. Supporting Internet browsing in Windows is a logical, incremental step in the evolution of the operating system. For 15 years, Microsoft operating systems have included as core technology the capacity to locate and use information from local sources—such as the hard drive or the CD drive—as well as remote sources, such as local area networks. Windows 95 simply permits users to get information from the newest remote source—the Internet.

The DoJ's strongest argument appears to be based around adverse comments from Microsoft executives in how it attempts to combat competition. If the DoJ can prove that Microsoft only 'bundled' Internet Explorer with Windows to put

Netscape out of business, its anti-trust case is strengthened. If this occurs, the logical progression for the DoJ may be to call for the break-up of Microsoft into two distinct business: operating systems and applications. Paradoxically, this could evolve into a free-market situation, with the two companies aggressively competing in the market unfettered by government officials and regulation.

Further Reading

Alexander, G. (1998) Battle of the browsers, *The Sunday Times*, 11 January, p. 7.
Check, D. (1996) *The Case Against Microsoft*.
http://ourworld.compuserve.com/homepages/spazz/mspaper.htm
Computing (1998) Sleepless in Seattle. Microsoft in Court, 9 July, pp. 29–35.
Maldoom, D. (1996) The Microsoft Anti-trust Case, *London Economics*.
http://www.londecon.co.uk/pubs/comp/microsft.htm

SUMMARY

This chapter has focused on the role of government in the development of a legal and regulatory framework to govern global Internet commerce. The discussion shows that while there are some differences in priorities and objectives both within and between the United States and the European Union, the overall consensus is for the private sector to take the lead in developing the global information society with governments only imposing rules and regulations where necessary. What is evident from the above discussion is that global Internet commerce will only be successful if governments worldwide can agree on a variety of legal, market and technical parameters for the protection of businesses and consumers. Much progress has already been made, in particular with the Uniform Commercial Code (UCC) and other measures to safeguard the interests of buyers and sellers. However, more needs to be done if the Internet is to make significant inroads into business-to-consumer Internet commerce.

4
Market as Opportunity: Developing Business-to-Business Internet Commerce

INTRODUCTION

The growth and development of Internet commerce will have profound effects on business organisations worldwide, in particular how they are structured, organised, managed and controlled in an electronic (virtual) rather than physical (traditional) environment (Feher and Towell, 1997). The literature is replete with examples of how technology can be utilised as a strategic resource for business (Currie, 1995a). The Internet is no exception. Precepts such as the strategy–technology connection (Kantrow, 1980), competing through technology (Porter, 1985), and the information resource (Davenport, 1993a) all suggest that technology should be placed at the forefront of the business. As with other technologies, e.g. computer-aided design (CAD), computer-aided manufacture (CAM), advanced manufacturing technology (AMT), and philosophies and techniques for improving operational efficiency, e.g. just-in-time (JIT), total quality management (TQM), business process re-engineering (BPR), process innovation (PI) and outsourcing, practitioner and academic interest in the Internet is equally intense.

In the past few years, governments on both sides of the Atlantic have sought to examine the phenomenon of Internet commerce in the context of its potential to enhance economic performance. Task forces, steering committees, quangos, pressure groups and other interested parties (trade associations, journal and magazine editors, etc.) have also begun to consider the wide-ranging implications of Internet commerce for business and the wider society. There are now numerous conferences, workshops and seminars on Internet commerce, which are sponsored by a range of organisations, some with a non-commercial (information dissemination) focus and others with a view to advertising and selling their products.

The hype surrounding Internet commerce, however, is disproportionately large compared with hard evidence from companies of tangible economic and practical benefits. In this chapter we examine three interrelated areas on Internet commerce. First we consider some of the literature on whether the Internet can be perceived as a strategic marketing resource for business (Brannbach, 1997), or simply just another high-tech fad, which will cost businesses a lot of money with few tangible benefits. Second, we examine the growing phenomenon of business-to-business Internet commerce. Whilst this form of Internet commerce is treated by some as a new development, it is important to remember that the EDI private networks have been around for many years. To this end, Internet commerce is perhaps more appropriately viewed as offering additional functionality to existing systems. However, Internet commerce is likely to be more accessible to small and medium exterprises (SMEs), partly because of its reduced cost. Third, we consider the Internet and the role of intermediaries. This is a contentious area and one that is open to much debate. So far, the debate appears to be divided into two distinct camps, namely those that believe that intermediaries will be eliminated as a consequence of Internet commerce (disintermediation), and those who believe the opposite. Whilst the true picture is perhaps much more complex, it is apparent that whereas some intermediaries are likely to become obsolete (Brenner *et al.*, 1997), there will be a continuing growth in high-tech intermediaries. This will be partly due to the continuing trend of outsourcing. Fourth, an overview of three international companies engaged in either business-to-business or business Internet commerce is considered. They are Dell Computer Corporation, Cisco Systems, and Federal Express. These companies comprise a growing list of success stories in the design, development, implementation and management of Internet commerce, and illustrate some of the many benefits of this new medium.

THE INTERNET AS A STRATEGIC MARKETING RESOURCE FOR BUSINESS

One of the key questions is whether the Internet is simply an electronic marketing channel like direct mail or home shopping or instead a revolutionary new technology to create a global marketplace (Quelch and Klein, 1996). At the present time there is an immense amount of hype about the possibilities of using the Internet as a marketing tool. This is marked by the development of numerous company Web sites, many of which provide little or no real value-added information or services for customers. More sophisticated Web sites, however, provide customers with an expanded range of products and services, and this removes potential communication barriers between businesses and customers which are created by distance and location (geography), time zones, and cultural differences (language and customs). According to Quelch and Klein (1996), 'Much of the current expansion in Internet use, accelerated by the emergence of the World Wide Web (WWW), is driven by marketing initiatives—providing products and product information to potential customers.' These authors further claim that in future, more and more businesses will utilise the Internet for a wider range of services and thereby exploit this medium for its potential for enhancing information (communication) and transactions. To this end, the Internet has the potential to transform retailers from their traditional marketing role as product-led merchants to consumer-driven marketeers. This is important given the market saturation that exists in many mature marketplaces (e.g. North America, Europe and SE Asia).

A recent survey by Forrester Research (1997a,b) contrasts the growth in Internet shopping for 1997 and 2000, respectively (see Table 4.1). As we can see, all categories are expected to grow, especially those of PC hardware and sales, travel and entertainment. One of the consequences of this growth will be *disintermediation* (the elimination of intermediaries as more and more customers purchase goods and services directly from companies with interactive Web sites).

Whilst there has been a considerable amount of hype about on-line shopping, one area that requires further development is on-line shopping malls. In the physical world, on-line shopping malls offer the customer a relatively seamless shopping experience. A wide range of stores and shops operate under one roof and shoppers can also take advantage of other services (post offices, restaurants, crèches, rest areas, etc.), all of which contribute to a more satisfying and convenient day out. Free car parking is another facet of some shopping malls which is a further factor in encouraging people to travel to do their shopping rather than use local shops in congested areas.

In the virtual world, on-line shopping malls are intended to make people's lives even easier since they can do their shopping from the comfort of their own homes. However, recent research shows that on-line shopping malls require further development as some evidence suggests that people find that some Web sites are boring and confusing. Virtual on-line shopping has also to take into account the fact that many people perceive a visit to a physical shopping mall as a day out and enjoy being able to sample the products for sale.

On-line (virtual) shopping malls are an attempt to recreate a successful real world retail model on the Internet. To the extent that customers are becoming less fearful of giving their credit card details over the Internet, it would appear that the potential for on-line shopping malls should increase. Recent experiences, however,

Table 4.1   *The Internet shopping marketplace*

Internet shopping marketplace	1997 (US$ million)	2000 (US$ million)
PC hardware and sales	863	2901
Travel	654	4741
Books and music	156	761
Gifts, flowers and greetings	149	591
Clothes and footwear	92	361
Food and beverages	90	354
Jewellery	38	107
Sporting goods	20	63
Consumer electronics	19	93
Entertainment	298	1921
Other (toys, home, etc.)	65	197

Adapted from: Forrester Research (cited in *Computing*, 26 February 1998, p. 54).

show that two on-line shopping malls were deemed to have failed when IBM closed its World Avenue site after failing to attract large retailers. In addition, US based Shopping.com also ran into trouble when auditors called into question the financial viability of the company (*Financial Times*, 3 June 1998, p. 7). One of the key problems in setting up on-line shopping malls is the failure to provide retailers and customers with a seamless service. Web sites can be confusing and difficult to operate with the result that the user simply loses interest. It is therefore important for Web site developers to combine the front office with the back office operations of a retailer. This has yet to be achieved by many retailers. Most commentators believe that large companies should set up their own Web sites and possibly outsource some services to specialist intermediaries. For small and medium companies (SMEs), it is likely that they will benefit by joining an existing on-line shopping mall—one that is set up and known to be successful.

What is critical in the area of on-line shopping is that Web sites must offer the customer an interesting and value-added service, possibly one which can transfer cost savings onto the customer. For example, retailers with on-line shopping will not have to pay exorbitant commercial rates for sites as they do in physical shopping malls since their needs will be different. In a virtual on-line shopping environment, the retailer will need an adequate warehousing facility with good distribution channels. A good example of this is the company Amazon.com which sells books over the Internet. Its owner decided to set up the company in the US state of Seattle where procurement and distribution (of books) was easier compared with other US states. This company has proven to be one of the more successful examples of Internet commerce. Less successful examples are in the areas of luxury goods and designer clothes where people have been more reluctant to purchase items.

A recent survey from US market research firm Cyber Dialogue claims that customers look at on-line retail sites to gather information about products, but then buy them from local retailers. The survey estimates that US$4.2 billion of US consumer goods and service sales were influenced by on-line information in 1997, compared with US$3.3 billion in actual on-line sales (*Financial Times*, 3 June 1998, p. 7). This survey points to the Internet becoming an important element in the purchasing process irrespective of whether the purchase is made on-line or off-line.

In a study that considers the Internet as a strategic resource in the European retail sector, Reynolds (1997, pp. 408–409) differentiates between the informational and transactional uses of the Internet. At present, the Internet is used largely for informational rather than transactional purposes although this balance may change over time as buyers and sellers become more confident about Internet commerce.

Informational uses offer the opportunity

- to better inform the customer's buying decision (by clarifying choice in the emerging transactional environment);
- to better understand the needs of an increasingly sought-after market segment; and

- ultimately to build presence at an early stage in a new and potentially powerful distribution channel.

Transactional uses offer the opportunity

- to use existing skills to develop value-added retail products and services specifically designed for the electronic environment;
- to make shopping for essential goods easier; and
- to improve the quality of the non-essential shopping trip (by providing additional choice within the home).

The author suggests that

> Retailers seeking to invest in Internet ventures need to devote as much (if not more) care and attention to researching and understanding the market, to the design and crafting of their offers and to their skills and capabilities in delivering the offer as they would in the development of more conventional physical storefronts.

Research of this kind shows that, although the Internet offers many new possibilities for retailers to expand their markets, it is important that they thoroughly understand consumer behaviour in a virtual and not just a physical environment. Indeed, there are many examples of failed Web sites as consumers have found that poor Web site design and difficulty of use has deterred them from using them for transactional (as opposed to informational) purposes (Chesbrough and Teece, 1996).

BUSINESS-TO-BUSINESS INTERNET COMMERCE

Internet commerce encompasses a range of electronic interactions between organisations and their upstream and downstream (business-to-business) trading partners. As we saw in Chapter 1, transactions of this nature are not new and have been occurring for many years prior to the Internet being opened to commercial traffic. Platforms for Internet commerce that precede the Internet include the use of the Teletel in France for interorganisational commercial transactions, as well as the use of EDI over private networks. We noted in the previous section that marketing on a network requires that new strategies, methods and approaches are adopted to ensure that businesses fully exploit this new medium (Deighton, 1996, Granger and Schroder, 1996). Networks can facilitate the co-ordination between buyers and sellers, reducing transaction costs that are passed on to the customer in the form of reduced prices for goods and services. Therefore accelerated information flows across the network may significantly reduce administrative overheads and thereby eliminate traditional intermediaries—a subject we shall consider in more detail below. This has already occurred to some extent in banking and insurance in the form of *direct* marketing of products and services to customers. The level of automation (or lack thereof) in the financial securities industry is an impediment to the further progress of electronic commerce. These markets should be among the first to become fully automated, given their commodity-like attributes and lack of physical goods to transport. Yet automation has not been fully implemented in these markets. Fully automated transactions over networks will be difficult to achieve, mainly because the network removes the ability of actors (buyers and sellers) to behave strategically, especially during the price discovery phase of a transaction.

Notwithstanding the lack of automation in some business sectors, the further diffusion of the Internet is likely, over time, to call into question traditional theories and practices of buyer–seller relationships. Some argue that one of the main effects of networks linking business trading partners will be a reinforcing of existing relations, and the formation of electronic hierarchies, rather than the creation of large electronic marketplaces. Contrary to expectations in much of the previous literature, they suggest that this is likely to be true even on ubiquitous, public network infrastructures like the WWW (Steinfield et al., 1995). Other writers point out that organisations will exploit an NII to create closed interorganisational networks characterised by Intranet work co-operation and interdependence. Their many case studies in the Netherlands help to illustrate this trend. Together, these two papers suggest that visions of a vast electronic marketplace, on which buyers shop around for the best deal among a large set of sellers, do not take into account the real dynamics of interorganisational relations. So while the Internet has been described as a haven of consumer choice and opportunity by some, it is likely that some buyer–seller relationships over time may become more cemented rather than unstable. This of course will depend on the design and implementation of effective *seller* marketing strategies to lock *buyers* into repeat purchases of products and services.

The Internet has the potential to greatly expand the value of goods and services businesses that trade electronically. Estimated at more than US$8 billion in 1997, the value of goods and services traded between the businesses over the Internet (excluding the transfer of funds or financial securities purchased) far exceeds on-line transactions between businesses and consumers. Given the pace at which businesses are beginning to use the Internet to manage interactions with their business partners, it will continue to grow very rapidly. Analysts predict businesses will trade as much as US$300 billion over the Internet in the next three to five years. Forrester Research (1997a) estimates that Internet commerce between businesses in the United States could reach US$327 billion by 2002. This will be an increase of as much as US$319 billion in only a five-year period.

There are some business analysts who believe that given the pace at which companies are adopting the Internet in key business applications and processes, the figures presented in Table 4.2 could be much higher. In a recent report, Price Waterhouse (1998) claimed that, 'between 1996 and 1997, business-to-business trade doubled every six months and this is accelerating to double every 3 to 4 months in 1998. By 2002, the value of goods and services traded via the Internet globally will increase to US$434 billion'.

Internet commerce between businesses is not a new phenomenon. Businesses began sending and receiving purchase orders, invoices and shipping notifications electronically via EDI in the late 1970s. Analysts estimate that businesses already trade well over US$150 billion in goods and services using EDI over private value-added networks. This was initially expensive and required considerable training and

Table 4.2 *Forecasting the growth of business-to-business Internet commerce over a six-year period*

	1997 (US$ billion)	1998 (US$ billion)	1999 (US$ billion)	2000 (US$ billion)	2001 (US$ billion)	2002 (US$ billion)
Internet commerce (all business-to-business)	8	17	41	105	183	327
Manufacturing	3	8	17	41	68	116
Wholesale/business retail	2	6	18	48	89	168
Utilities	2	2	3	5	7	10
Transport	—	—	—	—	—	—
Services	1	1	3	11	19	33

installation. It was therefore financially unviable for many small and medium-sized businesses. In 1997, it was estimated that the worldwide value of goods and services traded between businesses via EDI over private networks was US$162 billion (Input, 1997).

One of the advantages of the Internet is that it is more affordable to very small companies, and even to individuals working from home. Companies of all sizes can now communicate with each other electronically, through a web of interconnected networks including the public Internet, intranets, extranets and value-added networks. The rapid growth of business-to-business electronic commerce is being driven by:

- reduced transaction costs;
- reduced inventory (stock);
- more efficient logistics; and
- lower sales and marketing costs, and new sales opportunities.

Reduced Transaction Costs

The traditional way of procuring goods and services by companies was time-consuming and expensive, and often led to double invoicing (being charged twice for the same goods and services) and other forms of financial miscalculation and irregularity. With the use of EDI channels, companies have been able to systematically reduce transaction costs incurred by procuring goods and services. These costs are lowered in three important ways to do with information-gathering, selection and rationalisation. First, by undertaking a thorough search of the marketplace for potential low cost sources of supply, more informed decisions about suppliers can be taken by companies. Companies may find they contact or are contacted by overseas suppliers who are able to offer goods and services at a reduced rate. In the past these suppliers may have been deterred from widening their customer base because of the high telecommunications costs (telephone, fax, telex, etc.). Second, by developing strong relationships with a number of preferred suppliers, it is likely that companies will receive better service and support. With EDI channels, software can be developed which streamlines the procurement process, thus reducing the potential for human error. Third, by taking advantage of volume discounts offered by preferred suppliers, companies will reduce their internal costs in the areas of labour, administration, office space, printing and mailing. By applying business-process re-engineering techniques *vis-à-vis* the Internet, companies will also be able to reduce procurement costs by automating previously manual tasks. Real-time communication will also offer significant advantages to companies, particularly where just-in-time (JIT) methods and techniques are implemented.

It has been estimated that US businesses spend about US$250 billion each year on materials, services and supplies not used in the production process. Buying office supplies, computer equipment, and parts for maintenance, repairs and operation of equipment (otherwise known as MRO supplies) is typically a manual process and can be very costly and inefficient. Purchase orders for indirect and MRO supplies are often for low-dollar-value amounts.

Reduced Inventory (Stock)

In the 1980s there was significant interest in the concept of JIT manufacturing methods and techniques (Cobb, 1991; Currie and Seddon, 1992). Rising inventory (stock) costs incurred by manufacturing companies, particularly those operating in North America and Europe (Hayes and Jaikumar, 1988), fuelled part of this interest. In the United States and the United Kingdom, academics began to quantify inventory overheads with a view to identifying ways to reduce these costs. Kaplan (1985) claimed that much of the problem was caused by obsolete management accounting systems which could neither measure nor evaluate the source of production and operating costs. Whilst it is outside the scope of this section to examine the merits and demerits of this debate, suffice to say that companies now realise the importance of performance measurement systems for providing timely and useful management information. EDI private networks and, more recently, the Internet are likely to play a major role in determining and monitoring inventory levels in a variety of industries. We now consider two examples from the airline and computer industries, respectively.

In recent years, EDI private networks and, to a lesser extent, the Internet, have been used to provide accurate forecasts of sales and inventory levels. These technologies are a useful means of ensuring that real-time data and information are provided to managers to allow them to take more informed decisions. An example of this is found in the airline industry. A few years ago the airline industry attempted to make their suppliers responsible for spare parts inventory. Boeing saw its overall order volume increase, most notably for priority orders. (The longer a priority order remains unfilled, the longer an aeroplane could be grounded.) Boeing took the decision to move its own inventory closer to its customers, where it used historical data and information based on customer needs to determine stock levels. The company further reduced its response time on routine orders from 10 days to next day and for priority orders from same day to 2 hours only. Data and information based upon historical experience is generally believed to be useful for ensuring that the most appropriate level of inventory is available for airlines at the point at which it is required. What is even more useful is to combine historical data and information with forecasts about future requirements so as to ensure that inventory levels do not fall short or exceed requirements.

Given that aircraft servicing is a highly regulated activity, the Federal Aviation Authority (FAA) has guidelines about how often and how thoroughly aircraft must be serviced. This means that many future needs can be anticipated, but that information has to be communicated from the airline to its suppliers. Boeing envisages a system in which airlines would incorporate needs for scheduled maintenance activities directly into their spare parts ordering processes. For instance, if a part was needed, the system would first scan the database of parts in the inventory and, if a match was found, assign that part to the future order. If the required part was not already in stock, a production order could be generated and sent to the supplier well in advance of the need. All links in the chain would be better served. Airlines would have the parts when they needed them (and would be able to track the status of the parts they ordered); Boeing would be able to plan its inventory more effectively (currently, 50% of Boeing's orders are high priority; if Boeing cannot find the parts in the inventory, it has to place an emergency or *expedited* order, sometimes meaning higher production and shipping costs that affect adversely Boeing's profit margin); and Boeing's suppliers would benefit from having to respond to fewer expedited orders. For this strategy to be successful, communication from the airline to the aeroplane manufacturer to the supplier is critical. With the Internet's potential to reach all participants at a low cost, it will play a key role in making this work.

Another example of business-to-business Internet commerce is found in the computer industry. As many as 75% of personal computers (PCs) are sold through third-party distribution, and this figure is likely to decrease over time. In the mid-1980s two computer companies emerged which challenged the concept and practice of third-party distribution which was common practice in the industry. Dell Computer Corporation, founded in 1984, and Gateway 2000, which followed a year later, have become serious players in the marketplace. By the 1990s, both companies had become multi-billion dollar corporations. Their key strategy was to sell directly to businesses and individuals through catalogues, over the telephone, and, more recently, via the Internet. The 'build-to-order' model was implemented in place of the more traditional 'build-to-stock' model which was commonly used in third-party distribution. In the build-to-order model, a computer is produced only after a customer orders it. With the price of integrated circuits and other key components dropping radically from month to month with new technological advances, postponing the ordering of these parts can significantly reduce the product's overall cost. As a result of these initiatives, Dell and Gateway typically have a 100% advantage in inventory levels over their competitors, resulting in lower inventory carrying costs and less risk associated with price protection and returns. Over the past year, Compaq, IBM and Hewlett-Packard have begun to modify their sales and inventory practices to lower their costs and, at the same time, offer more value to their end customers. The Internet plays a key role in their strategies. It is used to locate and purchase parts, link suppliers into up-to-the-minute inventory and design information, and collaborate with suppliers and resellers on more accurate and flexible forecasts and production plans.

More Efficient Logistics

EDI private networks and the Internet further serve a useful role in ensuring that business processes work seamlessly and efficiently. The process from procurement to delivery is a critical element of the logistics operation and one in which Internet technologies in particular can play a vital role. Logistics has become increasingly important as companies have de-layered and restructured with the result that many now outsource significant parts of their business, including logistics (Currie and Willcocks, 1997). Logistics may involve the use of warehouses and various consolidation points (where products from different parts of the country or the world are transferred to trucks or containers along with other products going to the same place). A company's logistics operation will usually liaise with customs agents and freight forwarders, delivery companies and handling companies. Depending on where the product comes from, and whether it gets sent via express mail, truck or ship, some products can be shipped from point to point in a few hours. Other products may take several weeks. Being able to track a product each step of the way from the factory to the end customer has meant that the logistics function has become much more sophisticated. Orders placed over the telephone, by fax or the Internet are electronically communicated to the logistics company's internal system. If the product is in a warehouse, a picking order is automatically generated, the product is loaded onto a truck or mailed to the customer's home. Each of these processes gets recorded in the system for tracking purposes so that whoever needs to see its movement, whether the customer service representative at the logistics company or the manufacturer, or the end customer, knows where it is and when to expect its arrival.

Recent evidence shows that Internet technologies are now making large savings to companies, particularly where integrated logistics, planning and manufacturing across the entire supply chain, from supplier to customer, and beyond to their suppliers and customers, has led to dynamic scheduling and lower inventory. Furthermore, Internet technologies not only support existing business processes, but they may also drive new business opportunities (Kalakota and Whinston, 1997). Many businesses that use the Internet now look to partners to supply and distribute their products (Currie, 1999b; Kurbel and Teuteberg, 1998). As retailing of tangible goods over the Internet grows, so too will opportunities for logistics and delivery companies.

Lower Sales and Marketing Costs

Throughout the 1980s and 1980s, many companies have directed large resources into their sales and marketing operations. This is also reflected in business schools which treat marketing as a core part of the curriculum. The discipline of marketing, however, is undergoing vast changes, and this is summed up by Deighton who writes:

> The profession of marketing, its theories, its practices, and even the basic sciences that it draws on are determined by the tools at its disposal at any moment. When the tools change, the discipline adjusts, sometimes quite profoundly and usually quite belatedly ... Clearly,

marketing's tool kit is experiencing unsettling amounts of innovation today. The boom in direct and database marketing, the dawning of electronic commerce, new ways to automate sales force management, and the sudden blossoming of the WWW all suggest that the discipline is under pressure to reshape (Deighton, 1996, p. 151).

Theory and practice concerning sales and marketing is therefore likely to change markedly with the move from traditional (manual) to electronic (virtual) methods and techniques. Traditionally, companies have set up large sales and marketing functions where personnel are charged with the responsibility of handling as many customer accounts as they can physically undertake in person or by telephone. The greater the number of accounts, the greater the sales force. Even direct marketing companies whose businesses rely on people to take orders by telephone increase staffing as order volumes increase.

By using the Internet, companies will find they can take on board new customers without incurring additional costs. Since the sales function is located within a computer server as opposed to a physical environment like an office, its ability to serve customers is restricted only by the capacity of the servers to receive and respond to their inquiries and orders. Many computer companies now use the Internet for a variety of sales and marketing purposes. Customers can therefore access a Web site and read all the sales and marketing information about new and existing products and services. Many companies have also set up a FAQs (frequently asked questions) facility, and this has the advantage of saving staff time and offering the customer a 24-hour service. Some computer companies have interactive sites where customers (e.g. software developers) can liaise with other customers about their products.

The discussion in this section has considered the potential benefits to companies from business-to-business Internet commerce. Reduced transaction costs, reduced inventory costs, more efficient logistics, and lower sales and marketing costs, are just four areas where companies are likely to reap the rewards from EDI private networks and Internet commerce more generally. Prior to examining three case histories on business-to-business Internet commerce, namely Federal Express, Cisco Systems and Dell Computer Corporation, we will consider one of the important debates emerging in the field. This debate concerns how Internet commerce is likely to change the role of intermediaries.

THE ROLE OF INTERMEDIARIES

In recent years, practitioner and academic circles have begun to consider the impact on intermediaries from the growth and development of Internet commerce. Intermediaries (or cybermediaries as they have been called) are companies that serve both the customer (buyer) and the company (seller). For example, travel agents, estate agents, insurance sales staff, stockbrokers, recruitment consultants, financial advisers, among others, all occupy a *traditional* intermediary position between buyers and sellers. *Virtual* intermediaries by contrast are likely to be start-up high-tech firms which see a commercial opportunity to provide goods and services to larger firms wishing to establish an Internet commerce facility. As we saw in Chapter 2, companies which are developing an Internet commerce facility will need to consider the effects on their existing intermediaries, in addition to determining the need for new capabilities and skills. The debate about the Internet and intermediaries is currently highly contentious and appears to be divided into two distinct camps.

The Reduction of Intermediaries (Disintermediation)

On the one hand, some commentators argue that as Internet commerce continues to grow at an alarming rate, intermediaries will be systematically eliminated from the value or supply chain. This process has been labelled *disintermediation* and it will be characterised by the buyer procuring goods and services direct from the seller. For example, Internet users can now purchase a range of goods and services from companies operating in a variety of business sectors from retailing, financial services and computing. As we saw in Chapter 2, physical products (clothes, electrical goods, flowers, etc.) may be procured electronically, although they will be delivered via traditional methods (e.g. postal services, rail, road and air). Virtual (non-physical) products and services (bank statements, newspaper articles, software, flight information, etc.), on the other hand, may be procured and delivered via the Internet. Both categories of product and service (physical and virtual) may therefore result in undermining the role of intermediaries over time. Such *progressive disintermediation* will transform companies in terms of their markets, hierarchies, structures, size, personnel requirements and operations.

In some cases, intermediaries will be eliminated from the whole process and this is likely to benefit both the company and the customer. This is likely to occur to a large extent in companies offering virtual (non-physical) or informational products and services, and to a lesser extent in companies offering physical or tangible goods. However, the jury is still out on the extent to which disintermediation will occur. According to Buxmann and Gebauer (1998), 'When the Internet started to establish itself in the corporate world, some observers foresaw a diminishing role for, if not the end of, intermediary functions, i.e. market players located between manufacturers (sellers) and end consumers (buyers).' Similarly, Gellman (1996) contends that, 'With the Internet cutting information costs and facilitating direct connections between businesses and consumers worldwide, the question arises whether a replacement of intermediaries might be the result.' A more practical example is offered by Benjamin and Wigand (1995) who claim that the elimination of wholesalers and retailers from the existing value chain system in the high quality shirt market would reduce the retail price by more than 60%. To this end, manufacturers may use the Internet and related technologies to reduce costs. They may also establish closer links with their customers by bypassing firms that have hitherto played an intermediary role in the traditional value chain. Clearly, disintermediation is an attractive proposition for business and commerce, particularly in so far as it can contribute to rationalisation strategies. Whether cost savings will be transferred to the customer, however, is another matter, although this is likely to occur in highly competitive markets such as computing, financial services and the leisure industries.

The Growth of Infomediaries

The other side of the debate argues that Internet commerce is likely to create new intermediaries (*infomediaries* or *cybermediaries*). Two interrelated reasons are paramount. First, with the trend towards outsourcing, particularly in the IT function, it is conceivable that companies will find they do not possess sufficient in-house technical expertise to design, maintain and manage an Internet function. So it is likely that they will seek to outsource or insource technical expertise to undertake this work (Currie and Willcocks, 1998a). Second, the Internet will open up many new opportunities for existing and start-up companies to enable them to offer their products and services. Time and distance may not pose a problem, particularly where information handling can be undertaken electronically (e.g. data warehousing is one example). As Buxmann and Gebauer (1998, p. 71) point out,

> The ubiquity of the Internet and the ease of market entry allow the spread and integration of so far geographically separated market places. As a result, the number of buyers and sellers entering the market space might increase. Lower transaction costs and the availability of higher quality information would encourage potential sellers and buyers to actually join the market, which, in turn, might positively influence market characteristics such as size, purchasing, frequency, and in the case of the real estate market maybe even people's overall mobility.

In the case of outsourcing, an important trend emerging from the expanding global information infrastructure (GII) is that companies will need to procure the products and services offered by a network of suppliers to fulfil their innovation strategies. No single company is likely to possess all the relevant managerial and technical skills necessary for it to play an active part in the global information society (GIS). Most industrialised nations suffer from skill shortages in the computing and information systems fields, and this will continue to act as a key impediment to implementing innovation and technology strategies. High-tech intermediaries have therefore become increasingly common. Moreover, the trend towards IT outsourcing by larger firms has fuelled a growth in software start-up companies, and this is supported by government who, realising their importance to the economic performance of the country, are considering various initiatives designed to offer these firms tax breaks and other financial incentives. Many of these firms are self-styled high-tech SMEs positioning themselves as *niche players* operating in a wider business community that has become increasingly perplexed by the numerous offerings of the computer industry. The portfolio of services offered by these SMEs is wide and ranges from Web site development, networking, installation, telephone applications, data warehousing, security/risk assessment, maintenance and training. According to Rayport and Sviokla (1995) SMEs will need to forecast technological changes in the marketplace so that they can develop their own specific technical expertise to enable them to serve their client base. Those SMEs that succeed in doing so are likely to become major players in the GIS.

The debate about intermediaries in the context of Internet commerce is complex and should take into consideration wider factors such as government policy (e.g. financial support for large companies and SMEs) (Poon and Swatman, 1997), international trends in business and commerce (e.g. globalisation, outsourcing, skill surpluses and shortages), and technical developments (e.g. information and communications technologies [ICTs]).

BUSINESS TRANSFORMATION FROM TRADITIONAL TO VIRTUAL METHODS AND TECHNIQUES

Much of the literature on Internet commerce suggests that a second information technology revolution is taking place,[16] although the nature and scope of how businesses will be transformed is the subject of much speculation. Clearly, the development of Internet commerce will transform different business activities at varying degrees. Table 4.3 lists seven key business activities and tracks their potential changes from traditional to Internet commerce methods/techniques. The *conceptual* category, for example, shows that traditionally, businesses sourced data and information from books, trade journals, magazines, conferences and seminars, etc. With the new medium of the Internet, companies may use various on-line services to acquire up-to-date information. Many of these services are free or low cost.

The extent to which the above key business areas will be transformed will depend on the levels of trust and security of Internet commerce methods/tools.

Table 4.3 *The changing shape of seven key business activities*

Business activity	Traditional methods/techniques	Internet commerce methods/ techniques
Conceptual	Books, trade journals, magazines, conferences, seminars	Free or low cost on-line services (Delphi, Lexus/Nexus, etc.)
Design/development	'Best practice', professional organisations, standards	On-line consulting, design, testing services and marketing specialists
Marketing/advertising	TV, trade journals, exhibitions	On-line services (TradeWave, Galaxy, Yahoo, Alta-Vista, etc.)
Evaluation	Credit investigation, public image, benchmarking	Dunn and Bradstreet on-line
Ordering/purchasing	Post Office, telephone system, telemarketing, EDI private networks (business to business)	EDI private networks/WWW (business to consumer)
Delivery	Delivery through retail outlet, a service delivery or an electronic medium	Using digital information (text, audio, video clips)
Payment	Electronic funds transfer (EFT), credit cards	Credit-card-based settlement services, digital cash

Low risk activities may involve obtaining marketing/advertising information via the Internet. Companies wishing to sell their services on the Internet may do this as an alternative to advertising in trade journals or through exhibitions. At a more sophisticated level, payment systems may pose greater risks to both buyer and seller, and it is in this area where trust and security will need to be nurtured. As we saw above, the Internet is largely used for informational purposes, although many companies wish to develop the transactional side to this medium by encouraging their customers to purchase goods and services direct from their Web sites.

Whilst many theories and perspectives exist within the field of innovation management and technology, few are directly relevant to the phenomenon of Internet commerce. Angehrn (1997) has recently made this point. Within the information systems literature, theories will need to address whether the impact of the Internet is the second IT revolution within this century. In particular, the rapid pace at which Internet technology has developed since 1994 suggests that new theories and perspectives will need to address the changes to markets, hierarchies, organisation structures, cultures, knowledge generation, learning, and job design (Evans and Wurster, 1997).

CASE STUDIES—BUSINESS-TO-BUSINESS INTERNET COMMERCE

Dell Computer Corporation

The concept of the Dell Computer Corporation is one that has changed industry structure. While the rest of the industry was building personal computers to stock, and selling them through value-added resellers, distributors and retail stores, Dell was creating a new business model. Dell decided to build-to-order and sell the computers through its own sales force, mail order and telephone centre. By so doing, the distribution and retail costs in the traditional supply chain would be avoided. As a result, Dell would reduce its inventory costs substantially. As of December 1997, Dell was the second largest supplier of desktop PCs, with 9.7% of the market and a 10%–15% price advantage compared with its major competitors who distribute their products through the indirect channel. Dell identified the benefits of using the Internet and was one of the first to exploit them. As of July 1996, Dell's customers could configure and order a computer directly from Dell's Web site. A further six months later, Dell was selling US$1 million worth of computers via the Internet each day. Its volume doubled a few months later. Dell reports having sold US$6 million per day several times during the 1997 holiday selling season. The company's Web site also provides technical support and order status information, including the ability to download software directly from the site. The site responds to more than 120 000 technical support queries each week (see Table 4.4).

About 90% of Dell's overall sales are to businesses and 10% to consumers. On-line, the customer mix is very different: about 90% of its sales are to small businesses and consumers. Dell's large corporate customers use Dell's Web site to get product information, order status and technical help. Most still do not place orders electronically. Dell is working to make its on-line service attractive enough

Table 4.4 *Dell's daily on-line sales and weekly technical support volumes tripled during 1997*

	1Q97	2Q97	3Q97	4Q97
Sales per day	US$1m	US$2m	US$3m	US$3m+
Technical support queries per week	30 000	45 000	60 000	120 000
Visitors per week	213 000	255 000	250 000	400 000
Sales outside US (%)	0	5	10	17

Adapted from: US Department of Commerce (1999).

for its large corporate customers to use for purchasing and customer service. Customised 'premier pages' allow major customers to purchase Dell computers from the company's own intranet. The premier pages incorporate the customer's corporate discounts, specific computer configurations and codes identifying those authorised to make purchases on the company's behalf. MCI estimates it has saved 15% in computer procurement costs due to this service. In the past, 16 purchasing agents in four different locations were responsible for purchasing computers. When working with Dell to develop the rules for the on-line service, MCI consolidated its computer purchasing (and realised a greater discount due to their higher volumes). The company also cut its purchase order cycle time from four to six weeks to within 24 hours (US Department of Commerce, 1999).

Benefits of the Internet

Additional Revenues. Eighty per cent of the consumers and half of the small businesses that purchased on Dell's Web site had never purchased from Dell before. A quarter of customers claim that the Web site was the major reason they made a purchase, and their average purchase was higher compared with the typical Dell customer.

Lower Sales/Marketing Costs. Dell's Web site gives enough product, pricing and technical support to help guide a customer through the purchasing process. This information was previously accessed by calling a telesales representative. As a result, Dell has been able to generate an increased sales volume to its consumer market with lower labour costs. Dell expects that its advertising costs should also be lower for its Internet customers, as 30% of these customers had not seen a Dell advertisement, yet still bought on-line.

Lower Service/Support Costs. Dell saves several million dollars each year by having basic customer service and technical support functions available on the Internet. Such an offering gives customers relevant and timely information and is therefore a major benefit. Each week, about 20 000 customers use the Web site to check their order status. Some of these would have come into the call centre, at a cost of US$3–5 per call. If just 10% of these customers had called rather than using the on-line service, those 2000 calls would have cost Dell US$6000–US$10 000 per week. Some 30 000 software files are downloaded each week from Dell's site.

Answering these requests by telephone and then sending each customer the software by mail would cost US$150 000 per week. Customers who access troubleshooting tips on-line save Dell a US$15 call to a technical support person. If 2%– 3% of the 30 000–40 000 technical information queries the Web site receives each week had reached Dell's technical support staff, it would have cost an additional US$9000–US$18 000 per week. One large customer in the auto industry reports saving US$2 million in its own technical support 'help desk' costs. Rather than calling up Dell's telephone support centre and usually holding for about 3–5 minutes, they go to Dell's Web site for help.

Customer Relationship Building. Perhaps the greatest potential Dell sees for the Internet is its ability to enhance the company's relationship with its customers. One-to-one, targeted marketing and tailored customer service can be used to shorten the repeat purchase cycle and therefore generate more revenue for Dell from their corporate accounts. The Dell Channel is a customer service feature tailored specifically to a customer's computer model and specific configuration. Dell believes that the ability to tailor customer service solutions and product offerings to individual customers will improve customer service and satisfaction and open up new opportunities for selling its products and services. Dell expects to conduct half its total business (sales, service and support) on-line shortly after the year 2000.

Cisco Systems

Cisco Systems is the worldwide leader in networking for the Internet. Cisco's networking solutions connect people, computing devices and computer networks, allowing people to access or transfer information irrespective of variations in time, place or type of computer system. Cisco provides end-to-end networking solutions that are used to build a unified information infrastructure, or to connect to other networks. An end-to-end networking solution is one that provides a common architecture that delivers consistent network services to all users. The broader the range of network services, the more capabilities a network can provide to users connected to it. Cisco offers: the industry's broadest range of hardware products used to form information networks or give people access to those networks; Cisco IOS^{TM} software, which provides network services and enables networked applications; expertise in network design and implementation; and technical support and professional services to maintain and optimise network operations. Cisco is unique in its ability to provide all these elements, either by itself or together with partners. Cisco serves customers in three target markets.

1. *Large enterprises*, i.e. organisations with complex networking needs, usually spanning multiple locations and types of computer systems. Enterprise customers include corporations, government agencies, utilities and educational institutions.
2. *Service providers*, i.e. companies that provide information services, including telecommunication carriers, Internet Service Providers (ISPs), cable companies, and wireless communication providers.

3. *Small/medium enterprises* (SMEs), i.e. companies with a need for data networks of their own, as well as connection to the Internet and/or to business partners.

   Cisco Systems sold US$6.4 billion worth of routers, switches and other network interconnect devices during its 1997 fiscal year. As its business forms the underpinning of the Internet and private networks, it is not surprising that Cisco is at the forefront in making the Internet a major player in transforming the business processes of its customers. From employee self-service stock options, training seminars and work team collaboration to customer service and ordering, the company develops new applications for business processes on-line. It tends to avoid large-scale projects. Rather, it opts for new applications which can be installed within three to six months. As with many of its customers, Cisco has developed its Web site over a long period of time. It was first to give customers technical support. It later evolved into the largest Internet commerce site worldwide. Currently, Cisco offers nearly a dozen Internet-based applications to both end use customers and reseller partners.

Customer Service

Cisco began providing electronic support in 1991 with a pre-Web system using the Internet. Software downloads, defect tracking and technical advice were the first applications. In the spring of 1994, Cisco put its system on the Web, and re-named its site Cisco Connection On-line. Today, Cisco's customers and reseller partners log onto Cisco's Web site more than 900 000 times a month to receive technical assistance, check orders, or download software. The on-line service has been very successful. Some 70% of all customer service inquiries are dealt with on-line. As with Dell, this saves time and money—benefits which can be passed on to the customer.

On-line Ordering

One of the main attributes of the virtual society, which is discussed by many writers, is the electronic transfer of goods and services from supplier to customer. Like Dell, Cisco builds virtually all its products to order, so there are very few off-the-shelf products. Before the Cisco Web site, ordering a product was a physical and complicated process. It was subject to many human errors as many different procedures were involved in the process. For example, an engineer at the customer site knew what type of product was needed and how it should be configured. This information was communicated to the procurement department who then created a purchase order and sent it to Cisco via fax, phone or e-mail. A Cisco customer service administrator keyed the order into Cisco's system. If the order went through without problems (clean) it would be booked. From here, production was scheduled within 24 hours. Nearly one out of four orders was problematic. So when the system at Cisco tried to validate the order, it discovered an error in how the product was configured. The order would then be rejected. Having contacted the customer, the procurement cycle would begin again. The time spent in processing what was termed a 'dirty' order cost time and money to both Cisco and its customer.

Cisco's relationships with its customers were also affected, so a more efficient and fast ordering system was needed.

Cisco began deploying Web-based commerce tools in 1995. In 1996, the Internet Product Centre allowed users to purchase any Cisco product via the WWW. The change has vastly improved the ordering system. Nowadays, an engineer can use a PC to configure a product on-line. He will know immediately if there are any errors. Once corrected, the order is sent to the procurement department. The customer's pricing details are already programmed into the Cisco site. An authorised purchaser can complete the order within seconds. Rather than calling Cisco to find out the status of the order, invoice or account information (including the exact installation site of the equipment the customer has purchased from Cisco), a customer with the proper authorisation can access that information directly on the Web site. Cisco's largest customers would like to take advantage of the features of immediate and automatic access to Cisco's on-line ordering, configuration and technical support tools. Because of their large volumes, however, they do not want to go into Cisco's Web site each time they place an order or have a question. A program that was launched in 1997 interactively links the customer and Cisco's computer systems over the Internet and private networks, so that before an order is placed, Cisco configuration and pricing tools have already validated it. With the on-line pricing and configuration tools, about 98% of the orders go through Cisco's system the first time, saving time both at Cisco and at the customer's site. Lead times have dropped two to three days, and customer's productivity has increased an average of 20% per order. In the five months of its operation in 1996, Cisco booked just over US$100 million worth of sales on the Internet. For the first 10 months of 1997, the figure grew tenfold, to top US$1 billion. Net sales for the first quarter of 1999 were US$3.88 billion with US$2.60 billion for the same period in 1998, which was an increase of 49%. According to John Chambers, President and CEO of Cisco Systems, 'The Internet continues to be a powerful force fuelling the ecomony ... In the US, the Internet grew 68 per cent from the first quarter of 1998 to the first quarter of 1999.'

Order Status

Each month, Cisco's Web site receives about 150 000 order status inquiries. When will the order be ready? How should it be classified for customs? Is it eligible for NAFTA? What export control issues apply? Cisco gives customers the tools to find all this information on its Web site. In addition, Cisco records a shipment date, the method of shipment and the current location of each product. The company's primary domestic and international freight forwarders regularly update Cisco's database electronically with the status of each shipment, typically via EDI. The new information in the database automatically updates Cisco's Web site, keeping the customer current on the movement of the order. As soon as the order ships, Cisco sends the customer a notification message via e-mail or fax.

Business Benefits

In total, Cisco estimates that putting its applications on-line has saved the company US$363 million per year, or approximately 17.5% of total operating costs. With

Table 4.5 *Financial savings at Cisco in a networked business*

Operating costs	Savings per year (US$ million)
Technical support	125
Human resources	8
Software distribution	180
Marketing materials	50
Total	363

Adapted from: US Department of Commerce (1999).

70% of its technical support and customer service calls handled on-line, Cisco's technical support productivity has increased by 200%–300% per year, translating to roughly US$125 million lower technical support staff costs. Customers download new software releases directly from Cisco's site, saving the company US$180 million in distribution, packaging and duplicating costs. Having product and pricing information on the Web and Web-based CD-ROMs saves Cisco an additional US$50 million in printing and distributing catalogues and marketing materials to customers (see Table 4.5).

Federal Express

Federal Express (or FedEx) is the world's largest express transportation company, with 605 aircraft and service to over 212 countries. There are 46 call centres across the globe handling over 600 000 telephone calls daily. FedEx employs over 140 000 people, including 39 500 couriers who deliver more than three million packages every single working day. In 1973, FedEx became the first company to offer overnight delivery in the United States. By 1986, the company was the first express company to introduce a money-back guarantee. In 1994, FedEx achieved the ISO 9001 quality certification for its entire worldwide operation. It was the first major carrier to be recognised in this way. In 1996, the company launched FedEx International First, an 8 am door-to-door delivery service to nearly 5000 zip codes across the United States. During the same year, it expanded its European service, further improving the range of solutions offered to customers and its international capabilities.

FedEx is one of a number of delivery and logistics companies in the United States, including United Parcel Service (UPS) and the US Postal Service. Like these companies, FedEx is using the Internet in key business processes. The example of FedEx illustrates the role played by the Internet and EDI private networks in improving efficiency and customer satisfaction. Internet commerce has been at the centre of FedEx's operations for more than a decade. In 1982, the company rolled out a program called FedEx PowerShip® that gave its major customers a window into FedEx's computer systems. Employees at shipping docks could place orders for package pick-up directly into their FedEx PowerShip terminals, automate the paperwork and track the status of their orders electronically. In 1995, FedEx introduced FedEx Ship, a free software program that would work on any PC with a modem connection. Because it could be used on any PC, FedEx Ship made its way from shipping docks into other departments. Production planners that needed access to delivery status information for a rush order could now see when a supplier shipped the part and when it was due to arrive. FedEx PowerShip and FedEx Ship® soon became the standard way of doing business with FedEx. Two-thirds of the company's shipping transactions from 550 000 customers came via these two on-line services.

In 1996, FedEx launched FedEx InterNetShip K, extending on-line capabilities to the Internet. Within eighteen months, 75 000 customers were using the service. A fedex.com customer can request a parcel pick-up or find the nearest drop-off point, print packing labels, request invoice adjustments and track the status of their deliveries without leaving the Web site. Recipients of deliveries can request that FedEx send them an e-mail when the package has shipped. The company's Web site is only part of FedEx's extensive use of networks. Its own proprietary network, FedEx COSMOS®, handles 54 million transactions a day. Through the information available on the network, the company can keep track of every package from the point a customer requests a parcel pick-up to the point it reaches its final destination. When a customer enters a pick-up request, a courier is notified electronically of the time and location. Once at the customer's office, the courier scans the bar code on the package into his hand-held system, recording that the package has been picked up. FedEx employees record and track the package's progress electronically from the van to a FedEx plane to a sorting centre where it gets sorted and loaded onto another FedEx plane, to the truck that it gets unloaded onto, to the customer's home or office.

FedEx also plays a role in the core logistics processes of other companies. In some instances, FedEx operates the merchant server on which a retailer's Web site runs. In others, FedEx operates warehouses that pick, pack, test and assemble products as well as handle the delivery, which sometimes involves consolidating products with other shipments and clearing customs. And the nature of FedEx's customers' products (high-tech, high value or perishable) means that the orders they process have to be filled almost immediately. The information network that enables FedEx's core business to meet its delivery commitments is the same foundation for its growing logistics business as well. Hundreds of thousands of tracking requests per month come from links from over 5000 Web sites to fedex.com. These FedEx customers can add a product tracking feature to the other services they offer to their on-line customers. If a customer buys a router from Cisco Systems and wants to know when it is supposed to arrive, he does not have to make any phone calls to get the details. Instead, he can go to Cisco's Web site, enter the order number, and find out that the router is on a FedEx truck and will arrive the next morning. This information appears directly in the Cisco site in a matter of moments.

Up until five years ago, National Semiconductor (NatSemi) used to deal with a variety of different companies to get a product from its Asian factories to customers across the world, including freight forwarders, customs agents, handling companies, delivery companies and airlines. Five years ago, they decided to outsource this entire process to FedEx. Today, virtually all of NatSemi's products, manufactured in Asia by three company factories and three subcontractors, are shipped directly to a FedEx distribution warehouse in Singapore. Each day, NatSemi sends its orders electronically to FedEx. FedEx makes sure the order gets matched to a product and the product is delivered directly to the customer when promised. By going with FedEx as a one-stop shop for their logistics needs, NatiSemi has seen a reduction of the average customer delivery cycle from four weeks to one week and their distribution costs drop from 2.9% of sales to 1.2%. Not only does FedEx handle all the back-end logistics for its customers, it also leverages its vast network of technical couriers to handle customer service functions like repairs and returns. If a customer notifies a retailer that the computer he just purchased has a malfunctioning hard drive, the retailer sends an electronic message to a FedEx courier to go to the site and try to repair the hard drive, swap it for a new one, or collect the computer and return it to the company.

Benefits to FedEx

FedEx's proprietary network forms the underpinning of the company's Internet commerce today. The Internet extends the reach of the proprietary network, electronically connecting customers that had communicated with FedEx by phone, paperwork or not at all in the past. And, as more companies sell tangible goods over the Internet with the promise of quick delivery, FedEx benefits from increased business opportunities. For competitive reasons, FedEx has not publicly shared the full extent of benefits it has realised from information technology and electronic networks, except to say that it has enabled FedEx to continuously lower its cost to deliver each package.

Reduced Operating Costs

If it had not developed FedEx PowerShip®, FedEx would have had to hire an additional 20 000 employees to pick up packages, answer phone calls at the call centres and key in air bills. With PowerShip®, many of the routine tasks are automated or transferred from FedEx to the customer. Couriers spend less time recording information at the customer's site, and phone service representatives spend less time answering calls from customers who now place orders and track their own shipments on-line. Also, customers use FedEx InterNetShip K to track over one million packages per month (and the volume increases at double-digit percentage levels month on month). Approximately half of those calls would have gone to FedEx's toll-free number instead.

Improved Customer Service

FedEx has developed a sophisticated communications system for its customers which enables them to interact with the company in a variety of ways, e.g. by phone, fax or other means. Nearly 950 000 of them find it easier and more convenient to communicate with FedEx electronically. The ability to track parcels and packages at every stage of their journey is a major benefit to customers, and clearly is part of the trust relationship between supplier and customer.

SUMMARY

This chapter has explored four related areas on Internet commerce, namely the issue of whether the Internet is a strategic marketing resource for business, or simply just the latest high-tech fad; the development of business-to-business Internet commerce; the Internet and the role of intermediaries; and now three international companies engage in business-to-business Internet commerce (Dell Computer Corporation, Cisco Systems, and Federal Express). In the following chapter we continue with these themes by considering the emergence of business-to-consumer Internet commerce.

5

Gaining Competitive Advantage from Business-to-Consumer Internet Commerce

INTRODUCTION

In the last few years the Internet and its possibilities for business and commerce have become inextricably linked with the concept of competitive advantage.[17] It is interesting to note that, since the 1980s, new technology in its various forms—i.e. personal computers (PCs), computer-aided design (CAD), computer-aided manufacture (CAM), flexible manufacturing systems (FMSs), decision support systems (DSSs) and electronic data interchange (EDI)—have all been promoted for their potential to enhance business performance. A cursory glance at some of the recent literature on Internet technology shows that a similar logic applies, as some writers analyse the impact of Internet commerce in the context of its potential to maximise competitive advantage (Glazer, 1991). Much of this analysis is upbeat and tends to equate the impact of Internet commerce with success stories rather than failure scenarios. For example, Attal (1997, p. 25), writing about the benefits of the Internet for small businesses, claims that, 'The Internet and new technologies associated with it enable small businesses to compete and gain access to markets previously reserved for large global corporations.' Assuming this is the case, one key advantage for the small and medium enterprise (SME) is that it will be able to establish a Web site and compete with its larger rivals by appearing *larger than it really is*. Traditional business variables used to measure performance, such as size, structure and geographical proximity to customers and suppliers, will become less important in a virtual society. This is because an SME, like its larger rival, will be able to communicate much more effectively with its customers and suppliers in what has been described as a *networked-based businesses* (Coyne and Dye, 1998). As a consequence, other performance measures will replace traditional ones. These may include, customer relations, new product and service development, flexibility, managing intellectual property and knowledge assets (Christiaanse and Venkatraman, 1998).

By all accounts, companies are investing in Internet technology across the spectrum of business sectors (Iansiti and MacCormack, 1997). Although there is a wide variation in the design, quality and functionality of these Web sites, the evidence shows that businesses are keen to make an investment in this new medium, if only to demonstrate to their customers that they, like their competitors, have a Web site. It is predicted that there will be 320 million people with Web access by 2002 (IDC, 1998b). This confirms that many companies are making some form of investment in Internet technology, and it is likely that those who help create and define the marketplace, or marketspace, will achieve the most competitive gains.

One company which hopes to play a significant part in the evolution of Internet commerce, is the computer giant IBM. At IBM global services, 10 000 out of 130 000 employees are dedicated to e-commerce—an area that brought in 25% of IBM's US$78.5 billion revenue in 1997. Fundamental to IBM's strategy is a focus on three cross-industry solutions: electronic commerce payment systems; supply chain services and software; and customer-relationship solutions, including business intelligence and call-centre technologies. According to Lou Gerstner, the Chairman of IBM,[18] 'The mantra is growth, globalisation, cycle times, speed, and competitiveness. What we say to our customers is that it is a fundamental change in the way business will be done in their industries, aided, abetted, supported, and enabled by technology.' He asserts that, 'When the e-business industry moves from just a browser opportunity to a commerce opportunity, it's coming our way.' Similarly, Guthrie and Austin (1996) argue that the Internet has great potential to achieve competitive advantages for businesses, though much depends on how it is managed. They identify four areas critical to this process:

1. communications—electronic mail, customer service, customer focus groups, product feedback from customers;
2. personnel—employee searches, job searches, industry-specific interest groups for professional development;
3. sales/advertising—low cost marketing and advertising, electronic commerce;
4. intelligence—on-line research for tracking competitors and industry trends, information about customers and markets.

These authors contend that the Internet will become much more useful since its capacity to generate useful data and information will enhance the negotiating power of a business. They assert that 'the Internet offers businesses the ability to track customer needs and access niche markets at the touch of a button. Small home-based businesses can appear as corporate giants and operate internationally in ways that previously were impossible' (p. 90). Similarly, Cronin (1996, p. 1) claims that it is important for companies to develop a strategic framework that links Internet connection with the issue of competitive advantage. Thus, 'The most valuable Internet applications allow companies to transcend communication barriers and establish connections that will enhance productivity, stimulate innovation development, and improve customer relations.'

In this chapter we focus on four key issues, which are related to the concept of competitive advantage. First we consider whether Internet commerce has created a power shift from supplier to customer. This thesis has been advanced by Hagel and Armstrong who claim that, 'Virtual communities have the power to re-order greatly the relationship between companies and their customers. Put simply, this is because they use networks like the Internet to enable customers to take control of their own value as potential purchasers of products and services' (Hagel and Armstrong, 1997, p. 8). With the growth of business-to-consumer Internet commerce, this view contends that customers will, over time, become more powerful and discriminating in their evaluation of products and services offered over the Internet. Clearly, much depends on how the Internet develops and how businesses target new and existing customers. Notwithstanding these points, the notion that customer power will increase is an important one in the literature and therefore worthy of attention.

Second, we examine the topic of the new economics of Internet commerce. This is often placed within the wider domain of the virtual society or the economics of networked-based businesses. The central argument that binds this work is based on the premise that, as the Internet expands into core and peripheral business processes and functions, new performance indicators will be required to measure success and failure factors. This is an important issue given that Internet commerce may realise cost savings in some parts of the business and increase costs in other areas. So an important question is likely to be: Who will benefit from the virtual or network based economy? So far, there appear to be few definitive answers to this question, albeit much speculation and hype.

Third, we examine the digital delivery of goods and services and how business-to-consumer Internet commerce is likely to change the commercial landscape. Forecasts for the growth of business-to-consumer Internet commerce look impressive with IDC predicting that the number of people buying on the Web is expected to increase from 18 million in December 1997 to 128 million by 2002, representing more than US$400 billion worth of Internet commerce transactions (IDC, 1998b). This discussion is linked to our fourth area which considers key business drivers of growth (for digital delivery of goods and services). The main purpose of this section is to show that the development and implementation of Internet commerce is not merely a technological phenomenon but an all-embracing one which encapsulates all business processes and activities. Finally, we consider case studies on business-to-consumer Internet commerce.

A POWER SHIFT FROM SUPPLIER TO CUSTOMER

In this section we explore the merits and criticisms concerning the thesis that Internet commerce will shift power relations from the supplier to the customer. Many writers who contend that the Internet and WWW will become a major benefit to consumers worldwide adopt this view. The logic to this debate is relatively simple. In short, it is believed that suppliers have, over many years, taken advantage of their customers since the latter has not had access to information from which to take sound commercial decisions. The benefits of information have tended to be weighted against the customer in favour of the supplier, who has been able to control and shape consumer choice. However, if the customer gains access to timely and relevant information, there may be a shift in the power relations between customer and supplier. According to Hagel and Armstrong (1997, p. 17) vendors or suppliers use

> information to target the most attractive customers for their products or services and to engage in what economists call *price discrimination*—the practice of charging one customer one price and other customers another, depending on what the market will bear. Price discrimination is perfectly legal, to be sure, but it does illustrate one of the ways in which vendors tend to capture market surplus at their customers' expense.

These authors claim that such a situation may be reversed in the advent of virtual communities since the customer will be able to capture and evaluate information more readily. The concept of reverse markets is an important one, although the evidence to support it is so far limited.

Whilst it is apparent that consumers will be able to use the Internet to generate information about products and services, the extent to which they will compare and contrast the different offerings of competing businesses is the subject of much debate. For example, many customers of banks tend to stay with the same institution even though they may experience consistently poor service. They may take the view that competing banks offer equally poor service so there is little point in spending the time transferring from one bank to another. The impetus to thoroughly research the products and services offered by different banks is usually low, and customers tend to take a reactive rather than proactive approach. Even with the estimated growth of Internet users, it is doubtful that individuals will exercise their powers of choice about the products and services they purchase unless other factors prevail. In the case of the financial services sector, it is likely that banks will have to target their customers much more closely and entice them with new and improved products and services if they are to see any benefits to their competitive advantage.

So banks will need to give their customers a more personalised service rather than treat them simply as an *account number*. In the past 20 years it is certainly the case that the banking sector has become much more streamlined and routinised, with many existing customers complaining that, 'I don't even know my bank manager any more!' Such views in the light of the sums of money banks spend on information technology have done little to enhance their image. Whilst this trend towards customer anonymity has led many to criticise the banks for becoming *faceless institutions*, the extent to which Internet technology would reverse this situation is unclear (Crane and Bodie, 1996). At the positive end of the spectrum, banks will need to target specific customers and offer them personalised or targeted banking services rather than continue with their blanket marketing and advertising approach. Whilst some banks are already doing this, it is likely that those financial services institutions which can develop a product and service differentiator (unmatched by their rivals) will be the ones that gain a competitive advantage.

Recent surveys point to the relative lack of progress in exploiting Internet commerce. For example, the management consultancy firm Ernst and Young (see Nua Internet Surveys, 1998) found that banks have no concrete conception of how to structure themselves on-line or generate profit from on-line transactions. They claim that after the year 2000, banks will be spending the same amount of money on Web applications to develop their on-line presence as they currently do on branch networks. Despite this, the report found that banks displayed an apparent ignorance of the Internet. Jonathan Charley, Banking Partner with Ernst and Young, added that while most banks were willing to invest in on-line technologies, very few had any kind of strategy outlined for the future and even fewer had any idea of how to generate profit on the Internet.

Similarly, a survey of the leading banks in over 26 countries found that 96% did not expect to generate more revenue from on-line transactions. Only 34% believed that the Internet would help them maintain existing customers (Nua Internet Surveys, 1998). These findings suggest one of two things. First, that banks are conservative and risk-averse institutions which are slow to jump on the bandwagon of Internet commerce. Second, that banks are doing their home-work on the potential advantages and disadvantages of Internet commerce and have come to the conclusion that a cautious approach is the best policy. Notwithstanding the hype that surrounds Internet commerce, an important factor underpinning the take-up of Internet banking services is the number of people connected to the Web. Whilst estimates vary, one prediction is that a total of 320 million people worldwide will be on-line by 2002 (IDC, 1998b). We will explore some of these issues in the next section.

NEW ECONOMICS OF INTERNET COMMERCE

Another important thesis that has emerged in recent years concerns the shift in economic relations and Internet commerce in the wider global information society (GIS). Many writers contend that traditional theories of the economics of information will become obsolete. As more and more people communicate electro-nically using universal open standards, this expansion in connectivity will change people's behaviour and, in turn, alter the cost structures of companies. According to Evans and Wurster (1997, p. 71), the rise in connectivity is the most important issue confronting business strategists for several years, and certainly with regard to the latest 'wave in the information revolution'. They claim that managers in the past decade tended to be preoccupied in adapting operating processes to IT (business process re-engineering). Whilst this was significant in itself, they claim that more profound changes are to come. Managers will need to re-evaluate the 'strategic fundamentals of their businesses'. The new economics of information will change existing industry structures and how specific business sectors compete.

Much of the literature on the economics of information has explored dynamic changes in the traditional value chain (Porter, 1985). As we saw in Chapter 2, Internet commerce offers companies the opportunity to reduce operating costs by simply developing much closer links with their customers. The process of disintermediation is therefore one that has significant implications for the debate surrounding the economics of information. However, the process of deconstructing a vertically integrated value chain does not automatically transform the structure of existing industries and companies. On the contrary, many companies will need to develop a well planned business strategy before they place too much faith in the perception that Internet commerce is the latest panacea to enhance competitive position.

At the present time, there are few detailed, longitudinal case studies on the new economics of the virtual or networked-based economy within specific business sectors. This is because Internet commerce is relatively new and many companies have yet to decide if they should invest in this area. Tried and tested business models on the economics of Internet commerce are thin on the ground. Some are too general to be useful for specific business sectors, and others measure only tangible assets and costs. Since many of the benefits and pitfalls of Internet commerce are thought to be intangible, it appears that companies should attempt to develop their own cost and information management systems. A tailored approach will help them develop a reliable picture of their overall business performance.

As Internet commerce develops, each business sector will define its own dynamics, and economic transformation will vary in speed, intensity and scope. It is therefore unwise to make hard and fast predications about how these changes will affect specific business sectors as a whole. Table 5.1 identifies eight fundamental strategic implications of the changing economics of information.

It is well documented in the literature on Internet commerce that traditional markets and hierarchies governing companies will undergo much transformation. Terms such as globalisation, outsourcing, information and communication technologies (ICTs) and international economic markets and conditions are all said to play a part in reshaping existing value chains of companies. Traditional business models tend to draw a distinction between company and supplier. Traditionally, companies have been described as having a functional, product or matrix organisation structure (Child, 1984). Companies have been viewed as separate entities from their suppliers and customers. This has now become a misleading picture since company structures, and their economic relationships with their suppliers and customers,

Table 5.1 *Strategic implications of the changing economics of information*

1. Existing value chains will fragment into multiple businesses, each of which will have its own sources of competitive advantage
2. Some new businesses will benefit from network economies of scale, which can give rise to monopolies
3. As value chains fragment and reconfigure, new opportunities will arise for purely physical businesses
4. When a company focuses on different activities, the value proposition underlying its brand identity will change
5. New branding opportunities will emerge for third parties that neither produce nor deliver a primary service
6. Bargaining power will shift as a result of a radical reduction in the ability to monopolise the control of information
7. Customers' switching costs will fall, and companies will have to develop new ways of generating customer loyalty
8. Incumbents could easily become victims of their obsolete physical infrastructure, and their own psychology

have become much more complicated. Equally, concepts such as *vertical integration*—where all the materials and parts that make up a product are sourced and controlled by one or even a few organisations—is a business model which is becoming somewhat dated. Traditionally, a company's assets were measured simply in terms of raw materials, capital equipment and property. Human assets were not always included in this evaluation.

In a virtual company the value chain is likely to fragment into multiple businesses, networks and short-term ventures. There is a shift towards a horizontal (rather than vertical) supply chain that is less integrated. Since a company's assets are not only tangible but also include intangible assets such as brand value, intellectual property, human capital (people), virtual integration, information management, quality of service and customer relations, they need to be factored into performance measurement exercises. Otherwise, a company may end up with a distorted picture of its overall economic value, market position and future potential.

Since the structure and configuration of companies continues to undergo vast changes, acquiring a detailed understanding of the economics of information may be akin to trying to capture an image of a moving target. For example, companies wishing to focus on their core business competencies (Prahalad and Hamel, 1990) may choose to outsource all their non-core functions and operations. Whilst outsourcing is not new and has been a major activity in many industries for some time (e.g. automobiles, insurance, construction), it may change the economics of ownership and control within companies and, by so doing, inject greater complexity into existing cost structures. With the growth of Internet commerce, it is likely that outsourcing will increase as companies procure a range of goods and services, which are critical to their business, from a wide network of suppliers. Examples of this may be found in a variety of business sectors like financial services, retailing and publishing.

In the banking sector—which is often described as risk-averse, cautious and resistant to change—the development of Internet banking increasingly involves the creation of partnerships. Banks no longer provide all their products and services from in-house resources since they are becoming more dependent upon external partners, suppliers and agents. The major high street banks are fast becoming invisible as money becomes increasingly electronic. Some people have even posed the question: Are we moving towards a cashless society? The development of digital cash systems, which allow payment of bills through home computers and the introduction of smart cards that automatically debit charges from checking accounts, are becoming more widespread in society.

Direct payment systems and automatic teller machines (ATMs) have reduced the need for banks to dispense cash in large quantities. For customer convenience, ATMs are increasingly located away from banks, in supermarkets, railway stations, cinemas and other locations. The need for bank branches is disappearing as more complex transactions can be handled over the telephone, or on-line. This suggests that the entire economic structure of the financial services market is being transformed by Internet commerce.

Banks are being disintermediated at every stage in the supply chain (*Financial Times*, 1999). On-line brokerages, such as Charles Schwab and E*Trade, are reporting huge levels of transactions at cut-price rates. On-line brokers of basic banking services, insurance and stock trading are likely to replace traditional agents rapidly, as the level of on-line trading is forecast to rise by a factor of four by 2000. By that time, almost every US bank plans to have an on-line service available on the Web, with 42% offering advanced services such as on-line bill payments. Most notably, Citibank have stated their ambition to have one billion customers for its banking services by the year 2010, from their current position of 60 million. They have made it clear that this can only be achieved through on-line growth (IMRG, 1998).

Whilst the evidence suggests that the percentage of on-line banking is currently small and is therefore unlikely to threaten the existing revenue streams of banks, banks may increasingly come under threat as new entrants become serious competitors. These new businesses will take advantage of network economies of scale as banks face new competition from outside the traditional banking sector. This will be encouraged by low barriers to market entry. For example, the retailing sector in the United Kingdom has made inroads into the financial services with some supermarkets now offering their customers banking services. This is likely to continue. The management consultants Booz-allen & Hamilton claim that 'a transaction over the Internet costs one-tenth of what it does at the bank'. In addition, 'Independent researchers have estimated that finding a high rate certificate of deposit can take 25 minutes on the telephone, but only one minute using an electronic agent on the WWW' (Edmondson, 1997, p. 76). Banks will therefore have to re-evaluate their existing products and services with a view to seeing whether they can offer them on the Internet to increase their profit margins.

With the increasing fragmentation of value chains, new opportunities will arise for purely physical businesses. As we saw in Chapter 2, people may procure goods and services electronically, though their delivery will be via a traditional route (road, rail, postal services). Books, computers, flowers, etc. are examples of this process. Since retailers will not have the need to position these goods in expensively decorated stores and shops, but use a warehouse instead, cost savings may be transferred to the customer. As Evans and Wurster (1997, p. 80) point out, 'The new economics of information will create opportunities to rationalise the physical value chain, often leading to businesses whose physically based sources of competitive advantage will be more sustainable.'

Clearly, connectivity will be a major factor in stimulating changes to physical value chains. For in spite of the success of ventures such as electronic bookselling at Amazon.com, the vast majority of people continue to purchase their books from high street bookstores and even through mail order (Kotha, 1998). So far, the advantages of electronic bookstores are: enhanced information about the products (reviews of books, customer bulletin boards), superior choice compared with traditional bookstores (Amazon.com has over 2.5 million books listed), reduced inventory (no need for book store), ease of access (customer can order books at any time of day and night), superior search facilities (well-designed Web site), and discounted goods. Cost savings therefore accrue to both company and customer.

Evans and Wurster (1997, p. 81) claim that, 'Because a brand reflects its company's value chain, deconstruction will require new brand strategies.' They cite the example of banking where brand identity is tied up with the importance of branches and ATMs rather than being based upon products. As more banks develop their Internet sites, it is likely that brand identity will become increasingly related to product provision. These authors also stress that new branding opportunities will emerge for third parties that neither produce a product nor deliver a primary service. Information providers, e.g. a restaurant reviewer, is one example. Another important element, which will alter the economics of information, is that bargaining power will shift as a result of the radical reduction in the ability to monopolise the control of information.

Given that the Internet has been labelled an unregulated 'Wild West', where individual searches for information can generate many thousands of 'hits', an important service involves the selection, categorisation and sorting of information. New intermediaries may be well positioned to provide such services, and they may end up building up a considerable power base in their ability to monopolise the control of information. For example, people planning a holiday would find it very useful for an intermediary to seek out the best deals in the marketplace. Assuming that customers' switching costs fall, companies will need to seek new ways of generating customer loyalty. Traditional ways of exchanging and processing information will be phased out as people gain access to networks that facilitate a reduction in switching costs. Companies that fail to address these potential changes will become 'victims of their obsolete physical infrastructure, and their own psychology', according to Evans and Wurster (1997). These writers claim that traditional barriers to entry, which were once the key to achieving competitive advantage to a company, become liabilities. This is likely to occur where companies provide information in a physical format that can now be delivered more effectively and inexpensively electronically. An example is the physical part of sales and distribution systems, such as branches, shops and sales forces. The authors state that: 'As with newspapers, the loss of even a small portion of customers to new distribution channels or the migration of a high-margin product to the electronic domain can throw a business with high fixed costs into a downward spiral' (p. 82). A recent example of a company moving to a different form of selling its product is *Encyclopaedia Britannica*. This multi-volume product which has been prepared in a physical form for the last 200 years has now been placed on a CD-ROM. The company found that very few customers were purchasing the physical product (e.g. the cumbersome book volumes). To avoid a potentially disastrous situation, the company moved towards providing this material in a much neater CD-ROM format, the contents of which can be accessed much more easily.

The new economics of Internet commerce will be more pronounced in the virtual (digital) delivery rather than the physical delivery of goods and services. Whilst companies will need to identify key performance indicators which reflect changes in their markets, products, services, operations, logistics and customer profiles, it is apparent that many old business models will no longer be relevant for Internet commerce. In the next section we consider some more examples of goods and services that will be delivered to customers in an electronic or digital format.

DIGITAL DELIVERY OF PRODUCTS AND SERVICES

In the business-to-consumer side of Internet commerce, the digital delivery of goods and services is critically important and one that is likely to permanently change industry structures, standards, markets and hierarchies across different vertical markets. In the case of computer software, CDs, magazine articles, news broadcasts, stocks, airline tickets and insurance policies, these are all intangible products whose value is not dependent on a physical form. Intellectual property of this type is typically produced, packaged, stored and then physically delivered to its final destination. Examples include books, theatre tickets, and airline and hotel reservation information. Currently, this is changing as the technology now exists to transfer the content of these products in digital format over the Internet. For example, shares and securities may now be purchased over the Internet as well as airline and theatre tickets. The trajectory is for these activities to expand. Other industries, such as consulting services, entertainment, banking and insurance, education and health care, face some challenges, but are also beginning to use the Internet to change the way they do business. Over time, the sale and transmission of goods and services electronically is likely to be the largest and most visible driver of the new digital economy.

Information Retrieval

The traditional way of acquiring information retrieval services for many people is by visiting a local library. For example, researchers seeking relevant academic material usually follow a multistep process which starts with a keyword search on-line to find relevant journal articles or books. Such an activity produces a list of publications, some of which will be more useful than others. This is followed by a walk to the floor and section containing each publication (book, journal, magazine, pamplet, etc.). This is a time-consuming activity since the individual will have to seek out each and every publication, and it is likely that some will have been removed. In the case of journals, the researcher will have to find the relevant volume, month and year, and this may take some considerable time. If a quick read shows that the article contains interesting information, the next step is to walk to the photocopying machine and make a hard copy. This is expensive and time-consuming.

Information retrieval services such as Dialog Information Services, Lexis-Nexis, Westlaw, and others made a business by streamlining this process, pulling together a variety of sources and allowing librarians, law students and businesses to search electronic databases for information on-line using a dial-up connection. Publishers are also considering the benefits and pitfalls of offering content over the Internet, although how they charge for these services is still yet to be decided. Web-based information retrieval services find and organise content. They also shop around for the best possible deals. They may further inform the customer by e-mail when new products and services become available. Some perform the service only when someone requests it; others can be programmed to continue providing the information until the user stops the service. There are sites for people interested in technology with searchable databases crossing a variety of technology magazines.

News and Information Services

A recent study shows that nearly 90% of people use the Internet to gather news and information and another 80.5% use it for research (Maddox, 1997). Some of the Internet's most popular sites offer news, information and entertainment content and services. For example, Time Warner's Pathfinder, Warner Brothers, CNN, C/NET, USA Today, Disney, ABC and HotWired all rank among the top 20 most popular Web sites in the United States. Similarly, *The Times*, Microsoft UK, *Financial Times*, *Daily Telegraph*, *Computer Weekly*, BBC, *The Guardian*, Hewlett-Packard and *Daily Mail* are popular Web sites in the United Kingdom. This information is free to individuals as many sites simply ask a non-fee registration prior to releasing any information.

At the present time, US Web sites will generate more hits than their UK counter-parts (notwithstanding population size) partly because local telephone calls in the former country are free. The distinction between on-line daily newspapers and weekly or monthly magazines becomes blurred as content is usually updated as often as 24 hours a day, and editors use colour graphics and photos, video and audio and other techniques to make their sites more attractive to visitors. The Editor & Publisher Company's on-line newspaper database lists more than 2700 newspapers which have on-line businesses, with over 60% being US-based. The top 25 daily newspapers all have Web businesses, featuring the day's stories from the paper, some special Web-only sections, searchable on-line archives, as well as reviews of books or movies. A few work in partnership with other local businesses to highlight a given city, in addition to the general news.

For instance, Boston.com features news from the *Boston Globe*, *Boston Magazine* and other local print and radio channels, classified advertising for cars, homes and job listings in the Boston area, local sports highlights, and traffic and weather reports. The most widely circulated daily newspaper in the United States is the *Wall Street Journal* which launched its *Interactive Edition* in April 1996. The *Interactive Journal*'s coverage includes politics, economics, technology news, marketing, in-depth sports reporting and features, an extended editorial page, and weather. US readers receive the Journal's national edition, and can also access content from the European and Asian editions on-line. The *New York Times* on the Web offers readers the day's print stories on-line, along with AP Breaking News and AP radio, 50 000 book reviews dating back to 1980, hosted and unhosted on-line fora, and 'Web specials' covering women's health, sports and special in-depth features. Readers do not pay for general access. Small fees are charged for crosswords and archived news stories. Customers are given a user ID and password to gain access to the site. If the customer forgets the password, they simply type in their e-mail address and then receive the relevant information to enable them to gain access to the site once again.

Most on-line newspapers have not made a profit up till now. However, newspaper proprietors are keen to exploit the potential of the Internet and WWW as a new form of content delivery. Knight-Ridder, a US publisher with newspaper holdings across the country, invested US$27 million in its 32 Web sites in 1997 while generating just US$11 million in revenue. The *New York Times Interactive*

Edition 1997 revenues grew 66% over 1996, but the company's on-line ventures lost between US$12 and US$15 million for the year. C/NET's 1997 third quarter revenues, while two-and-one-half times greater than its revenues for the same period in 1996, still did not cover its costs (US Department of Commerce, 1999).

Television and Radio

Whether people access the Internet from their PC or television screen will not detract from the importance of this medium for purchasing goods and services or acquiring information on a whole range of topics from sport to wildlife to business news, etc. In the United States, more than 800 television stations have set up their own Web site. All the major broadcast networks have Web sites that combine information about TV programming and a host of other information. The cable channels offer their customers on-line information and services. One estimate is that 151 US cable channels exist, including CNN, fX, HBO, MTV, and the Weather Channel (US Department of Commerce, 1999).

Business Information Services

Companies that provide news and information to the business community have their own stand-alone Web sites. They provide information feeds to enhance other companies' on-line businesses, and they provide feeds into internal business processes through corporate Intranets. Reuters has its own site with on-line news reports, quote data, market snapshots and other products and services. In addition, Yahoo! readers can keep up-to-date with breaking news provided by Reuters. Personal investors on some on-line brokerage sites may see Reuters' delayed stock quotes, historical pricing charts, and portfolio tracking services. Small and medium-sized companies use Dun & Bradstreet's (D&B) Web site to access standard business reports including credit and risk management reports for evaluating buyers, purchasing products reports for evaluating sellers, and database marketing reports for evaluating prospective markets.

Larger companies also get information feeds directly into their corporate Intranets or private networks. Individuals comparing life insurance policies can see how different insurance firms are evaluated by independent analysts. The securities industry has long subscribed to proprietary newswires and business reports transmitted over private networks. Institutional traders use these services to track stock prices, currency fluctuations, and commodities prices, all in real time.

The digital delivery of goods and services within a business-to-consumer context will have the most major impact on informing debates on power shifts from suppliers to customers and the new economics of the virtual society. The above examples are just a few that illustrate the revolutionary changes that are currently taking place in a variety of business sectors from news and information services to television and radio. In the next section we examine the drivers of growth for digital goods and services.

BUSINESS DRIVERS OF GROWTH

Currently, there is a shortage of rigorous academic research on the growth, development, implementation, evaluation and outcome of Internet commerce in specific business sectors (Ghosh, 1998). Yet there is no shortage of hype and speculation about how Internet commerce will revolutionise the international business community. Whilst the technical capability exists to transform business processes, many companies remain reluctant to spend large sums of money on Internet technology before they are sure of a financial return on their investment. This is particularly true for SMEs who do not have the financial resources, or the in-house skills, to facilitate Internet commerce. Notwithstanding these points, a range of interrelated market, business and technical factors is driving the movement of business information services to the Internet. To the extent that the *automate or liquidate* debate plays its part in encouraging senior executives to invest in Internet technology, an overview of existing practitioner and academic literature on the subject points to at least 10 key business drivers of growth in business-to-consumer Internet commerce, which are outlined in Table 5.2. These business drivers will of course vary both within and between different business sectors and companies.

Enhance/Sustain Competitive Position

An ongoing message in the management literature for the past 20 years has urged senior executives to develop effective corporate strategies to both enhance and sustain competitive position in increasingly difficult economic markets. The work of Porter (1980) was highly influential in highlighting the importance of five key forces underpinning competitive strategy. They included: the bargaining power of buyers; the bargaining power of suppliers; the threat of substitute products and services; potential new entrants; and existing industry rivals. This logic is still being used to justify investment in Internet technology (Guthrie and Austin, 1996), although few business models and strategies currently exist that capture how the Internet will enhance and sustain a company's competitive position (Angehrn, 1997).

Table 5.2 *Business drivers of growth for business-to-consumer Internet commerce*

Enhance/sustain competitive position
Generate new markets
Consumer demand
More efficient distribution channels
Disintermediation
Loss of existing revenue sources
Develop and retain customer base
Enhance company image
Desire to innovate
Cost reduction

Generate New Markets

One of the key drivers for developing Internet commerce is the desire to generate new commercial offerings and even new markets. Whilst the concept of globalisation is overplayed in the literature, it has relevance in the context of the Internet given that companies can develop a Web presence to target or attract new customers for their products and services. One market which has been stimulated by the growth in the use of the Internet is advertising. Forrester Research predicts that on-line revenue sources from advertising, subscriptions and transactions fees will grow from just over US$520 million in 1997 to US$8.5 billion within five years. Jupiter Communications projects that on-line advertising and direct marketing will grow from US$1 billion in 1997 to US$9 billion by 2002. Though less than US$1 billion was spent on advertising on the Internet in 1997, a number of traditional media companies are preparing for the time when existing revenue sources, particularly local business and classified advertising, will in part shift from traditional media to the Internet. Other non-traditional competitors are using the Internet to position themselves to tap into the US$175 billion advertising industry. Companies started using the Internet to advertise in late 1994. Two years later, 46 of Advertising Age's 100 Leading National Advertisers had purchased Web advertising and nearly all had corporate Web sites. Advertising in 1996 reflected the characteristics of early Web users: computer literate, high income, and male.

The top advertisers on the Web were computing products (38%), consumer-related goods (20%), new media (17%), telecommunications (9%), and business services (6%). In the space of a year, Internet advertising has begun to reflect the interests of more mainstream audiences. Consumer goods companies' share of spending surpassed that of computer hardware and software companies, with 32% and 22% of the total advertising dollars, respectively. Financial services had a strong on-line ad presence in 1997, contributing 20% of the total. Yahoo!, a leading Internet search engine and one of the top recipients of advertising dollars, confirms the shift: its mix of advertisers went from 85% technology companies in 1995 to close to 80% consumer brand companies in 1997.

The fact that very few consumer-oriented Internet content businesses are making money today does not reveal much about the long-term viability of the industry as a whole. In the early stages of a high-growth market, it is often wise to focus on capturing market share rather than making profits. Even the most mature Internet-based content companies have only four years of experience. Most date back only two to three years. Many have come and gone in a shorter period of time. During this early stage, companies will try different sales techniques, marketing approaches, and product adaptations to determine the most effective business model. Every couple of months, a visitor to a Web content site may find an entirely new layout, new product additions, technology enhancements, or speciality sections that did not exist before. The sheer number of Internet content businesses suggests that the Internet will become a significant market.

Analysts believe that the revenue streams will soon materialise to support these businesses, with on-line revenues from advertising, subscriptions and transactions fees growing from just over US$1 billion in 1997 to over US$8 billion within five years, or close to 5% of today's advertising expenditures (Jupiter Communications, 1998). Long-term success for the on-line content industry is tied to solutions for protecting copyrights and improvements in the Internet infrastructure. Uncertainty about whether digital copies sold over the Internet will be prone to copyright infringement and piracy impedes growth. How quickly the speed and convenience of Internet access for the home user improves will also drive the size and growth of the Internet content marketplace.

Technological solutions, including watermarks and digital object identifiers, are being developed to protect copyright. A treaty negotiated at the World Intellectual Property Organisation (WIPO) in December 1996 addressed the question of how copyright should be legally recognised and protected in global Internet commerce. Legislation to ratify this treaty is now underway in the US Congress and in legislative bodies in other countries around the world. Until users can download a video in a matter of seconds, Web sites will not create many video products to sell on-line and Web users will prefer to read text, watch television or use their VCR.

As broadband Internet access becomes possible from the home via faster telephone connections, cable, satellite and wireless technologies, the demand for multimedia content will increase. Publishers point out that the lack of portability and difficulty in reading lengthy articles or magazines from cover to cover on a computer limits the potential of the on-line content market. Their readers like being able to buy a newspaper or a magazine on their way to work and read it during the journey. People also like to have their newspaper delivered to their home. These limitations may diminish as opportunities to access the Web from other devices increase, whether from a television set, telephone, car console, wearable computer or lightweight, portable screen.

Forrester Research predicts that US$1.5 billion in local ad purchases will shift to the Internet in the next three to five years. More than 60 corporations crossing different industries, including on-line services, broadcast and cable, directory providers, search engines, telephone companies and newspaper networks have announced plans to tap into the US$70 billion in local advertising with Internet-based services. Classified advertising represents 37% of a newspaper's total advertising. In order not to lose this revenue, most of the on-line dailies have at least some portion of their classifieds on-line.

Forrester Research claims that subscriptions for Internet content will grow from US$22 million in 1997 to US$89 million by 2000 and US$158 million by 2002. According to the company, revenue from on-line subscriptions will grow from US$22 million in 1997 to more than US$158 million by 2002. Subscriptions currently generate about 30% of a newspaper's and 40%–60% of a magazine's revenues. On-line, newspapers and magazines are weighing the trade-off between enticing people to look at their Web sites free of charge or levying a charge for their content. So far, they tend to do both. To attract advertising dollars, Internet businesses attempt to amass as large an audience as possible, even if that means their businesses operate at a financial loss for a period of time. Imposing a fee to access the content on the Web site could result in greater short-term revenues, though the audience may decrease over time. So far, most content sites are opting for building audiences rather than imposing subscriptions.

One issue that needs to be addressed by those wishing to set up content Web sites is that of information overload. Many people are tempted to join a Web site, be it a newspaper or magazine. They then find they simply do not have the time to access the Web site on a regular basis. Charging for content may simply mean that people use the Web site even less, or may only consider paying for content if it is absolutely necessary, e.g. they need to purchase a backdated article for professional reasons.

The *Wall Street Journal Interactive Edition* is one of the notable exceptions. Launched as a free service in April 1996, the site attracted 650 000 non-paying subscribers. Five months later the site was relaunched with a subscription fee of US$49 per year for non-print subscribers and US$29 if the reader also subscribed to the print edition (an additional US$175/year). Thirty thousand people subscribed to the relaunched site. As of November 1997, the *Interactive Edition* had 150 000 on-line subscribers, the largest group of paid subscribers for any on-line publication. In addition to traditional advertising and subscriptions revenues, Web publishers anticipate that they will be able to generate a growing amount of revenues by charging transactions fees (also called 'commerce' fees). This works as follows: visitors to one site go to another to purchase a CD, book travel, buy stock. The 'host' company receives a fee for renting the space on its site, a percentage or flat dollar amount for each lead or purchase that results at the other company, or some combination of the above.

Consumer Demand

Much has been written about consumer demand for Internet-based products and services. Many writers perceive the *customer as king* in the context of business-to-consumer Internet commerce, with some offering a cautionary message, namely that unless businesses rush to set up a Web site, they will lose market position to their more innovative rivals. So far, publishers, educational establishments, news groups, radio broadcasters and many others who are able to offer a digital delivery of their products and services have quickly established an Internet presence.

The key advantages of Internet-based content from the consumer's point of view are choice and convenience, savings, and timely, carefully targeted news and information. The Internet's selection of news and information is so vast that it would be impossible to find its equivalent in any other place due to physical constraints and the costs of carrying such a wide inventory. Traditional chain stores tend to stock the publications they can sell to a general audience. Small, speciality shops tend to sell the books, magazines or journals that serve a more targeted community of interest. The Internet provides the umbrella for both types of stores. Internet users can find obscure or limited circulation journals on-line along with the top sellers. What is limited to text and perhaps a picture in a print edition may be supplemented with video or audio clips, maps or in-depth background research. At present, Internet users can access most newspaper, magazine, TV and radio content free of charge. Businesses offering content from trade and technical publications, investment advice and other specialised content targeted to particular audiences may charge a fee or bundle it with other products and services.

Because the on-line content industry is not yet mature, pricing structures will continue to evolve. Internet businesses may begin to charge for general news and information if they think they can maintain and grow their audience even after they impose a fee. Timeliness and personalisation are two other factors that may influence consumer demand for Internet-based content. Books can take several months or years to go from concept to publication. Magazines come out weekly or monthly, and newspapers once a day. Almost as soon as a new story is written and approved, people can start reading it on-line. With Web news, readers can also choose to skip an article in today's news and still find it again tomorrow, next month, or next year in the site's searchable archives. Internet users can select only the news, entertainment and information they want and have it 'delivered' to their personalised Web page, to an e-mail box, or as a service that the computer defaults to when at rest.

More Efficient Distribution Channels

Distributing newspapers and magazines can cost as much as 30%–40% of the retail price. By contrast, an Internet version of that newspaper or magazine avoids the expense of the trucks that move the papers from the printing plant to the city news stands or the cost of postage to send a magazine to a subscriber across the country. Instead, the publisher's distribution costs include paying off the investment in the Web servers and other technology that makes sure that when someone clicks on the Web site that it responds quickly. Unlike newspaper or magazine content that gets used once, content stored digitally can be repackaged and used again. Storing content in a digital library means that it can be used not only on the Internet, but can be called up on TV as a broadcast feed or video-on-demand, made into customised CD-ROMs or electronic games.

Disintermediation

One of the more convincing theories about Internet commerce is that traditional organisation structures will cease to be based around business functions and products (Benjamin and Wigand, 1995). Instead, the virtual or network-based business will be structured around electronic distribution channels in remote locations. Whilst companies have been using EDI for several years as a means of ordering, reordering, and monitoring and paying for supplies, the Internet will develop this process further as supplier and customer bases expand.

Loss of Existing Revenue Sources

One issue that has received much attention in recent years is the growing competition and dynamism of emerging virtual markets and traditional physical markets. Whilst there is much hype surrounding this topic, it is apparent that the digital delivery of goods and services will disrupt existing marketplaces and transform some of them into marketspaces. Such a transformation will result in the loss of current revenue sources for many businesses. As we saw above, the new economics of Internet commerce will mean that traditional performance indicators will no longer be relevant. In a virtual or network-based economy, companies will need to isolate the various elements of the value chain and determine which ones are more important than others. For example, many companies are finding that setting up a Web site does not automatically add value to their business. A poorly designed Web site may actually deter customers from purchasing products and services from the company, particularly if they find the information misleading or incomplete.

To some extent, the fear of losing existing revenue sources may lead some companies to invest in Internet technology although they do not have a clear strategy of how it will add value to their business activities. As with other investments in new technology, the cost justification of Internet technology needs to demonstrate *real* as opposed to *theoretical* business benefits (irrespective of whether they are tangible or intangible in nature). Whilst the evidence which shows a direct correlation between loss of existing revenue sources and the growth of Internet commerce is thin on the ground, the perceived fear that a link exists may provide the impetus in some companies to develop and retain their customer base. Some of these new initiatives will support existing revenue streams and others will involve developing new products and services to be digitally delivered over the Internet.

Develop and Retain a Customer Base

The desire to develop and retain a customer base is central to the rhetoric and hype which supports Internet commerce. There are now many examples in various business sectors, from financial services, computing, retailing and publishing, where companies are using the Internet to widen their customer base. Notwithstanding the many popular examples, there is a shortage of rigorous empirical research on how specific business sectors are using the Internet to win new customers. A recent research study of the Australian insurance sector offers a cautionary note by stressing that

> of the 21 largest Australian insurance companies, only 18 have Web sites. These sites are mainly used for promotional purposes and not for directly generating sales. Only six companies offer customer-specific pricing of their products. And of these, only four companies sell any of their products over the Internet (Costello and Tuchen, 1998, p. 153).

The authors conclude that

> Paradoxically, despite pressing business drivers in the insurance sector and a favourable electronic commerce environment in Australia, these findings demonstrate a significant gap between appreciation of the importance of electronic commerce and realisation of commercial potential (p. 153).

Enhance Company Image

Given that new technology in its various forms is inextricably linked with images of progress, innovation and forward thinking, the Internet is no exception. To this end, many businesses have rushed to set up a Web site to enhance their company image. Although this business driver is difficult to measure in any tangible way, many companies realise the importance of developing a positive image and they use technology to achieve this aim.

Desire to Innovate

One of the key challenges which underpins the development of Internet commerce is a desire to turn *Web surfers* from passive browsers into active consumers (Zwass, 1998). This will only be achieved through a process of innovation. Although the cost of building an interactive, transactional and dynamic Web site is estimated to be more than US$1 million, companies will also need to re-engineer their existing business processes in order to realise any Internet-based return on investment (ROI). The risks involved are significant and, as we saw above in the section on the new economics of Internet commerce, there are few reliable financial performance indicators that can measure the success or failure of virtual or network-based economies. Notwithstanding this point, the desire to innovate is a strong business driver in most companies, with some claiming that a direct correlation exists between expenditure on R&D and bottom line profit. Yet the concept of innovation is much misunderstood in the literature, with many writers often adopting a narrow, technical perspective. In the context of Internet commerce, innovation is an interdisciplinary phenomenon which encapsulates markets, hierarchies, people, processes, functions, networks, supply chains and technologies.

Cost Reduction

As with all investment in new technology, the desire for cost reduction (fixed and variable) is a common business driver. Whilst there are few detailed empirical studies on Internet-based cost reduction, there is widespread speculation. So far, cost reduction from Internet commerce is likely to arise in the five areas outlined in Table 5.3.

CASE STUDIES—BUSINESS-TO-CONSUMER INTERNET COMMERCE

As we have observed above, the transition from physical to virtual (digitally delivered) products and services is making significant inroads in countries where

Table 5.3   *Potential areas for cost reduction from Internet commerce*

Disintermediation	By establishing more direct links with customers, a company will reduce the need for intermediaries and, in turn, reduce business transaction costs
Outsourcing	More business and technical services will be procured from the marketplace, such as technical expertise in the form of Web site developers. This will eliminate the need for an in-house IT department
Administration	More orders processed electronically will reduce paper-based processes
Product and service innovation	Products and services which are digitally delivered (books, CDs, flight tickets, insurance premiums, etc.) will generate cost savings
Staffing	Virtual or network-based companies will be able to locate staff in remote/low labour cost areas. Many staff will be able to work from home (teleworking)

Table 5.4   *Top five domains from home and work*

Top five domains from home	Top five domains from work
aol.com—46%*	Yahoo.com—49%
Yahoo.com—40.5%	Netscape.com—40.0%
Microsoft.com—27.3%	aol.com—34.1%
Geocities—25.9%	Microsoft.com—33.0%
Netscape—25.4%	Excite.com—30.3%

*Percentages refer to people who used Web site in July 1998—$N = 10\,975$.
Adapted from: Nua Internet Surveys (1998) 'Media Metrix: Amazon.com remains top shopping site.'

more advanced Internet commerce markets exist. Recent evidence shows little difference between home and work use of the Internet, as the same popular Web sites are used in both categories. For example, Media Metrix have released their figures for the most trafficked Web sites during mid-1998 (see Nua Internet Surveys, 1998). Table 5.4 shows that aol.com was used by 46% of the sample from home and by 34.1% of the sample from work. The figures are similar for the Yahoo! and Microsoft Web sites, respectively.

Another survey carried out by Media Metrix (see Nua Internet Surveys, 1998) claims that the top three shopping sites from home and work were almost identical. As Table 5.5 shows, Amazon.com and Bluemountainarts.com were the most trafficked Web sites irrespective of whether people were accessing them from home or work.

Whilst the above survey data offer interesting insights into the most popular or trafficked Web sites, an interesting observation is that the distinction between home and work use of the Internet is becoming blurred. Clearly, those people responding to the survey have Internet access and may therefore work from home for some or even all of the time. In this respect, the Internet offers them the opportunity to undertake Internet-related work and leisure activities, and this may ultimately benefit businesses wishing to develop digitally delivered products and services.

In this section we explore two case studies of companies who are currently offering on-line products and services to their customers. First, we consider how the *New York Times* (a US newspaper) is seeking to expand its customer base by tailoring its services to specific readership categories. Second, we examine the case of Dun & Bradstreet who deliver a growing number of their current products and services over the Internet or through corporate Intranets. Responding to customer

Table 5.5   *Top three shopping sites from home and work*

Top three shopping sites from home	Top three shopping sites from work
Amazon.com—8.1%	Amazon.com—11.3%
Bluemountainarts.com—7.4%	Bluemountainarts.com—5.6%
Cnet software Download Services—5.4%	Barnes & Noble—4.8%

Adapted from: Nua Internet Surveys (1998) 'Media Metrix: Amazon.com remains top shopping site.'

demand, D&B is also developing a new range of products and services specifically designed to be delivered over the Internet.

New York Times

In anticipation of highly profitable classified advertising revenues leaving the print media for the Web, the *New York Times* Company (along with hundreds of other newspapers) launched its on-line business in early 1996. Newspaper circulation is very different in the United States compared with the United Kingdom. In the United States, with its 52 states, newspapers tend to serve a state (regional) audience rather than a national one. However, at the *New York Times*, the strategy has been to position itself as more of a national paper than a regional paper, drawing a larger share of its revenues from national advertisers. In addition, it is creating an on-line business. Like other newspaper Web sites, the *New York Times* offers readers daily print stories on-line. It also offers various 'Web specials' which cover health issues for women, sports and special in-depth features. Offering content of this nature dictates a different dynamic from a physical (paper-based) product.

In an on-line business model, the supply chain is very different. The need for a large premises and plant is greatly reduced. People may work remotely, unlike in the traditional newspaper environment with a large printing works and offices attached. The barriers to entry to the Internet are also low. Yet this is the same for competitors. In the traditional business model, the high cost of setting up a plant and office infrastructure acted as a strong barrier to entry for potential new competitors. However, with the relatively low costs of doing business on the Internet, low capital costs mean that more competition will result. What becomes important is building a brand. At the *New York Times*, the success in capturing a national audience will be a major factor in attracting advertising revenue from major clients. So far, newspapers have found it difficult to generate revenue streams from their on-line business. Whilst the main revenue comes from advertising, additional revenues come from a subscription fee charged to the international audience, along with fees to print stories from the archives and an annual fee for on-line crossword puzzles. The more attractive and versatile the Web site for customers (readers), the more advertisers will come. Another key factor in the on-line business is the speed with which news can be placed on the Web site. An event such as a major environmental disaster or even the death of a celebrity can be placed on the Web site within minutes. One of the problems with newspapers is that the news is often out of date at the point of sale. Traditionally, newspapers have tended to compensate for this with other content, such as features (interviews with celebrities), TV guides and regulars (the gardening or health section). With the on-line Web site, all the additional content can be included as well as *real-time* news stories.

James Terrill, Vice President and Controller of the *New York Times*, discussed the preparation of a newspaper thus:

> Before noon on the day before, we decide the shape of the newspaper. Once you know the advertising spend, you know the size of the paper. The look and feel of the newspaper does not change—everyone knows the positioning of articles on a page and what should go in each section. Where it goes says, 'this is today's news, this is what's important.' We have to

make sure that 365 days of the year, we go through the sequence properly. Once every 20 years we reinvent the newspaper.

Cris Zukowski, director of business operations at *New York Times* electronic media company, discusses the on-line approach thus:

> Our business is a 24 × 7 operation. It's much more dynamic. The key is to attract viewers and get them to stay, while at the same time deciding what's worthy of the *New York Times'* brand name. We're very informal and have to be because of the speed this market moves at.

One of the most important differences between the traditional (print) and on-line versions of the *New York Times* is in the cost structure. Essentially, the two approaches represent two different types of business, and the business model used for the former will not be appropriate for the latter. In the traditional business, the largest forms of expenditure are: the newsprint, the physical distribution, and the costs to manufacture and print the paper. One estimate is that these combined costs represent 30%–40% of the total cost structure. The major expenses of the on-line business are content creation, sales and marketing. The *New York Times* claims that marketing expenses are the most difficult to predict. Depending on how the Internet marketplace evolves, marketing expenses could be higher as a percentage of total operating expenses for the on-line business than for the print business, particularly if users continue to access the Internet via a handful of Web sites. The *New York Times* plans to expand its on-line Web site, pulling together speciality Web sites under the strength of the *New York Times* brand name. With its large base of print subscribers and growing base of registered on-line users, the *New York Times* is making good progress in expanding its audience. A recent offering to its subscriber is as follows:

> Hello New York Times Subscriber,
>
> INTRODUCING a new way to stay informed and entertained, whenever and wherever you like. Audible lets you listen to today's top stories from THE NEW YORK TIMES, catch-up on Stephen King's latest thriller, and tune-in to your favourite public radio shows like FRESH AIR and MARKETPLACE. All in digital audio format. Direct from the Internet (*New York Times*, 30 July 1999).

Dun & Bradstreet

For over 155 years, Dun & Bradstreet (D&B) has provided information services to assist businesses in buying and selling decisions. Today, D&B is one of the leading providers of business-to-business credit, marketing, purchasing, receivable management and decision-support services worldwide. Supplementing reports and products available in CD-ROM, proprietary software and via direct electronic feeds, D&B delivers a growing number of its current products via the Internet or via corporate Intranets. Responding to customer demand, D&B is also developing new products and services designed for the Internet. D&B positions itself as 'organising the business space' on the Internet much as it does in traditional markets. Buyers and sellers need information to validate the identity and legitimacy of a potential business partner. They also need a basic corporate profile to determine credit worthiness, size, geographic presence, management and ownership structure.

D&B's D-U-N-S$^{®}$ Number, a registry for 46 million businesses around the world, is used by governments, standards organisations and industry associations to verify a business's identity on-line, whether for an Internet or EDI transaction. Small and medium-sized companies use D&B's Web site most often to access standard business reports, including credit and risk management reports for evaluating buyers, purchasing products reports for evaluating sellers, and database marketing reports for evaluating prospective markets. Larger customers also use D&B's standard reports, but they have begun to request more specialised information and customised solutions their employees can access from corporate Intranets and the Internet.

In the past, a buyer of solid wood products would have asked the corporate librarian to print out a supplier evaluation report on each mill being considered for the pine contract for the company's North Carolina furniture factories.

Today, the buyer is no longer satisfied with a printed report. Instead, he wants to pull up information about different mills right from his desktop computer, store certain fields of data and compare data across companies to qualify them and look for opportunities to negotiate better prices. A large telecommunications company in the process of deciding which vendor to lease computer equipment for a year uses D&B's Financial Stress Score, a statistical model that predicts the likelihood of that supplier's business failing in the next 12 months. The D&B information is built right into the workflow. Instead of having to interrupt the process to call up a D&B report, the information is fed directly into a vendor scorecard that the procurement officer uses to evaluate different vendors. The Internet has given the company a number of benefits.

The corporate customers of D&B traditionally consisted of a few key individuals within purchasing, credit and marketing departments who controlled a company's access to D&B reports. With the Internet and corporate Intranets, the 'gatekeeper' mentality is changing. Customers now request hundreds or thousands of passwords for their employees to access D&B products from the Internet. In fact, D&B have had a 6%–11% growth in revenues from customers accessing information from the Internet while its traditional business has remained flat. Customer demand has led the company to develop new products and services to integrate into business applications on corporate Intranets. At the same time, D&B is working with Internet companies to provide businesses with D&B's D-U-N-S$^{®}$ Numbers system when they register for a domain name. They also provide their services to certification authorities to validate businesses conducting commerce on the Internet. This has led to greater integration between D&B and their customers' business processes. Clients have asked for new products that allow them to directly incorporate D&B information into key business processes. Because it is easier to charge vendors for a standard report than it is to change a business process, D&B is becoming more of a strategic partner than it has been in the past. Another benefit is reduced data acquisition and labour costs. In the past, data collection was a time-consuming procedure, and meant maintaining a labour force in different geographical locations who physically visited courthouses and government offices to request and photocopy documents. With automation and electronic feeds for much of its data-collection process, D&B has been able to centralise its collection activities and reduce costs. Data acquisition via the Internet will be more efficient. Individual companies will register and update their profiles with D&B on-line rather than by fax or mail, and a greater share of public information will be transmitted to D&B electronically. The company believes its business will continue to evolve from producing standard reports to providing customised services that rely heavily on collecting, interpreting, storing and presenting information in ways that are meaningful to individual customers. D&B expects that more than half of its business will come through the Internet shortly after the turn of the century.

SUMMARY

This chapter has considered the issues of gaining competitive advantage from the Internet and WWW. It gave an overview of the debate on whether Internet commerce will generate a power shift from supplier to customer. At the present time, the jury is still out on this issue, since business-to-consumer Internet commerce is still evolving. As we saw in our case study discussion on the *New York Times*, Web sites need to encourage subscribers with a whole range of services if they are to maintain their interest. At the current time, many subscribers to on-line newspapers are inconsistent in their use of such Web sites. This may change over time, particularly as Web sites become more sophisticated in their offerings to customers. With regard to the debate about the new economics of Internet commerce, it appears that new business models will be needed to evaluate the performance of virtual businesses. However, the benefits gained from reducing administrative costs, etc. will be widespread and will not therefore be restricted to only a few companies. For example, publishers, newspaper proprietors, and airlines, to name just a few, all offer their products and services on-line. As such, competitive advantages will not be gained even though an on-line offering may reduce a company's operating costs. So to identify any competitive advantage, it will be important to isolate the key competitive or business differentiators. This may be in the form of brand name, marketing and sales strengths or content creation. It is unlikely that numerous Web sites offering similar products and services will survive. Rather, some will go from strength to strength and others will perish. In view of the changing commercial landscape, an important question is: How revolutionary is the Internet and WWW in changing industry structures and cultures? Whilst business-to-business Internet commerce is becoming well established, the business-to-consumer side offers many opportunities and threats to existing and new businesses. In the next chapter we explore some of the popular management innovation and change panaceas of the post-war period. By placing the Internet and WWW in this context, a key question will be: Is Internet commerce a significant development in the business world or simply just another passing fad or panacea?

6
Revisiting Management Innovation and Change Programmes

INTRODUCTION

The subject of managing innovation and change has been widely discussed in the business and management literature for several decades (Vedin, 1994). Every few years a new management philosophy, method or technique is developed which is believed to enhance business performance and competitive advantage. Many of them emanate from North America and are developed by practising management consultants. In the last few decades writers have focused upon the merits and demerits of total quality management (TQM) (Oakland, 1995; Rao et al., 1996), just-in-time (JIT) production management (Schonberger, 1982, Voss and Robinson, 1987), and activity based costing (ABC) which is a revised cost management system to identify cost drivers to enable managers to differentiate between value-added and non-value-added activities (Kaplan, 1984, 1985; Cooper and Kaplan, 1991). More recently, the concepts of business process re-engineering (BPR) (Hammer, 1990; Hammer and Champy, 1993), process innovation (Davenport, 1993b, 1994), organisational learning (Stata, 1989) and knowledge management (Alvesson, 1995) have been championed. These ideas, or *panaceas*, have generated numerous quantitative and qualitative academic research studies, many of which are intended to evaluate their theoretical relevance and practical application to the business community. Whereas some studies have focused upon evaluating the results of different methods and techniques at the organisational or national levels, others have adopted a cross-national (comparative) perspective. What is central to all of this work is the notion that by developing and implementing new philosophies, methods and techniques, businesses will become more efficient, competitive and profitable in the long term (see Table 6.1).

Table 6.1 *Some influential organisation and management theories, concepts and practices in the twentieth century*

Structures, systems, technology	Management, organisation and strategy	People, culture, behaviour
Scientific management (Taylor, 1911)	Executive functions (Barnard, 1938)	Industrial conflict
Legitimacy, authority, bureaucracy (Weber, 1947)	Giving of orders	Human relations (Mayo, 1949)
Authority and communications networks	Principles of management (Fayol, 1949)	Socio-technical systems (Trist and Bamforth, 1951)
Technology of production (Woodward, 1958)	Management at General Motors (Sloan, 1963)	Motivation and personality (Maslow, 1970)
Dysfunctions of bureaucracy (March and Simon, 1958)	Decision-making (bounded rationality) (Simon, 1960)	Formal organisations/ individuals (Argyris, 1957)
Mechanistic and organismic structures (Burns and Stalker, 1961)	Strategy and structure (Chandler, 1962)	Muddling through (Lindblom, 1959)
Organisation growth and development (Nystrom and Starbuck, 1981)	Business strategy (Ansoff, 1965)	Theory X, theory Y
Structuring of organisations (Mintzberg, 1973)	Top management planning	Supportive relations (Likert, 1961)
Strategy–technology connection (Kantrow, 1980)	Corporate planning (Ackoff, 1970)	Organisational choice (Trist et al., 1963)
Micro-electronics revolution (Forrester, 1980)	Competitive strategy (Porter, 1980)	Motivation-hygiene theory (Hertzberg, 1966)
Just-in-time (Schonberger, 1982)	Critical success factors (Shank, 1985)	Total quality management (Crosby, 1979)
Business process re-engineering (Hammer and Champy, 1993)	Activity-based costing (Kaplan, 1984, 1985)	Local incrementalism
Process innovation (Davenport, 1993a,b)	Knowledge management (Alvesson, 1995)	Organisational learning (Stata, 1989; Nonaka, 1991)

The chapter is divided into three main sections. First, it considers seven management innovation and change programmes which have emerged in the post-war period. These include, TQM, JIT, ABC, BPR, process innovation, organisational learning and knowledge management. They are discussed in chronological order beginning with TQM and ending with knowledge management. Second, an attempt is made to compare and contrast the seven approaches. What emerges from the discussion is that they share a common set of key characteristics:

1. they advocate a company-wide approach to managing change;
2. they seek to change the philosophy or culture of the organisation;
3. they are focused upon achieving business improvements;

4. to be successful, they must be top-down led and managed; and
5. they are prescriptive and developed from a management consultancy rather than an academic perspective.

In comparing the seven approaches, the chapter questions their authenticity and originality and suggests that panaceas of this kind rarely achieve the spectacular results advocated by their supporters. Third, we conclude the chapter with a case study on managing large scale innovation and change at Royal Bank of Scotland. Here it can be shown that virtually all the innovation and change programmes described can be applied to this company.

SEVEN MANAGEMENT INNOVATION AND CHANGE PROGRAMMES

Table 6.2 gives an overview of the seven management innovation and change programmes discussed in this section. As we can see, they are presented in chronological order beginning with TQM and ending with knowledge management. Some key texts/articles relating to each one are also given, as are the business drivers, enabling technologies, and benefits and improvements. The table is intended to show the similarities in the scope and content of the seven programmes.

Total Quality Management (TQM)

Of the innovation and change programmes that have emerged over the last few decades, total quality management, or TQM, as it is often called, is perhaps one of the most popular. First developed by US writers such as Crosby (1979), Deming (1982) and Juran (1986) in the post-war period, TQM has widespread appeal in both the academic and practitioner communities. This is largely because it offers a company-wide perspective on managing change which includes all members of an organisation, from top management to operational and clerical personnel. TQM is sometimes referred to in the literature as an example of Japanese management methods and techniques. Indeed, there was a spate of management books in the early to mid-1980s which linked Japanese manufacturing success with the effective design and implementation of TQM. Such a position led to confusion and misunderstanding since the roots of TQM are found in the United States, though the theory and practice were later transferred to Japan in the post-war period along with other Western-based management methods and techniques, such as management accounting and practice (Currie, 1994). Japanese writers later published books about TQM as it applied in their own economic, social and organisational contexts (Ishikawa, 1985).

   In essence, TQM is concerned with quality improvement on a company-wide basis. It is a comprehensive approach to improving competitiveness, effectiveness and flexibility through planning, organising, and understanding all the activities and tasks undertaken by people within an organisation. The core of TQM is about improving customer and supplier relationships. In this context, customers and

Table 6.2   A chronology of seven innovation and change programmes

Concept	Key players	Business drivers	Enabling technologies, improvements and techniques	Business benefits and improvements
Total quality management (TQM) 1980–	Crosby (1979); Deming (1982); Juran (1986); Ishikawa (1985)	Quality/continuous improvement; Customer/supplier relations; Supply chain management; Team-working	Statistical process control (SPC); Benchmarking; Quality circles (QCs); Plan, do, check, act (PDCA)	Quality enhancement; Customer satisfaction; Zero defects; Culture change; Better communications; Cost reduction; Flexible working practices
Just-in-time (JIT) 1980–	Pascal and Athos (1981); Schonberger (1982, 1986); Hall (1983); Voss and Robinson (1987)	Production, logistics and supply chain management; Team-working; Process/product technology improvement; Innovation; Quality/continuous improvement	Materials requirements planning (MRP); Manufacturing resource planning II (MRP II); EDI, reliability centred maintenance (RCM); Total preventive maintenance (TPM)	Reduced machine downtime, waste and re-work (of stock); Reduced cost; Fulfil innovation strategy; Improved customer/supplier relationships
Activity-based costing (ABC) 1989–	Kaplan (1984, 1985, 1986)	Improved financial monitoring and control; Identify cost drivers; Performance measurement	Cost management systems (CMSs); Value-added analysis of business processes; Benchmarking	Eliminate non-value-added activities; Reduce cost, identify profitable and loss-making products
Business process re-engineering (BPR) 1990–	Hammer (1990); Hammer and Champy (1993)	Competitive pressure; Eliminate/transform business processes; Cross-functionality; Automate or liquidate; Outsourcing	Strategic vision; Top-down process analysis; Management information systems (MISs); Customer perceptions	Eliminate non-core business processes; Achieve functional integration; Greater worker empowerment

Programme	Authors			
Process innovation 1990–	Davenport (1993a)	Competitive pressure Processes improvement and innovation Customer demand Financial restructuring Quality, flexibility service levels Outsourcing	Identify change levers Customer perceptions Work redesign Groupware Brainstorming Critical success factors (CSFs)	Eliminate non-core business processes Fuse IT and HRM Encourage cross-functional team-building
Organisational learning 1980–	Argyris (1977); Fiol and Lyles (1985); Stata (1989)	Desire to change culture/behaviour Training needs analysis Organisation development (OD) Skills shortages Global competition Intellectual work replacing manual work	Encoding inferences from history into routines Use of memory Team-building Mentoring Sharing of ideas	Create a learning culture Sustain competitive advantage Build on past knowledge and experience Empowerment Knowledge transfer
Knowledge management 1990–	Drucker (1946); Nonaka (1991); Alvesson (1995)	Focus on core competencies Intellectual property protection Intellectual capital and assets Knowledge as a commodity 'Knowledge-creating companies' Continuous innovation	Relationship-building/management Develop 'digital nervous system' Managing worker autonomy Contract negotiation/management Codifying 'tacit' knowledge	Protect intellectual property Codification of knowledge Translate data/information into knowledge Better understanding of performance Focus on key customers Knowledge as strategy

suppliers may be either internal or external to the company. For example, a purchasing manager may deal with an external supplier, or an internal accountant may liaise with the sales department of the same company. Whatever the exchange, the notion of suppliers serving their customers is central to the practice of TQM. The key objective is for suppliers to continually seek to improve the way they deal with their customers (internal and external). This is thought to have a positive effect on a company's overall performance as all employees are engaged in the change process.

A Strategic Vision

TQM further encourages senior management to develop a strategic vision of quality and focuses upon the prevention of problems rather than their detection and resolution once they have arisen. To this effect, TQM is not about 'firefighting' (i.e. waiting for fires to occur and then putting them out). Rather, it is about predicting potential problem areas by a process which is described as 'continuous improvement'. Since TQM is perceived to have wide-ranging benefits, senior management is expected to change the mindset of people in an attempt to break down existing barriers between hierarchies, functions and departments. The beliefs, behaviours, norms, dominant values and rules to which people subscribe form the culture of an organisation. So, to be effective, the philosophy and practice of TQM should have the total commitment of senior management, as well as the 'buy-in' from all members of staff, customers and suppliers. This may be facilitated through education and training programmes run by external consultants and/or internal staff and other stakeholders. To this end, TQM is not a 'quick fix' management innovation and change programme, but one that is carefully planned and implemented over time. Oakland (1995, p. 21) advocates that senior management should develop a 'quality policy' which aims to:

1. establish an 'organisation' for quality;
2. identify the customer's needs and perception of needs;
3. assess the ability of the organisation to meet these needs economically;
4. ensure that bought-in materials and services reliability meet the required standards of performance and efficiency;
5. concentrate on the prevention rather than detection philosophy;
6. educate and train for quality improvement;
7. review the quality management systems to maintain progress.

Other writers (Rao *et al.*, 1996) have identified five approaches to defining quality drawn from the existing literature. They are labelled as the

1. transcendental approach
2. product-based approach
3. user-based approach
4. manufacturing-based approach
5. value-based approach.

In short, the *transcendental approach* is defined as 'a condition of excellence implying fine quality as distinct from poor quality... Quality is achieving or reaching for the highest standard as against being satisfied with the sloppy or the fraudulent.'

This definition can be applied to the arts, sciences and manufacturing contexts since it is largely about achieving the highest quality or standard as measured by these different fields. The *product-based approach* identifies specific features or attributes that can be measured to indicate higher quality. For example, a Rolls Royce car and its various features (leather upholstery, engine capacity, bodywork, etc.) would be considered to be a higher quality product compared with a cheaper model. The same logic can be applied to many other products such as electrical goods, furniture and clothes. The *user-based approach* is attributed to Juran (1986) who developed the concept, 'fitness for use'. Since the product or service that best satisfies the user is the higher quality product, it is important for companies to develop data and information about the user (or customer). The user-based approach links customer satisfaction with quality. Customer attitudes and preferences can be incorporated into product and service offerings, so it is important for companies to develop close relationships with customers. Crosby (1979), who focused upon production and operations, espoused the *manufacturing approach*. He developed the concept of 'conformance to requirements' from his observations of the automobile industry. As Rao *et al.* (1996, p. 27) point out:

> Engineering specifies the product characteristics, and the more closely manufacturing can conform to those requirements, the better the quality of the product. If a process results in a product that has a precision of $\pm$ half-an-inch, it is considered worse than the process that makes a product with a precision of $\pm$ one-tenth of an inch ... This definition has the advantages of providing objectively measurable quality standards and of reducing the costs of quality.

The advantage of this approach is that it encourages a 'right-first-time' (reduced waste/zero defects) attitude to production output, but it tends to overlook the important issue of customer preferences, since it assumes that customer satisfaction is based upon 'the precision of meeting the target specifications of a product or service' (Rao *et al.*, 1996, p. 28). Finally, the *value-added approach* introduces the concept of price as a key determinant of quality. According to Broh (1982), 'Quality is the degree of excellence at an acceptable price and the control of variability at an acceptable cost.' In this approach, there is a trade-off between quality and price. As such, customers may choose to purchase a lower quality product if they believe it offers value for money. Conversely, they may choose a more expensive product if they feel it offers greater value for money in the long term.

The TQM movement gained a considerable following in the 1980s, with numerous publications, conferences and training and consultancy offerings advising senior managers to develop and implement TQM in their own organisation. Whilst TQM continues to be an important and popular management innovation and change programme in the 1990s, it has found competition from new rivals in the form of BPR and process innovation which we shall discuss later. The following section considers the concept of JIT which became popular with TQM in the 1980s. To some extent, JIT and TQM were seen by many Western academics as two sides of the same coin, since many of the ideas which underpin them are complementary.

Just-in-Time (JIT)

Throughout the 1980s, many writers concentrated their attention on the advantages to be gained by incorporating just-in-time (JIT) methods and techniques into their production management strategies and operations. The background to much of this interest was a fear that manufacturing in the Western world, North America, Canada and Europe, in particular, was experiencing industrial and economic decline (Gerwin, 1982; Drucker, 1988, 1990; Hayes and Jaikumar, 1988). Hayes and Abernathy (1980), for example, published an influential article entitled, 'Managing our way to economic decline', which argued convincingly that North American manufacturing industry was being seriously challenged by overseas competitors who could compete more favourably on labour, price, quality and cost. This fuelled further interest in the 1980s with the publication of work, some theoretical and others empirically based, on how industrialised nations could avoid further economic decline (Hirst and Zeitlin, 1988; Hirst, 1988).

World Class Manufacturing

Faced with serious economic problems such as rising unemployment, poor investment in education and training, skills shortages, severe global competition for manufacturing goods, lack of investment in new technology, and inefficient manufacturing and production methods and practices, many writers embarked upon research into cross national comparisons to distinguish between those countries, industries and companies with 'world-class' manufacturing strategies (Hayes and Wheelright, 1984; Schonberger, 1986). One conclusion of much of this research was that Japanese manufacturing methods, which included TQM and JIT, which were being used in some of the more successful Japanese manufacturing companies, were producing benefits resulting in greater efficiency, productivity and profitability than could be observed in many US and European manufacturing firms. Schonberger (1982, 1986, 1990), for example, compared automobile production in the United States and Japan. He found that Japanese firms out-performed their US rivals in a number of areas, including inventory, technology performance, operator productivity and manufacturing output (product). Schonberger's (1986) findings were later compared with another study on cross-national comparisons on manufacturing performance in Japan, North America, Britain and West Germany (Currie, 1991). As Table 6.3 shows, comparisons between Schonberger's findings on the Toyota, Kamigo, car plant in Japan, Ford, Dearborn in the United States, and research by Currie and Seddon (1992) on the Ford, Dagenham, car plant in the United Kingdom, show marked differences in productivity and performance.

As Table 6.3 shows, there were significant differences between the three car plants, with the Japanese far outstripping its Western competitors on many performance indicators. Interviews with Japanese manufacturing managers found that JIT production management methods and techniques were believed to be partly responsible for achieving this enhanced performance (Currie, 1994). However, the Japanese conceptualisation of JIT differed from the Western approach. For example, in Japan, JIT comprised three elements: JIT production management, total quality

Table 6.3   *A cross-national comparison of car engine plants in Japan, the United States and the United Kingdom*

Performance indicator	Toyota, Kamigo (Japan)*	Ford, Dearborn (US)*	Ford, Dagenham (UK)†
Products	2.4 4-cyl 2.0 4-cyl	2.4 4-cyl	1.6 4-cyl 1.8 4 cyl 2.0 4-cyl 2.5 6-cyl
Plant (ft^2)	0.3 million	2.2 million	2.6 million
Shifts	2	1 assembly 2 machining	2/3 assembly 2/3 machining
Inventory	4–5 hours	9.3 days	4 days
Wages (per hour)	US$11	N/A	£6–8
Robots	None	N/A	15
Operators	180	1360	2000
Line rate (per day)	1500	1960	2550
Labour-hours (per engine)	0.96	5.55	6.27

* Schonberger (1986).
† Currie and Seddon (1991).

assurance (TQA) and total preventive maintenance (TPM) (Wu *et al.*, 1992). This holistic approach to JIT was believed to succeed only if all three areas were taken seriously. That is, they were supported by clearly defined and thought-through manufacturing strategies. To this end, JIT was not merely a 'tool-box of techniques' (Cobb, 1991) but rather a management philosophy of integrated manufacturing planning and control (Wu, 1992).

JIT in Japan

Like TQM above, JIT was developed in the West and has been adapted by the Japanese to suit their culture (Shingo, 1989). On a comparative level, there is some evidence to show that, in Western countries (North America and the United Kingdom in particular), the JIT philosophy is perceived in much narrower terms. Gilbert (1989) contends that many commentators on JIT in Western manufacturing companies concentrate on a single JIT method or technique, such as inventory control, and so fail to grasp the 'JIT philosophy'. JIT is also discussed in the context of its cost advantages in manufacturing (Voss and Robinson, 1987; Inman and Mehra, 1990). However, surveys have shown that companies introducing JIT which seek fast and painless financial benefits have allowed 'short term monetary pressures to drive major operational decisions' (Zipkin, 1991, p. 44). Zipkin (1991) offers two definitions of JIT—*romantic JIT* and *pragmatic JIT*. The first is 'idealistic' and 'promises a factory where workers and suppliers will be in harmony and goods will flow like water' (p. 42). This is a more complex form of JIT and one which is often misunderstood in Western manufacturing industry. The second form—pragmatic JIT—focuses on the practical application of basic manufacturing methods and techniques and does not prescribe 'revolutionary' change. This focus on simplicity offers one explanation as to why the Japanese have been able to adapt JIT to their own manufacturing culture. At the broader level, JIT aims to develop an all-encompassing philosophy which encapsulates:

1. production management methods and techniques
2. total quality assurance (TQA)
3. total preventive maintenance (TPM)
4. customer–supplier relationships
5. technology/innovation strategies
6. flexible working practices
7. machine performance (uptime/downtime).

As with TQM, there were numerous offerings on the philosophy and practice of JIT from the academic and practitioner communities throughout the 1980s. Whilst JIT continues to be of interest, it too has been somewhat eclipsed by the more recent concepts of BPR and process innovation. More recently, however, the concepts of the virtual society and other, Internet-related ideas have attracted much attention. Before discussing this in more detail, the next idea, which emerged within academic and practitioner communities in the 1980s, was ABC. Once again, this concept, like TQM and JIT, attracted much attention as the latest 'panacea' to resolve business-related problems.

Activity Based Costing (ABC)

The impetus behind the development of ABC is the realisation that traditional management accounting fails to provide adequate cost management information in contemporary organisations using a range of new technologies, including computer-aided design (CAD), computer-aided manufacture (CAM) and robotics, as well as management methods and techniques, such as JIT, TQM, MRP, MPR II, among others. Against a backdrop of industrial and economic decline, many US writers argued that traditional cost management systems used in manufacturing companies were unable to capture a reliable picture of overall financial performance. In short, traditional cost management systems, which measured 'direct labour and machine hours to allocate to products the expenses of indirect and support activities', were becoming less relevant over time (Cooper and Kaplan, 1991). The supporters of ABC claimed that direct labour was now less than 10% of overall costs. New technologies were altering much of the cost management landscape. As direct labour costs were declining, indirect or variable costs were burgeoning. Many manufacturing companies were therefore losing their grip on measuring and monitoring costs, and this was seen to be a major impediment to the strategic planning and control processes.

A Comprehensive Cost Management System

As with TQM and JIT, ABC was developed as a major management change programme which could be implemented with far-ranging results. Developed by Harvard Business School academics in conjunction with a management consultancy firm, ABC was intended to complement other innovation and change programmes, but was also deemed to be more than just a new cost management system. In short, ABC has five key objectives, namely to

1. understand the relationship between costs and products;
2. identify cost drivers;
3. isolate overhead costs;
4. differentiate between value-added and non-value-added activities; and
5. provide useful data and information to inform strategic decision-making.

Whilst ABC is likely to be initiated by the finance department, most writers argue that it must be supported politically and in practice by senior managers throughout the organisation. This is because the process of conducting an ABC analysis is politically contentious and likely to highlight poor performance in some areas. Writing on the advantages of ABC, Jeans and Morrow (1989) outline five areas where ABC is a foundation from which improved information can lead to better decision-making in contemporary organisations. First, they state that 'ABC is concerned with understanding the cost activities and their relationship to products'. In this capacity, one could argue that ABC is concerned with micro-manufacturing economics in that it breaks down costs into their component parts rather than using only a few traditional measures such as direct labour, materials and indirect costs. ABC is therefore a 'basic for product costing, performance measurement and profitability analysis'.

Second, they state that, 'ABC uses multiple cost drivers as a means of attributing overhead costs to activities and then to products.' Coopers & Lybrand, Deloitte give the definition of a cost driver as the 'identification of the root cause (source) of cost'. The costs of activities, which support production, are identified so that an organisation can acquire reliable information on product costs, price formulation and profitability. Using the example of machine set-up times (a cost driver) an ABC analysis may show that the machine set-up time for product A is 185 minutes, whereas it is 350 minutes for product B. Utilising an appropriate cost driver will thus demonstrate a 'meaningful relationship between the amount of overhead attributed to the product and the consumption of resources by that product via the activities performed'.

Third, the authors argue that ABC is not functionally restricted to the shop floor—rather it is concerned with company-wide 'overhead costs'. In this capacity, ABC can be introduced in all organisational settings.

Fourth, it is contended that ABC is designed for a complex business environment in that it uses 'multiple cost drivers and attributes the resulting costs to the products and customers which cause it'. As a more sophisticated cost management system compared with traditional management accounting methods, ABC is perceived by its supporters to offer improved information from which strategic decisions may be taken (i.e. those concerned with product profitability and life cycle).

Finally, the authors say that ABC provides 'meaningful product and cost and profitability analysis and information'. Thus, by identifying a multiplicity of cost drivers, identifying those activities that consume resources and their relationship to a firm's products, it is contended that information for strategic and operational decision-making will be vastly improved.

Another salient feature of ABC is its aim to differentiate between 'value-added' and 'non-value-added' activities. By identifying the whole range of activities pertaining to each product from its development, manufacture, marketing, after-sales support, etc. decisions may be taken about the 'relevance' of such activities. The CAM-I organisation states that, 'Activities can be identified as non value-added when they contribute nothing that the customer is willing to pay for. This provides a focus for cost improvement that is not available from traditional accounting systems.' All such non-value-added activities should therefore be eliminated. Bromwich and Bhimani (1989) state that, 'The manufacture of a product entails many processes which add cost to the product but not all such activities necessarily add value to the product.'

Since ABC is process orientated rather than functionally focused, activities that consume resources may be identified and evaluated. CAM-I state that

> Activities represent the real work done by the organisation, not the shadows represented by costs . . . Activities are understood; they are what we do and they are actionable. The resource consuming behaviour of an organisation and its processes is best revealed by Activity Analysis and a structured investigation of drivers and causes.

Those activities that are deemed to add value to a product may be returned and assessed for improvement while resource-consuming 'wasteful' activities are eliminated. The focus on 'activities' is important here, since it has been found that people cannot manage costs, they can only manage activities that cause costs. Similarly, Cooper and Kaplan (1991) state that 'ABC has emerged as a tremendously useful guide to management action that can translate directly into higher profits. Moreover, the ABC approach is broadly applicable across the spectrum of company functions and not just in the factory.' The authors say that ABC invites managers to 'separate the expenses and match them to the level of activity that consumes the resources'. Such an approach is contrary to the tradition of allocating all expenses to individual units.

ABC implemented in conjunction with TQM and JIT was seen as an important contribution to improving overall business performance. Whilst many writers on ABC focused upon its advantages in a manufacturing setting, it was considered to be relevant also to other sectors, notably the service sector. Through the late 1980s and early 1990s, ABC was discussed widely in the finance and accounting literature. Some companies claimed to have success with implementing ABC programmes, and others saw it as a useful 'adjunct' to their existing cost management systems. Since the development of ABC, other process orientated management innovation and change programmes have emerged. The following two sections consider BPR and process innovation, respectively. Once again, it is interesting to observe that many of the ideas from TQM, JIT and ABC are reproduced in the following offerings.

Business Process Re-engineering (BPR)

Business process re-engineering (BPR), or *re-engineering*, emerged in the late 1980s and early 1990s as a new approach to managing innovation and change. Essentially it was designed to be highly prescriptive since it advocated that managers should constantly seek new and improved methods and techniques for managing and controlling core and service business processes. A more cynical interpretation is that BPR was a euphemism for 'Big Personnel Reductions' (Kavanagh, 1994) since it called for the ambitious restructuring of organisations through *downsizing* and *delayering* of managerial hierarchies and functions (Conti and Warner, 1994). In an article entitled 'Re-engineering work: don't automate, obliterate', Hammer (1990, p. 107) claims the essence of re-engineering is about 'discontinuous thinking' and the relinquishing of 'outdated rules and fundamental assumptions that underlie operations'. It is a move away from linear and sequential thinking to an holistic, all-or-nothing perspective on strategic change in organisations. Managers are criticised for *thinking deductively*. That is, defining a problem and then seeking its resolution by evaluating a number of possible remedies. Instead, Hammer and Champy (1993) make the case for *inductive thinking*. This is to 'recognise a powerful solution and then seek the problems it might solve, problems the company probably doesn't even know that it has'. Other writers suggest that re-engineering is about serving the external environment through improved customer service and not simply about meeting a narrow range of internal performance targets (Harrison and Pratt, 1993). Thus, 'Re-engineering is a radically new process of organisational change that many companies are using to renew their commitment to customer service' (Janson, 1993, p. 45). But some writers question re-engineering's claims to radicalism and novelty, and also the notion that organisations can engage in a process of 'collective forgetting', of wiping the slate clean, and starting with *a blank sheet of paper* (Grint *et al.*, 1995).

A Radical Innovation and Change Programme

Breaking away from incremental and piecemeal approaches to strategic planning and change, Hammer contends that re-engineering is not a step-by-step, incremental approach. Rather it is a radical innovation and change programme. It is intended to *revolutionise* all the components which make up an organisation. This includes processes, products, services, people and technologies. Neither is it about *fixing things*, nor propping up a 'creaking management process or functional structure' (Kavanagh, 1994). It can be applied in private and public sector organisational settings and is therefore not simply about improving bottom-line performance. According to its supporters, re-engineering is not simply a quick-fix approach for managers seeking to improve the efficiency of outdated administrative functions, since its fundamental message concerns long-term organisational transformation. Outlining his *Utopian* vision, Hammer (1990) concentrates on 10 wide-ranging areas which are critical to the success of re-engineering. These areas are not ranked in order of priority in Table 6.4, but comprise the core focal points pertaining to the re-engineering goal.

One of the key elements of re-engineering is a focus on business processes. This is defined as 'a structured, measured set of activities designed to produce a specified output for a particular customer or market' (Davenport, 1993a). The re-engineering activity described in the literature varies in the scale and type of change contemplated, and is not restricted to any one type of market, product, organisational size

Table 6.4   From the traditional to the re-engineered organisation

	Traditional organisation	Re-engineered organisation
Organisational structure	Hierarchical	Flat
Work units	Functional departments	Process teams
Nature of work	Simple tasks	Multidimensional work
Employee roles	Controlled	Empowered
Managerial roles	Supervisors	Coaches
Executive roles	Scorekeepers	Leaders
Value system	Protective	Productive
Job preparation	Training	Education
Promotion criteria	Performance	Ability
Performance measurement	Activity (inputs)	Results (outputs)
Compensation systems	Salary, perks	Salary, share options, equity

Adapted from: Hammer and Champy (1993).

or technical capability (Heygate, 1993; Morris and Brandon, 1993). Central to re-engineering practice, according to most sources, is an holistic approach to strategy, structure, process, people and technology (Galliers, 1994; Hammer and Stanton, 1995; Johannsson *et al.*, 1993). As such, a re-evaluation of all these areas is likely to produce significant changes to the entire organisation in terms of management control, co-ordination and reward systems.

Implementing BPR

Re-engineering as theory, i.e. a set of prescriptions for management, and as practice, can be assessed in several ways and at several different levels (Currie and Willcocks, 1995). A major concern must be to compare the theory against what is actually being achieved in re-engineering programmes. A major issue that arises from surveys, case study research, and also from anecdotal evidence is why, despite the large sums being spent on re-engineering by some high profile organisations, and a deluge of prescriptive management literature and consultancy activity, BPR so often seems to fail to live up to expectations (Burke and Peppard, 1995). Even Hammer and Champy cautioned against the 'disappointing results' from poorly conceived re-engineering projects. Champy (1995), for example, claimed that, 'Re-engineering works—up to a point. The obstacle is management.' So against a backdrop of mixed results, the authors estimate that between 50% and 70% of re-engineering attempts fail to deliver the intended dramatic results, although they point out that this figure is not rigorously arrived at, and implies 'nothing about the expected rate of success or failure of subsequent re-engineering efforts' (Hammer and Stanton, 1994). Other studies show that most re-engineering projects consistently fall well short of dramatic or even expected benefits (Bartram, 1992; Hall *et al.*, 1993; Harvey, 1995; Moad, 1993).

Notwithstanding these problems Hammer (1990) describes two examples of IT-enabled re-engineering initiated by the Mutual Benefit Life (MBL) Insurance company and the Ford Motor Company. Both these examples demonstrate how re-engineering can successfully transform a business to achieve enhanced competitive advantage and increased profitability. At MBL, for example, procedures for administering insurance applications were perceived to be highly bureaucratic, time-consuming and inefficient. The process was essentially linear, where multistep processing, credit checking, quoting, rating and underwriting absorbed the activities of 19 staff working across five departments. The process was broken down into some 30 sequential steps. The average turnaround of insurance applications was between 5 and 25 days, and paperwork was at risk of being lost along the way. An interesting observation of the entire process was that only 17 minutes of actual work was required to complete the insurance application procedure. Yet the entire process lasted as many as 25 days.

Further complexities fuelled the inefficiency problem. For instance, customers wishing to redeem existing insurance policies and execute a new policy were met with further delays. Payment for the old policy was in the form of a cheque made payable to MBL and was sent to the new policies department along with the paperwork. This meant that more staff time was used in the cancellation and generation of insurance policies. Hammer contends that top managers became increasingly concerned with the delays and bottlenecks of the procedure and 'demanded a 60% improvement in productivity'. This was to be achieved by using the latest information technology to re-engineer the insurance applications process.

Senior managers at MBL created a new job title of 'case manager'. These individuals were charged with the responsibility of overseeing the entire insurance applications processing procedure. But, unlike clerks who were required to work under the strict supervision of a supervisor, the new case managers would work autonomously. This eliminated the supervisory role and also reduced the number of clerks originally used to handle the process. According to the author, information technology in the form of expert systems and relational databases enabled this process to be re-engineered. Relevant customer, product and service information was at the fingertips of the case manager which resulted in a reduced processing time of only four hours with an average turnaround of only two to five days. Some 100 field office positions were eliminated as a direct consequence of the re-engineering exercise. This example of re-engineering, according to Hammer, was to reduce organisational hierarchy, cut operating costs and develop 'self-managing', technically competent personnel. Thus, 'as doers become self-managing and self-controlling, hierarchy—and the slowness and bureaucracy associated with it—disappears. Organisational hierarchies thus become flatter thereby rendering the traditional pyramidal structure a thing of the past.' Grint (1993, p. 181) aptly sums up the fundamental objective of re-engineering, which is 'to develop systems built around teams that are configured to mirror the processes that the business actually works around rather than the functions it may use to execute these processes'.

In a survey on the economics, benefits and impacts of BPR which targeted a random sample of medium and large UK organisations, it was found that high risk, radical re-engineering approaches were generally not being undertaken, in spite of the rhetoric that BPR is an all-encompassing change activity (Willcocks, 1995a, 1996). One indication of this was the low size of spend, with 43% of medium and large organisations each incurring BPR-related expenditures of under £1 million. In fact, many of the processes being re-engineered seemed to be existing ones to which improvements were being sought rather than those identified as a result of a radical rethink of how the organisation needed to be reconfigured and managed. Radical BPR resulting in sizeable job losses were fewer than expected since the survey found that for all completed BPR projects and all types of process, staff redundancies averaged less than 5% of total BPR costs (Willcocks, 1996). Generally, whatever the process being re-engineered, organisations did not seem to be aiming high when they looked for improvements from BPR. Actual improvements being achieved were also relatively low. Very few organisations were achieving what could be called *breakthrough results*. Thus, of the organisations that had completed BPR programmes, if a relatively conservative benchmark of significance of 20% profitability gain, 20% revenue gain and 10% decrease in costs of doing business is used, only 18% of organisations had achieved significant financial benefits from BPR on all three measures. Organisations were achieving, and in most cases aiming for, tangible improvements rather than radical change. This would suggest that the picture of discontinuous change represented in the BPR literature is not clearly underscored in BPR practice. In short, a wide gap is apparent between the strategic vision of BPR and its implementation.

The Rhetoric and Reality of BPR

This position is also adopted in the literature on re-engineering which seeks to contrast the rhetoric underpinning BPR with the reality (its implementation). Here, it is shown how radical approaches, or the way in which espoused radical aims become emergent, incremental improvements, may be related to the difficulties inherent in realising any practical benefits from BPR programmes (Currie, 1995b; Currie and Willcocks, 1996; Davenport, 1993b; Grint and Willcocks, 1995). Whilst the survey research is only a snap-shot of re-engineering in 100 organisations, one issue only just emerging is the extent to which BPR efforts fail to link closely with business strategy and with effective organisational processes for strategy formulation. This is a feature also of a number of texts ironically concerned with securing the business strategy–BPR linkage (Belmonte and Murray, 1993; Hammer and Champy, 1993; Johannsson *et al.*, 1993; Morris and Brandon, 1993).

This has led some to posit the need to go beyond BPR and focus on business systems engineering (Galliers, 1994; Watson, 1995). Furthermore, a prime question raised by the multidisciplinary approach at the heart of BPR study and practice is whether there are robust methodologies and tools available to facilitate the outcomes required from BPR activities. The conclusion has been that despite many approaches, there is an immaturity and a lack of integratedness on the methodological front (Earl and Khan, 1994; Klein, 1994). Indeed, most methodologies do not encapsulate all the elements associated with re-engineering, and thus fall short of providing the all-embracing 'catch-all', which is central to the BPR message. Moreover, such a *blank sheet of paper* approach to managing innovation and change would surely render prescriptive methodologies highly problematic.

Research that considers the results of re-engineering was conducted by Mumford (1999) who claims that four reasons explain why many firms experienced serious problems with re-engineering. They are:

1. the tendency to copy others,
2. the absence of a theory,
3. the lack of management involvement,
4. the lack of concern for people.

She claims that

> Because US industry had misinterpreted the goals of business process re-engineering and focused on short-term financial gains, its results were not very positive. A series of large-scale surveys carried out by different consultant groups between 1993 and 1996 charted its progress from initial euphoria, through increasing doubts about its benefits, until, finally, Davenport published an article in a US management journal stating that the approach should now be abandoned (Mumford, 1999, p. 35).

According to Davenport the re-engineering genie had become:

> So ugly that today, to most business people in the United States, re-engineering has become a word that stands for restructuring, layoffs, and too often failed change programmes . . . The rock that re-engineering foundered on is simple: people. Re-engineering treated the people inside companies as if they were just so many bits and bytes, interchangeable parts to be re-engineered (Davenport, 1996).

He asserts that

> As is always the case with any fad, there was a kernal of truth to re-engineering. Over time that truth got lost. But that doesn't make it any less true. The most profound lesson of BPR was never re-engineering, but business processes. Processes are how we work. Any company that ignores its business processes or fails to improve them risks its future. That said, companies can use many different approaches to process improvement without ever embarking on a high risk re-engineering project . . . When the Next Big Thing in management is, try to remember the lessons of re-engineering. Don't drop all your ongoing approaches in favour of the handsome newcomer (Davenport, 1996).

Criticisms of BPR are are now common in the literature (Galliers, 1994; Galliers and Swan, 1999; Hammer, 1996; Willcocks and Currie, 1996), and many of them can also be directed at Davenport's thesis of process innovation which we discuss next.

Process Innovation

In what appears to be direct competition with Hammer and Champy (1993), Davenport (1993a) developed the concept of *process innovation*, which was different from process improvement. In short, process innovation was an ambitious management change programme designed to 'fuse information technology and human resource management' for the purpose of improving business performance. As with BPR, process innovation focuses upon company-wide innovation and change and is not intended to be a managerial 'quick fix' to resolve short-term, functionally-based, operational problems. According to Davenport (1993a, p. 1):

> process innovation combines the adoption of a process view of the business with the application of innovation to key processes. What is new and distinctive about this combination is its enormous potential for helping any organisation achieve major reductions in process cost or time, or major improvements in quality, flexibility, service levels, or other business objectives.

The author cites a number of examples where firms have gained competitive advantage through process innovation. At IBM Credit, the preparation time for supplying potential customers with a quotation for either purchasing or leasing a computer was reduced from seven days to only one. The result was a tenfold increase in the number of quotes prepared for customers. Another example cited by the author is the insurance company, Mutual Benefit Life, which was trying to offset a declining real estate portfolio and, with the use of IT, actually halved the costs associated with its policy underwriting and insurance process. Similarly, the US Internal Revenue Service made significant gains through process innovation by collecting 33% more dollars from taxpayers with only half its former staff and as many as a third fewer branches.

Unlike functionally-based innovation and change programmes, process innovation is deemed to work only if it is supported by senior management, all of whom buy into a carefully thought-through strategic vision of where the business *is* going, and where it *should* be going. Table 6.5 draws a distinction between the less ambitious process improvement, which Davenport (1993a) asserts will not achieve significant improvements in business performance, and process innovation, which is all encompassing and designed to equip companies to compete more effectively with their rivals.

Davenport recognises that process innovation has a competitor in the form of business process redesign or re-engineering (BPR). However, he argues that the term *process innovation* is more appropriate for encapsulating an ambitious innovation and change programme for a number of reasons. Thus,

> Re-engineering is only part of what is necessary in the radical change process; it refers specifically to the design of a new process. The term process innovation encompasses the envisioning of new work strategies, the actual process design activity, and the implementation of the change in all its complex technological, human, and organisational dimensions (Davenport, 1993b, p. 2)

He asserts that process management was discovered and successfully implemented by Japanese companies. This, he believes, is an important factor in explaining the success of many Japanese manufacturing firms throughout the 1980s and 1990s. In particular, Japanese firms have improved the processes of product development,

Table 6.5   *Process improvement and process innovation*

	Process improvement	Process innovation
Level of change	Incremental	Radical
Starting point	Existing process	Clean slate
Frequency of change	One-time/continuous	One-time
Time required	Short	Long
Participation	Bottom-up	Top-down
Typical slope	Narrow, within functions	Broad, cross-functional
Risk	Moderate	High
Primary enabler	Statistical control	Information technology
Type of change	Cultural	Cultural/statistical

Adapted from: Davenport (1993a, p. 11).

logistics and sales and marketing. This logic reinforces the work of Schonberger (1982) who argues that Japanese manufacturing companies' interest in breaking down (isolating) business processes into their component parts, and measuring their performance with a view to improving them (continuous improvement), has been a major contributory factor in securing worldclass competitive success. Notwithstanding these points, the work of Schonberger was published in the early to mid 1980s when the Japanese economy was still booming. In more recent years, Japan's economy has undergone major economic shocks with a downturn in manufacturing performance, increased unemployment and uncompetitive goods (Hori, 1993; Currie and Yoshikawa, 1995). To this end, cross-national comparisons of innovation and change programmes, such as BPR, should not preclude an analysis of the bigger picture, i.e. one that considers the national and international economic climate.

A Customer-Driven Approach

Davenport asserts that process innovation is invariably 'customer driven'. He cites the automobile and retail industries as two key examples. He contends that, due to the intense global competition in the 1980s, automobile manufacturers forced their suppliers to improve the quality, speed and timeliness of their manufacturing and delivery processes. This was done in a number of ways from just-in-time (JIT) production management and control systems to materials requirements planning (MRP) and manufacturing resource planning II (MRP II) initiatives. However, the result was a general improvement in operations between customer and supplier, as suppliers were invariably forced to accept lower profit margins than before. In the retail industry, Davenport shows how Wal-Mart has established practices of 'continuous replenishment, supplier shelf management, and simplified communications that have significantly influenced its suppliers, including such giants as General Electric' (p. 3). He asserts that both the automobile and retailing industries demonstrate that IT-enabled innovation and change has played a crucial part in achieving business benefits. He cites this as further evidence of the success of process innovation.

Like Hammer and Champy (1993), Davenport places senior management at centre stage in defining the strategic vision for innovation and change. He contends that process innovation is a company-wide programme that relies on effective management and leadership. Companies are seen as comprising a variety of important and not so important business processes. Davenport asserts that it is the responsibility of business managers to identify the key processes and seek ways to improve them. He recognises that this may be difficult given the complex nature of many organisations. However, he claims that even if only 10–20 business processes are improved, this will greatly enhance overall performance and, in turn, vastly improve the bottom line. By advocating the development of 'cross-functional solutions', Davenport believes he is offering an alternative from traditional business approaches which he considers are too 'functionally based'. In adopting this position, he seeks to outline the fundamentals of process innovation. He claims that a 'process view of the business' is a change in perspective. It means turning the organisation 'on its head', or 'on its side'. A process view takes into account 'elements of structure, focus, measurement, ownership, and customers'. He claims that

> In definitional terms, a process is simply a structured, measured set of activities designed to produce a specified output for a particular customer or market. It implies a strong emphasis on *how* work is done within an organisation, in contrast to a product focus's emphasis on *what*. A process is thus a specific ordering of work activities across time and place, with a beginning, an end, and clearly identified inputs and outputs: a structure for action. This structural element of processes is key to achieving the benefits of process innovation. Unless designers or participants can agree on the way work is and should be structured, it will be very difficult to systematically improve, or effect innovation in, that work (Davenport, 1993a, p. 5).

Similarly, Earl (1994, p. 7) differentiates between core and support business processes. He asserts that core processes are those which are 'central to business functioning, which relate directly to external customers. They are commonly the primary activities of the value chain.' Support processes, on the other hand, are those 'which have internal customers and are the back up (or "back office") of core processes. They will commonly be more administrative secondary activities of the value chain.' Davenport asserts that 'hundreds of firms' in the United States and Europe are introducing some form of process innovation. But he cautions that this form of innovation will only be successful if managers in these firms change the 'existing Western paradigm' which perceives performance improvement and innovation as two activities in isolation from traditional managerial work (p. 23). He voices a common criticism about Western management that innovation and performance improvement is placed in the hands of '*ad-hoc* cross functional teams' or project teams, task forces, steering committees or even individuals rather than being managed and co-ordinated by senior executives. Here innovation is treated as a 'one-off' activity which leads to the adoption of various 'off-the-shelf' initiatives which are rarely successful. This is also witnessed by the Western managerial paradigm where management consultants are commonly brought in to manage innovation by developing IT strategies, JIT production management and control systems, TQM and team-building, re-engineering programmes and a whole host of other initiatives designed to improve performance. Yet according to Davenport, process innovation is only likely to be successful if senior managers are fully involved and committed, and can motivate their staff. He outlines a framework for process innovation which consists of five steps (p. 24)

1. identifying processes for innovation;
2. identifying change levers;
3. developing process visions;
4. understanding existing processes;
5. designing and prototyping the new process.

This framework shows many similarities with the work of Porter and Millar (1985), McFarlan (1984) and Earl (1989), not to mention BPR as advocated by Hammer and Champy (1993), since it invites managers to consider carefully their innovation and change strategies. Along with the previous authors, Davenport's (1993a) work is prescriptive since it advocates that senior managers should engage in 'process orientated thinking'. Yet unlike the previous studies, the above framework for process innovation places a greater emphasis upon perceiving business activities as a series of interrelated processes, with the recommendation that firms should reduce their processes and eliminate or incorporate other processes. One of the attractions of process innovation as a complement to existing frameworks arises because recent developments in information and communications technologies have led to greater possibilities for functional integration between and within companies, suppliers and customers. However, the potential scale and scope of BPR in an organisational setting have led to criticisms about the concept that it is inherently difficult to implement (Davenport and Stoddart, 1993).

Organisational Learning

The concept of organisational learning became popular from the late 1970s to the early 1990s (Senge, 1990a,b). It is a difficult concept to define since it embodies intangible processes of knowledge and skills generation, and shared insights, experiences and memory (Argyris, 1977; Stata, 1989; Huber, 1993; Garvin, 1993; Fiol and Lyles, 1985). There seem to be many competing interpretations of organisational learning, with some writers even referring to *the learning organisation* and its advantages for business (Senge, 1990a). According to Garvin (1993, p. 80) 'a learning organisation is an organisation skilled at creating, acquiring, and transferring knowledge, and at modifying its behaviour to reflect new knowledge and insights'. Alternatively, 'organisational learning means the process of improving actions through better knowledge and understanding' (Fiol and Lyles, 1985), or, 'an entity learns if, through its processing of information, the range of its potential behaviours is changed' (Huber, 1993). Levitt and March (1988) state that, 'organisations are seen as learning by encoding inferences from history into routines that guide behaviour'.

Argyris (1977), on the other hand, says that 'organisational learning is a process of detracting and correcting error'. Another interpretation is given by Stata (1989) who states that 'organisational learning occurs through shared insights, knowledge, and mental models ... (and) builds on past knowledge and experience—that is, on memory'. Irrespective of the definition adopted, organisational learning tends to address cultural issues about how people work together, share ideas and use their experience. Whilst the concept places people at centre stage of organisations, it tends to ignore some of the political processes that influence behaviour, in particular how people may choose not to share ideas and information for their own political or career objectives (Hibbard and Carrillo, 1998). To this end, the notion of a shared value system or shared *organisational objectives* which underpins so much of the literature on organisational learning becomes problematic when placed in an individual, personal organisational context.

Knowledge Management

The concept of knowledge management first emerged in the 1960s (Drucker, 1969) with the recognition that post-industrial society was characterised more by intellectual as opposed to manual work. Since then, the concept has been adopted by many writers and has become increasingly popular at the end of the twentieth century (Inkpen, 1996). Knowledge management is best understood as complex, multilayered and multifaceted (Blackler, 1995). It is about, 'creating, acquiring, capturing, sharing and using knowledge'. Nonaka (1991) divides knowledge into two forms: *explicit* and *tacit*. He claims that explicit knowledge is formal and systematic. It is therefore easily communicated and shared throughout the organisation. For example, explicit knowledge is embodied in a computer program or set of procedures for hiring staff, etc. Organisations are full of examples of explicit knowledge, indicated by their various administrative procedures and controls.

Tacit knowledge, on the other hand, is defined as 'highly personal' and not amenable to formalisation and standardisation. In addition, tacit knowledge is not easily communicated to others. Nonaka (1991, p. 98) claims that

> tacit knowledge is also deeply rooted in action and in an individual's commitment to a specific context—a craft or profession, a particular technology or product market, or the activities of a work group or team. Tacit knowledge consists partly of technical skills—the kind of informal, hard to pin down skills captured in the term 'know-how'. A master craftsman after years of experience develops a wealth of expertise 'at his finger-tips.' But he is often unable to articulate the scientific or technical principles behind what he knows.

Nonaka (1991) argues that the knowledge-creating company should attempt to make tacit knowledge explicit. This is likely to be achieved in the ubiquitous team approach adopted by Japanese companies where individuals work together in an attempt to create and share knowledge for product development and technological innovation.

In recent years, many companies have incorporated knowledge management policies into their corporate strategies (Davenport *et al.*, 1998). Many software and computing services companies sell knowledge-based systems (KBSs), tools and techniques to their clients. Such systems (among other things) attempt to codify tacit knowledge into formal systems. Yet this may 'generate its own pathology [as] the informal and locally situated practices that allow the firm to cope with uncertainty, may become rigidified by the system' (Scarbrough, 1999). Swan *et al.* (1999) claim that paradoxically, 'whilst knowledge management tools may increase the effectiveness with which existing knowledge is exploited, they may simultaneously reduce the knowledge creating potential of the organisation'. They argue that knowledge management must not neglect 'human issues and people management practices'. Otherwise, it may simply be another panacea or 'fad to forget people' (Swan *et al.*, 1999).

A COMPARATIVE ANALYSIS OF MANAGEMENT INNOVATION AND CHANGE PANACEAS

It is apparent from the above discussion that the management innovation and change panaceas that have emerged in the post-war period all share a common set of characteristics which we include under seven themes:

1. company-wide approach,
2. philosophical change,
3. business improvement,
4. top-down led and managed,
5. IT-enabled,
6. management consultancy driven,
7. formulaic application.

Company-Wide Approach

As we have witnessed above, the seven panaceas from TQM to knowledge management all recommend that successful results will only occur if a company-wide, or processual approach is adopted. The terminology varies from programme to programme, yet the message is the same in each case. For example, the literature on TQM contends that quality improvements will only arise if all members of the organisation 'buy-into' the TQM philosophy. This includes top management right down to the shopfloor, with the latter offering their ideas and suggestions for continuous improvement. Similarly, BPR and knowledge management, both coming some years later, adopt the same rhetoric. In the case of BPR, senior managers should begin the analysis of their organisation using a 'blank sheet of paper', and not be distracted by existing hierarchies, information flows and other factors which may impede change.

Equally, knowledge management can only be successfully implemented if management seeks to 'stockpile workers' knowledge and make it accessible to others via a searchable application' (Cole-Gomolski, 1997). Even the more cost-focused concept of ABC asserts that managers need to identify cost drivers across the entire organisation if they are to understand 'cost consuming activities'. In addition, process innovation argues for the same all-encompassing approach where change incorporates a thorough examination of people, processes, technologies, structures and markets. Organisational learning also presumes an important role for senior management in creating cultures which are conducive to the sharing of ideas, information and experiences. The all-embracing, company-wide approach is a common theme in all seven panaceas, the only identifiable difference being the priorities and practices managers attach to organisational change.

Philosophical Change

Another common characteristic running through the seven panaceas is their focus upon philosophical change, or cultural change. BPR is perhaps the most revolutionary approach since it calls for a complete departure from the past and a new beginning exemplified by the 'automate or liquidate' scenario. TQM, JIT and organisational learning, on the other hand, are less radical since they perceive change in a more evolutionary way. Continuous improvement, which is a key objective of TQM, is a departure from the radical and revolutionary approach of BPR and process innovation. All seven panaceas claim that a philosophical change is necessary to achieve real benefits in business performance. In the case of TQM, the focus is upon quality improvement, broadly defined. In this context, managers and staff are expected to continuously seek ways to improve the quality of products, and the business processes that support them. JIT is equally about a change in the way people carry out their work, with the emphasis upon maximising the way manufacturing resources are used. ABC is intended to be a move away from measuring costs using traditional management accounting methods and techniques. It also recommends that managers change their 'mindset' from measuring direct labour, materials and overheads, to measuring multiple cost drivers as a means of attributing overhead costs to activities and then to products. Both BPR and process innovation are labelled as new 'philosophies' rather than a narrow set of tools and techniques for management. Organisational learning is, in part, a response to the changing shape of organisations, from tall, hierarchical structures to flatter, networked structures. Similarly, knowledge management is about 'empowering' people to make decisions rather than simply to follow rules. By advocating philosophical or cultural change, each of the seven panaceas stresses they should not be seen narrowly as a 'toolbox of techniques', but instead, as a complete departure from traditional organisational and managerial methods and practices.

Business Improvement

Business improvement is another theme that is central to all seven approaches. The scale and scope differs considerably, and it is apparent that contradictions arise when comparing the revolutionary approach to organisational change of BPR to the more subtle approach of TQM and organisational learning. An overview of the literature from TQM to knowledge management highlights a somewhat 'Utopian' message that companies will vastly improve their performance if they embark upon a comprehensive management change programme. All seven panaceas are intended to achieve both quantitative and qualitative benefits. TQM will enhance quality, JIT will improve customer and supplier relationships, ABC will improve cost monitoring and control, BPR will make business processes more efficient, process innovation will fuse IT with HRM and lead to 'dramatic improvements in business performance' (Davenport, 1993a, p. 1), organisational learning will result in the sharing or ideas and experiences, and knowledge management will help project intellectual assets by the codification of tacit knowledge. Many writers attempt to evaluate the contribution of specific panaceas, yet few empirical studies exist which pinpoint their results over a lengthy period of time (three to five years). Indeed, the usual approach for writers is to speculate the success or failure of specific panaceas in different organisational settings (e.g. business sectors), but without following this up with longitudinal research. This often creates a somewhat uneven interpretation between the rhetoric and reality of different panaceas.

Top-Down Led and Managed

All seven panaceas assert that it is essential to win top management support if they are to be successful in practice. This circular and prescriptive view stresses that management should have a strategic vision of how to design and implement a successful change programme. Such rhetoric tends to be based upon apolitical and one-dimensional logic, since success stories are those companies that *effectively* implemented a specific panacea, and unsuccessful ones are those that have failed in the process! To support this argument, those who advocate change programmes tend to select only those companies that qualify as either successful or unsuccessful examples, often explaining the differences in a glib or superficial way. Few studies report that results were partially successful. Writing about process innovation, Davenport (1993b, p. 285) asserts that,

> A clear vision of what is wrong and how to fix existing management processes is a necessary prerequisite for management process innovation. The vision may be of either the management process or its result, but it must be clear, measurable, and inspirational enough to motivate behaviour change; because managers will have to change substantially before a process orientation can take hold, the vision must be even more compelling than for most operational processes.

Similar logic is used in TQM and other change programmes. One problem with such rhetoric is that management is treated as an homogeneous group, all sharing the same ideological, political, organisational and practical objectives. Clearly, research on management has shown that such a group is highly differentiated by hierarchy, ambition, power, politics, status, qualifications, etc. (Knights and Murray, 1994), and can therefore not be treated as a cohesive group, all of whom desire similar outcomes from change programmes.

IT-Enabled

The role of IT or 'new technology', broadly defined, is central to the development of all seven approaches. For example, in the case of TQM and JIT, new process and product technologies play an essential part in spearheading the need for change. Customers are seen to demand higher quality products, at a reasonable price and on the expected delivery date. The process technologies which make new products must also be of a high standard. Achieving the goals from TQM and JIT are therefore dependent upon a range of new technologies from CAD, CAM, robotics and others, and also from information systems such as MRP and MRP II. Similarly, the concept of ABC is based upon rhetoric which claims that new technology has significantly altered the way costs can and should be measured in manufacturing industry. For example, the reduction in direct labour costs in manufacturing brought about, in part, by the introduction of advanced manufacturing technology (AMT) should be reflected in changes to the cost management system, where the cost drivers for indirect or variable costs are properly understood. Equally, BPR and process innovation also place IT at centre stage of the change process. Writing on BPR, Hammer and Champy (1993, p. 83) claim that 'A company that cannot change the way it thinks about IT cannot re-engineer. A company that equates technology with automation cannot re-engineer. A company that looks for problems first and then seeks technology solutions for them cannot re-engineer.' These authors claim that 'modern, state of the art IT is part of any re-engineering effort, an *essential enabler*, since it permits companies to re-engineer business processes'. Knowledge management also emphasises the role of IT in helping to codify tacit knowledge, even to the point of overlooking some of the more political and self-seeking behaviours or people.

Management Consultancy Driven

The influence of management consultancy is a further factor which combines the seven approaches. In the case of TQM, North American writers such as Crosby, Deming and Juran spearheaded the quality movement with a view to improving business performance in their own country. TQM was then transferred to Japan in the post-war period and later transferred back to the United States, when manufacturing industry was perceived to be in a state of chronic economic decline. JIT has also been peddled by a range of management consultancy firms—as a method and technique to control inventory in the West, and a *philosophy* which incorporates production management methods, quality assurance and total preventive maintenance (TPM) in Japan (Wu *et al.*, 1992). ABC, BPR and process innovation were all management consultancy *inventions* of the late 1980s and early 1990s. Organisational learning spawned a management consultancy *industry* in organisational development (OD) and, more recently, knowledge management has been 'black-boxed' as technology for implementation in client companies (Scarbrough, 1999). Since management consultancy firms are keen to develop *new and innovative business solutions* for their clients, it is little wonder that each successive panacea invites criticism for being simply a *re-tread* (mixture) of past ideas and approaches.

Formulaic Application

An interesting observation about the seven panaceas is how they are all driven by a set of formulaic methods and techniques. Notwithstanding the fact that organisational change is a complex process, marked by different market, technical and managerial contexts, each approach tends to follow a linear or sequential path. Issues about context, size and environment tend to be lost by the rhetoric, which assumes that *one size fits all*. Indeed, the advocates of all the panaceas rarely address contextual differences such as business sector, company size, country of origin (of company), etc.

Using some of the language and terms associated with the seven panaceas, Table 6.6 compares them in six ways. First, the starting point of TQM tends to focus upon quality issues, whereas JIT is aimed at improving manufacturing performance and ABC aims to identify cost drivers. The later panaceas of BPR and process innovation are wide-ranging, with the former assuming that managers can design business processes using a *blank sheet of paper*. Organisational learning is more obscure since it stresses the importance of shared meanings in spite of the complexity of modern organisations. At a more technical level, knowledge management embraces the core competency debate (Hamel and Prahalad, 1994) since it assumes that managers can identify what is useful knowledge in addition to being about to codify such knowledge using technology.

Writing on the similarities between TQM and BPR, Hammer and Champy (1993, p. 216) recognised that some people questioned the authenticity of the latter approach and so put forward the view that

Table 6.6   *A comparative analysis of the key business drivers for seven innovation and change programmes*

Business drivers	TQM	JIT	ABC	BPR	Process innovation	Organisational learning	Knowledge management
Starting point	Quality audit/assessment	Manufacturing performance	Identify cost drivers	Blank sheet of paper	Clean slate, multidimensional	Shared insights	Core competencies
Scope of change	Continuous	Incremental	Ongoing	Revolutionary	Radical	Evolutionary	Multilayered/multifaceted
Typical slope	Company-wide	Cross-functional	Total cost control	Broad, cross-functional	Processual, cross-functional	Dominant culture	Worker empowerment
Risk	Medium	Medium	Medium	High	High	Low	Medium
Primary enabler	Customer focus	Supply chain management	Performance measurement	HRM/IT-enabled	IT	History, memory, experiences	Codifying knowledge
Type of change	Cultural	Technical	Administrative	Structural	Processual	Behavioural	Systemic

Re-engineering and TQM are neither identical nor in conflict; they are complementary. While they share a focus on customers and processes, there are also important differences between them. Re-engineering gets a company where it needs to be fast; TQM moves a company in the same direction, but more slowly. Re-engineering is about dramatic, radical change; TQM involves incremental adjustment. Both have their place. TQM should be used to keep a company's processes tuned up between the periodic process replacements that only re-engineering could accomplish. In addition, TQM is built into a company's culture, can go on working without much day to day attention from management. Re-engineering, in contrast, is an intensive, top-down, vision driven effort that requires non-stop senior management participation and support.

Whilst the authors are optimistic about the ease with which BPR and TQM can be implemented and work successfully in the same organisation, they provide virtually no empirical evidence to support their view.

LEARNING FROM PAST IDEAS

A cursory glance at the management literature shows that managing change is a dominant theme. What tends to change are the ideologies, methods and practices of managing change (Keen, 1981). This has continued throughout the last century and will no doubt continue into the twenty-first century. The seven business and management panaceas discussed above have generated much interest in the business and academic communities in recent years. The extent to which they offer fresh analysis to problems related to technology, organisation and management is open to question. By and large, each *new* panacea tends to attract much interest, albeit for a relatively short space of time. This has happened with ABC, BPR, process innovation and organisational learning, and to a lesser extent with TQM and JIT. Knowledge management is still popular, but for how long remains open to speculation. Two important questions arise from our overview of the above panaceas. First, do they each offer a distinct approach to understanding and resolving issues and problems in the field of business and management? Second, why is their value to the business and management community relatively short?

With regard to the first question, it is apparent when we refer to past ideas within the field that each panacea addresses issues and problems that are not in themselves new. Indeed, if we divide earlier work into three overlapping categories, we find that numerous studies emerged. For example, Taylor (1911) developed the concept (panacea) of scientific management. This work was instigated to elicit data on how work was carried out in the context of time and motion studies. Taylor's ideas continue to be discussed today and are very relevant to current thinking about BPR (Mumford, 1999). Fayol's (1949) study on the principles of management has further influenced later studies on corporate planning (Ackoff, 1970) and competitive strategy (Porter, 1980). Even the current interest in knowledge management makes assumptions about the type of people who should be in positions of power and authority, their capabilities and skills, and how intellectual assets are used. Similarly, the socio-technical approach (Trist and Bamforth, 1951) offers insights into human behaviour in the context of their working environment, which is relevant to TQM and organisational learning. Unlike latter-day panaceas, some of the more enduring earlier ideas were not to be dressed up and packaged solely as the products of management consultancies, but were instead the output of large-scale academic research work.

The answer to the second question is possibly found in the previous sentence. The influence of management consultants in developing and promoting recent panaceas has had very mixed reviews. As many companies *implement* BPR and knowledge management (or at least their own versions of them), some of these companies claim to have previously introduced TQM and JIT. Yet TQM and BPR share many similarities; so do JIT and knowledge management given that both are intended to provide management with timely, reliable and useful data. This suggests that by viewing the different panaceas as the *products* of management consultancy firms, their popularity and usefulness can be explained in terms of a product life-cycle approach. To this end, once BPR has served its purpose in redesigning and rationalising business processes, it is no longer useful. Since few people are prepared to look to past ideas for an explanation of a current technical, organisational or managerial issue or problem, it is little wonder that each new panacea seems to offer the desired solution (or quick fix). This is in spite of the fact that the methodologies and techniques relating to each panacea tend to remain underdeveloped (Currie, 1999a).

CASE STUDY—BPR AND THE 'NEW BANK' VISION

The Columbus Project at Royal Bank of Scotland

As a consequence of intense competition in the financial services industry, Royal Bank of Scotland embarked on the Columbus project in 1992. As an exercise in radical BPR, the project was conceptualised as a wide-ranging solution to growing competition, not just from other banks but also from building societies and insurance companies. Senior managers at the bank conceded that lifetime customer loyalty was no longer guaranteed. Indeed, customers were becoming more in-tune with the range of financial services offered by competitors, and were becoming fickle in their choice of financial institutions. With Columbus, the bank hoped to become 'the best retail bank in the UK by 1997', and this would be achieved by implementing major changes to structures, products, services, job titles and roles, training policies, technology and marketing/sales. A summary of the key strategic objectives of the Columbus project are given below:

- The Branch Banking Division (BBD) would be organised around three customer streams—retail, commercial and corporate.
- New managerial roles would be introduced network-wide during 1995.
- Each branch would have ready access to specialist centres and knowledge without having to house all the traditional back office functions.
- Five branches would test the New Branch Design.
- Well over £100 million would be committed to developing new technology.
- HR policies and processes would be designed to reflect the new organisation.

Essentially the Columbus project team was set up to identify how these changes would be achieved. According to senior managers, it was crucial that line management were the 'focus for building the New Bank'. Comments made by senior managers in the business units and Technology Division stressed that, in spite of millions of pounds invested in new technology, few tangible benefits had arisen in the business units. Columbus was intended to be more than simply a large-scale IT project. Instead it was a re-engineering project conceptualised and planned by senior executives with the aim of revolutionising the entire bank. Six key inter-related areas were identified as comprising the Columbus project. They are discussed in sequence.

A New Philosophy for Work Organisation

Perhaps the most important challenge of Columbus involved changing peoples' attitudes to encourage them to embrace *new philosophies* of work organisation. People were expected to be 'empowered' in the new banking environment. Banks were renowned for being highly bureaucratic and regimented and senior managers were aware that some customers were intimidated by this image. It was pointed out that the old emphasis on geographical splits was no longer appropriate and this had given way to a different structure which established three distinct but interrelated businesses—retail (for personal and business customers), commercial and corporate. To facilitate this structural change, new managerial roles were required which clearly distinguished between sales and service responsibilities. Corporate customers were believed to require a different service level from personal/domestic customers. Several interviewees at the bank were sceptical about these changes, particularly where they viewed empowerment as detrimental to their own status, career and promotion prospects. This issue is discussed later.

New Technology

In common with the proponents of re-engineering, new technology was perceived as an enabling factor for translating BPR vision into practice. With over £100 million invested in new technology the bank was hoping to achieve a *seamless service* for its customers. Irrespective of the type of services required, technology would integrate services across the network. One senior manager cautioned that

> Technology is a key component of our change programme but we have not fallen into the trap of seeing technology as an end in itself. Rather it is being used as a means of improving business performance and of producing that essential seamless service.

The bank was aware of the high-profile, large-scale IT disasters such as the Taurus fiasco which beset the International London Stock Exchange in 1993 (Currie, 1994) and, to this end, attempted to impose more stringent checks and balances for evaluating IT performance. As one senior IT manager pointed out, 'IT should not be perceived as a quick fix panacea for BPR or any other large scale project.'

The Outlet

The Columbus project was designed to improve service levels throughout the entire banking outlets. IT-enabled re-engineering was planned to achieve consistent levels of services where entire transactions would be conducted in front of the customer. Senior managers hoped to reduce the risk of fraudulent transactions by improving customer identification methods. The New Branch PC-based system would have three main components: Customer Service, Cashier/Teller and Account Opening. In the past, technology was perceived by senior managers as 'not always delivering appropriate technical solutions to a particular business problem'. As such, technology developments would no longer be planned in an 'ivory tower'. Communication between project sponsors (those who commission IT systems), project managers, analyst/programmers (those who manage and design IT systems) and users would need to improve. According to one project manager, 'technology developments should not be left to the Technology Division alone, but to the business users as well'.

Improvements from IT-enabled re-engineering were sought in three areas:

1.   proposed technology developments would be *user friendly*;
2.   staff would feel confident about using the new system; and
3.   customers would equally wish to use the technology.

Facilitated by current technical developments, changes to the outlets were planned to enable staff in branches to become more directly involved in serving their customers. The new branch design was being tested in five different prototypes and was designed to utilise space to, 'create more flexible surroundings for staff to work in and a welcoming environment for customers to conduct business . . . Gone are the forbidding exteriors, regimented queuing zones and glass screens. Instead, a more welcoming layout invites customers to feel comfortable.'

According to one senior manager, BPR should not simply be perceived in terms of how it changes bureaucratic or technical systems of the banking business. It is also about changing customer perceptions of the bank. Customers should not feel intimidated when they enter a bank, nor should they be faced with long queues. An important activity was to monitor customer perceptions about the new look of the bank. Thus the physical appearance of the new branches was another element of BPR and though it was accepted that some customers would not like the new set-up and withdraw their custom, others would be won.

The Network

Major changes to the network were a further element of the Columbus project. The traditional set-up where each branch was a *mini-bank* in its own right was gradually being phased out. Instead, each branch would have access to specialist centres and knowledge without having to house all the traditional back office functions. New specialist centres would be set up such as a Mortgage Centre serving the whole network, and UK-wide Mortgage Shops. Some 18 Corporate Centres housing specially selected relationship managers were planned where these individuals would develop close links with corporate customers. In addition, 15 Service

Centres strategically located throughout the United Kingdom would deal with traditional back office functions. At the time of interview, centralised cheque returns would initially be handled by the Service Centres, but ultimately outsourced to EDS (a major outsourcing supplier). Part of the rationale for these changes was to facilitate a situation where customers would become customers of the bank and not of a branch. These changes were described as 'a total re-engineering of current practices', where many services would move from a manual system 'with all its inevitable inconsistencies' to a computer-based system.

Credit Processes

Credit processes were further being re-engineered primarily to achieve efficiency gains and consistency in credit policies and lending decisions. Technology was essential for this goal to speed up processes and automate administration. A document obtained from the bank stressed that 'Our credit process will comprise an effective team-lending approach between relationship manager, analyst and sanctioner.'

Human Resources and Teamworking

The final element of the Columbus project concerned major changes in human resource policies and practices. This was recognised by senior managers as the most challenging of all six elements of the Columbus project, yet arguably one which was given least detailed attention by the bank. A document obtained from the bank repeated a popular slogan expressed by many organisations:

> None of our planned improvements are possible without the support of our staff. It is only through our people that we can hope to reach our goal of becoming the best bank in the UK by the millennium.

Theoretically these changes would encourage staff to take charge of their own careers, in that promotion would no longer be based upon *keeping your nose clean*, but on achievement and ability. The same document observed that

> No industry or sector is immune from market forces. Banking is no exception. The current competitive situation calls for different skills and much more flexible working practices. In a world where technological improvements can be copied, it is the people element which is often the only true differentiator . . . We believe that it is through our staff that true change will occur.

The above six elements of the Columbus project were wide-ranging and politically contentious. To enact such changes demanded the attention of numerous bank personnel from the Business Units and Technology Division. To this end, several multidisciplinary teams were formed to translate the New Bank vision into a practical reality.

Implementing the 'New Bank' Vision

Initial interviews with senior managers from the Business Units and Technology Division confirmed that IT-enabled re-engineering was a major element of the

Columbus project. As suggested elsewhere, senior managers were cautious about large-scale investment in IT given past failures. IT-enabled re-engineering was no exception and was not perceived as a technical 'quick fix' for the various business units. Sentiments of this nature reinforce Hammer and Champy's (1993) claim that as many as 70% of radical re-engineering projects fail, many involving large-scale IT investment. According to the Head of the Technology Division, there was no correlation between level of investment in IT and project success. With over £100 million invested in new technologies, Columbus was not simply a large-scale IT project, but a large scale BPR project to 'revolutionise existing business processes'.

Unlike past failures in IT, senior managers from the Business Units were keen to align IT with the corporate strategic vision. In the past, users had complained that computer systems had simply been imposed upon them from the Technology Division with little regard to their relevance for the business. Technical staff, on the other hand, complained that users changed their minds frequently about what it was they required (e.g. what a computer system was intended to do and how it would be developed).

Sometimes IT projects spun out of control. The consequences were escalating costs, a failure to meet delivery dates, a loss of management control, low morale among users and the technical team, and the emergence of a 'blame culture'. Failed IT projects were viewed by the Business Units as the responsibility of the Technology Division. IT managers were accused of not listening to their customers, poor project management, not following procedures and methodologies, and failing to understand the *business situation*. The Technology Division usually responded with comments that business customers did not know what they required as a technical solution for a specific business problem, were technically 'illiterate', were 'lunched to death' by large computer suppliers (therefore purchased hardware and software which was not appropriate for their requirement), and constantly imposed system changes even though the functional and technical specifications for the proposed computer system had been authorised. The Columbus project was intended to deal with the problems engendered by the separation of the Business Units and Technology Division. With Columbus, all staff were expected to become involved in re-engineering the business.

Aligning Business Strategy With Technology Through Re-Engineering

Tracking the development of the Columbus project over a two-year period suggested that aligning business strategy with technology through re-engineering was still a distant goal. What emerged from interviewing senior managers from the Business Units and IT managers and technical staff from the Technology Division, was that a wide gulf existed between the two areas. The Technology Division was perceived as a *support function* for the business and one that was not strategic or even necessary according to some senior executives who thought it should be outsourced. These views are well documented in the literature (Currie, 1995a; Friedman and Cornford, 1989). Yet they are important in this context since structural and cultural divisions engendered by the separation of technical services from the business are significant for our understanding of large-scale, IT-enabled re-engineering.

For the Columbus project to be effective, it was highly dependent upon the design and implementation of effective computer systems, designed in-house by the Technology Division and externally by software suppliers and consultancies. In recent months, the bank had shed about 2000 jobs, with a further 1500 planned job losses over the next two years. Against a background of large-scale redundancies, the role of technology was becoming even more political. Many of the job losses were in middle management where *old skills* were perceived to be redundant in the New Bank environment. Within the Technology Division, the bank hired as many as 40% external IT contractors for some projects. Two reasons were paramount for pursuing such a strategy. The first was to hire IT staff according to the peaks and troughs of computer projects. As stated elsewhere, some senior managers viewed IT as a support function that was not critical to the core activities of banking. As such, hiring IT contractors reflected the desire of some senior managers to pursue an IT outsourcing policy. The second was to hire *expert* technical skills, which were not available internally. Many IT contractors possessed scarce PC-based skills which were perceived as essential for the realisation of the New Bank Columbus project.

Developing Project Management Skills

In 1994 the bank had hired a firm of consultants to develop and administer core competency tests to its senior and middle managers. Some 44 managerial jobs were shed as a result of these *pseudo-scientific* tests. Interviews carried out with managers and technical staff suggested that, against a backdrop of large-scale job losses, the bank was suffering from serious skill shortages in project management and technical skills (client–server). These skill shortages were perceived as an impediment to the re-engineering efforts of the bank. Yet perceptions about the type of skills required varied within and across managerial and technical grades.

At the project management level, the new PC-based technical environment was threatening managers with traditional skills acquired in previous decades. In some cases, project managers with a mainframe background were not considered to possess the *right skills* for managing client–server technology. Many of these criticisms were voiced by IT contractors who, in some cases, formed an unholy political alliance with senior executives wishing to find legitimate reasons to shed managerial positions in the Business Units and Technology Division.

Interviews with IT staff (permanent and contract) suggested that new skills were needed for project managers which emphasised self-managing teams and autono-mous working practices rather than those that were based on a command and control approach. But the bank was considered to be an old-fashioned establish-ment which continued to be structured according to hierarchical and functional demarcation boundaries. Criticisms about project managers from technical staff (particularly analysts/programmers) suggested they were *out of touch* with the latest technologies. But some technical staff went further by arguing they were poorly placed to manage technology since they had abandoned their technical skills to become managers in the first place. Many technical staff rejected the view that technical knowledge was not essential for managing large-scale, IT-enabled re-engineering projects.

The rigid methodologies used by project managers were also considered to be obsolete by technical staff and even by some of the project managers themselves. According to one senior analyst/programmer:

> My project manager usually asks me to set my own deadlines. He doesn't really understand what it is I do, even though he is responsible for my performance. This works because we have a good working relationship. It's all about trust and respect, not charts, checklists and performance indicators.

In other examples, the opposite was the case where interpersonal relationships between project managers and technical staff had broken down. Interviews suggested that autocratic, rigid project management methods and techniques were inadequate for large-scale computer projects where IT staff were working with the latest client—server technology. As one IT contractor commented:

> Project management is too concerned with rule-based, linear approaches to measuring performance. Just because you measure something doesn't mean you can manage it. The best management practice involves understanding what it is you can't measure. It is very difficult to manage the work of technical people when you don't understand the technology.

Similarly, many project managers were critical about the demands placed upon them to manage large-scale IT projects in a constantly changing business environment. In the past two years the bank had undergone significant organisational, managerial and technical change. The business had been restructured and part of the Columbus project was to see through further fundamental changes in how banking services were offered to customers. This had placed significant demands on managers, many of whom remained nervous about the recent redundancies. Project managers were the interface between the Business Units and Technology Division and had to ensure that appropriate technical solutions were delivered to business customers. But this was proving increasingly difficult in an environment of constant flux. The situation for project managers was worsening since senior executives were attempting to impose stringent performance targets on project managers. In turn, their own performance would be judged according to the outcome of the IT projects they managed. Pressures on project managers were growing and were not ameliorated by the severe skill shortages in specialist technical areas.

Developing Technical Skills

Paradoxically, the technical skills shortages of the bank were not helped by the increasing tendency to hire external IT contractors on short-term (six months to one year) contracts. From a financial perspective, this approach was viewed by senior executives as the most appropriate given the inevitable peaks and troughs of IT work, not to mention the financial constraints on the technical choices of the Business Units. Whereas many permanent IT staff were seen to have traditional mainframe skills, IT contractors were brought in to work on new client—server and other applications. Yet the problems of interfacing programming code written in Fourth

Generation Languages (4 GLs) with the mainframe (COBOL code) proved technically challenging and politically contentious, particularly where people interpreted the development of client—server to be detrimental to their own career interests.

Interviews with the technical team working on the New Branch computer system at the bank raised many issues which were more than just technical quibbles. For example, this project was intended to develop a customer-based system to replace the existing account-based one used by the branches. This would mean that staff would be able to call up all the customer accounts on one screen to carry out fund transfers and monitor transactions, among other tasks. In turn, processing time would be greatly reduced. This would involve the development of many new programs written in SQLWindows which would interface with the legacy (mainframe) system.

Many of the technical staff working on this project were IT contractors, brought in for only six months. During their contract period they encountered numerous obstacles in the development process. An important constraint was that the mainframe was essentially account based and could not easily be changed. Thus each customer enquiry was handled by a separate program pertaining to a particular customer account and the complexity of attempting to call up numerous customer information only added to the intense traffic on the network.

As a result of these problems, the technical team was unable to meet the original business objective of developing a customer-based system within the time and budgetary constraints of their project. This meant that senior managers from the business, and project managers working within the Technology Division, were faced with the dilemma of either (a) developing a less ambitious account-based system, or (b) pursuing the expensive option of developing a full customer-based system. In the end managers decided to follow the first route and dilute the original project spec. But this was felt to be detrimental to the original New Branch computer project. To this end, senior executives attempted to justify their decision on the grounds of changes in the business situation. IT staff, on the other hand, took a different view. One IT contractor commented:

> Senior managers think they know what the business requires, but they don't understand how it can be achieved technically. They seem to think that technical solutions are just a matter of pressing a few buttons on a keyboard. This happens all the time. They come up with a great idea and then we have to tell them it is not technically feasible!

Case study research on developing the Columbus project at Royal Bank of Scotland raised many organisational, managerial, strategic and technical issues which produced a complex picture of a large-scale re-engineering project. We now attempt to address some of these issues and discuss their relevance for existing studies. Notwithstanding the critical literature that has emerged on the theory and practice of re-engineering (Grint and Willcocks, 1995) our case study research highlighted a number of issues that are relevant for the management of large-scale IT projects in general and not just re-engineering projects (Beer *et al.*, 1990; Sauer, 1993; Currie, 1995a). The claim of re-engineering that organisations can embark on process innovation using a *blank sheet of paper* (Hammer and Champy, 1993) is clearly misguided in the context of the organisational, strategic, managerial and technical antecedents of contemporary organisations (Willcocks and Smith,

1995). At Royal Bank of Scotland, re-engineering was not a definitive strategy for addressing important external competitive business and labour market pressures in the banking industry, but a complex, *ad hoc* and fragmented response which was constantly being revised.

The *multidisciplinary holism* at the heart of BPR was little more than a melting pot of conflicting disciplines, coalitions, and interests across managerial and technical groups (Willcocks, 1995b). At the organisational level, the separation of the Business Units from the Technology Division seemed to hinder re-engineering efforts, particularly where managers and technical staff interpreted strategic and operational change in line with their own political interests. Traditional hierarchical and functional boundaries in an industry which is historically conservative did not assist those wishing to enforce new working practices and attitudinal change on its staff. Senior managers from the Business Units perceived the Technology Division as separate from core banking activities even though IT-enabled re-engineering was intended to further integrate technologies throughout the organisation. These views led some senior managers to a position where they felt that outsourcing IT could achieve greater cost efficiencies. Attitudinal differences between business managers and technical staff on the role of IT in re-engineering were wide and reflected institutional communication barriers between the two groups. This was demonstrated by analysing the nature of project management of computer systems development within the Technology Division. Senior managers' attempts at developing the New Branch project were inhibited by their own lack of understanding of technology and also by how computer projects were managed and co-ordinated.

The case study shows that one important organisational issue for re-engineering was the separation of the Business Units from the Technology Division. This influenced the roles and relationships between these two areas and, in turn, the perceptions about the roles of technology and technical staff within BPR and the wider organisation. By perceiving the Technology Division as a support function, senior managers removed decision-making powers from this part of the organisation, although technical considerations were critical to the re-engineering effort. This was witnessed by the realisation that ambitious business objectives involving technology developments were not feasible within the time and budgetary constraints of the New Branch project. Clearly, this demonstrated poor communication between the Business Units and Technology Division.

Project managers who provided an interface between the business and Technology Division faced a difficult challenge as few methodologies and techniques existed which reflected the complex nature of managing large-scale re-engineering. Whilst formal—rational project management and software development methodologies have been heavily criticised for not addressing the 'soft' issues of managing projects and people, these methods and techniques were outdated for the present organisational and technical environment. Client—server technologies apparently demand a new project management style which emphasises a more autonomous and iterative approach to software development rather than one based upon a formal, autocratic *command and control* management style.

The above discussion suggests that a wide gulf exists between the rhetoric and reality of re-engineering. There is no *one best way* of introducing re-engineering since our case study found that no cohesive or comprehensive methodologies or techniques were available for BPR. Traditional project management methodologies were outdated. Yet senior managers were unable to ascertain what new skills and competencies were needed in a re-engineered environment. Senior bank personnel also underplayed the social and political processes of re-engineering, and this appeared to manifest itself in poor communication between the Business Units and Technology Division. In conclusion, the case study research on BPR has not produced the wide-ranging organisational, managerial and technical changes espoused by those who advocate radical, revolutionary change. Whilst some process improvements were apparent, there was little evidence of wide-ranging process innovation. Finally, as organisational, managerial and technical transformation proved difficult to implement, elements of the re-engineering project were simply diluted to accommodate these problems, a phenomenon which explains 'why change programmes don't produce change' (Beer *et al.*, 1990).

SUMMARY

This chapter has given an overview of seven recent business and management panaceas. It offers a comparative analysis of their key business drivers, enabling technologies, methods and tools, and intended business benefits and improvements. This discussion showed that the distinctiveness presupposed by these panaceas is not altogether clear. The rhetoric behind TQM and BPR is very similar, even though the advocates of these approaches stress their uniqueness as solutions for technical, organisational and managerial problems. Similarly, JIT and knowledge management each highlights the importance of information management, yet the overlaps between the two are rarely mentioned in the literature.

Few longitudinal research studies exist which report findings on the development and implementation of panaceas in a specific business sector in comparison with competing panaceas. For example, the introduction of BPR may be similar to TQM a decade before, and it is not clear where one panacea ends and another begins. In addition, the legacy of past ideas is rarely mentioned in terms of how they influence the success or failure rates of new panaceas. Socio-technical systems are relevant to the problems faced by management today, yet their message seems to be eclipsed by the popularity of current panaceas, namely BPR and knowledge management. However, the pace at which panaceas come and go in the latter half of the twentieth century is alarming and unexplained by those who seem to promote them.

The rhetoric that panaceas are unsuccessful if they are not implemented properly (Davenport, 1996) is inadequate and fails to address the issue of their overall usefulness to management in the first place. In conclusion, it seems that if we are to avoid the twenty-first century becoming littered with tried and failed business and management panaceas, we should adhere to some of the lessons from past research, and particularly some of the more enduring ideas (cf. Currie and Galliers, 1999). This is not to suggest that the recent panaceas have no value in diagnosing problems and offering solutions to the modern corporation. Rather, it is to stress that some of these problems may not be new ones, nor do we always need a new panacea or *product* as the solution.

7
The Global IT Outsourcing Marketplace

INTRODUCTION

The concept of IT outsourcing is not new and is related to the use of a third party for the provision of products, services, capabilities and skills. According to Applegate *et al.* (1996, p. 556): 'IT outsourcing is a harbinger of traditional IT department transformation and provides a glimpse at the emerging organisational structures of the information economy.' IT outsourcing dates back to about 1963 when a US company, EDS, signed its first customer (*Computer Weekly*, 1998). Yet companies in a variety of business sectors, from manufacturing to financial services, had been using the services of third party agencies and suppliers for many decades. So terminology to describe the use of third parties has evolved over time and has been mixed. For example, facilities management, contracting-out, supply-chain management, competitive tendering, resourcing and market testing, all indicate the use of third parties. IT outsourcing is perhaps different given the extent to which companies use third parties in their resourcing activities (Loh and Venkatraman, 1992). In the early days (pre-1980s) companies tended to use outsourcing suppliers for what has been described as a *quick fix*. During this time, the term *facilities management* tended to be used instead of outsourcing, and the main business drivers were to reduce costs and gain access to technical capabilities and support.

Companies often used a supplier to manage a large database or network, and these activities could easily be separated from other business processes and operations. The 1980s saw a shift in emphasis where companies started to use outsourcing suppliers for a wider range of services. This corresponded to wider economic and societal changes which saw the emergence of global competition, the further diffusion of information and communications technologies, rationalisation and downsizing of companies, and the need to develop new capabilities and skills in the workforce. According to one source (*Computer Weekly*, 1998), this post 1980s era 'saw the first US$1 billion (US$625 billion) contracts, right through to the Xerox mega-deal' (worth US$3.2 billion).

In the last decade, many companies have justified outsourcing as a desire to focus on their core business competencies[19] (Hamel and Prahalad, 1994). As IT was not seen as a core competence, they reasoned that it could be outsourced to a third party without incurring any loss in overall business performance. Indeed, outsourcing would give management more time to concentrate on more pressing business issues. Such a view has become popular in the 1990s, and has encouraged people to perceive IT as something which is separate from other business processes, functions, and activities (Currie and Glover, 1999). Equally, it has fuelled the tendency to treat IT as a commodity which is readily available in the market-place.

Against this background, this chapter focuses upon IT outsourcing from the client perspective or 'demand side' (Evans, 1994). Chapter 8 looks at the supply side by reviewing the key outsourcing service providers in the software and computing services industry. In what follows, the literature is examined mainly from the United States and the United Kingdom, where outsourcing has become very popular. We begin by looking at how the global IT outsourcing marketplace has expanded in recent years. Forecasts on the growth of IT outsourcing vary considerably, yet it is apparent that outsourcing is expanding both in terms of financial cost (size of contracts) and scope (range of services). A conceptual frame-work on four distinct types of IT sourcing is introduced. This includes: total outsourcing; multiple/selective sourcing; joint venture/strategic alliance outsourcing; and insourcing (i.e. retaining an in-house IT department/facility). This typology is developed from extensive empirical research on US and European experiences of IT sourcing decisions, which found that the outsourcing marketplace is becoming increasingly diverse and complex as companies negotiate second and third generation contracts with their suppliers (Currie and Willcocks, 1998a). The rationale for each type of IT sourcing decision is analysed along with its corresponding risks and rewards.

Finally, the chapter considers four case histories, each of which illustrates a different type of IT sourcing experience. They include: the total outsourcing deal between British Aerospace plc and Computer Services Corporation (CSC); selective sourcing at Grand Metropolitan plc; joint venture/strategic alliance sourcing at Crestco Ltd (a company set up by the Bank of England); and the UK Post Office's decision to retain a large in-house IT department, where it chooses to *insource* technical capabilities and know-how.[20] The findings from this research suggest that companies need to develop their own IT sourcing strategies based upon a thorough market analysis which includes an understanding of the strategic positioning of outsourcing service providers (suppliers), IT skills surpluses and shortages, employment law, and new developments in technology and business practices. This is because *off-the-shelf* IT outsourcing contracts, designed by suppliers, rarely produce the tangible (value-added) benefits which companies seek from their outsourcing experiences.

THE GLOBAL IT OUTSOURCING MARKETPLACE

The 1990s witnessed the growth and maturing of the IT outsourcing market (Saunders *et al.*, 1997). In the late 1980s and early 1990s, senior executives sought ways to leverage outsourcing to control and shape IT costs in conjunction with changing business requirements. Cost savings were often at the root of many outsourcing deals (Takac, 1994). Conversely, many Chief Information Officers (CIOs) and IT directors resisted outsourcing initiatives which they interpreted to be against their interests. Many IT service providers won their initial outsourcing contracts by positioning themselves as the lowest bidders. Their rivals were not only other external IT service providers but also large in-house IT departments. Yet many in-house IT departments found themselves outsourced, as external suppliers often won contracts through their slick presentations to senior executives, many of whom had little knowledge, understanding and experience of IT.

As more companies entered into outsourcing arrangements, they often found external suppliers offered additional value-added services in the form of improved quality of service, more flexible and responsive design and implementation of IT infrastructures and systems, faster access to properly skilled technical staff, better alternative schemes for using technology to improve business functions, and far fewer difficulties in managing organisational and internal political issues. The ongoing drive to re-engineer legacy systems (mainframe and data centres) to alternative architectures (client–server and distributed networks) tended to destabilise many in-house IT departments, thus rendering them vulnerable to the threat of outsourcing (Venkatraman, 1997). Some CIOs and IT directors lost control of IT costs as a trend emerged in North America and, to a lesser extent, in the United Kingdom, where senior management actively decentralised the responsibility for IT to managers and staff across the various business and administrative units (Adler *et al.*, 1992; Boynton *et al.*, 1992). But even this decision was not always effective in controlling costs, particularly where companies were attempting to invest in new technologies while at the same time supporting their legacy infrastructures. As a result, CIOs and IT directors in the mid-1990s onwards increasingly turned to outsourcing as a *panacea* to manage the dilemma of maintaining existing systems and applications and introducing new ones at only a marginally increased cost.

Financial Forecasts

Within the information systems (IS) community and the wider business and management arena, IT outsourcing has become a fruitful research area, not least because of the increase in the size and scope of outsourcing contracts. Whilst the statistics on the IT outsourcing marketplace need to be treated with some caution, it is apparent that an upwards trend has been in place for several years. The global IT outsourcing market is estimated to be growing at a compound annual growth rate (CAGR) of 20.1% to reach US$151 billion in the year 2000. The Yankee Group claim the market was worth about US$121 billion in 1999 (Yankee Group, 1998), with the US market comprising US$116 billion of this figure (see Figure 7.1).

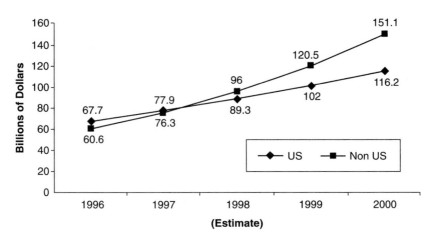

Figure 7.1   *The global IT outsourcing market. Source*: Yankee Group

According to IDC.com, the Western European market is expected to reach US$33.6 billion by 2001. This is approximately a 30% increase from US$22.7 billion in 1996. IDC (1998d) claims that the Western European market represents 26% of the global market and that four of the top ten outsourcing companies are European in origin. Similarly, Infoserver claims that total European IT outsourcing was estimated to be US$15 billion in 1997 and expected to rise to around US$27 billion by 2001. Whilst the United States is the largest global market, the most active markets in Europe are found in the United Kingdom, France and Italy, with the UK market expected to be US$3.7 billion. This is expected to rise to US$7.6 billion in 2000. Another study claims that spending on IT services will increase from US$335 billion in 1997 to nearly US$860 billion by 2002 (CSC.com).

In Western Europe, the IT outsourcing marketplace is also predicted to grow to US$33.6 billion by 2001, a figure which represents approximately 26% of the global outsourcing market; with the 'outsourcing reluctant' countries in Europe such as Germany, Belgium and Italy becoming more interested in outsourcing. In other parts of the world such as SE Asia, Australia, Canada and India, large outsourcing suppliers are eager to win new business with companies keen to reduce their costs and gain access to new capabilities and skills.

In the United Kingdom, privatisation witnessed through market testing, compulsory competitive tendering (CCT) and contracting out have led to large outsourcing contracts in central and local government (Currie, 1996b). Even the more recent Labour government initiative of *Best Value*[21] promotes the idea that public sector bodies should continue to secure value for money contracts with their private sector suppliers. One of the most high-profile public sector outsourcing contracts was between the Inland Revenue and EDS at an estimated cost of US$1 billion over 10 years. (This subsequently rose to US$1.6 billion.) Other UK public sector organisations are also considering IT outsourcing. For example, National Savings, which issues premium and children's bonds, is considering the contracting out of up to 4000 people. This is twice as many as the previous record-breaking Inland Revenue deal where 2000 IT specialists were transferred to EDS (*Computer Weekly*, 14 May 1998, p. 27).

A UK sector-specific analysis of IT outsourcing shows that in the year 2000, investment companies will spend £1.2 billion a year on IT, which is 8% higher than the estimated figure for 1996. The trend in this sector is to increase the outsourcing of operations, maintenance and applications development, thus forcing in-house IT departments to reduce staff. So while £491 million, or 42% of the total, is currently spent on internal staff and maintenance, that proportion will decline to less than a third in 2000 (*Computer Weekly*, 1996). Central government remains the largest IT outsourcing customer in the United Kingdom, accounting for £324 million of the £1393 million total value of contracts.

Yet, not all vertical markets, nor companies within them, embrace outsourcing in quite the same way. One estimate is that US$94.2 billion worth of outsourcing contracts will be signed in five vertical markets within the period 1996–2001. This is broken down as: manufacturing (US$44.4 billion); utilities (US$17 billion); state/local government (US$9.9 billion); insurance (US$12.3 billion) and communications (US$10.6 billion) (Yankee Group, 1996 [YankeeGroup.com]). To a large extent, cost control is no longer the paramount issue, and there is much evidence to show that future outsourcing deals will be based more on joint risk and reward between client and supplier as well as containing a value added/pricing component (Currie and Willcocks, 1998a).

Table 7.1 gives a breakdown of some of the more high-profile IT outsourcing contracts signed in recent years. Every year, it seems the size and scope of outsourcing contracts is increased. However, the 'mega deals' are still the minority as most companies tend to prefer to enter outsourcing contracts which are smaller (in money), shorter (in duration) and more narrow in scope (range of IT services).

Range of IT Services

Coupled with the burgeoning global outsourcing marketplace, the scope of IT services being outsourced is also expanding. Two reasons are paramount. First, increased offerings in the IT marketplace from enterprise resource planning, Internet and communications technologies (ICTs), etc. have led to an increase in customer demand for outsourcing. This is because companies do not have the in-house capability to introduce and maintain such a wide portfolio of technology. Recent evidence shows that some companies are expanding the range of activities they wish to outsource to include not only technical work but also managerial activities. For example, a recent IDC report advocates the advantages of business process outsourcing (BPO), and extended to functions like human resource management, accounting, logistics and customer services. In essence, BPO refers to the combined outsourcing of an IT system and the business process it supports (IDC, 1998b). This is much more ambitious and wide ranging than simply outsourcing a database or telecoms network. Second, IT service providers are eager to *cash-in* on offering their customers both business and technical services. Whilst the large players like EDS,

Table 7.1   *The value and duration of IT outsourcing contracts in the United States and the United Kingdom*

Client	Supplier	Value (US$)	Duration (years)
JP Morgan	Four vendors	2 bn	7
Inland Revenue*	EDS	1.6 bn	10
MetraHealth Companies Inc.	IBM	540 m	10
BHS	CSC	200 m	11
British Petroleum	Anderson Consulting	120 m	10
Indianapolis Government	Sys/Comp Technology Corp.	81 m	7
Oceanic Control Centre, UK*	EDS	80 m	—
London Stock Exchange	Anderson Consulting	—	5
John Menzies Retail	CSC	60 m	10
Hyatt Hotels	CSC/Sabre Group	45 m	5
Ford UK	Logica	43 m	3
UK Ministry of Defence*	Unisys	38 m	—
3 Clients	Sykes Enterprises	18 m	Annual
European Chemical Company	CSC	13 m	10
BC Gas Inc.	DMR Group	10 m	5
Cotswold District Council, UK*	Data Sciences Corp.	8 m	5
Honeywell Inc.	Bull/Integris	3 m	3–5
Columbia Pacific Division Hospitals	Transcend Services Inc.	—	3
Connecticut Childrens Medical Centre	Transcend Services Inc.	650 000	2

Adapted from: hppt://www.tekptnr.com/tpi/newsroom/s_arch.htm
   * UK public sector.

IBM and CSC offer their clients a full range of services, small and medium-sized suppliers are attempting to do the same. As we will see in Chapter 8, many IT service providers are using mergers and acquisitions as key strategies to leverage their position in the software and computing services industry.

A large-scale research study on new strategies in the IT outsourcing marketplace found that outsourcing was becoming more complex as client companies had learned the lessons from previous outsourcing contracts, and were now attempting to seek more lucrative deals with their service providers (Currie and Willcocks, 1998b). Some of the case studies from this project are given below. Table 7.2 gives an overview of the research findings in addition to some predictions from other research bodies or industry analysts. It points to the growing complexity of market, business, legal, technical and human resources issues that will need to be addressed by companies with existing and potential IT outsourcing contracts.

A CONCEPTUAL FRAMEWORK FOR UNDERSTANDING IT SOURCING DECISIONS

This section discusses four distinct types of IT sourcing which emerged out of extensive empirical research conducted in the United States and Europe (Currie and

Table 7.2 *An overview of the current and predicted IT outsourcing marketplace*

By year 2000, it is estimated that 75% of all enterprises will outsource in some form (Gartner Group)

Gartner Group claims that 63% of US companies and 72% of European companies said they were already outsourcing or considering outsourcing options

The range of IT activities outsourced is growing to include business process outsourcing (BPO)

A desire to focus on the *core business* continues to be a major reason for outsourcing

Value-added outsourcing is becoming a top priority in many companies

Few organisations enter into total outsourcing deals with the majority choosing multiple suppliers

Only about seven outsourcing suppliers have the capacity to provide a full suite of IT services

The average profit margin for all outsourcing services is estimated to be 10%–12%

The human resources dimension of outsourcing continues to be mismanaged or overlooked by some companies

New capabilities and skills need to be developed to manage outsourcing contracts

Loss of control over the supplier can lead to the failure of outsourcing contracts

Willcocks, 1997). They are: total outsourcing, multiple supplier/selective sourcing, joint venture/strategic alliance sourcing, and insourcing (retaining an in-house IT department). Table 7.3 summarises the key points of each form of IT sourcing. Whilst some organisations select only one type, e.g. total outsourcing, others enter into different types of arrangements. For example, a financial services company

Table 7.3 *An overview of four types of IT sourcing*

Total outsourcing	Multiple supplier/selective sourcing
• Develop 'partnership' with single supplier	• Create competition between suppliers
• Sign long-term contract with supplier	• Standardise/co-ordinate operations
• Focus on core business	• Focus on core business
• IT perceived as a service/support function	• Formulate framework agreement
• Reduce IT costs	• Nurture an alliance of suppliers
• Share risk/reward with supplier	• Develop short-term contracts with suppliers
• Eliminate IT (problem) function	• Suppliers given management responsibilities
• Access to managerial/technical expertise	• Transfer fixed costs to variable costs
• Retain strategic control	• Relationship management critical

Joint venture/strategic alliance sourcing	Insourcing
• Take 49% share ownership of IT supplier	• IT is seen as core business
• Client retains control over partner	• High level of in-house technical expertise
• IT supplier may be new or existing company	• Retain centralised IT department
• Shared risks and rewards	• Inadequate supplier/market conditions
• Develop sector-specific knowledge	• Synergy between business/technology
• Generate new business opportunities	• Lack of trust about supplier motivation
• Access to specialist technical expertise	• Manage contractors as permanent staff
• Two companies/two cultures	• Retain up-to-date technical expertise
	• Manage peaks and troughs of IT work

with a large centralised in-house IT department which undertakes most of its IT work in-house may also outsource specific IT applications development projects to specialist suppliers (Buck-Lew, 1992). Alternatively, another company may enter into an arrangement with several outsourcing suppliers. In doing so, it may seek to reduce its internal IT facility over time. Some companies may decide that neither of these arrangements is suitable and instead choose to enter into a partnership with a supplier. Such an approach may be described as joint venture or 'strategic alliance' sourcing (Willcocks and Choi, 1995). Others may perceive outsourcing as too risky and therefore retain a large in-house IT function. An overview of the four types of IT sourcing is given in Table 7.3.[22]

FOUR TYPES OF IT SOURCING

Total Outsourcing

A small minority of companies including the Inland Revenue/Electronic Data Systems (EDS), the London Stock Exchange/Anderson Consulting, and British Aerospace/CSC adopt this approach to IT sourcing. The publicity surrounding total outsourcing, however, is immense, particularly where landmark deals are agreed between client and supplier. Huber (1993) discusses total outsourcing in his *Harvard Business Review* article, where he examined the case of Continental Bank and its contract with IBM. Total outsourcing is where an organisation chooses to outsource as much as 70%–80% of its IT facility, usually to a large single supplier. These contracts are usually between five and ten years. A common assumption underpinning total outsourcing deals is the nurturing of a 'partnership' between client and supplier (Henderson, 1990). This is sometimes called a 'strategic alliance' (Willcocks and Choi, 1995). This notion is treated with scepticism in some quarters of the outsourcing literature. This is because the supplier may seek to maximise its financial return from an outsourcing contract, sometimes to the detriment of the client (Lacity and Hirschheim, 1993a).

Currie and Willcocks (1998a,b) found that part of the rationale for total outsourcing was so that the client could focus on core business activities, thus leaving the supplier to manage the IT facility. This is supported by other researchers (Quinn and Hilmer, 1994). Total outsourcing commonly involves the transfer of a significant proportion of IT staff from the client organisation to the supplier. The client receives a large payment for IT assets (hardware, software, networks, databases, etc.) from the supplier and, in doing so, removes the burden of having to manage and control what it perceives to be a non-core, 'service' activity. Concerns about relinquishing strategic IT systems to the supplier may be overcome when the client reasons that even a *business-critical* activity can be outsourced to a third party. In this capacity, the strategic versus commodity argument evaporates (Lacity *et al.*, 1995). But, as we shall see below, large-scale IT outsourcing engenders significant risks to the client, particularly where the lines between strategic and operational activities are unclear. In this chapter we consider total outsourcing at the London Stock Exchange. Here, we consider some of the opportunities and pitfalls of outsourcing to a large single supplier, and pose questions about the long-term viability of this arrangement.

Multiple Supplier/Selective Sourcing

Some companies have entered into IT sourcing arrangements with a variety of suppliers. The British company ICI plc adopted the view that IT should be 'business-led and business-managed'. According to this company, IT outsourcing is a 'commercial relationship' and not simply a partnership based only on trust and co-operation. Grand Metropolitan plc (which we examine below), developed what they described as 'tight contracts' with their suppliers to ensure that service level agreements (SLAs) were met. Part of the rationale for multiple supplier/selective sourcing has been discussed by Cross (1995) who analyses the situation at British Petroleum Exploration. This company negotiated a framework agreement with its suppliers who outlined the procedures and policies of how each party would work together. Contracts were not expected to exceed five years in duration. Suppliers were encouraged to form an alliance and compete with each other for business with the client. The difference between total outsourcing (above) and multiple supplier/selective sourcing is significant. First, the client organisation tends to safeguard against being dependent upon a single supplier, who may ultimately control all its IT assets. Second, this type of sourcing encourages competition and innovation by ensuring that contracts are short-term and liable for renewal not necessarily with the same supplier (or combination of suppliers). Third, this approach enables the client to concentrate on its core business activities in that the suppliers manage and provide IT services. Fixed costs become variable costs as the client reduces its in-house IT staff and instead purchases a portfolio of IT services from selected suppliers. The client intends to retain strategic control of IT, although significant management responsibilities are transferred to supplier organisations. Multiple supplier/selective sourcing tends to mitigate the risks of using only one supplier. However, some companies have experienced difficulties in managing and co-ordinating different suppliers.

Joint Venture/Strategic Alliance Sourcing

An organisation either selects an existing IT supplier or creates a new company for the purpose of outsourcing some of its IT work. This may involve the organisation taking a 49% share ownership in an existing IT supplier. For example, CRESTCo Ltd was an independent company set up by the Bank of England to design, implement and maintain the Crest electronic settlement system. Given the demise of the Taurus project in 1993, City of London institutions that funded this project in conjunction with the London Stock Exchange sought an alternative approach to developing a large-scale information system in-house with significant help from management consultants. Instead, CRESTCo Ltd was set up with the strict brief of developing a much more scaled down version of the Taurus system. Whereas the budget for the Taurus project falls somewhere in the region of £75–100 million (with some estimates claiming an overall cost of up to £400 million), the Crest system was given a budget of about £35 million (Currie, 1997).

The key advantage of the joint venture/strategic alliance sourcing approach is to reduce the risks of outsourcing contracts where suppliers are perceived to exert too much power. Here, the organisation may own a large share in an IT supplier and will therefore be able to influence its strategy and planning processes. It will also gain access to specialist managerial and technical skills, which it may not have in-house. Such an approach delineates the core competencies of both organisations in question. On the one hand, the organisation seeking the joint venture with an IT supplier will be able to retain its own core competencies by obtaining this resource elsewhere (Hamel and Prahalad, 1994). On the other hand, the IT supplier, which may be a small company looking to develop a partnership with a larger company (not necessarily in the same business), will be able to concentrate on its own core competencies of supplying IT services and also benefit from additional funding and support. By entering into a joint venture, an organisation can control the activities of the supplier company and share risk and reward. In this chapter we consider the joint venture between the Bank of England and CRESTCo Ltd, as part of a strategy to retain control over the development of the Crest equity settlement system to replace the failed Taurus project.

Insourcing

An organisation opts to retain a large centralised IT department and insource management and technical capabilities according to the peaks and troughs of IT work. Contractors may be given employment contracts between three months and a year, although there are many examples of them staying with an organisation for several years. The Royal Bank of Scotland hired as many as 40% of contractors to work on some IT projects (Currie and Willcocks, 1996). Although IT outsourcing is fast increasing in all sectors including central government, financial services, manufacturing, etc. a significant proportion of private and public sector organisations retain a large centralised IT department. Some of these organisations remain deeply sceptical of the division between the business and technology functions by suggesting that IT should instead be perceived as part of, not separate from, the business. In the UK Post Office, discussed below, technical innovation was perceived by management as critical to the future of the business. A decision was therefore made not to outsource a significant proportion of IT work to one or more suppliers. This organisation further holds the view that it has a high level of technical capability which is equal to, if not greater than, many supplier organisations. To outsource a large proportion of IT work would therefore not achieve any real value-added benefits.

SCALE OF IT SOURCING DECISIONS AND CLIENT–SUPPLIER INTERDEPENDENCY

The academic and practitioner literature on IT outsourcing is broadly concerned with two related issues. The first is the scale and growth of IT outsourcing predominantly in the last 10 years (*Financial Times*, 1994). The second is concerned with the experiences of organisations entering into outsourcing arrangements and the debates surrounding their related advantages and disadvantages (Lacity and Hirschheim, 1993a). In this section we consider some of the literature in relation to the second issue by examining the four types of IT sourcing decision in the context of the relationship between the scale of IT sourcing and client–supplier interdependency.

Figure 7.2. locates different types of IT sourcing decisions in a matrix, which links the scale of IT sourcing in the marketplace with client–supplier interdependency. The scale of IT sourcing decisions refers to the percentage of IT work done by external supplier(s); resources attributed to the contract(s) (financial, staff, technology, etc.) and length of contract(s). Large-scale total outsourcing carries with it the greatest interdependency between client and supplier. Unlike multiple supplier/ selective sourcing, total outsourcing deals are usually with one large single supplier, the success of which therefore depends upon the development of a successful partnership between the two parties. Multiple supplier/selective sourcing, on the other hand, is a strategy which intends to create an alliance of suppliers who compete with each other for business with the client. Interdependency between the client and supplier is reduced, although the client may be faced with problems of lack of co-ordination and logistical issues since commissioning and managing the various contracts takes precedence over providing the IT services.

In the case of joint venture/strategic alliance sourcing, it is a common problem that IT applications development work invariably goes over time and budget. Numerous examples of this problem have been well documented in the literature (Currie, 1994, 1996b; Sauer, 1993). The decision to outsource a large-scale IT applications development project to an external provider tends to increase client–supplier interdependency given that the outcome is almost entirely dependent upon the supplier's ability to deliver a fully functional system. Failure to do so can create innumerable problems for the client organisation as was the case at the

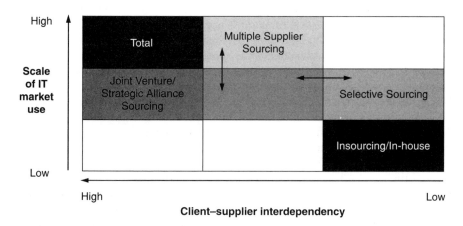

Figure 7.2   *The relationship between the scale of IT sourcing and client–supplier interdependency*

London Stock Exchange in 1993, the London Ambulance Service, and Wessex Health Authority (Currie, 1995b). To reduce these risks, some organisations choose instead to retain an in-house IT department and insource technical capability in the form of contractors (project managers and programmers, etc.). But while this reduces client–supplier interdependency, there is no guarantee that an in-house IT department, even with contractors being managed internally as permanent staff, will produce more effective IT projects.

What emerges from this discussion is that risks are associated with all forms of IT sourcing decisions. Whilst significant client–supplier interdependency is not in itself a risk, the risks to the client organisation may increase where disagreements emerge about the provision of IT services. To the extent that some large-scale IT sourcing deals are successful, others are less so (Lacity and Hirschheim, 1993b). It therefore becomes important to consider in some detail the case histories of specific IT sourcing decisions. This is best illustrated by examining the experiences of four companies which have selected one of the four types of IT sourcing. We begin by considering the case history of British Aerospace which entered into a total outsourcing deal with CSC. This outsourcing arrangement is ongoing and it offers a rich example of many of the benefits and pitfalls of total outsourcing.

CASE STUDIES—EXPLORING FOUR TYPES OF IT SOURCING

Total Outsourcing at British Aerospace plc

Context and Overview

The pursuit of a single supplier IT outsourcing contract rested upon 'a fundamental decision to outsource rather than not'. The financial background shows that, as a company, 75% of the turnover of £8 billion a year is represented by the contribution of partners and suppliers. Against this background, the company achieves its business objectives with the ongoing involvement of third parties. This has been the case for some 20 years. Culturally it is not a difficult thing for the company to come to terms with—that activities which are central to the business involve other organisations that are not under the direct management control of British Aerospace. The origins of the decision to outsource are historical and lay within the structural and financial position of the company in the early 1990s. British Aerospace was formed in 1978 by nationalisation from various disparate parts of the UK aerospace industry at that time, and was de-nationalised by the Conservative government in 1981. It was de-nationalised in a way that left it substantially decapitalised, and whilst this was not apparent for some years, it became so in the late 1980s to early 1990s with the economic recession affecting many of the key markets of the aerospace industry. The cold war had ended which had significant implications for the defence budget of the United Kingdom, in addition to that of the United States and elsewhere. In fact, the US defence budget had declined by 45%, which was broadly parallel to the decline experienced in other parts of the world. Defence was about 70% of British Aerospace's business.

Coupled with the decline in business in the defence area, other areas of the business, like commercial aerospace, which amounted to about 30% of British Aerospace's business, also saw a decline. In the early 1990s, the major airlines all stopped buying aircraft. This meant that a major re-evaluation and readjustment was necessary. During this period, the company found itself in serious difficulties. At the end of 1992, it declared a loss of just over £1 billion. This was the biggest corporate loss in British corporate history. It reduced the net worth of the company by about 50% at a stroke. The share price plummeted from a high of about £4.50 to just under £1. Faced with these problems, the company set about constructing a strategy for survival which had two threads to it. The first was to dispose of businesses that were judged to be non-core. This included a number of businesses that were non-performing. For example, the Rover car company and construction businesses were sold to enable the company to return to its core business of aerospace and defence. Second, in respect of the businesses that were set to continue, a programme of cost reduction, efficiency improvement and rationalisation was initiated. The company is currently at the end of implementing those two streams of activity. In the course of doing so, staff numbers have been reduced from 125 000 to about 44 000. The company continues to retain a high level of technical expertise given that, out of the 44 000 staff, some 20 000 are qualified engineers. Recognising that 'leading edge' technical skills should be rewarded, new pay and grading systems are being introduced to reduce the financial disparity between specific managerial and engineering grades.

Evaluating the IT Infrastructure

With the implementation of the changes described above, the company is now the most profitable aerospace business in Europe. In terms of the review that was done to seek opportunities for efficiency improvement and rationalisation, an evaluation of the role of IT was included. Historically, IT along with many of the other activities in the business, was run as a heavily decentralised service. If businesses delivered a profit, than there was a tendency for the main board to leave them to their own devices, and that included how they organised and managed their own IT requirements. Each business had its own IT department with very little cross-fertilisation. There was no systematic planning of IT service delivery across the organisation as a whole. Payroll was done locally by each business. There were examples where certain businesses had let out some contracts for distributed maintenance and other bespoke activities. But this was done on a localised and *ad hoc* basis. An evaluation of the infrastructure that had emerged over the years led management to conclude there was over-capacity and structural inefficiencies. A decision was taken to instruct a multidisciplinary team drawn from the individual business units to evaluate the entire organisation to discern whether something could be done to improve the cost efficiency of the IT service delivery in a collective rather than independent way. The focus at that time was related to the business pressures facing the company. The accent was therefore on cost reduction. As such, a number of people were brought together with a background in commerce, finance, human resources, IT, and engineering, and collectively they evaluated the IT capability infrastructure and what might be done in the interim to reduce costs. It was apparent that there were significant cost economies that could be yielded. The real issue was not whether the review group maintained the status quo but whether they could set about realising cost economies through some form of terminal rationalisation or by using an external third party to enable that process. The latter was not easy to assess for two reasons. First, the review group and wider organisation knew very little about the outsourcing marketplace such as the capabilities and skills of the supplier organisations. Second, and related to the first issue, it was not easy to evaluate the outsourcing marketplace in a short period of time. Faced with these issues, a decision was reached to develop a full-scale in-house rationalisation proposal and, in parallel, run a full-scale outsourcing competition. Only at the end of these activities would the review group draw together the conclusions and make a recommendation to the board about the best way forward.

At the outset, the review group looked at about 20 potential suppliers on a superficial basis. Information was requested from each one, and this enabled 10 suppliers to be eliminated from the exercise. The remaining 10 suppliers were called in to receive intensive briefings from the company about the services required and to question the suppliers how they would deliver such a service. The suppliers were sent away to prepare bidding documents. However, without any encouragement from the company, the suppliers formed themselves into five groupings for the purposes of engaging further discussion. One reason for this was that each supplier was stronger working together with other suppliers to form a group rather than working independently. In addition, very few suppliers had the full capability to offer the wide range of services needed by the client. Yet the company was absolutely insistent that it wanted to have a single prime contractor to deal with, and it was therefore for the suppliers to manage as they thought appropriate. It is common in the aerospace business for a major company like British Aerospace to be a prime contractor. As such, much of its skill and competence lies in organising teams and suppliers up and down the value chain. The advantage of this approach is to organise the co-ordination, control and accountability around a single supplier rather than have multiple suppliers, which is a strategy followed by other companies.

At the end of the first phase the company narrowed the suppliers down to only three, each of whom was considered capable of doing the full range of services required. They were CSC, EDS and IBM. So that left two streams of activity. The in-house proposal was not intended to be a bid to compete with the other suppliers but rather to inform the company what might be possible internally, and also to provide useful benchmarking information to use in the discussions with the other outsourcing parties. That process ran for about 11 months. The CEO and finance director allowed this time given the importance of the decision. During this period the focus of attention tended to shift. At the outset, it had started off as a cost driven exercise. Whilst this remained part of the agenda, it became increasingly clear that the company was going to survive. The share price was recovering fairly rapidly. So some of the immediate urgencies were receding. As the exercise was drawing to a close, it became clear that outsourcing was likely to be a more appropriate option that doing things internally. However, the focus had shifted to one described as 'value-added'. In looking at a comparison of the cost model between internal and external performance, it became clear that either option could be equally cost effective. However, the key question for the company was: Is there something that a third party (whose core capability lay within exploiting IT) could bring to the business that we could not otherwise acquire? This question was considered for a period of some two to three months and key people were brought from the various businesses to interview the suppliers on all aspects of their service. Such in-depth questioning caused some bad feeling with the suppliers as their services as well as their managerial approach was placed under scrutiny.

The Tendering Process

The company has within its mainstream engineering organisation genuine leading-edge capability in some IT-related areas, e.g. product embedded software within the aeroplanes and missile systems. Such capabilities and skills would not be outsourced under any circumstances. Indeed, they were considered to be a core competence. The company boasts a software development capability which goes far beyond anything that external suppliers are able to provide. In this capacity, IT is seen as part of the business. It was only after those very rigorous series of meetings that the view came back that there was probably some additional capability to be gained for the benefit of the business provided they could be targeted correctly. At this stage, there were two remaining suppliers—CSC and EDS. Both suppliers came up with a bid with only 1% difference in price. CSC eventually won the contract partly because they have a wide range of experience within the aerospace industry.

Given the extent of the services required by British Aerospace, one relevant issue concerns the fluctuating pricing structure. Two areas were examined. The first considers the quality of the forward planning exercise. It was considered important to build in a clause that covered unforeseen changes to the IT service delivery. Pricing algorithms were negotiated with the supplier for most of the mainstream areas. This was done as a safeguard for any future changes and is contractually binding with the supplier. The second area concerns the need for independent benchmarking. Contained within the outsourcing contract is a commitment from the supplier to deliver prices for all the services they deliver either now or in the future. These prices will be located in the top decile of the industry peer group, and are independently assessed. Benchmarking is applied to the range of IT services covered in the outsourcing contract. Four broad areas of work are currently out-sourced. They are:

1. Datacentre services provision: this embraces IBM computing, DEC computing and Craig supercomputing.
2. Networks (WAN, LAN).
3. Distributed Computing Environment: acquisition of new hardware and software and the maintenance and support of the distributed environment.
4. Applications development, support and maintenance.

The company has a policy to subject each of the four areas to independent benchmarking every six months. It is a lengthy process as it takes about six months to complete a thorough audit of each area. The two most problematic areas are the distributed computing environment, particularly the acquisitions side of it, and applications development. Although the company applies benchmarking to those areas, there was a concern at the time of outsourcing three years ago that the state of the art in benchmarking would not keep pace with the changes in those areas. As a pre-condition, the supplier was given the right to supply in those two areas on a non-exclusive basis only. This enables the company periodically to ask other suppliers to compete with the major supplier for a specific project.

To provide a framework for analysing their single supplier outsourcing contract, British Aerospace draws from the work of John Henderson. This framework categorises activities into three types: core, necessary and basic. Whilst it is outside the scope of the present case study to analyse this framework in detail, suffice it to say that managers at British Aerospace concluded that developing evaluative (quantitative) measures such as service-level agreements (there are currently 650 in operation) was only part of managing the outsourcing contract. It was equally important to consider qualitative issues such as people's perceptions of the outsourcing relationship.

To help the company gather more information about IT outsourcing, it formed a major outsourcing user group of 15 companies to include Xerox, McDonnell Douglas, American Express and Kodak, among others. Notwithstanding the sectoral differentiation between these businesses, it is a useful exercise to pool information about managing outsourcing relationships. Indeed, the same problems tend to arise in each participating company irrespective of sector, market and technology factors.

It was stressed that one of the main considerations of a single supplier oursourcing deal was that it would be a relationship that 'touches at various points'. A British Aerospace spokesperson commented that, 'It is important to define your requirements, ask the contractor if they can deliver and monitor the service. If we find the contractor is failing at any point, they are tackled about non-performance. But we are doing other things.'

It was stressed that service-level agreements (SLAs) are a vital element of managing the supplier, but they are inappropriate for understanding the subjective nature of the outsourcing relationship. A British Aerospacee spokesperson said that

> I think we judged that many of the things we need to deliver 'best in class' services are not easily definable in terms of hard quantitative measures. Rather you are moving into subjective territory . . . What are people's perceptions of how this company is providing the service on a day to day, seven days per week basis? We decided we were missing a series of measures (addressing this issue) so we instituted a new regime called the customer performance assessment reporting system (CPARS).

CPARS is a framework intended to capture subjective information about people's perceptions of the service they receive from the supplier. It seeks to identify a range of key users of IT in the business areas. These people arrange a meeting with their counterpart from the supplier organisation and set out to discuss a wide range of issues about the service provision. There are two key objectives underpinning these meetings. The first is for both parties to agree how the service will be provided in the coming month or quarter. This discussion will exclude the application of hard measures such as SLAs, because it is intended to generate new ideas rather than simply discuss what is already in place. The second objective is to formulate an agreement that is acceptable to both parties. It will then be implemented and will be the subject of the next meeting. So far, the company has set up some 250 meetings between key users of the services and the relevant representative from the supplier organisation.

The evaluation process of the IT outsourcing delivery now considers both hard and soft information. This is shown in Table 7.4.

The British Aerospace spokesperson pointed out that the 250 meetings per month between the individual user and his/her counterpart at the supplier organisation were not a 'bureaucratic nonsense'. Rather, they were part of the day job of all the people in question. Such an activity was seen to impose discipline on the organisation and focus attention on contemporary issues and concerns. Moreover, it amounted to a useful dialogue which enables users to align their objectives which those of the supplier. Notwithstanding the frameworks that were in place for analysing information on both quantitative and qualitative aspects of the IT service delivery, the company had experienced some problems with its outsourcing contract. They were divided into two categories. The first was in the Desktop Computing Environment (DCE). This was a major problem where performance had been judged to be unsatisfactory. There were a number of contributory factors. One was the rapid explosion in scale and complexity of DCE, from 6000 to 20 000 devices in two and a half years. Complexity had grown exponentially. For example, two years ago a person may have used only a spreadsheet and word-processing package. Now there was e-mail, Lotus Notes, Internet access, and a range of other functions. The support model for the DCE was now much greater and more complex. The company admits that forecasting this growth had not been easy. The supplier was now left behind a power curve in responding to that demand. In spite of this, performance levels were not acceptable.

In discussions with the 15-strong outsourcing user group discussed above, the particular problem affected all of these organisations. An essential question was:

Table 7.4 *The evaluation process of the IT outsourcing delivery*

Hard measures	Service delivery specification (SDS) business critical • 10% or more below (red) serious • less than 10% below target (yellow) • on target or less than 10% above (green) • 10% more above (blue)
Soft measures	Customer performance assessment reporting system (CPARS) based upon perceptions • excellent • fully satisfied • some problems • poor

How effectively can we do upgrades, moves, changes, etc.? Irrespective of whether this service was offered internally or externally, managers concluded that the whole operating model of managing the DCE was changing and that would mean getting the business to agree to a more standardised environment. One option was to reduce the DCE to a single software suite to the same issue standard. General Motors who manage some 80 000 devices currently use such a model. This restricts the user from loading software on their PC since all software is accessed from a central server which, in turn, reduces the cost since it is managed centrally. This eliminates viruses, and improves maintenance times. However, the user will find their freedom to use their computer as a 'personal' computer somewhat restricted. One issue that had been a problem was software licences. At the time of outsourcing, the company had to negotiate changes to some 350–400 different software licences with the relevant companies to use their equipment. Each one had to be approached to seek a reassignment of the licence rights to the supplier. Whilst all but 10 were straightforward, these companies wanted to renegotiate the licences. This problem had not been fully anticipated before embarking upon outsourcing. The company now builds in a provision regarding the software licence before procuring and implementing new software products.

The second concern was potentially more critical and longer term than the first one. It concerned the so-called 'value-added ticket'. The company had reached a stage where it found that after a year it could not identify any value-added service from the supplier. When approached, the supplier said it believed it was offering such a service. However, there was some debate about this between the two parties. The outcome was that a definitional problem was identified. The supplier claimed it was delivering a value-added service by way of reorganising and consolidating data centres. This activity was delivering a 30% cost improvement. However, the company took this as a given and argued it did not necessarily constitute value added. What was needed was a demonstration by the supplier of how they were applying their expertise for the benefit of exploiting the potential of IT for their client's business. What was eventually agreed was a three-tier definition of value added, with the first tier being the most critical:

1. business (identifying ways to exploit IT for the client's business);
2. capacity (infusing new skills, methodologies, capabilities in the staff who transfer to the supplier);
3. basic (doing better, more efficiently and cheaper IT services which can also be done by the client in-house).

From the outset, the supplier sent a number of people from North America to advise on a whole range of issues. The company wanted to know how it could access the expertise contained within the supplier organisation. A decision was made to integrate carefully selected people from the supplier with the IT planning and business planning processes of the company. IT planning had been poor (see above) prior to outsourcing. The company's forecasting requirements were short-term which tended to indicate a wide gulf between IT, the business areas and strategy development. To execute this plan a few individuals from the supplier were identified who could work with the business management teams to identify and understand the key business drivers. These people were either senior managers or subject-matter experts (e.g. a specialist in implementing manufacturing systems for the business). So if a key business requirement was to reduce aircraft billing times by 50%, then the relevant individual would suggest what had been done in other parts of the aerospace industry. According to a British Aerospace spokesperson:

> This was culturally quite difficult for us because this was the acid test—whether we would be able to acquire real value added from our supplier. The supplier has now been involved in this for 18 months. We have seen in various parts of the business quite substantial IT-enabled change propositions. These are much broader business change projects.

Managing the Outsourcing Relationship

The company recognised the importance of developing new skills for managing the outsourcing contract. These skills fell into two broad categories. At the time of interview, the company was going through a resourcing review of people who were retained in the company's IT facility. These people were largely responsible for managing the relationship with the supplier. The competencies and skills were managerial and technical in nature. First, people were needed with the skills of negotiating, influencing and co-ordinating. It was necessary to articulate business requirements to the supplier on a continuing basis. Second, people were needed with good technical skills who could also undertake an internal consulting role. These people were needed to articulate the IT-related solutions within a business context to the supplier.

At the time of the outsourcing contract, the company retained a number of people who could manage the outsourced relationship in terms of IT service delivery. This was appropriate at that time. There was a requirement for people with experience of mainstream service delivery. As the outsourcing contract progressed, a need had arisen to develop people with the skills at the strategic end of IT such as relationship management skills. People with these skills were becoming very marketable.

The company built a competency and a skills model to identify those attributes which it felt were important for the future. A workshop was planned to do IT job profiling against those competencies and skills that were identified. For example, an IT director to be head of the airbus division will require competencies and skills which are sector, business and technically specific. The questions to ask would therefore be: What is the match and mismatch in the organisation? What is the gap analysis? What is the resourcing plan to deal with this gap? Training requirements would then be identified to fill these gaps. Clearly, there will be some gaps that training will not be able to fill. As such, people will be moved around the organisation to gain experience and expertise. The company believed it was below critical mass in some smaller business areas, so it would have to combine some resources in order to provide the full portfolio of capability that was required. Five aspects of skills profiling were developed. They were:

1. bespoke training requirements;
2. behavioural area;
3. inter-redeployment of people;
4. selection, recruitment;
5. organisational implications if below critical mass in some business areas.

It was pointed out that one of the problem areas was that some people could not easily make the transition from a technical background into the business. However, for those who could, they would become very marketable as IT was now considered capable of providing a value-added service. Offering advice for other companies wishing to outsource with a single supplier, a company spokesperson made the following comments:

> The point I would make is don't expect you can define a single contractual regime from a monolithic contract that will satisfy all your requirements. Just as you need SLAs, you need to look at different forms of contracting based upon risk and reward where the outsourcer is incentivised according to the business results which flow, rather than the IT performance that is delivered. You have to be ready and have people on both sides of the fence who are capable of having a dialogue. I recently spent one and a half hours talking to my counterpart at the supplier organisation about a large project. I had a list of about eight points at the performance level. But we were also talking of the strategic advantages. It is a relationship which has many facets. We would not want to be bothered with managing the interfaces. In our business, we tend to have specific suppliers for specific projects. It is a long term business. Sourcing is strategic, not tactical.

He also added the following comments relating to negotiating applications development projects:

> If you have a large system which costs about £15m, how do you negotiate it? We negotiate rates up front, like set labour rates which are benchmarked against industry competitiveness. We will then talk to our supplier about possible technical aspects of the project and ask them if they want to quote. We would typically expect them to give a quote using those labour rates. We might go to other outfits as well. What is central is the core infrastructure. It is important for one outfit to run that. But we can populate infrastructure with systems which we may procure from suppliers other than our major supplier. But we would expect the supplier to have an input, particularly in managing the interface between suppliers.

A common mistake which potential outsourcers make is attempting to rush a deal through. The spokesperson, who acts as an 'unofficial adviser' to those companies thinking of outsourcing, commented:

> You can usually tell within five minutes if a company who comes here for advice is having problems. These outfits sometimes say 'we have to get it done by the year end, and we do not have too much time to negotiate!'. This is a shambles. Culturally you have to make sure that what you are putting in place is going to work. You need to manage staff expectations and be able to communicate. There is no substitute for selecting an outsourcer through competition. Some say this is not conducive to forming a partnership, but I think it is the only way. You have to have clear objectives. Also to be able to manage expectations. There is a tendency that on the day you press the button, the grass will be greener. But the resource after outsourcing will be pretty much the same as before.

On the issue of where IT outsourcing decisions originate in the organisation, the spokesperson said

It is important to determine where ownership of outsourcing lies, e.g. a business leader or a person who heads up the IT organisation. The latter may be more reluctant to relinquish control and may target best of breed suppliers. Whereas a CEO would be more open to something more radical. It is important to ask—what has to be done in IT terms? We had a massive amount of infrastructure rationalisation to do and a decentralised IT service organisation. It may be the case that there is a correlation between the higher the level in the organisation a decision is taken the more likely it will be total outsourcing. But they may take a more strategic view anyway.

The company believed that we would increasingly see more outsourcing of complete business processes. These outsourcing decisions would probably be taken at a more strategic level. The rationale was that you need to access the right capabilities and competencies, but you do not need to own the resources. However, one consideration would be how the outsourcing suppliers would manage what has been remarkable annual growth as they have acquired new assets and resources by way of equipment and labour. Sooner or later, the outsourcing suppliers may have to rationalise their own operations.

Like other companies, the issue of mitigating risk in outsourcing deals was given some attention. The company spokesperson said that

It pays to retain non-exclusivity of suppliers. You need to retain leverage over the supplier— maintain benchmarking about pricing and the ability to influence and develop the organisation. We are an important account for the supplier. I think mega-deals can work but they take a lot of hard work.

Multiple Supplier/Selective Sourcing at Grand Metropolitan plc

Context and Overview

The company has traditionally had an internal centralised IS support function. This has now become the Grand Metropolitan Information Services (GMIS) group which sits in the middle of the organisation and provides the technical infrastructure for global communications across the company. It does all the operational support, mainframes, AS400, mid-range machines, and LANS. In addition, it runs the help-desk and voice and data telecoms. GMIS has contracts to provide services to the three major businesses of Grand Metropolitan, namely Pillsbury, International Distillers & Vintners (IDV) and Burger King. So to some extent the three businesses outsource their IT services to an internal supplier. They each pay for those services, and GMIS's mandate is to break even to cover its costs every year. The historical situation was that Grand Metropolitan, through GMIS, actually operated a separate business which sold IT services to an internal as well as external market. This was when the company operated like a conglomerate organisation.

The IT budget is just under £100 million per year. Each of the three businesses have their own information systems facility and carry out design and development, and applications support and maintenance. Whilst the company uses the services of a range of computer suppliers, it has not hitherto ventured into any large-scale outsourcing deals with a single supplier. For example, one of GMIS's large outsourcing arrangements is with a telecoms supplier and this contract is for the duration of one year. The company also uses a range of computer suppliers for mainframe, mid-range and PCs. Each of the three businesses has the freedom to procure computer equipment from a range of suppliers provided they can justify their decisions. In recent years, the company has moved much more towards package solutions and almost exclusively uses external suppliers to develop systems. The rationale for selecting suppliers was described as one based upon commercial awareness of what a supplier could offer rather than one taken from a 'vendor selection guide'. The company first looked at the functionality of the system. In other words, what it can deliver and what is required as an IT-enabled business solution. The cost of the system must be understood in full, and this includes the cost for ongoing support and maintenance provided by the supplier. It was pointed out that when selecting any supplier, the company made an assessment of the service offered on a global basis. This was because the commercial interests of the company were spread internationally.

Developing an Outsourcing Strategy

The approach to outsourcing IT services at the company has proceeded with some degree of caution. The company has spent about a year developing a strategy for outsourcing. It has drawn upon experiences and work from a wide range of sources, from concrete examples of other organisations with existing outsourcing contracts, such as British Aerospace, Chase Manhatten Bank, among others, to reports from management consultancies and research from business schools. The company has also entered into lengthy discussions with a range of outsourcing suppliers.

The company believed it was possible to learn from the experiences of those organisations with outsourcing contracts, even those operating in different sectors. Having identified all the IT services, GMIS developed a model that looked at the potential benefits and risks associated with outsourcing. It was decided that certain areas of the IT service could be outsourced. These areas were all owned by GMIS on behalf of the businesses. This excluded core administrative systems. Data centres were considered but it was decided that to outsource this area would pose too many risks in the present climate. However, this area would need to be continually assessed as the market is constantly changing. Data centre benchmarking had been done and the results of this exercise showed that the company would not receive any additional cost or value-added benefits from outsourcing this facility. Currently, the company was benchmarking data invoice networks with a view to outsourcing this area. The key criteria for outsourcing was to discern whether a supplier could provide the service more efficiently and with enhanced quality than the in-house team. The company's approach to outsourcing was described as one of 'smart sourcing' as the following comments suggest:

> It would be smart sourcing rather than outsourcing. I find it hard to see a situation where we could move to one supplier lock, stock and barrel. It seems to me that single supplier deals are driven by some other imperative . . . you are in the mire so deeply you can't handle it yourself . . . that you have not got the confidence to do it . . . or rightly or wrongly, it may be a business decision to say we have not got the right internal competencies here to do this . . . and we decide that someone else should take the problem away and do it for us. But, how do

you change a single supplier? With multiple suppliers, it is manageable. Changing from a single supplier? I don't know how you do it. We buy services on a business driven, more ad hoc basis, not on a long term basis.

Benefits and Risks of Outsourcing

In order to assess the potential benefits and risks of outsourcing, GMIS has undertaken this activity on behalf of the board. Three areas were considered. They were:

1. the use of management time;
2. service quality; and
3. access to new technology.

On the first issue, GMIS looked at the relationship between management time and value added from IT services. In other words, could an outsourcing supplier save management time by providing some of the IT services which were currently run by in-house managers? Second, service quality was an issue that was examined using a similar rationale. That is, could an outsourcing supplier improve IT services? Third, the issue of access to new technology was evaluated, particularly since Grand Metropolitan was 'not a hugely technology literate organisation'.

A company spokesperson commented that

> Making some sort of step change in how you are doing IS/IT delivery is important ... the quality and delivery of service. This was a bit of an issue for GM, certainly because of the problems associated with geographical regions. If we haven't got critical mass, it is difficult getting people on the ground out there to support the organisation. Equally, a lot of the outsourcing suppliers haven't got critical mass in these places either. But a large supplier with a big contract with us would seek to supply the service. So these are the interesting issues for us. The other one is that you understand better the cost that you are getting because it becomes real money, not just internal money. So if things need to be changed, you have to be aware of the dollars that will go out of the door to the supplier to do this. That focuses attention. When we have looked at risk, we have concluded that we want to retain IT governance, the technical architecture and the technical capability. Although we haven't got any really large outsourcing contracts, we still think it is important to address these issues. In order to retain the level and control, we would have to maintain control of these things ourselves.

Commenting on whether the IS needs of the three businesses were compatible given their differences, the spokesperson said:

> Yes, they are all doing different things and they are all driven by their own business strategy. So we do not from the centre attempt to lay down any formal systems or applications strategy. Those decisions are all made by the businesses themselves. But we have agreed a strategy that we get maximum levels at GM by continuing to run this sort of organisation, because the businesses do not want to spend their time running telecoms operations, LANs, supporting AS400 or HP boxes, etc. So we have got a lot of leverage out of centralising these services, and brought a lot of data centres into GMIS without dictating to the businesses what they should do with their applications. This has resulted in economies of scale.

Commenting on the difficulties of managing IT outsourcing contracts, the spokesperson said:

> Obviously the issue of supplier and contract management gets right to the top of the agenda. In all the things that we picked up in terms of our research last year, one school of thought was that you really do need to have a phenomenally detailed contract, down to the last fine detail, or that you will get taken advantage of. So tie it all down. Another issue is the more euphemistic partnership approach. We came to the view that the notion of 'partnership' was misplaced because you have to have a tight commercial contract. It now seems that building benchmarking into the contract is critical.

He continued:

> Some things are more difficult to define ... I think you can benchmark service provision which is what the majority of your outsourcing is about. Benchmarking as an activity is maturing all the time. We started off with data centres and that was a relatively straightforward thing to do. Now we are looking at benchmarking networks and PC operations, which you can do very well now. Applications development is a difficult one but you can do it. In some way, shape or form, it is possible to benchmark most things and there are commercial offerings out there that will do it for you. So I think it is good practice to build benchmarking into a contract. At least it gives you leverage to avoid being left behind by the marketplace. So if it is a good rate now, you must remember that it may not be so good in five or ten years time. Contracts will therefore need to reflect possible changes in the marketplace and be linked to contemporary benchmarking figures rather than historical ones.

Grand Metropolitan tended to favour risk and reward arrangements with outsourcing suppliers. The company was currently looking at other companies that have tried this arrangement. One such company was a popular retailer. Making a comparison between Grand Metropolitan and this organisation, the company spokesperson said:

> They (the retailer) have referred to it as soft equity. With this arrangement, the supplier has a strong interest in the client doing well. We saw their chief executive and the rest of the board and they were very enthusiastic about this. They talked positively about it. Their IS Director had started off fairly cynically, but had decided that the contract was working fairly well. So the risk–reward situation seemed to be doing very well. They had a driving reason to do it. They needed to make strategic changes to their business. They needed a step change in terms of how their IS department was to operate in the future. They were doing traditional 1970s work and had to move IS into the retail era of the 1990s. It was a strong piece of strategic thinking on their part. Cost was not the main driving force. It was the need to make a step change. In a Grand Metropolitan perspective, you could do a similar thing but we need to ask 'what is the real strategic imperative here?'. We haven't got one. We are not in a cost disaster. We do not need an influx of cash. We are not in a service disaster ... But we needed to manage things a bit more smartly. There is no right or wrong here.

Whilst the company advocated the development of tight outsourcing contracts with suppliers, it recognised that it did not possess much internal legal expertise in designing and negotiating such contracts. This was compared with other organisations which had signed major single supplier outsourcing deals. These organisations were seen to possess much greater levels of legal expertise. So given the shortfall of legal expertise at the company in conjunction with its relative inexperience of negotiating outsourcing deals, it was recognised that legal expertise would need to be accessed from the marketplace. Fortunately, there were now many legal firms able of offer such advice—a situation that has grown with outsourcing.

Skills Shortages

The company said that there was a skills shortage in areas of contracts management and strategic planning and management in an outsourced environment. It was mentioned that businesses with a history of using external suppliers such as aerospace, the oil industry and construction, would probably be better placed to negotiate outsourcing contracts. This was because these businesses have a history of project management skills development, whereas retailing, financial services and the major areas of the public sector do not. In addition, companies with major strengths in project management also tend to use structured methodologies for systems development. Notwithstanding the criticisms of structured approaches, the spokesperson said:

> If you elevate project management as an issue and you have some sort of uniformity of approach, you start to define the problem. It does not resolve the problem but it helps you to define it. It starts to give project management a role which is possibly more than it is at the moment. It helps you define what the role of the business is . . . the role of technology, etc.

The company recognised the human resources issues relating to outsourcing, one of which was the wide gulf often present between the business and technology areas within a company. Reflecting on the issue that a lot of good technical people leave their technical specialism to become managers (for promotion purposes), the spokesperson said:

> This is an interesting question. I think at the end of the day you don't gain anything by forcing people out of an avenue in which they are productive. I think there is a lot of merit in the professional recognition approach. If a person is a great analyst, and they can bring on other people, and they want to stay in that, there should be scope to do so. You can lift the ceiling of their salary and add to their responsibility, i.e. use them to retain the development and standards being used, and reward them for developing younger people who will add value to the business by virtue of their technical skills. Project management is a very important role. There should be no ceiling on salary for this work, particularly if you are managing major computer projects. I don't see why these people should not be paid as much as a director.

On the subject of the hybrid manager (someone who theoretically blends both business and technical skills) the spokesperson said:

> I am supposed to be one of these people. I do wax a little bit hot and cold on this because I personally feel that it is easier to learn to be an effective general business manager from an IS background than the other way around. I would say that I suffer in some areas for not being able to keep up to date with all the technologies in the marketplace. But I can access this information from the people I manage. But I would feel exposed if I had no technical background whatever.

IS strategy was developed by the board with a major input by GMIS. The IS strategy developed at this level provides a global architecture and vision for the business which includes the three major businesses within the group. However, each business may choose to present a proposal to outsource part of its IS facility if it so wishes. For example, Pillsbury may decide to outsource their LAN, PC support and helpdesk, and there should be no reason why the board at Grand Metropolitan would disagree with this approach. It would be illogical for the board and the business to come to a different conclusion.

Joint Venture/Project Sourcing at CRESTCo Ltd

Context and Overview

This case history offers a new angle to IT outsourcing in that a specialist company was set up with a clear objective to develop a large-scale computer system. CRESTCo Ltd was created in 1994 to 'establish, design, construct, acquire, own, manage and operate, or, in whole or in part, arrange for the management and operation of, the CREST settlement system in accordance with the principles and requirements published by the Bank of England' (CRESTCo Ltd, Memorandum and Articles of Association, October 1994). It is an independent company, owned by a consortium of 69 firms across the United Kingdom. Unlike other large-scale computer system development projects undertaken within organisations, the CREST system was the core activity of CRESTCo Ltd, with all its employees working towards a common goal. Coming three years after the failed Taurus computer project (abandoned in March 1993), the CREST system went live in the summer of 1996 (notwithstanding some teething problems). Part of the success of the CREST system was that applications development work and outsourcing activities formed part of a clearly defined business strategy from the outset.

A Joint Venture Approach to Systems Development

The CREST equity settlement system began operations just three years after the Board of the Stock Exchange announced it was abandoning the Taurus computer project. The CREST system is the new computer system released by CRESTCo Ltd in the summer of 1996. CRESTCo Ltd was set up by the Bank of England to run the CREST system. With the implementation of CREST, securities are now progressively de-materialised from paper records into an electronic format. The first transactions were settled using CREST one month following its implementation. The transition was scheduled to culminate in April 1997 when the Stock Exchange's Talisman settlement system was decommissioned, some 17 years after it first began operating. CREST marks a new phase in strategic IT developments for the securities industry. It will put the industry on a new platform that can support wholesale changes in the way it operates. Examples include links from CREST to other international settlements systems, or using CREST to handle other instruments such as unit trusts. Many of its international competitors in the United States and elsewhere already have paperless settlement systems (*Financial Times*, 1996).

CREST has three major advantages over Talisman. First, it should eliminate the everyday risks of settlement. A certificate moves through an average of 25 pairs of hands each time it is traded. It can get lost or mis-filed. It may also be lost through transportation. Second, it will allow a reduction in financial risks. The biggest risk in settlement is that the investor who buys a share will go out of business before money is paid. The longer the delay between the transfer of shares and payment—known as the settlement cycle—the greater the risk. The London market has already moved to a shorter cycle, in which trades are settled five days after the transaction, a system known as T + 5. CREST intended to move to T + 3 by autumn 1997, and already allows the same day transfer of cash and shares. A reduction in settlement time will be in line with other world markets. Third, it will lower the overall cost of settlement. The system itself will require about £35 million in income a year to break even (including network costs) compared with Talisman's £65 million in revenue. Although Talisman includes some settlements services not available on CREST, it still costs nearly twice as much when services are properly compared.

Unlike the Taurus system that was managed by the London Stock Exchange, the responsibility for CREST shifted to the Bank of England. Whereas the Stock Exchange struggled to accommodate all the interests of its members and ended up with a 'requirements creep' problem, the Bank of England set up a task-force which was given two months to originate the CREST proposal. The new proposal was a 'descoped' version of Taurus, since the task-force specified a much simpler systems architecture. The task-force, which put together the proposal for CREST, learned the lessons from Taurus by creating highly structured functional and technical specifications. In turn, they excluded some of the more ambitious aims of Taurus which were politically contentious. For example, unlike Taurus, where shareholders would be forced to relinquish their paper share certificates, this becomes optional under CREST. However, paper-backed transactions are more expensive, particularly for the small shareholder (private investor). The key functions of the CREST are outlined in Table 7.5.

The business strategy for the CREST computer project was finalised in May 1994. The key functions of CREST are outlined above. Software development was completed in December 1995. The development process was audited by both the Bank of England's internal auditors and Price Waterhouse. During this period,

Table 7.5 *The key functions of CREST*

- CREST will respond to electronic messages from members to transfer stock between accounts.
- It will authenticate the messages and compare the instructions input by the buyer and the seller—and match them.
- On settlement day, it will check the availability of stock and cash in the CREST members' accounts, and move the stock from the seller's account to the buyer's. The buying member's bank will be instructed to pay the selling member's bank and will be unconditionally obliged to do so.
- CREST will notify the stock's registrar who will commit to register valid transfers within two hours of the electronic transfer within the system.
- The contents of each member's accounts on the register, and in CREST, will be a mirror image of each other.

Adapted from: Documentation from CRESTCo Ltd. See also, *Financial Times*, Survey on IT, 3 July 1996, p. 8.

CRESTCo Ltd grew from six employees of the Bank of England, working on the Bank's premises, to a staff of more than 120 with offices in the City of London.

The total cost of developing the CREST system was £30 million. The annual operating costs were estimated to be £18 million. Any surplus in profit would be passed on to the users. The de-commissioned Talisman system gave the Stock Exchange an income of £55 million a year. The securities industry should see its processing costs fall dramatically. CREST was financed through the private sector, with 69 member firms contributing £12 million in equity, and a £17 million borrowing facility. Full control of the project remained with the Bank of England until completion of development when the system was handed over to the shareholders. Details of all transactions are transmitted directly from CREST to the Stock Exchange to allow it to police the market and ensure that trades and settlement data marry up. Shareholders in CRESTCO will be able to dictate future enhancements since they will eventually control the company.

Joint venture/project sourcing by the Bank of England witnessed by the development of CRESTCo Ltd was, in part, a reaction to the failure of the Taurus project that was managed by the London Stock Exchange. CRESTCo Ltd was set up with the primary aim of developing the CREST equity settlement system. Unlike other large-scale computer projects, the CREST system had a clearly defined technical and business specification, budget and delivery date. Although there have been some delays in the implementation of the CREST system, these problems have not been insurmountable. One advantage of this type of IT sourcing has been the Bank of England's ability to retain control over the activities of CRESTCo Ltd. This would not have been the case if the project had outsourced to an independent supplier. In some respects, joint venture/project sourcing is a hybrid between external and internal IT sourcing.

Insourcing at the UK Post Office

Context and Overview

The UK Post Office is a £5 billion business, with over 200 000 employees, structured into four divisions with a corporate head office function which includes IT. Its core business remains within the public sector, although many of its functions and services are being exposed to privatisation. As with other public sector organisations, the focus in the last five years has encouraged a commercial approach rather than one based entirely on the traditional public sector ethos of serving the community. Issues such as cost reduction, developing projects with suppliers, enhanced flexibility of service provision, and value for money have all become important.

The organisation culture at the Post Office has generally been risk averse and hierarchical which is a reflection of its civil service heritage. This has not been the case within the IT department. The approach to IT strategy has tended to focus upon the development of a robust and adaptable IT infrastructure to provide a wide range of applications rather than being driven by a predetermined applications portfolio. The business units have operated within a climate of dynamic market and political changes and this has initiated moves towards outsourcing which have been witnessed in other organisations. According to one spokesperson:

IT is becoming an integrated part and driver of the core business. It is an enabler of new products. Not just a support function but integral to the main fabric of the organisation.

The role of the Corporate IT function has undergone many changes over the last 10 years. In the mid-1980s it was a centrally funded headquarters department. In 1986, an internal charging mechanism was introduced, and many functions such as PCs and LANs devolved to local business units. In 1990 it became a business unit in its own right, selling its services both internally and in the external market place. Whilst this was effective in making the unit more businesslike, senior management perceived that it was causing too much diversion of effort, and over the next few years the focus moved back to concentrating on internal needs. Today, the model is of a customer-owned service unit, and it no longer sells its services externally. Whereas in 1990 IT was widely seen as a commodity service, it is now seen as core to the business.

The central service function has about 1000 staff, with another 500 IT-related people in the businesses. Over the last year, the distribution of staff has been charged with a tendency to recentralise operational activities, while devolving those associated with business analysis.

The Changing Nature of the IT Department

The IT group was set up as a business in 1990 and moved from being centrally funded to one that sold its services for profit maximisation. It was subsequently established as a business unit jointly owned by its customers. It is not driven to make a profit but instead aims to break even each year. Essentially, the strategy and policies of the IT department are set by a board, on which customers and Group Headquarters are represented.

Prior to the late 1970s, there were only about 100 people employed within IT, and this grew to about 1000 in the mid-1980s. Managers accounted for about 10% of this figure and this included business analysts. In addition, project managers were employed in various parts of the business. Although the figure of 1000 people in IT dipped slightly during the recession, it has now returned to this figure. There is a high capability and skill level within the IT department, albeit some of these skills are not in the latest communications and information technologies but in legacy systems.

During the early 1990s, the philosophy of an 'internal market' evolved to regulate what was described as a set 'of rather antagonistic relationships'. The policy was to protect the internal services from external competition for a period, during which time the internal services would attempt to reorganise themselves, improve quality, and achieve 'best in class' standards. If this had not been achieved by the end of the period, the role of the internal service would be reassessed and possibly disappear, with customers then being able to use the external marketplace.

Benchmarking

This move encouraged the IT group to focus on benchmarking its services against the external marketplace. Benchmarking came out of the internal market philosophy. It was an attempt to understand and improve the services and the position of the in-house supplier in relation to the market. It focused on a series of very detailed criteria across the range of services and prices offered. Value for money was a key objective of this exercise. The benchmarking of mainframe services, voice and data networking, and development has now been in place for several years. The benchmarking was not an easy task and many problems were encountered, such as ensuring like with like comparison. The in-house IT group provided a 'cradle to grave' service. This meant a lot of services, and the management of these services was difficult to separate out, or disentangle for comparative purposes. On the mainframe side, an external benchmarking service was used to help in the evaluation as they quickly found that they needed some independent credibility for their evaluation. One spokesman commented:

> One of the things we found was that doing your own reviews doesn't really work ... customers feel you are just fixing the figures.

The benchmarking of development was found to be a particularly difficult area:

> I think the development productivity area was the knotty one to tackle. It's often the one where you have most customer perception issues, which are related in and around customer management rather than actual delivery and results.

This meant that they encouraged their customers to become involved in the benchmarking process and to devise their own metrics. This helped them to manage and control their own use of resources and to look at things from a business perspective, rather than just using traditional measures. Even the traditional measures proved problematic in benchmarking, particularly in a changing technical environment. As the spokessperson observed:

> We do development productivity analysis with comparisons of input measures, function points, daily rates, and so on, but clearly as you move into case tools and rapid application development, the less the traditional methods of measuring function points are really appropriate.

Service-level agreements were created and were put in place for all services and customers. Some included penalty clauses and other criteria more commonly associated with external contracts. An annual customer satisfaction survey of the internal provision produced a rating of 6.9 out of 10, comparable with an industry average of 7. In general, technical competencies were highly rated, but areas such as marketing, sales and customer management were not. Overall, the benchmarking process was believed to have been successful. The spokesperson added:

> We found when we set up as a business centre customers felt that anywhere was better than the in-house supplier. In some places it was and that's fair enough. In other cases they found it wasn't. What I think it's done is lead to quite significant maturing of the relationship into a strategic customer/supplier relationship. But I think the challenge for us is to stop pretending we can do everything best in class and really be quite rigorous about benchmarking ourselves.

The benchmarking effort was seen as a way of moving towards a more commercial, externally comparable service with a view, subsequently, to establishing an outsourcing strategy. In some ways it was a prerequisite for moving towards an outsourcing strategy. Although, following the benchmarking exercise two years ago there still remain a number of outstanding issues to resolve. Because of the political uncertainty in which the organisation operates, conventional strategic planning is difficult. For example, the political issue of privatisation of the Post Office remains unresolved. IT strategy has to be based on the provision of an IT infrastructure. A spokesperson commented:

> What I have said to the board is that, as regards both networking and mainframe services, provided we are competitive, we visit the outsourcing issue in two years time when we are clear on our electronics services strategy rather than doing it now and suddenly finding we have given away a core capability to a potential competitor.

The second issue was about staffing, and the consequences of finding that certain people might not be needed. The culture of the organisation was to look after its staff and there had not been a compulsory redundancy in over 350 years. There had been voluntary redundancies, but experience had shown this could mean losing the very people and skills needed by the organisation.

A third issue was that the in-house IT saw itself as a genuine competitor in any outsourcing; it did not wish to be outsourced as a whole or in any of the key areas.

In the early 1990s, the IT department tended to be technology focused. During 1994/5, the organisation attempted to identify its core competencies at the same time as embarking on a reskilling/training programme to develop people to become more service/customer aware. It also needed to improve its contract management skills since it did not have a strong tradition of using external suppliers on a large scale.

During this period, a framework for the future of the IT structure was developed. It envisaged that if and when a decision was made to outsource, it would be on a partnership basis for non-core activities in the event of the organisation not having the relevant in-house skills, or where the in-house capability was not competitive.

At the present time the Post Office has undertaken its own research into the advantages and disadvantages of outsourcing. It has entered into a large-scale joint venture with the Benefits Agency to automate its counter services. The supplier is a consortium called Pathway. Under this contract the supplier provides a complete service. Risk and reward are shared so that if there is a benefits fraud which can be directly attributed to administrative problems caused by the supplier, then the supplier is responsible for part of the risk. About 100 people are engaged to manage this contract. Some parts of the contract are with the Post Office whereas others are with the Benefits Agency. There is an umbrella contract which both organisations for certain aspects of the contract.

A spokesperson at the Post Office said that,

> The Post Office has been considering its attitude to outsourcing. Our approach will be selective, and a number of opportunities are currently under consideration.

Business Drivers for Outsourcing

One such area related to the provision of mainframe services, where a number of possible benefits were identified:

1. *Improving the balance sheet*: 'Outsourcing enables capital expenditure to be substituted by a revenue stream. This can be attractive, but is not currently a major issue.'
2. *Moving to a variable cost base*: 'This is theoretically attractive, but in practice there is a limit to the rate at which existing mainframe systems could realistically be phrased out or moved to another environment. The trade-off here is likely to be that a high level of variability can only be achieved at the expense of giving up technical control to a public bureau style of operation, or being prepared to sacrifice service coherence and continuity by relying upon other organisations' spare capacity. A realistic compromise is probably to avoid commitments in either duration or capacity which extend beyond the period over which the equipment would normally be depreciated.'
3. *Cost saving*: 'Whilst there is a widespread perception that mainframe out-sourcing can reduce costs, this needs to be treated with caution. In the Post Office there are few further economies of scale as this installation has already been consolidated on a single site. Most of the savings an external supplier can achieve are equally available in-house, where there are no marketing overheads, profit requirement or VAT. Clarity must be obtained as to how they expect to achieve any savings that they claim, and that the Post Office is not exposed to unexpected additional charges once the contract is operational.'

In particular

- Do the in-house costs cover a wider range of services, or greater service flexibility, than the supplier is committed to provide?
- Has an initial cost reduction been achieved by moving some of the charges to a later stage in the contract, when costs will be lower due to technology improvements or full depreciation? Will he/she be able to charge extra for renewal of software licences or software updating which would have been covered in internal budgets?
- Have we taken advantage of all opportunities to reduce costs in-house?
- Is the vendor planning to reduce costs by re-engineering our appliances?
- Are we sure that the supplier is contractually committed to service levels that are at least as good in all respects as those achieved in-house? Alternatively, if a lesser level of service would be acceptable, does this provide an opportunity for further savings in-house? Would our in-house process of continual improvement have led as a matter of course to enhancements that will cost extra in an outsourced environment?
- Have we budgeted for the cost of future changes on a like for like basis between the outsource and in-house options?
- Outsourcing contracts that are driven by cost saving need to ensure great clarity in the definition of the services to be delivered, the prices to be charged and the service levels to be achieved. The basis upon which changes to these services will be charged for needs to be clearly established, and benchmarking

provisions included to ensure that prices remain competitive in the future. Workable exit provisions are essential as an ultimate sanction.

- Outsourcing cost estimates need to include an allowance for the costs of in-house functions needed to manage the technical, service and financial interfaces with the supplier, and for renegotiation or transition to another supplier at the end of the contract.

Core Competencies

One aspect of the rationale for considering outsourcing is the proposition that the presence of major enterprises which do not form an integral part of core business is a distraction for top management, as well as requiring them to make decisions in areas where they have limited expertise. Given the growing dependence of the Post Office upon IT in its day-to-day operations, together with its emerging role as an enabler of new Post Office services as well as a source of competition, there can be little doubt that understanding and exploiting IT is a core competence. The core nature of day-to-day operations is more controversial. 'The management of large networks' has been recognised as a core competence, but current thinking tends to take the view that it is acceptable to outsource operational activities, provided that an adequate level of control is retained. Outsourcing arrangements driven by core competencies arguments tend to focus on off-loading as much responsibility and accountability onto the supplier. Research shows that this has often been done at the expense of maintaining essential core internal expertise and control to safeguard the future of the client organisation.

Access to World Class Expertise

This is often claimed as a benefit of outsourcing but seldom delivered. Where this is a driver, contracts need to be based around the supply of individuals with defined levels of experience and expertise in the relevant areas, rather than around basic service delivery. This is not particularly applicable to mainframe outsourcing. The Post Office operation is sufficiently large and well respected to be able to attract high-quality expertise, and stands up well in international benchmarking. The area in which major outsourcing companies may possibly excel is in process refinement and cost management. This will be established during preliminary benchmarking activities.

The spokesperson claimed that the issue of retaining control is another challenge of the outsourcing relationship.

> Too much control will reduce the supplier's capability to add value, but too little will result in a deal that is uncompetitive in the long term, and could seriously constrain future development of Post Office IT infrastructure.

In general terms, the type of outsourcing relationship that is most amenable to future business and technical change will be one that avoids long-term commercial commitments and maintains control over the technical environment. At the very least, the commercial arrangement must be concluded in such a way that, if there is a major drop in mainframe usage for some reason, the Post Office will be no worse off than if it had retained the function in-house.

Retaining Technical Capabilities and Skills

The Post Office is clearly addressing the key opportunities and pitfalls of outsourcing. It is tending to proceed with some caution on all fronts. Unlike many other organisations that do not perceive IT as part of the core business, the Post Office values its strong IT infrastructure, technical capabilities and skills. At the time of writing, the Post Office continues to use the external market for benchmarking its own internal activities, while at the same time developing the competitiveness and quality of the internal service. It is increasingly adopting a commercial awareness more akin to the private sector by attempting to address its structure, and identify the skills needed for the future. These measures have proved invaluable to internal customers. In terms of mainframe services, economies of scale have been achieved similar to those of external suppliers. Internal charging mechanisms have also been set up on a more commercial footing using service level agreements (SLAs) and internal contracts. The organisation has clearly observed the experiences of other high-profile outsourcing deals and, in so doing, is attempting to develop strategies which are compatible with its own organisational culture, structure and technologies. As the Post Office approaches the millennium, it is apparent that the degree of political and business uncertainty remains. This poses questions about the viability of outsourcing.

Given that some technology-related activities are perceived to be part of the core business, such as the management of large networks, it is not easy to separate business and technology matters along the lines of the core competencies model. Some activities, such as those relating to the core businesses and the customer interface systems, are potentially strategic. Owing to the wide range of activities currently undertaken, many fall into the 'useful' category and are never likely to become strategic. As such, they are commodity systems and services and may therefore, potentially, be outsourced. Others, however, may not. Technological maturity at the Post Office is relatively high. However, this situation is not static and whereas capabilities and skills in legacy technologies (some aspects of mainframe computing) are high, new skills will need to be developed in communications and information technologies.

SUMMARY

This chapter has sought to examine IT outsourcing by considering theoretical and empirical material on the subject. Our discussion of the global marketplace shows a steady increase in outsourcing with about seven suppliers offering a full range of IT services. The four different types of IT sourcing may be seen as mutually exclusive since the advantages of total outsourcing, for example, may be perceived as disadvantages by those opting for selective sourcing. Company strategies for IT sourcing depend on many factors, not least whether they can find a suitable supplier who is able to offer a value-added service. In reviewing existing literature and empirical research on outsourcing markets, business and technical strategies, it is apparent that many challenges lie ahead if companies are to gain advantages from outsourcing.

Recent research on the results of first and second generation IT outsourcing contracts shows that some organisations are now learning the lessons from hindsight. Yet one survey indicates that few of them are fully aware of the 'real options available at contract expiry' (OTR Group, 1998). This report shows that many outsourcing contracts are created with inadequate provisions concerning termination. However, it warns that very few outsourcing contracts due to expire over the next two years will be given to different suppliers, even if there is deep dissatisfaction with the present supplier. This is because companies often leave it too late to begin the renegotiation phase and end up negotiating with existing suppliers from a position of weakness. Some suppliers also make it difficult for companies to move to another supplier by arguing that intellectual property (e.g. information contained on databases) cannot be handed over to the client nor the rival supplier. Whilst the reletting of outsourcing contracts is an important issue, so too is the management of ongoing contracts, some of which last for a 10-year period. As the British Aerospace case study shows, managers and staff need to spend some time negotiating ongoing issues with their counterparts at the supplier organisation. Whilst this company has made an attempt to quantify this time, and believes it to be beneficial to both client and supplier, many companies often underestimate the management costs of so doing. One estimate is that companies should spend as much as 3% of the total outsourcing contract value on management costs.

From the research studies examined in this chapter, there is a general trend towards using multiple suppliers in favour of other IT sourcing options (Currie and Willcocks, 1998b). The risks of handing the entire IT function to a single supplier is less attractive to many companies, particularly if they perceive this to result in higher costs and reduced control. Notwithstanding this point, all forms of IT sourcing carry certain risks and it is the responsibility of the client company to ensure that risk-avoidance strategies are in place (Lacity and Willcocks, 1998). In concluding the chapter, it is apparent that IT sourcing is a complex activity; one that encapsulates market, business, organisational, human resources and technical factors. Within the global information society, IT outsourcing has become a major phenomenon and one where many lessons are yet to be learned. In the next chapter we consider the supply side of outsourcing by focusing upon the strategic positioning of companies in the software and computing services industry.

8
Strategic Positioning of Companies in the Software and Computing Services Industry

INTRODUCTION

The supply side of IT outsourcing has received little attention in the academic research community since the focus has been largely on client strategies. This has tended to produce a one-dimensional approach to the study of IT outsourcing. Especially, since our understanding of large 'mega' deals is just as much a reflection of the strategic positioning of the large, well resourced IT service providers, as it is on client strategies to restructure, re-engineer and reshape their businesses to compete more effectively in vertical markets from aerospace to banking. This chapter looks at the strategic positioning of mainly large IT service providers in the software and computer services industry. It offers a model of how these companies are attempting to gain leverage in providing outsourcing services through a series of mergers, acquisitions and joint ventures. Medium and small players in this market are generally following their lead, although many are finding themselves victims of take-overs by their larger counterparts. If this trend continues, it is likely that the software and computing services industry will become dominated by supplier 'cartels'. Such a situation will have significant implications for the industry, as fewer, yet more powerful service providers will determine price, quality, choice and competition.

For the majority of suppliers, outsourcing has so far been highly profitable (Terdiman, 1996). But now the market is moving into a new phase and is rapidly reshaping itself. Until now, data-centre outsourcing represented the core element of the business given the large investments in mainframe infrastructure. But over time, profit margins have fallen in data-centre outsourcing. This has encouraged suppliers to become more selective in pursuing this business area. Larger numbers of suppliers are now declining to bid for data-centre contracts. Instead, they are seeking higher profit margins from offering their services in areas of applications development, systems integration, distributed systems technologies and associated consultancy work (Currie, 1999b). This will leave the second tier suppliers (with annual outsourcing revenue of up to £200 million) to bid for the remaining large-scale processing work which their more ambitious and larger rivals have left behind.

It is estimated that value-added services such as consulting, business process reengineering, distributed support and application development offer operating profit margins of 15% and above, thereby making these activities more profitable for vendors. The average profit margin for all outsourcing services is estimated to be between 10% and 12% (Terdiman, 1996, pp. 2–3). Another salient point is that new forms of outsourcing will be generated by emerging technologies. As we saw in Chapter 4, Internet commerce will spawn a new generation of supplier companies (or high-tech intermediaries) which will provide a range of technical and support services to their customers. The large outsourcing suppliers are also exploring this market (Currie, 1998).

This chapter is divided into three parts. First it considers the maturing global IT outsourcing market and, in particular, some of the new 'mega' deals that have occurred in recent years. Whilst selective sourcing continues to be the most popular model adopted by client companies, an industry analysis shows that the large deals are becoming more complex as the industry leaders attempt to offer a wider portfolio of products and services to their customers. Second, the discussion introduces a typology of outsourcing companies in the software and computing services industry. It shows that many companies, like traditional hardware manufacturers, systems houses and generic outsourcers, are attempting to enhance their product and services portfolios by signing more lucrative outsourcing contracts involving business process outsourcing (BPO), knowledge management and relationship building. Third, we consider the key players in the UK IT consultancy/service provider sector. Since the late 1980s, these companies have enhanced their strategic position through a series of mergers and acquisitions. Having considered the supply side of IT outsourcing, the chapter concludes by suggesting that the software and computing services industry will become increasingly complex and difficult to define as the key players strengthen their strategic positioning in vertical markets from banking to health care.

THE TREND TOWARDS 'MEGA' OUTSOURCING DEALS

As we saw in Chapter 7, the trend towards IT outsourcing continues to grow. A recent snapshot of the five largest UK private sector outsourcing deals ranged from £70 million to £1.8 billion (see Table 8.1). These deals are usually for a long period of time, often up to 10 years' duration. The largest UK public sector deal is between the Inland Revenue and EDS, and is worth about £1.6 billion. This deal is now in its fifth year, which is halfway through. The deal has attracted some criticism given that the cost of the contract increased by 60%. John Yard, Inland Revenue Director of IT, said:

Table 8.1   *Top UK private sector IT outsourcing contracts*

Cable and Wireless Communications	IBM	10 years	£1.8bn
British Steel	Cap Gemini	9 years	£400m
Transco	ICL	5 years	£160m
Bradford & Bingley	IBM	10 years	£100m
ICO	CSC	2 stages	£70m

Adapted from: Computing, 26 November 1998, p. 18.

> The price increase is blamed on new government tax policies—such as the introduction of tax credits. The contract is good value for the taxpayer. I'm confident that the current investigation by the National Audit Office (NAO) will vindicate that.

The NAO is investigating the deal's value for money, following a previous price increase from the original projection of £1 billion to £1.6 billion. The first price increase, on what is not a fixed price contract, was due to the increase in IT workload to ease the introduction of the self-assessment tax system in 1997. EDS claims that it receives a reduced baseline fee each year and is greatly reducing unit costs. 'The base workload fee of £1 billion is £225 million less than if the Revenue had stayed in-house. Unit costs for systems development will be 50% cheaper when the contract ends. (*Computing,* 13 January 1999, p. 13).

As the IT outsourcing market continues to grow in terms of the number of contracts signed and their relative increase in price, it is apparent that few IT service providers are able to meet the demands of 'mega' outsourcing deals. To some extent it may be the case that demand for outsourcing exceeds supply. This is likely where small and medium size companies (SMEs) wishing to outsource all or part of their IT facility find that only a few suppliers offer the range of services they require. For example, an analysis of emerging trends towards outsourcing in vertical markets shows that the propensity to outsource is high in utilities, government and telecommunications, but low in the insurance industry. Manufacturing has traditionally used outsourcing, but healthcare, which has not, is now undergoing major changes due, in part, to financial pressure. As such, IT service providers are likely to find new opportunities in this market over the next five years. The large players will therefore look towards developing new markets (Birkinshaw and Fry, 1998), such as healthcare, rather than tailor their offerings to smaller (lower margin) contracts with SMEs.

Globalisation, Deregulation and Consolidation

Three major forces have been driving change in the business world and the software and computer services industry in particular. They are globalisation, deregulation and consolidation. These forces have generated the growth and demand for information technology outsourcing, and systems consulting and integration services (Eisenhardt and Brown, 1998). Companies like IBM, EDS and CSC, to name only a few, have extended their global reach by entering into a variety of strategic arrangements with other suppliers, largely for the purpose of serving their clients' growing demands for products and services. There has been an increase in serving clients in vertical markets worldwide, ranging from aerospace and automotive companies to chemical, oil and gas, to financial services, utilities and, more recently, healthcare. These global suppliers now have a significant presence and scale in such markets through securing large outsourcing contracts and entering into joint ventures and by making strategic acquisitions. This trend was set in place from the late 1980s (Henderson, 1990). To this end, large IT service providers have been very instrumental in deciding their strategies for making inroads into vertical markets. An example is EDS's positioning within the defence industry. Such a move enables EDS to develop core competencies relevant in defence contracts, not least to serve its clients, but equally to help define and shape the future of the global defence industry.

Deregulation in the financial services industry has also fuelled outsourcing, particularly where companies have turned to external IT service providers to tackle competition from potential new entrants to this market. Consolidations, mergers and acquisitions have enabled these new entrants to gain access to markets and customers in ways which were not possible prior to privatisation and deregulation. Table 8.2 gives a breakdown of the top 10 suppliers of software and computing services to the UK market in 1998. As we can see, EDS retains the top position, followed by IBM. Three of the top companies are US in origin, and there are only two European companies in the list. There is also a wide differential between the

Table 8.2   *Top ten suppliers of software and computing services to the UK market in 1998*

1998	Company	Nationality	1996 (£m)	1997	1997 Rank	1998	Growth % 1997/8
1	EDS	US	765	1000	1	1270	27
2	IBM-UK SCS	US	600	800	2	1100	38
3	ICL-UK SCS	Japan	575	620	3	750	21
4	CAP Gemini (UK)	France	320	386	6	596	54
5	Anderson Consulting UK	US	350	445	5	545	22
6	CSC UK	US	323	380	7	500	32
7	Microsoft UK	US	260	343	8	450	31
8	Oracle UK	US	234	335	9	440	31
9	Sema Group	UK/France	361	476	4	419	−12
10	Compaq/Digital UK SCS	US	160	270	15	310	15
Overall growth				25%		26%	

Note: Excludes hardware, operating software and own hardware maintenance and associated support. Revenue relates to financial year ending in 1998—*not* calendar year 1998.
Adapted from: Holway (1998).

top two companies and the rest in terms of annual revenue, yet one company, CAP Gemini, showed a 54% growth from 1997 to 1998.

A TYPOLOGY OF OUTSOURCING COMPANIES IN THE SOFTWARE AND COMPUTING SERVICES INDUSTRY

The IT services market has undergone many changes in the last 30 years. From 1970 to 1987 the market consisted of three distinct types of IT service provider. They were: hardware suppliers; systems houses supplying and developing software; and IT consultancies (Mitchell and Fitzgerald, 1998). From the late 1980s, many new entrants entered the outsourcing marketplace from the traditional IT service providers to other sources. The reasons for this vary. First, legislation passed in the United Kingdom and the United States to contract-out *white-collar* public services led to increased outsourcing as some in-house IT departments were transferred to an external vendor. For example, in the United Kingdom, central and local government were required by law to market test their public services through a process known as compulsory competitive tendering (CCT) (Currie, 1996b). This was seen as an opportunity by many IT service providers to reinvent themselves as experts in offering strategic outsourcing services from IT consultancy through to applications management and development (Quinn and Hilmer, 1994).

Second, economic recession and increased global competition has led many companies to seek cost-cutting measures (Takac, 1994). This, in turn, has led to increased outsourcing of IT and other business services (e.g. accountancy, HRM and marketing). The IT service providers have responded by shifting their offering of *stand-alone* services, such as mainframe, data centre and applications management to, more recently, IT consultancy (e.g. IT strategy formulation), business process outsourcing (BPO), customer relationship management and systems integration.

Figure 8.1 identifies six types of IT outsourcing service provider in relation to their strategic positioning in the software and computer services industry. They are: IT consultancies/service providers; hardware suppliers; systems houses; generic outsourcers; niche player consultancies; and niche player IT suppliers. The diagram further considers the relationship between market differentiation and client—supplier integration. Traditionally, the in-house IT department would serve its *internal* customers from the various business and administrative units. It would therefore be highly integrated with its customer base and may insource additional services (contract programmers) from the external (labour) market. In recent years, however, many internal IT departments have entered into outsourcing contracts with external suppliers. As we saw in Chapter 7, IT sourcing contracts are varied but generally fall into four distinct categories: total outsourcing; selective (multiple contract) sourcing; joint venture/strategic alliance sourcing; and insourcing (buying-in services) (Willcocks and Choi, 1995; Currie and Willcocks, 1998c).

With the advent of increased outsourcing, the in-house IT department has become less integrated with its customer base, especially since external IT service providers now undertake to do some of the work previously done by the in-house team. This poses both an opportunity and a threat to a company. It is an oppor-

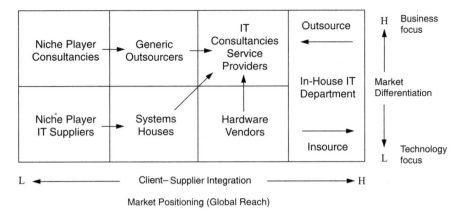

Figure 8.1 *Strategic positioning of IT outsourcing suppliers*

tunity since outsourcing may have the benefits of improving services, reducing costs and gaining access to new capabilities and skills. Yet it is a threat where a company finds that it is not easy to manage several suppliers, as is the case in some selective (multiple contract) sourcing arrangements (Currie, 1998). Client–supplier integration is thus an important element in the outsourcing relationship, and there is a current trend which shows that many IT service providers are seeking longer term relationships with their customers, albeit partly to generate higher margins from outsourcing contracts. Increased client–supplier integration is also enabled by the IT service providers offering highly differentiated business services, and not just by selling technical systems. This is explained in more detail if we consider the six types of IT outsourcing suppliers defined in Figure 8.1.

1. *IT consultancies/service providers.* These companies are global and most diverse in terms of offering a wide array of vertically integrated outsourcing services. They have developed from international consultancies specialising in business and IT consultancy including project management, software development and systems support and maintenance. They moved into the outsourcing market in the late 1980s to take advantage of the then lucrative margins and long-term nature of contracts. This international element has led to the import of mainly North American approaches to outsourcing, and large vendors achieved sizeable contracts by leveraging their North American outsourcing track record, experience and skills. EDS, CSC, and Anderson Consulting are examples. ISSC, which is part of IBM, is also an important player. Smaller companies are CAP Gemini and FI Group.

2. *Hardware vendors.* Traditional hardware manufacturers also moved into the market often through hardware maintenance outsourcing as hardware sales declined. In addition, software products have been increasingly commoditised, which has affected the PC hardware market. This has led many companies to turn to services to support future growth. IBM, HP, DEC, Siemens,

ICL, Unisys and AT&T all offer outsourcing services. IBM set up ISSC which now has many lucrative outsourcing contracts.

3. *Systems houses.* This is a dynamic and diverse group of mainly small and medium-sized companies (SMEs) offering a range of products and services. Many focus on a specific market sector, e.g. software development for the financial services sector. Others are regionally based, e.g. they operate in India and serve a regional market. AB Intersales and Computer Outsourcing Services are examples.

4. *Generic outsourcers.* Traditional services providers of security, facilities management (FM) and other services have expanded their outsourcing portfolio by offering desktop PC support and cabling services, etc. Synstar International offers a wide range of integrated services and solutions in the areas of computer services and business continuity services.

5. *Niche player consultancies.* These are usually small firms that offer consultancy in business process re-engineering, change management, organisational learning and other related areas. They also include *one-man-band* operators.

6. *Niche player IT suppliers.* These small firms offer specialist technical services such as Internet (Web site) design and development, software development, maintenance and support, among other areas.

There have also been instances where former in-house IT departments become IT outsourcing companies offering their services to a range of clients. ITNet and Barclays Computer Operations are two examples. To some extent, in-house IT management may see outsourcing as an opportunity to initiate a management buyout (MBO), especially if they are able to compete favourably with external IT service providers on price and quality.

As Figure 8.1 suggests, hardware suppliers, systems houses and generic outsourcers are all making inroads into the IT consultancy/solutions providers quadrant. As well as the major companies in this area (EDS, CSC, etc.), many medium and large companies are also expanding their outsourcing portfolios. The traditional hardware suppliers like IBM, HP, DEC, Siemens, ICL, Unisys and AT&T have all widened their outsourcing portfolios, often through mergers, acquisitions, strategic alliances and joint ventures. Similarly, systems houses are now more likely to seek long-term arrangements with their clients by offering additional outsourcing services. The generic outsourcing companies are also attempting to do the same. But systems houses and generic outsourcers are often inhibited by their limited size and service portfolios.

KEY PLAYERS IN THE UK IT CONSULTANCY/SERVICE PROVIDER SECTOR

Following a period of economic recession, the IT services market in North America and Western Europe gained strength towards the late 1990s. In Western Europe, there is some evidence to suggest that the IT services market is stronger than in the United States. It is apparent that economic conditions and growth cycles differ across countries. However, the United Kingdom has witnessed the strongest growth in recent years, but shows some signs of slowing down by the millennium. Conversely, France and Italy, which experienced an economic downturn during the mid-1990s, are projected to grow more than any other country in Western Europe. This is followed by Germany, a country which is among the relative late developers in the IT services market. Similarly, specific business sectors of the market are producing very different growth rates. Hardware maintenance suppliers are experiencing acute difficulties across Western Europe, although outsourcing continues to proliferate.

The supply side of the IT labour market (particularly freelance IT contractors) has also grown considerably as a consequence of the demands of the Year 2000 (Y2K) issue and the introduction of the euro. There is also a growing demand for services connected with e-commerce and the Internet/Intranet. The Western European market is now as important as the US market. This is shown by many US companies seeing Europe as the growth market for the future. IBM and EDS are now among the leading IT services suppliers in every country in Europe with Anderson Consulting and CSC among the fastest growing rivals. Many other companies are now looking to establish a presence in the European market, particularly by acquisition (Holway, 1998).

Whilst much of the academic research on IT outsourcing to date has concentrated largely on the client (demand) side, there have been few studies that focus directly on the supply side. To some extent, an understanding and analysis of the key players in the software and computing services industry is essential, since the industry is witnessing significant shifts with an increase in mergers, acquisitions, strategic alliances and joint ventures (McFarlan and Nolan, 1995; Willcocks and Choi, 1995). One prediction is that we are likely to see a growing tendency towards supplier 'cartels' in the IT outsourcing marketplace. Table 8.3 Gives a breakdown of the top UK outsourcers in 1998 as measured by outsourcing revenues alone. As we can see, EDS holds first place, although IBM, CSC and CAP Gemini are making significant inroads into the outsourcing marketplace. The following sections discuss EDS, IBM and CSC in some detail.

EDS

EDS is one of the world's largest information services companies with 110 000 employees working in 47 countries. EDS has about 9000 clients who range from small companies to the largest corporations and governments around the world. EDS serves most industries including manufacturing/distribution/retail, finance and insurance, communications, health, transportation, energy and chemicals, and government. According to one report, EDS takes home 25p in every pound spent on IT by UK civil government. The report claims that annual IT spending in civil government, excluding the Ministry of Defence (MoD), will rise from £1.39 billion to £1.44 billion in the next financial year. In addition, the MoD spends a further £800 million a year. The report concludes that EDS receives a 70% share of the government outsourcing market, worth a total of £514 million in 1998. That share

Table 8.3   *Top 10 UK outsourcers in 1998 as measured by outsourcing revenues*

Rank	Company	UK outsourcing revenue (£m)
1	EDS	850
2	IBM	450
3	CSC	400
4	Cap Gemini	360
5	ICL	280
6	Sema	255
7	Anderson Consulting	180
8	Capita	160
9	FI Group	110
10 =	ITNet	105
10 =	Perot	105

amounts to £360 million, which is a quarter of the total government IT spend of £1.39 billion. SEMA is the second largest government supplier with an 11% share, followed by ICL with 6% and Siemens with 4%. The bulk of spending is destined for external services, rising from £787 million in 1998 to a projected £850 million in 1999/2000.

In recent months, EDS has enhanced its position in relation to its key competitors, IBM and CSC, by buying SHL Systemhouse as part of a US$25 billion outsourcing agreement with MCI WorldCom. SHL Systemhouse is one of the largest Canadian computer service and consulting firms, and the agreement will significantly expand EDS's resources in its outsourcing, systems integration and electronic commerce businesses. EDS has gained a US$1.7 billion revenue company and will take over around 12 000 MCI staff. In a cross-outsourcing agreement that will bind them closely together, EDS will operate most of MCI Worldcom's information technology services, while MCI Worldcom will run EDS's global telecommunications network. Such a move is similar to IBM's recent deal with AT&T, which also involved cross-outsourcing of their non-core businesses. EDS's president Jeff Heller said that EDS's competitors—CSC and CAP Gemini—would look for similar alliances with telecommunications leaders. IBM has another close relationship with telecommunications company Cable & Wireless, having in 1998 won Europe's largest outsourcing contract with C&WC valued at £1.8 billion (*Computer Weekly*, 18 February 1999, p. 16). Although EDS has grown substantially over the years, largely through its adoption of staff from client companies as a consequence of outsourcing, it is likely that it will rationalise and reshape itself in the near future.

IBM/ISSC

IBM/ISSC has been the leading company in the global IT supplier market for several decades. It currently has 291 000 employees and under 300 000 wholly or partially owned subsidiaries. With revenues of US$81 billion, it is a truly international company. IBM, which was traditionally a hardware supplier, set up a company called Integrated Software Solutions Corporation (ISSC) to make inroads into the IT services industry. This company offers global core services ranging from business and IT consulting, business transformation, e-commerce (e-business), total systems management and strategic outsourcing. The latter (strategic outsourcing) is equally varied and includes services in business process management, application management outsourcing, network and IT outsourcing. IT outsourcing services provide management and support for IT operations. Outsourcing contracts include high end-server (host) operations, midrange services, distributed and desktop information technology services. Customers include large *Fortune 500* companies and SMEs. UK outsourcing revenues total £450 million. Given the backing of its parent, ISSC is likely to go from strength to strength as it makes further inroads into the software and computing services industry, largely through outsourcing deals.

CSC

Computer Sciences Corporation (CSC) operates from more than 700 locations on six continents. The company offers services that include management consulting, systems consulting and integration, operations support and information services outsourcing. CSC was formed in 1959. The company had revenues of US$7.4 billion for the 12 months ended 1 January 1999. This is an increase from US$6.6 billion for the previous year. CSC recently completed implementation of two of the largest IT outsourcing contracts. The first was with JP Morgan, where CSC led a team including Anderson Consulting, AT&T Solutions and Bell Atlantic Network Integration that won the contract. The team then joined with JP Morgan to form Pinnacle Alliance, which supports a large portion of JP Morgan's worldwide information technology structure. This alliance is continuing to expand and evolve. This agreement is a first in the IT industry and had provided CSC with knowledge and experience that no other information services company possesses.

The second contract was with DuPont, where CSC and DuPont have a shared goal of helping DuPont gain the greatest business value from its IT systems. Major accomplishments during the year include the incorporation of technology solutions such as SAP, Year 2000, supply chain and software engineering into the companies' businesses. The aim is to deliver global solutions to DuPont, which operates in more than 70 countries. Other large contracts were signed with CAN Financial Corporation and ING Financial Services North America, a unit of the Amsterdam-based ING Group, which is one of the world's largest diversified financial services companies. This contract is for the support of data-centre operations, automating help-desk functions and managing desktop support and local area network services (LANS). These large outsourcing contracts, along with others, significantly increased CSC's outsourcing revenue, contributing to an additional US$700 million during the year. A further US$300 million came from systems consulting and integration services. This includes electronic commerce via the Internet, Year 2000 services and enterprise wide solutions (which integrate disparate business functions across an entire company).

An overview of the recent mergers, acquisitions, strategic alliances and joint ventures by three of the leading IT service providers suggests a trend towards enhanced market differentiation. To this end, it becomes important to understand not only what the client company wishes to achieve through IT outsourcing contracts, but also how the various IT service providers may support a contract. In the very large 'mega' outsourcing deals, the major players in the software and computer services industry serve their customers through a complex web of global alliances and joint ventures.

MERGERS AND ACQUISITIONS IN THE FINANCIAL SERVICES SECTOR

To understand the growth in IT outsourcing contracts is to recognise the dynamic changes that have taken place in global markets. In the financial services sector, for example, there has been a spate of mergers and acquisitions which is part of a consolidation process that will reduce the number of physical banks by as much as 25% by the end of the millennium. These mergers and acquisitions in the banking sector have generated many opportunities for outsourcing suppliers with capabilities and skills to assist banks with their efforts to reorganise and consolidate their IT infrastructures. Over the last two decades, the banking industry has been transformed. An example is that seven of the ten largest US commercial-banking companies of 1988 have been acquired over a ten-year period.

There are three main reasons for the acquisitions in the US banking sector. First, federal restrictions were relaxed in 1994. Before deregulation, banks could acquire other banks in more than one state, but they had to operate as separate companies. When the new laws were passed in Congress in 1994, acquisitions outside the state of the parent bank could operate as branches of the parent bank. Second, there are a disproportionately large number of banks compared with the amount of money in the system. As a result, competition leads to consolidation. Third, with the growth in virtual banking, many customers no longer need to visit a physical branch since they can conduct banking transactions using their personal computer at home or at the office.

Outsourcing helps mergers and acquisitions where the supplier assists the merging institution to reach the new market quickly. A large outsourcing supplier can spend a couple of years with the client in managing the change process. Once an acquisition has been finalised, the acquiring bank has to run on two IT infrastructures, which includes two IT data centres, networks, helpdesks, cheque processing systems, and two sets of system engineers and business analysts.

The ultimate goal of the bank is to merge these two infrastructures into one integrated unit. A supplier can relieve the bank of the duality of the fixed-cost infrastructure that the financial institution has inherited and turn it into a variable rate service. So the supplier becomes very involved in the bank's change process since it manages the transformation. The advantage of a supplier taking up a short-term contract is that the bank does not inherit large additional costs. Instead, the supplier will take the risk and absorb the costs over a period of time. This outsourcing model mitigates the bank's risk by taking away any responsibility the bank would have of disposing of redundant assets after the overall conversion is completed. The extra assets after the hardware, software, and people may not be as valuable to the bank as they are to a supplier because they can deploy them to satisfy the requirements of other customers.

Mergers and acquisitions have now become an effective means of dealing with fierce competition, global expansion efforts, industry change, diversification, cutting costs, eliminating ineffective management, and increasing product and technological range. Over the last 10 years, outsourcing has played a critical role in merger and acquisition activities. Moreover, outsourcing can be a key element in increasing the chances of success for the new entity. The integration of staff and IT systems are pivotal areas where mergers often fail. Outsourcing may excel as a business tool to accomplish integration and efficiency in these areas (Bender–Samuel, `outsourcing.com`). Table 8.4 gives a summary of acquisitions in the US banking sector from 1991 to 1998.

An analysis of the mergers and acquisitions that have taken place in vertical markets like financial services (above) is symmetrical to the events that have taken place in the software and computing services industry. According to one analysis, there have been winners and losers. For example, IT staff agencies and those dealing in commodity items like hardware, third party software products, have not been very successful in increasing their margins. Conversely, companies with high, value-added earnings from long-term customer relationships (outsourcers like Capita and FI Group or products companies like Sage with high recurring revenues) have consolidated their position. UK-owned companies like Misys, Sage, Logica, RM, London Bridge and many others have shown that not only can they compete internationally, but can lead the world in their chosen markets. Although, as we have seen above, the United Kingdom continues to lack a global player in the software and computing services industry to rival US EDS and IBM Global Services, and French owned CAP Gemini, nevertheless the software and computing services industry market in Europe grew on average by 18% in 1998 to approximately E107 billion (euro). According to Holway (1998), the European market is forecast to be worth E173 billion in 2002. The United Kingdom and France had amongst the strongest growth in 1998, with Italy and Germany falling below average.

Table 8.4   *Acquisitions in the US banking sector—1991–1998*

Company	Acquired by	Date
Citcorp	Travelers Group	October 1998
Chase Manhattan	Chemical Banking	March 1996
Security Pacific	BankAmerica	April 1992
BankAmerica	NationsBank	September 1998
Manufacturers Hanover	Chemical Banking	December 1991
First Interstate Bancorp	Wells Fargo	April 1996
Bankers Trust	Deutsche Bank	December 1998

Adapted from: `Fortune/outsourcing-journal.com`

An effective merger and acquisition strategy where outsourcing is concerned is called 'roll-ups'. When a company which is acquiring numerous other companies has an alliance with an outsourcing supplier, the acquiring company can focus on integrating the core businesses, while the supplier focuses on integrating the non-core pieces of the business. This allows the consolidating company to do more acquisitions faster and still preserve its capital for integrating core businesses.

MANAGING THE CLIENT–SUPPLIER RELATIONSHIP

A salient issue that has emerged from research into IT outsourcing is how to manage the client–supplier relationship (Currie, 1998). This is an issue not just for the client company but also for the IT service provider. As outsourcing contracts have become more complex, particularly the 'mega' deals of recent years, client companies and their suppliers need to develop new managerial and organisational practices. An industry analysis of outsourcing deals shows that some client–supplier relationships have not been successful, which has led to the termination of some contracts. Powergen, which owns East Midlands Electricity, announced that it was ending its 12 year £150 million outsourcing deal with Perot Systems five years early. East Midlands Electricity claims the termination of the contract was 'a strategic decision' and was 'not a reflection on Perot Systems Europe's performance over the past seven years'. Perot Systems said in reply, it was 'a privilege for Perot Systems to work with East Midlands and Powergen'.

The history of this outsourcing contract is interesting since East Midlands first mooted the idea of ending the contract in the mid-1990s only three years after it began. The reason was that the outsourcing decision was taken when East Midlands considered IT to be non-core. It subsequently reached the opinion that IT was indeed a core activity. But the contract could not be ended early unless Perot Systems was in breach of contract over the quality of service or the utility was prepared to pay large sums in compensation. Quality of service has never been an issue and the payment of compensation was never an attractive option. (*Computer Weekly*, 1 April 1999, p. 44). The decision to end the deal raises questions over what will happen to more than 200 IT staff who are working on the East Midlands contract for Perot Systems. The supplier recently claimed that under the TUPE employment rules, it expected the staff to join East Midlands when the contract ends in October 1999. However, Perot announced in the United States that the skills of the East Midland team were in 'high demand' (*Computer Weekly*, 25 March 1999).

In another case of an unsuccessful outsourcing contract, British Gas Trading (BGT) is suing systems supplier SCT International for more than £10 million after the alleged failure of billing software. BGT claims SCT's customisation of software failed to deliver a working system, claiming also that it has been forced to maintain two separate billing systems. The client company believed that SCT was supposed to tailor the Banner Customer Information System (BCIS) package to meet 'unique billing procedures and processes'. BGT is claiming damages for installation and costs for running existing billing systems. BCIS has been installed at North West Water and 80 sites. SCT said the company had successfully under-taken customisation for other utilities and would vigorously defend the action (*Computing*, 11 February, 1999).

With more companies entering into multiple outsourcing contracts (for customer-facing parts of the business like call centres, as well as backroom support), the issue of relationship management has become an important one for senior management. Recognising this shift in attitude, large companies are creating new senior IT roles with the specific remit to manage outsourcing contracts. John Hetherington, manager of strategic contracts at Thomas Cook, says it is important 'to put commercial relationships in place and manage them contractually'. Much of Thomas Cook's business is outsourced already. It has about 10 IT and non-IT primary outsourcing relationships in the United Kingdom, keeping just application and project management and IT deployment in-house. There are two aspects to managing an outsourcing arrangement: service management and contract manage-ment. Service management is concerned with the day-to-day delivery of service levels. The contract manager, on the other hand, is someone who is more familiar with the wider issues of outsourcing and contracts. This trend towards sourcing directors or contract managers is very new. Robert Morgan, chairman of outsour-cing consultancy, Morgan–Chambers, estimates that there are only about 70 indi-viduals in the United Kingdom whose main job function is to manage the outsourcing contracts (*Information Week*, 13 January 1999, p. 24).

SUMMARY

This chapter has considered the strategic positioning of IT suppliers in the software and computing services industry. It is clear from the above discussion that signifi-cant changes are afoot as major IT consultancies/service providers enter into mergers, acquisitions and joint ventures to consolidate their strength and position within this industry. Equally, traditional hardware suppliers, systems houses and generic outsourcing suppliers are also attempting to extend their global reach, although it is likely that many of these companies will be subject to take-overs by the key players. As the large IT service providers consolidate their position in vertical markets by entering into increasingly larger, multidimensional outsourcing arrangements, significant changes will occur in the structuring and shaping of traditional industries. Industries such as telecommunications and healthcare will undergo major changes although consumer advantages of increased competition have to be weighed against potential 'cartels' forming between companies and IT service providers. This would suggest that, instead of considering outsourcing arrangements between clients and suppliers as two distinct research agendas, future research should address the issue that major IT service providers have also become key players in a host of other vertical markets.

9
Management, Technical Specialists, Competencies and Skills

INTRODUCTION

The IS and management literature, broadly conceived, has addressed the issue of developing competencies and skills over many years. As we saw in Chapter 6, all the management innovation and change programmes discussed, from total quality management (TQM) to process innovation, have prescribed concepts, methods and techniques to enhance the competencies and skills of managers, technical specialists[23] and other employees. This objective continues, although there is little consensus on exactly what competencies and skills are needed to manage the corporation of the 1990s and beyond (Schein, 1994). This chapter is concerned with this debate and examines some of the literature on managerial work, technical specialists, the need to develop new competencies and skills for the information age, and hybrid managers. The chapter is divided into four sections. First, it considers some of the contemporary problems facing organisations in hiring and recruiting skilled managerial and technical personnel. The so-called *IS skill shortage* is currently perceived to have reached a critical level in the United Kingdom (*PC Week*, 1998). This skill shortage is not confined to the United Kingdom, but is an international problem which is deemed to adversely affect the competitive advantage of companies and the balance of payments and general economic health of countries (HMSO, 1993, 1994).

Second, the chapter attempts to locate the IS skill shortage in a broader, historical, market and organisational context. To this end, it is important to understand the nature of managerial work by examining classical and contemporary definitions of how *management*, as a role, responsibility and activity, has been conceptualised (Carroll and Gillen, 1987). This is important since classical definitions of management, and their various derivatives, have influenced more recent debates surrounding the management of innovation, technology and technical specialists (Bashein and Markus, 1997). We explore how support for the thesis that management, as a generalisable 'core' competence, has defined and shaped common perceptions about the nature and role of technical specialists in contemporary organisations. For example, much of the Anglo-American literature asserts that technology and technical specialists are more appropriately *managed* by those with general, as opposed to technical, competencies and skills. This view is popular in the past and present management literature, although it has been questioned in recent years given the widely perceived divisions between managers and technical specialists, and the growing number of failed IS projects (Sauer, 1993; Currie, 1994, 1997).

Third, we examine the division of labour between managers and technical specialists, and address the issue of whether a *culture gap* exists between the two groups (Taylor-Cummings, 1997). This thesis has gained some credibility in recent years and is offered as an explanation for the productivity paradox concerning investment in new technology. That is, as investment in new technology increases, there is a corresponding decrease in productivity. In examining the management literature, it is interesting to note that a conceptual divide exists between the business and technology, with many writers perceiving the latter to play merely a supporting role to the former. Whilst this chapter does not argue that technology should be given centre stage in all organisations, it does, however, ask whether this dichotomy is symptomatic of the problems many organisations face in managing technology. It also relates the separation between the business and technology to other growing debates and trends, notably the core competence thesis which perceives technology as playing a supporting or peripheral role, and IS outsourcing, which is complementary to this thesis.

Fourth, we discuss the concept of the hybrid manager that has gained much interest in the business and management field over the last two decades. Essentially, a hybrid manager is intended to close the gap between the business and technology functions, processes and activities within an organisation. Recognising that a *culture gap* may produce adverse effects in performance and productivity, the hybrid manager is perceived as someone who can blend managerial and technical competencies and skills with the objective of aligning technology with business requirements (Skyrme, 1996). In assessing the theoretical and empirical evidence underpinning this concept, a critique of the hybrid manager is offered which highlights its many deficiencies in a labour market, organisational and practical context.

THE IS SKILLS CRISIS

The IS skills crisis has been a major concern to industrialised countries, particularly North America and the United Kingdom, for many years. As far back as the mid-1980s, government bodies were addressing the issue of how to develop skills and training programmes to meet the challenges of global competition, changing working practices and new technology (DTI, 1984a,b; Manpower Services Commission, 1985a,b, 1987). These reports urged companies to develop skills and training programmes to enable them to compete in an international marketplace. More than a decade on, managerial complacency towards the skills shortage crisis, which was identified in one report (Manpower Services Commission, 1987) seems to continue. For, according to a recent IDC report, the IS skill shortage in Europe alone is expected to reach 1.6 million by 2002. The report calls for a drastic improvement in training and reskilling (*PC Week*, 29 September 1998, p. 1). The IDC report, which was launched at the Summit on Employment and Training in the Information Society in Brussels, claims that the 1997 IS skills deficit of 32 000 could increase to 12% of the IS employment market. This would have an inflationary effect by causing an increase in labour costs, as well as serious delays in completing IS projects. An interesting observation in the IDC report is that, by the millennium, the IS skill shortage in Europe may be larger than the entire IS outsourcing industry.

Paradoxically, whilst there are high levels of unemployment in many industrialised countries, they also experience serious IS skill shortages. The reasons for this are varied and include skills obsolescence caused by the rapid pace of technical change, the nature of managerial work, which places a higher premium on general rather than technical skills, lack of investment in skills and training programmes on the part of government and companies, the view that IS is not a core competence—the capabilities and skills for this type of work therefore being perceived by managers as less important compared with other professional and occupational groups (i.e. strategic planning, HRM, marketing, finance, etc.), the culture gap between managers and technical specialists—where the former group do not fully understand the capabilities and skills requirements concerning the latter group, and the power differences between managers and technical specialists—where the former attempt to retain their status, position and influence as key decision-makers within organisations to the detriment of the latter group. Whilst the above statements are controversial and invite much debate, the impact and outcome of the current global IS skill shortage is very serious and adversely affects the performance of many companies, not least because they have to put their R&D and product development plans on hold whilst they search the labour market for people with the right skill mix. Part of the explanation for the current IS skill shortage may be found in an historical analysis of the nature of managerial work, particularly in so far as Anglo-American culture has seemingly encouraged the division of labour between managerial and technical work.

THE NATURE OF MANAGERIAL WORK

The current IS skill shortage discussed above can arguably be linked to classical and contemporary definitions of the nature of managerial work. Whilst this may not be immediately obvious, it is contended that the type of people running today's companies reflect the priorities and practices of both past and present management writers and practitioners. For example, traditional definitions tend to perceive management as broadly concerned with planning, organising, commanding, co-ordinating and controlling (Fayol, 1949). Against this interpretation, sector-specific knowledge and technical competence were not treated as essential requirements for occupying a managerial role.

Writing in 1961 in a book entitled *The European Executive*, Granick considered cross-national comparisons of management. In the case of Britain, unlike France and

Germany, he stressed that 'character building' was more important than developing intellectual or practical skills. The promotion of *narrow* specialists into managerial work was not encouraged since the 'talented amateur' was believed to be the appropriate role model for management (Gantt, 1919); in other words, a person with a good education who possessed the rather vague and impenetrable qualities of leadership, flair and decision-making ability. Being able to *fit in* was important, as was being a 'good team-player'. Notwithstanding the different interpretations of management throughout Europe and North America, many writers have attempted to delineate the key activities of management common to all organisational settings.

The traditional models of management promulgated by Fayol (1949) and Taylor (1911) have been examined by a number of writers. Kotter (1982), Mintzberg (1973) and Stewart (1961), for example, focused on behavioural aspects of managerial work and revealed that management was not simply about rational, systematic and reflective planning based upon the evaluation of hard information reminiscent of economic models of man (Carley, 1981). Rather it was characterised by responsive and intuitive decision-making processes. Here, complex tasks and decisions were initiated through political and informal processes where 'soft' information was considered vitally important. Unlike the former, more clinical approach to management advocated by Fayol (1949) and Taylor (1911), managerial decisions were taken at a hectic pace, and were constrained rather than innovative. To complicate the picture, Smith (1985) found that managerial jobs change over time, and posited a number of stages or cycles which they commonly pass through. As Mumford (1987) suggests, these studies seem to lie much closer to the reality of managerial experience both in the private and public sectors.

Table 9.1 contrasts earlier work on the key aspects of management with later writers. What is noticeable about this lexicon of key managerial activities is the similarity between the traditional and more recent definitions. For example, Fayol's five-point schema of planning, organising, commanding, co-ordinating and controlling is, in part, reproduced in the lists of Kotter (1982) and Luthans *et al.* (1988). Are we therefore to assume that in the light of sectoral variations and technological advances over the last 50 years that management activities remain unchanged?

Other research which reviewed 29 studies of what managers do, including only two from the public sector (of necessity because of the relative paucity of such studies), concluded that these revealed an immense diversity of behaviour, practice and job content, thus making for difficulty in identifying commonalities across different sectors and between organisations belonging to the same sector (Hales, 1986). Such findings at best contradict the *catch-all* interpretations of management outlined in Table 9.1, or at worst, render these studies too general to provide a meaningful interpretation of what managers actually do in the workplace. Key problems emerge in examining many of the traditional studies on management, since they rarely comment on whether their sample organisations share a common conceptualisation of management, or share categories for meaningful analysis. Crucially they tend to ignore important contextual and structural factors such as institutional sector; market position; technological capability; power relations between managers and non-managers (i.e. technical specialists); and internal,

Table 9.1   *Key activities of management*

Fayol (1949)	Mintzberg (1973)	Kotter (1982)	Luthans et al. (1988)	Hill (1992)
• Planning • Organising • Command • Co-ordination • Control	• Figurehead • Leader • Liaison • Monitor • Disseminator • Spokesperson • Entrepreneur • Disturbance handler • Resource allocator • Negotiator	• Setting goals and strategies • Allocating resources • Monitoring activities • Getting information, co-operation and support from superiors • Getting co-operation from other groups • Motivating, controlling and managing conflict	• Exchanging information • Handling paperwork • Decision-making • Controlling • Interacting with outsiders • Socialising • Managing conflict	• Team leader • Sales leader • Boss • Supervisor • Organiser • Liaiser • Politician • People manager • Negotiator

external social and economic factors which help explain managerial behaviour. Nor do they examine the extent to which tasks done by those called managers were not labelled managerial in other settings (i.e. the public sector), or the degree to which management tasks were assigned to and accomplished by those who did not hold the title of manager (i.e. technical specialists with responsibilities for supervising others). As such, they tend to perceive management as an homogeneous group rather than an heterogeneous one, comprised of individuals with competing and conflicting interests, unequal status and power, and different career trajectories and motives (Knights and Murray, 1994).

What emerges as significant here is the degree to which management is a social construction within organisations. This may be particularly important in public services, where the lack of people with the title manager has too often and too easily been taken for a corresponding dearth of relevant management activity. This is to simply accept the labelling of organisational members as either managers or non-managers without questioning the nature of roles and responsibilities, and their approximation to common definitions of management. This would suggest that many people undertake activities which approximate to those which are labelled management, yet are not given the title of manager. If this were the case, we would therefore suggest a revision in the concept of management to include the activities undertaken by other groups, for example technical specialists with supervisory responsibilities[24]. Alternatively, we may wish to redefine our understanding of management and managerial work to include activities which hitherto have not been incorporated into these concepts, while at the same time eliminating some activities which seem to be common across all organisational roles. In making these points, the following section examines the concept of generalisable 'core' competencies, which seeks to reinforce the notion that management and managerial work can be defined by a common set of labels, prescriptions, roles and responsibilities.

Generalisable 'Core' Competencies

It is worth considering the issue of generalisable 'core' competencies and skills in more detail in a UK context. From the mid-1980s at least three influential reports pointed to the inadequacies of British private sector management practice. Somewhat surprisingly, Handy (HMSO, 1987) and Mangham and Silver (1986) remained largely silent about the competencies and skills needed by British managers to enable them to compete with their international rivals. But what do we mean by *core competencies*? By 1988 a series of research projects was launched with the purpose of identifying core competencies relevant to all forms of managerial work. By 1988 a Chartered Management Initiative (CMI) had been launched under the aegis of the British Institute of Management, The Confederation of British Industry and the Foundation for Management Education to devise a professional structure for management in Britain, based on the gradual attainment of those skills defined as core competencies. Prahalad and Hamel (1990) further promoted the thesis that contemporary business organisations should focus upon developing their core competencies and potentially outsource those that are perceived to be non-core, peripheral, and/or non-value-added activities. These authors defined core competence as, 'the collective learning in the organisation, especially how to co-ordinate diverse production skills and integrate multiple streams of technologies' (p. 82). They gave the following examples of core competencies which, they believe, are central to the competitive advantage of the companies in question

> In NEC, digital technologies, especially VLSI and systems integration skills, are fundamental. In the core competence underlying them, disparate businesses become coherent. It is Honda's core competence in engines and power trains that gives IS a distinctive advantage in car, motorcycle, lawn mower, and generator businesses. Canon's core competencies in optics, imaging, and microprocessor controls have enabled IS to enter, even dominate, markets as seemingly diverse as copiers, laser printers, cameras, and image scanners (p. 83).

Since the concept of managerial work embraces a wide variety of activities where skills, expertise and knowledge are inextricably linked by a complex web of external and internal conditions, the pursuit of generalisable core competences becomes problematic. Hirsh and Bevan (1988), for example, found that even where large companies used the same terms to describe specific management competencies, such as leadership or communication, each assigned a different meaning to them. Thus, 'If we ask "Is there a shared language for management skills?" the answer seems to be *yes* at the level of expression, but *no* at the level of meaning.' Similarly, a European-wide survey by the Ashridge Management Research Group attempted to identify the competencies and skills required for the manager of the future. This report found a mismatch between the competencies and skills advocated by the classical management writers and those put forward by the sample organisations. The main difference was the emphasis by the sample organisations that competencies and skills should become organisation specific. Managers of the future would need to learn about the specific business sector in which they are employed, in addition to acquiring in-depth knowledge about their organisation and technical capabilities. Whilst this view seems to be one of common sense, it is outside the scope of the ethos, curriculum and objectives of the popular and widespread generic

Masters of Business Administration (MBA) degree which is based upon a view that managers should learn a range of, usually, functional management specialisms which they can later apply to all organisational (private and public) and business sectors. We shall return to this subject later in the chapter.

A Conceptual Framework for Managerial Work

In recent years writers have sought to identify core competencies for the post-capitalist society (Drucker, 1993), the information revolution (Forrester, 1985), the learning organisation (Senge, 1990a; Mills and Friesen, 1992) and the knowledge-creating company (Nonaka and Takeuchi, 1995). A conceptual framework for analysis is given in Figure 9.1, which captures those activities commonly ascribed to management. This is related to sectoral and technical considerations, and it is postulated that a knowledge of all three areas will be important for managing in contemporary organisations.

This framework is developed from the work of Harrison (1979). Environment refers to external political, social, economic and technological factors, and 'task' environment factors such as suppliers, customers, labour market and competition. These, together with the dominant coalition, will influence the nature and scope of the management functions developed by the organisation. For Harrison they are essentially: setting objectives, formulating plans, organising, staffing, directing and controlling. These generate constraints on the technical core—where the prevailing technology is applied to raw inputs in the process of transforming them into

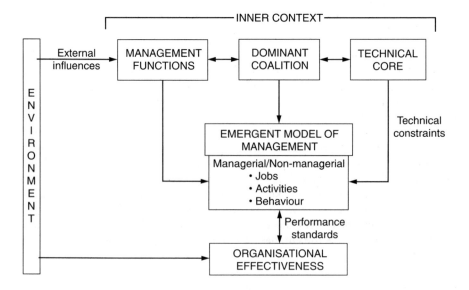

Figure 9.1   *A conceptual framework for understanding the nature of managerial work.*
Source: Willcocks and Harrow (1992)

finished outputs. The technical core thus consists of equipment, techniques, methods, procedures, skills and routines, and people. Essentially, the technical core is concerned with transforming innovative ideas into commercial realities. Technical factors, the dominant coalition, management functions and performance standards (largely set by managers) operate as constraints to produce an emergent model of management (Child, 1974). The figure is intended to be used as an heuristic devise. As such, it is a simplification and not intended to explain in detail the differences in organisations, but merely to recognise that they exist. Many contextual factors are not shown in detail, and the analytical constructs must be understood as dynamic and interactive where differences in environmental influences, objectives, dominant coalition, technical core and performance standards can influence the configuration of the management functions throughout the organisation. This becomes particularly important when considering differences in the nature of management both within and across private and public sector organisations.

The conceptual framework is a useful device which attempts to broaden our understanding of how external and internal factors shape the nature and scope of management. By incorporating external factors (competitors, suppliers, economic conditions, sectoral differences, etc.) and technical factors (hardware, software, expertise, knowledge, information flows, etc.) into the framework, a greater number of variables produce a complex picture of how management is conceptualised, structured and co-ordinated within different organisational settings. The conceptual framework, however, is unable to explain or evaluate the strategic choices (Child, 1972) taken by different management groups, nor indeed provide any meaningful understanding of the power relations inherent within managerial hierarchies (Knights and Murray, 1994).

In reviewing the management literature there emerges no coherent, systematic, shared conceptualisation of management, or what managers do, in both private and public sector organisations and across business sectors. In the past two decades, a number of contributions have prescribed generalised formulas and guidelines for *best practice*. Yet the rationalist approach, which pervades the generic management literature, fails to explain in detail how behavioural and attitudinal changes will translate into improved business performance. As a result, such approaches have engendered much criticism for offering glib and over-generalised interpretations of management and managerial work. However, such criticism has not halted the inexorable pace at which private sector managerialism continues to be imposed upon the public sector with a view to making it more *efficient, productive and cost effective*. To this end, there is some irony that in a period that sees the concept of generalised core competencies questioned as never before, the public sector is now being judged against traditional 'classical' management criteria, the essence of which is currently the subject of much contention and debate!

This is evident when we consider our conceptual framework which postulates a relationship between environment, managerial functions, the dominant coalition and the technical core. For although many writers concentrate upon the key activities of managers at the internal organisational level, they often overlook other key variables such as business sector context, and technical capabilities and skills. The pitfalls of overlooking these important variables are significant. This is because the continuing focus upon a narrow range of core competencies often based upon classical definitions of managerial work produce a distorted picture, which is outdated in the context of contemporary organisations. For example, in spite of the economic and structural changes to the world economy, coupled with the further diffusion of information and communications technologies (ICTs), many writers on management theory persist with the view that management is an homogeneous group, characterised by a narrow range of core competencies. As such, managers can move from one organisational context (i.e. business sector) to another, and be equally effective. This is irrespective of sectoral differentiation; market position; organisational size; products; services; and technical capabilities and skill. Yet, the justification that managers can move from one organisational context to another and retain their effectiveness as *managers*, has not been fully explained in the generic management literature, nor elsewhere. Neither are there adequate explanations as to why, in an age where innovation and technology is perceived as central to the success of many companies, not least national economies, there persists both a serious IS skill shortage and a *culture gap* between the work undertaken by managers and technical specialists. Such a culture gap, as we will see, is often seen as contributing to the poor overall performance of many companies, marked by their inability to compete in global markets.[25]

The Culture Gap Between Management and Technical Specialists

An important debate within the management literature concerns the relationship between the manager and technical specialist in the context of managing technology (Rockness and Zmud, 1989). For our purposes here, a technical specialist refers to someone with an in-depth knowledge of information systems and technology. Over the years, the labels attached to these individuals have changed considerably. For example, 20 years ago programming was perceived as a separate activity from analysis work. The term computer specialist was also widely used (Mumford, 1972). At the managerial level, the term DP (data processing) manager was popular (Friedman and Cornford, 1989). More recently, a variety of labels have been adopted which delineate management activities from technical work. Common labels for managers are: IS director; IS manager; project manager; and chief information officer (CIO—used largely in North America). Emerging roles for IS directors and CIOs would suggest an elevation in the status of technical specialists to reflect the growing importance of technology to the competitive success of a company. Yet the literature is replete with prescriptive messages advising senior and middle managers to become more involved in managing technology and technical specialists (Allen and Scott-Morton, 1994). Essentially, managers are advised to seize control of technology because it is now 'too important' to be left to technical specialists. The reasons for this are as follows:

1.   Global competitors are increasingly exploiting the potential and benefits from IS.
2.   A link exists between competitive advantage and IS.
3.   Corporate strategy should be aligned with the IS strategy.

4. Technology is too important to be left to technologists to manage and control.
5. IS outsourcing needs to be negotiated, co-ordinated and controlled by business managers.
6. IT-enabled business process re-engineering should be exploited for competitive advantage.
7. Technical specialists do not understand the business.

In the light of these considerations, some writers advocate that senior business managers, as opposed to technical specialists, should seek to exploit the strategic potential of technology (Rowe and Herbert, 1990). As such, their role should transform from one which is 'responsible for the performance of people' to one which is 'responsible for the application and performance of knowledge'. In this scenario, knowledge becomes 'the essential resource', and managers must devise ways of exploiting knowledge, as well as learning to manage knowledge workers (Drucker, 1993, p. 40). What is interesting about this line of reasoning is that managing technology continues to be discussed within a framework of dichotomous roles and relationships between managers and technical specialists. For example, Boynton *et al.* (1992, p. 32) claim that, 'over the last decade, general managers who report to functional areas other than information systems line managers have increasingly gained information technology management responsibilities'. This has occurred because of the growing requirement for line managers to 'manage interdependencies within and external to the firm in the light of:

• pressures to globalise operations
• new competitive requirements (increasing product quality and decreasingly time to market'.

Perceptions of Technology and Technical Specialists

Recognising the importance of technology as a resource with the potential to resolve business and strategic challenges, Boynton *et al.* rather thinly give their reasons why line managers (as opposed to technical specialists) should manage technology. Thus, 'Although IS managers possess important technical and systems know-how, IS applications are best led by line managers who thoroughly understand the business situation' (Boynton *et al.*, 1992, p. 32). Implicit in such a statement is that technical specialists do not possess adequate knowledge of the 'business situation', despite their in-depth knowledge of technology and their special status as *knowledge workers*. The authors do not propose that technical specialists should receive business training, but repeat their claim that, 'knowledge of the business' (which they do not define) is more important than 'technical and systems know-how'. By promoting these views, the authors serve to reinforce two points. First, that the business is something separate and distinct from technology, and second, that technical knowledge and expertise is of secondary importance to the business, broadly defined. These views are further supported by the various negative stereotypes which prevail about the capabilities and skills of technical specialists. For example, Currie (1995b) found that technical specialists were commonly perceived as:

- too narrow
- too specialised
- failing to understand the business
- only interested in the technology
- devoid of 'managerial qualities'
- boffins, techies, egg-heads, geeks, nerds
- disinterested in budgetary control or getting value for money
- poor communicators
- disliked teamworking or dealing with people.

These negative stereotypes seemingly produce a self-fulfilling prophecy which contributes to the low status of technical specialists in many organisations (Brooke, 1995). By the same token, the status of managers and managerial work is enhanced. Another writer who argues for greater managerial control over technical change is Rockart (1988, pp. 57–64). Whilst he supports the view that technology should be seen as part of the business, he believes that information technology has 'become the province not only of information systems professionals, but of every manager in the business no matter what his or her level'.

Implicit in the above discussion is that a power struggle exists between managers and technical specialists which, it seems, is more commonplace in North American and British managerial cultures. Yet the rationale for business managers to *manage* technology instead of technical specialists is rarely explained in detail. Rhetorical statements which suggest that managers understand the *business situation* better than technical specialists are, in themselves, superficial and rarely supported by strong evidence. Moreover, the dynamic changes within the business community, coupled with the inexorable rate of technological change, would suggest that new competencies and skills for managers and technical specialists are required (Willcocks and Feeny, 1995). Indeed, as we have seen above, definitions about management and managerial work are often so general and flexible that they cease to be meaningful in any market, business sector and organisational context. In recent years, many writers have become aware of the conceptual problem with the perceived dichotomy between the business and technology which is peddled in much of the management literature, and have instead sought to bring these two areas together, both theoretically and empirically (Currie and Galliers, 1999). This is discussed in the following section.

THE STRATEGY–TECHNOLOGY CONNECTION

According to many North American and British writers, managers should become involved in the strategic evaluation and management of technology (Rockart, 1988; Zmud *et al.*, 1987; Rockness and Zmud, 1989; Rowe and Herbert, 1990; Adler *et al.*, 1992; Smits *et al.*, 1993; Morone, 1993). Much of this research has been led by the five-year *Management in the 1990s* research programme funded by 12 industrial and government sponsors in the United States and Britain (Allen and Scott-Morton, 1994). The essence of this work is to reinforce the strategy–technology connection first identified by Kantrow at the beginning of 1980 (Kantrow, 1980). Since then, numerous prescriptive studies have sought to advise managers of the need to develop an IS strategy for business (Peppard, 1993); align the IS strategy with the corporate strategy (Henderson and Venkatraman, 1994); and avoid fragmented and piecemeal diffusion of technology. For example, Adler *et al.* (1992, p. 19) claim that

> Too many businesses leave the technical functions—research and development (R&D), management information systems (MIS), manufacturing engineering, and so on—out of the business strategy process and exempt them from senior management's expectation that all the functions manage their internal operations strategically.

Although Adler *et al.* (1992) caution against treating technology as an adjunct to the business strategy process, the failure of senior managers to recognise this suggests they are part of the problem rather than the solution. This is because their own lack of technical understanding and interest in these matters may preclude them from focusing upon technology and technical skills as a core competence within the organisation. This is particularly the case in North American and British companies, where managers treat technical capabilities and skills as commodities which can be contracted in (insourced), or contracted out (outsourced) according to the peaks and troughs of IS projects (Currie, 1995b). According to Earl and Feeny (1994, pp. 12–13), The IS/IT function should be seen as *part of the business*. These writers found that, 'the Chief Information Officer's (CIO's) ability to add value is the biggest single factor in determining whether the organisation views IS as an asset or a liability'. The findings of their research found two competing views which are outlined in Table 9.2.

According to Earl and Feeny (1994, p. 13):

> A recurring concern of the last several years has been how to connect IS investment to business strategy. All too frequently, the connections are attempted through special exercises led by IS—or they are not made at all because some missionary zealot drives through an investment unrelated to business direction (Feeny et al, 1989). By contrast, the most successful approach we have seen is where there are no IS strategies, only business strategies. Here, the CIO adds value by building informed relationships with key executives, making sure that IS requirements become an integral component of business strategy.

One strength of forging a conceptual link between strategy and technology is to fuse the business and technical functions of a company, thereby treating the latter resource as an essential ingredient for achieving competitive advantage and an improved market position. Few commentators could disagree that successful companies such as Microsoft have forged a strong link between the strategy and technology connection, and that such a link has contributed to the overall market leadership of the company (Cusumano and Selby, 1995).

Table 9.2   *Perceptions of IT*

Issue	IS as a liability	IS as an asset
Are we getting value for money?	ROI is difficult to measure, and the organisation is notably unhappy with IS as a whole	ROI is difficult to measure, but the organisation believes IS is making an important contribution
How important is IT?	Stories of strategic use of IS are dismissed as irrelevant to 'this' business	Stories of strategic use of IS are seen as interesting and instructive
How do we plan for IT?	IS plans are made by specialists or missionary zealots	IS thinking is subsumed within business thinking
Is the IS function doing a good job?	There is general cynicism about the track record of IS	The performance of IS is no longer an agenda item
What is the IS strategy?	Many IS applications are under development	IS efforts are focused on a few key initiatives
What is the CEO's vision for the role of IT?	The CEO sees a limited role for IS within the business	The CEO sees IS as having a role in the transformation of the business
What do we expect of the CIO?	The CIO is positioned as a specialist functional manager	The CIO is valued as a contributor to business thinking and business operations

Adapted from: Earl and Feeny (1994, p. 13).

Power Relations and Technology

The extent to which the business and technology can be brought together in any organisation depends not just on rhetoric, but also on the priorities and preferences of managers and technical specialists alike. Yet one disappointing outcome of the conceptual dichotomy between the business and technology, which prevails in much of the management literature, is that negative stereotypes about technical specialists, in particular, continue. To this end, the background to the debate is more appropriately understood by examining the power relations between managers and technical specialists, as well as suppliers and users (Knights and Murray, 1994). As the above discussion indicates, these relationships are influenced by the prevailing positive and negative stereotypes about the (perceived) differences in competencies and skills between managers and technical specialists. For example, Boynton *et al.* (1992, p. 33) construct an argument which stresses the importance of distributing IS management responsibilities to line managers to enhance the strategic capability of this *resource*. In doing so, they seek to enhance the position of line managers to the detriment of technical specialists:

> The best way to link IS consistently to a firm's day to day, core business processes is to centrally distribute IS management responsibilities to line managers. If the central IS function dominates IS management, this alignment will not occur for two reasons. First, in firms with dominant central IS functions, line managers have to place the fate of their operations and their careers in the hands of others. Thus they resist relying on IS resources that they neither control nor, most likely, fully understand. As the importance of IS resources increases, we believe that line managers will increasingly resist extreme dependence on a central IS func-

tion, even if the IS staff have been responsive to their needs in the past. With dispersed responsibility, line managers will use IS resources more effectively, learning to apply IS to business tasks just as they apply human, financial, and other key resources to business opportunities, problems, and threats.

This statement effectively treats IS as a political football where line managers wrest control of this resource, not because they understand it, but because it serves their political and career interests. What is central to their concern seems to be a fear that technical specialists may become more powerful if they control the IS resource. So by decentralising IS to line managers, the power base of a centralised IS function will be eroded, if not destroyed. What the authors fail to address is whether such a move, whilst serving the political interests of line managers, is actually beneficial to the organisation as a whole. Indeed, key questions that need to be answered are: 'Does it matter that line managers do not understand the IS resource they are required to manage?' 'How will line managers use IS more effectively if it is under their control as opposed to the control of technical specialists?' 'Should line managers (from the business functions/departments/units) and the IS function be in direct competition?, 'Will a change from a centralised IS function to a situation where IS is decentralised increase the risk of failure from IS projects?' 'How will performance and productivity from IS be measured and evaluated if it is dispersed throughout the organisation?' 'What are the core competencies and skills needed for managing complex IS projects and technical specialists?' In posing these questions, it seems that very few writers have considered the wider consequences of managing the IS resource and concentrate only on offering glib solutions from a narrow, managerialist perspective.

Education and Training

A cursory glance at existing education and training programmes shows that many of the above questions are overlooked by academics and practitioners alike, or are deliberately ignored with a view to preserving the *managerialist* status quo. Indeed, much of the management literature dogmatically accepts the view that general or line managers should be put in charge of technology and technical specialists without addressing how this may widen the well documented culture gap. Indeed, the routine acceptance of a distinction between the business and technology seems to reinforce the culture gap. This is also reflected to a large extent in higher education since the business schools have contributed significantly to cementing the division between managers and technical specialists through the development and promotion of the MBA degree—the rationale for which is grounded in the view that managers should learn a variety of competencies and skills from a broad disciplinary focus. As such, the general MBA degree commonly comprises core courses in accounting, finance, human resource management, organisational behaviour, business strategy, managerial economics, marketing, international business and quantitative techniques (international and national variations permitting). Courses in managing technology are only recently beginning to emerge alongside the more general core and optional subjects within MBA programmes. But the focus is often to impart a superficial understanding of the issues concerning managing technology rather than treating this area as a core competence in contemporary organisations.

What emerges from examining the popularity of the general MBA degree is the continuing tendency to place a high premium on acquiring general management knowledge, rather than business-sector-specific knowledge and technical capabilities and skills. North American and British management cultures are particularly noted for this tendency. Along the generalist–specialist continuum, therefore, strong evidence from government, academic and practitioner circles all seem to place a high premium on *general* capabilities and skills to the detriment of *specialist* ones. This has led to the comment that, 'In Britain, enterprise management has become the specialism of the generalists.' Similarly, Lawrence (1995, p. 1), writing about the United States, points out that

> The generalist approach views management as a generalisable activity, the practice of which calls for certain general qualities which then may be effectively deployed in a variety of contexts—functional, hierarchical, and branch of industry based. The USA is clearly an exemplar of this approach, and American managers like to think they can 'manage anything!', moving from purchasing to PR, forklift trucks to agri-business.

For many, managing technology is akin to managing any other organisational resource. A detailed knowledge of technology is not, therefore, the essential ingredient. Managers instead need to learn how to apply the general capabilities and skills of: aligning the corporate strategy with the IS or technology strategy; developing technical solutions to resolve business problems; applying effective project management techniques; motivating teams; ensuring that projects are running according to performance targets; managing the budget; and dealing with conflict, to name but a few (Yeates, 1991). So, according to this scenario, an educational background in technology (programming, analysis, software engineering, etc.) is not a prerequisite for being able to manage technology (equipment) or technical specialists (people). Such a view is reflected in many appointments for project managers which specify that a *general business background* is more important than technical competence and skill. Indeed, some companies even stipulate that a technical background disqualifies people from managing IS projects and people.

Whilst the position of the generalist manager seems secure in the light of prevailing attitudes towards managers and technical specialists, it becomes important to consider some of the more disquieting evidence that has emerged in recent years concerning the poor performance of many IS projects (Sauer, 1993; Currie, 1994). For example, a Price Waterhouse survey reported that 25% of companies claimed that *most* of their information systems were unsuccessful either because they were delivered too late and over budget, or because they did not meet user requirements (*Financial Times*, 1994). The reasons given by managers responding to this survey are interesting because the criteria for judging the success of IS projects is based on traditional project management performance indicators (cost, productivity, timescales) rather than on other criteria (the competencies and skills of managers and the technical team; experiential learning of new software packages/languages; quality of the code; relationship building, etc.). Since the publication of this survey, other studies have found little improvement in the success rate of IS projects (Sauer, 1999).

Whilst a popular solution to this problem is to impose greater management control, this in itself is not adequate given that IS project failures such as TAURUS, Wessex Health Authority and London Ambulance Service, to name a few, all had project managers assigned to them who reported to a traditional *command and control* managerial hierarchy (Currie, 1994, 1995b). To this end, the notion that more management control could have made a difference in the outcome of these projects is not an adequate explanation in isolation of other factors. One *solution* to the perceived *culture gap* problem which is offered as a reason why so many IS projects fail to meet their cost, performance and productivity targets, has emerged in the form of the *hybrid* manager. This concept is worth discussing in some detail given that it has gained popularity in recent years, with some organisations claiming to *employ* hybrid managers specifically to close the gap between the business and technology functions.

THE HYBRID MANAGER—A SOLUTION TO THE BUSINESS/ TECHNOLOGY DIVIDE?

The notion of the hybrid manager as someone to be put in charge of IS, and other technical operations has prevailed in UK management research in recent years, especially in the last two decades. The discussion is divided into two parts. First, we consider literature on managers and professionals in the United Kingdom from an historical perspective. Second, we offer a critique of the hybrid manager concept by suggesting that divisions between managerial and technical work essentially construct a false dichotomy. As we have seen above, this is often referred to in the wider management literature as a *culture gap*. This serves to reinforce the division of labour between what is perceived as managerial and technical work. The discussion concludes by arguing that, as opposed to constructing a barrier between the two areas by offering the hybrid manager in the form of *the solution*, we should instead seek to integrate managerial and technical work by re-evaluating the role and nature of work in the new information society. To this end, the concept of the hybrid manager becomes redundant.

The Literature on Hybrid Managers

By contextualising our discussion of the hybrid manager using historical, cross-national, labour market and organisational data and insights, it is not surprising that such a concept has found a place within business and management research. The literature on hybrid managers is an important component of a wider and, in recent years, burgeoning one on the management of innovation, technology and technical work in the United Kingdom. A central issue in these writings (whether explicit or implicit) is the relationship, in particular the communication problems, between generalists and specialists, or managers and technical staff. In the late 1970s to mid-1980s, fears about de-skilling through the use of IS were commonplace with the publication of alarmist literature on 'the collapse of work' and the 'leisure shock'. But during the mid-1980s to the present time, the notion of widespread de-skilling and unemployment as a consequence of technical change has given way to more considered discussion on how to develop appropriate mixes of capabilities and skills in managers and technical specialists.

In advocating the concept of the hybrid manager, it is believed that a blend of managerial awareness and technical skills will develop people who will counter the deficiencies of those with only generalist *or* technical capabilities. The corollary of this thinking is the hybrid manager. So in a 1990 British Computer Society (BCS) report, UK companies were exhorted to train approximately 10 000 people to become hybrid managers by 1995. This report suggested that at least 30% of all British managers will need to be 'hybrids' by the year 2000 (Palmer and Ottley, 1990). Such people would conceive and develop information systems to help their organisations compete in global markets. Earl (1989) defined hybrid managers as 'people with strong technical skills and adequate business knowledge or vice versa'. They would be 'able to work in user areas doing a line functional job, but adapt at developing and implementing IS application ideas'. The notion of the hybrid manager has been discussed, according to Earl and Skyrme (1992), in writings on IS, finance, R&D and general management, and on management roles and career development. Earl and Skyrme found that organisations that claimed to possess hybrid managers said they were usually business managers with IS experience rather than the other way around. They put forward four essential attributes for the hybrid manager:

1. business knowledge (detailed working knowledge);
2. IS knowledge (capabilities rather than detailed technical knowledge);
3. organisational knowledge (how to get things done);
4. management qualities ('soft skills', e.g. interpersonal and negotiating skills).

Whilst the concept of the hybrid manager has been discussed at some length by Earl and Skyrme (1992) and Skyrme (1996), these writers claim that such a concept represents 'a capacity for a role'. One writer who was involved with the CBI IS skills agency (ITSA) on the future demand of IS professionals suggested that hybrid managers should be responsible for 'Defining and determining the information needs of the business function in which he/she is specialised, for example, accounting, personnel, marketing, engineering, IS services; integrating IS into the function strategy; and assessing and evaluating IS performance within the business' Judd (1993). Willcocks and Feeny (1999) also found an increasing need by employers for staff who could combine business and IS experience, especially in customer-focused organisations which use IS to support the business.

In short, the central theme within the literature on hybrid managers is that contemporary managers need to blend business knowledge with technical awareness. Whilst this may not be the case for *all* managers, the assumption is that many organisations would be able to compete more effectively if they developed a cohort of their managers with *dual* skills. In reviewing the literature, it seems that the accent is more on the business than the technology. As such, hybrid managers are not expected to be *experts* in technology, but to at least understand how technology can be applied to support and improve the business. We shall now evaluate the literature on hybrid managers in the light of the wider business and management work discussed earlier.

A Critique of the Hybrid Manager Concept

Whilst the concept of the hybrid manager is intended to offer a solution to the so-called *culture gap* between generalist and specialist activities within organisations, it is apparent that such a solution is inherently Anglo-Saxon in design, scope and orientation. For, unlike the situation in West Germany where there is not such a fixed demarcation between managerial and technical roles, and in Japan where manufacturing success in the 1980s is attributed, at least in part, to the effective use and deployment of technical capabilities and skills (Currie, 1994), UK and US managers alike continue to delineate business activities from technical work. This is witnessed in several ways and, as we shall argue, sometimes to the detriment of the organisation. Four critical elements need to be addressed by those who espouse the virtues of the hybrid manager concept. They concern the dual career paths of managers and technical specialists in contemporary organisations; the role and status of IS in the context of the core competence debate; the freelance IS labour market; and education and training policies and the management of IS projects and staff. In considering these factors, new questions and concerns are raised about the usefulness of the hybrid manager concept.

Dual Career Paths of Managers and Technical Specialists

First, we consider the issue of organisational hierarchy, in particular the dual career paths that have hitherto existed for managers and technical specialists. In the post-war period, possibly up to the late 1970s, a dual career path had existed for managers and technical specialists. Career paths tended to take one of two distinct forms, managerial or technical. In the former case, individuals gained experience across the non-technical functions of accounting, finance, human resources, marketing and sales. This was common for graduate management trainees, particularly in Anglo-American companies. In the latter case, especially in regard to the IS function, individuals progressed from basic programming, systems analysis, into project management (Friedman and Cornford, 1989). It was very unlikely that anyone in the former group moved across into programming, or to any other *hands-on* kind of technical work in order to develop their careers. Yet movement in the opposite direction was commonplace and even encouraged by management. As we have seen above, the Anglo-American notion of *general management* (Lawrence, 1995), encourages promotion to senior management through a pre-defined career path which emphasises the traditional 'classical' skills of organising, co-ordinating, budgeting and planning, rather than technical capabilities and skills (Boynton *et al.*, 1992; Morone, 1993).

We suggest that one consequence of the delineation between management and technology within organisations has been to reinforce (as opposed to eliminating) the culture gap. Whilst some organisations have introduced more radical human resources strategies in recent years to break down this barrier, evidence from education, industry, professional organisations/agencies and academia all confirm the existence of this division. For example, promotion to senior management is, by and large, through a managerialist as opposed to a technical route. Few IS directors or managers sit on the main board of companies (Earl, 1989) and this continues today. Indeed, the rapid pace of IS outsourcing in the United States and the United Kingdom, and to a much lesser extent in wider Europe and elsewhere, has effectively reduced the opportunities for promotion for technical specialists (particularly in client organisations). Technical specialists are therefore more likely to further their careers by working for IS vendor/supplier companies, or by becoming freelance consultants/contractors, than they are by working for a company where IS is not seen as a core competence (Currie, 1995b). In fact, the very essence of IS outsourcing seems to confirm that, in the opinion of senior managers, IS represents a commodity which can be procured from the wider, external marketplace. Such a view further reinforces the conceptual and practical separation of the business and how it chooses to source IS resources (equipment, people, information, etc.).

Yet the danger for technical specialists who relinquish their technical capabilities and skills to become managers is pointed out by Earl and Skryme (1992). These writers caution that technical specialists may run the risk of not only losing their technical expertise by choosing a managerial route, they may also be perceived by others as not 'real business people'. This is more likely to occur in the United Kingdom and the United States, where people tend to value first degrees in non-technical subjects, such as business and management and postgraduate degrees such as the MBA, and to devalue technical qualifications such as engineering and computing as prerequisites for managerial careers (Ackroyd, 1995). Whilst the concept of the hybrid manager seemingly offers technical specialists in particular a 'capacity for a role' by blending both technical and managerial capabilities and skills (Earl, 1989), the success of this strategy will depend on the wider organisational context which includes culture, structure, hierarchy, power relationships, politics and control.

What is evident is that managerial and technical work continue to be perceived by senior managers as being unequal in terms of responsibility, status, promotion opportunities, pay and conditions. This is interesting given that the cost of sourcing technical capabilities and skills from the labour market can be extremely high for a company, particularly in the light of the current serious IS skill shortages. For example, contract IS staff (analyst programmers, database administrators, systems support, software engineers, etc.) can cost a company anything from £1000 to £3000 per week, per person. A full-time, permanent employee will not earn anything like this amount (possibly between £15 000 and £40 000 per annum depending upon job title and experience). Yet companies are reluctant to train and provide a career path for technical specialists, even though the cost of sourcing these capabilities and skills from the labour market depends on supply and demand. In the present climate, however, there is more demand than supply, and this only serves to increase the bargaining power (remuneration, terms and conditions, etc.) of freelance technical specialists. Indeed, a recent study has shown that many technical specialists now prefer to work as freelance consultant/contractors for three key reasons. First, they can command a high level of remuneration which they would not get by working for a company in a permanent, full-time capacity.

Second, they 'avoid the power politics' which is part and parcel of working as an employee for a company. Third, they enjoy the 'freedom' of being able to take time off (at the end of a contract) without having to leave a job (Currie, 1999a). In view of the continuing separation between management and technical capabilities and skills, and the relative *perceived* superiority of the former, the concept of hybrid manager becomes increasingly problematic, particularly where these people are neither *fish nor fowl* in contemporary organisations.

IS and the Core Competence Debate

Second, it is important to consider the hybrid manager concept in relation to some of the significant developments in business and management theory and practice in recent years. Here we shall consider the debate about generalisable 'core' competencies. As we discussed above, the IS function is usually perceived as peripheral to the core business functions or units within commercial organisations. This view has been widely promoted since the early 1990s by two US writers, Prahalad and Hamel (1990). Put simply, an organisation may seek to differentiate between what it believes to be its core competencies and those that it perceives to be peripheral. This may be in the form of intellectual property (patents, trade marks, brand names, technologies, competencies and skills, etc.) as well as other activities which cannot easily be done by a third party (vendor or supplier). The logic behind the core competency debate is that all those activities which may be provided more cost effectively and efficiently by a third party should be outsourced. Such a view is behind many of the large- and small-scale IS outsourcing deals worldwide (Currie and Willcocks, 1997). In fact, the prolific rate at which technical work (equipment and staff) has been outsourced in recent years is indicative that senior management do not perceive this activity to be part of the core competencies portfolio of their organisation. Moreover, large-scale outsourcing (more than 70–80% of the IS activities) will remove much of the technical capability and skill of the organisation.[26] In turn, a high proportion of UK and US organisations categorise IS departments as cost centres and service providers to the core businesses, thus making IS staff vulnerable when cost-cutting exercises are implemented (Currie, 1995b).

Given moves to outsource the IS function, the concept of the hybrid manager becomes problematic. Indeed, IS staff will be given a straightforward message from outsourcing initiatives that technical capabilities and skills are outside the scope of the core competencies of the organisation. This is likely to deter senior managers from developing technical capabilities and skills within their existing organisations. Whilst advocates of the hybrid manager concept will no doubt argue that it is important to retain people with a combination of business and technical awareness, the very act of outsourcing is likely to encourage people to overplay their business awareness whilst at the same time underplaying their technical know-how. It is also not easy to determine how people can become hybrid managers in a situation where IS is progressively stripped out of their organisation and put into the hands of a third party. To this end, IS people are more likely to find more lucrative career opportunities by either joining a company specialising in providing technical solutions (an IS vendor or supplier) or by becoming freelance IS consultants/contractors. What seems certain is that the hybrid manager concept sits uncomfortably in an environment of progressive IS outsourcing.

The Freelance IS Labour Market

Third, and related to the previous two issues, the hybrid manager concept needs to be examined in the context of the permanent and freelance labour market for IS professionals, the latter of which has expanded considerably over the last two decades. Here, we are more concerned with the freelance labour market[27] where many IS professionals work as freelance consultants or *contractors* on employment contracts ranging from three months to a year. Some contractors remain 'employed' with a client organisation for periods in excess of a year (sometimes as many as six years!) even though they do not enjoy the same conditions of employment as permanent members of staff (i.e. holidays, pension, sick pay, training, etc.). Given the growth of this important freelance or *peripheral* IS labour market, any discussion of the hybrid manager concept must surely take into account differences in employment conditions across organisations. It should also seek to reveal how IS professionals perceive their employment and career opportunities in a dynamic and changing labour market.

To some extent, the rapid pace of technical change has fuelled the IS skill shortage which now adversely affects many organisations. Equally, the problems of the management and technology gap and of constantly changing skill requirements have not been resolved. In fact, the rhetoric in favour of hybrid managers has, arguably, not helped the IS skills shortage problem, particularly where large numbers of IS professionals have actively relinquished their technical capabilities and skills to become *more rounded* business managers. Whereas an awareness of the latest technologies was seen by some as sufficient to qualify business managers for the role of hybrid manager, these people have also come under criticism by IS professionals for possessing what they describe as 'over-hyped and phoney technical knowledge'. Moreover, the hype surrounding new technology has shown that managers[28] with little direct technical experience (i.e. programming, systems analysis, databases, networking, testing, etc.), may resort to bluff in an attempt to retain their legitimacy in managing an IS project. One analyst/programmer at a UK bank summed up this situation well by stressing that

> A lot of so-called 'hybrid managers' know very little about IS, particularly the latest client server systems. Many of them have programmed in COBOL and have knowledge of legacy systems, but not the latest IS such as client server, networking and databases. Although some of them have read the 'idiots guide to IS', they come unstuck when they have to advise senior management about the intricacies of IS work. Having said that, they know all the buzzwords and can bluff their way out of a problem. But I am not surprised that a lot of poor decisions get taken about IS. If you don't understand what you are managing, I fail to see how you can know whether or not your technical decisions are sound. It is no use criticising IS people for speaking a language you don't understand. You should try to understand the language. That's what happens in the medical profession!.

Although much of the work on innovation and technical change over the last two decades has claimed that IS has a strategic role to play in achieving competitive advantage, with Kantrow (1980) writing about the *strategy–technology connection*, and Porter extolling the virtues of using technology for competitive advantage and market leadership (Porter, 1985), IS professionals, to some extent, continue to suffer from a poor commercial image. As we have seen above, IS people suffer from negative stereotypes since they are often perceived as being narrow, introverted and lacking in communication skills. This is seen to disqualify them from entering managerial positions. Some companies even employ graduates with non-technical degrees because they feel that these people are better at communicating across business functions compared with their computer graduate counterparts. So the historical separation between managerial and technical work, characteristic of a high population of UK and US organisations, with 'line positions depleted of technical tasks' (Sorge and Warner, 1986), seems to have been replicated in the information age.

Attitudes to Education and Training Policy

A fourth issue therefore broadly concerns education and training policy. Mirroring the views and practices of many US and UK companies shows that business and management courses in universities tend to be built partly on an assumption that technical capabilities and skills are not perceived as part of managerial work. Business and management schools have often eliminated production and operations and other technology-related subjects from the *core* management subjects of finance, strategy, human resources and marketing (Armstrong and Hagel, 1997). This is against a background of companies worldwide spending increasing amounts on innovation and technology since the 1970s where the management of this resource is now widely perceived as a strategic device which may enhance competitive position and market leadership (Allen and Scott-Morton, 1994). Against this background, the management of innovation and technology is often excluded from the agenda of senior management. Yet the often very different educational and occupational backgrounds of managers and technical specialists have contributed to the many problems in managing innovation and technology.

In attempting to make a virtue out of necessity by offering the concept of hybrid managers, those who advocate this *solution* to the *culture gap* between managers and technical specialists tend to overlook the inherent contradictions and anomalies mentioned above. The employment, and even credibility, of hybrid managers faces all kinds of difficulty, not least because of the very rapid pace of technical change, which suggests that it is difficult for people to keep up to date in their technical know-how while also undertaking managerial responsibilities. In reviewing the concept of the hybrid manager, such thinking seems to demonstrate a staggering *naïveté* about education, training, the division of labour between managers and technical specialists, and the current demand for IS capabilities and skills, which outstrips that for managerial positions. Such *naïveté* is not surprising given the origins of the hybrid manager idea in the mid-1980s, which borrowed ideas from project management in construction, shipbuilding and other business sectors in which teams of people are regularly brought together for the duration of contracts, projects, assignments and/or tasks. Indeed, project management has often been used to make working practices more flexible in times of rapid technical change, increased global competition and managing operations which are geographically diverse (Yeates, 1991).

Yet much of the literature on hybrid managers shows a profound failure to address the centrally important business-sector-specific requirements critical to project management. The notion that the person with technical skills and some business knowledge (e.g. the new MBA holder who has had technical education and experience) is capable of contributing both breadth and depth to the work of any business sector is often taken completely for granted by those who advocate the concept of the hybrid manager. Business knowledge is thought of, by such people, as MBA-type knowledge of functional specialisms and generic themes (globalisation, core competencies, etc.) not sector-specific business specialisms. An example of an effective hybrid manager in the eyes of such people would be an accountant with an MBA, and no sector-specific knowledge outside the practice of accountancy. Such a person, however, may be seriously deficient in experience of the details and peculiarities of all functions when employed in, or contracted to, a particular business sector. For example, compare the obvious differences of an accountant working for a software company as opposed to a toy manufacturer.

The study of comparative management suggests that superior competence is a product of breadth of education and practical understanding (neither of which is completely and necessarily best gained in formal education) and deep knowledge of the affairs and peculiarities of particular employment sectors (Glover and Hughes, 1996; Locke, 1996a). The job-hopping Anglo-Saxon with a first degree of varied and uncertain relevance, topped up with a generalist MBA and its promise of upward social and economic mobility, will normally fail to satisfy all or enough of these requirements. Yet the main point is that the self-styled hybrid manager who has some relevant skills and some practical knowledge but who lacks deep experience of their business sector is likely to find himself or herself at a serious disadvantage.[29]

What is certain from the above is that education and training policies in organisations continue to differ widely for managers and technical specialists, respectively. To the extent that some 23 UK institutions offer an undergraduate degree in Business Information Technology (BIT) which intends to combine business awareness with practical technical training, the wider labour market, and businesses in general, continue to draw a distinction between the business and technology, and their associated capabilities and skills. In doing so, they tend to reinforce the distinction between these two activities and, in turn, create a false dichotomy. Indeed, if we consider the activities of many companies, from financial services to manufacturing, it is evident that technology in the form of mainframe computers, personal computers (PCs), other communications and networking technologies are now embedded into core and peripheral business processes, functions, activities and structures. So to remove the technology infrastructure (equipment, staff, information flows, etc.) may render the business unable to compete in the medium or long term. For example, recent research into IS outsourcing has found that much confusion exists over what managers and technical specialists perceive to be the core competencies of their organisation (Currie and Willcocks, 1997). Whereas some believed that it was important to retain a technology infrastructure, others

Table 9.3 Comparison of Japanese-style vs. Western-style organisational knowledge creation

Japanese organisation	Western organisation
Group based	Individual based
Tacit knowledge-orientated	Explicit knowledge-orientated
Strong on socialisation and internalisation	Strong on externalisation and combination
Emphasis on experience	Emphasis on analysis
Dangers of 'group think' and 'overadaptation to the past success'	Danger of 'paralysis by analysis'
Ambiguous organisational intention	Clear organisational intention
Group autonomy	Individual autonomy
Creative chaos through overlapping tasks	Creative chaos through individual differences
Frequent fluctuation from top management	Less frequent fluctuation from top management
Redundancy of information	Less redundancy of information
Requisite variety through cross-functional teams	Requisite variety through individual differences

Adapted from: Nonaka and Takeuchi (1995, p. 199).

were convinced that this could be outsourced to a third party. As such, a variation of IS outsourcing deals were signed in a range of private and public sector organisations.

Whilst some banks outsourced more than 70%–80% of their technology infrastructure (total outsourcing), other banks chose to retain this facility and only outsource a small proportion of their IS work (selective sourcing). In fact, one manager at an insurance company said that, 'In my opinion, what is a core competence today may be a peripheral activity tomorrow. If you outsource all your IS work, you may end up losing your key assets. Outsourcing is a risky thing to do in the medium to long term.' These comments are interesting in the light of cross-national attitudes towards education, training and 'knowledge creation' in general. For if we consider the work of Nonaka and Takeuchi (1995), it is apparent that different attitudes prevail towards knowledge creation in Japan compared with the West (North America and Britain in particular).

Table 9.3 gives a breakdown of the commonly held attitudes in Japanese and Western organisations. What can be observed from this study is that Western cultures are much more individualistic and analytical than their Japanese counterparts, who tend to be more group-based and experiential in their approach to knowledge creation. It is also important to add that Japanese culture does not make quite the same distinction between managerial and technical roles and responsibilities, nor does it engage in separating the business from the technical functions, especially through outsourcing. In fact, few Japanese companies have engaged in large-scale outsourcing of their work compared with US and UK firms.

CASE STUDY—THE KNOWLEDGE GAP BETWEEN MANAGERS AND TECHNICAL SPECIALISTS

Royal Bank of Scotland

A longitudinal research study was carried out at a UK bank over a three-year period to explore relationships between managers and technical specialists. Over 50 interviews were carried out at the bank using a semi-structured interviewing technique. The primary focus of the research was to examine:

- the structure of the IS function;
- the division of labour between managerial and technical personnel;
- tensions between these groups;
- competencies and skills requirements.

In-depth interviews with a number of bank personnel were carried out with senior and middle managers, project managers, analyst/programmers, and end users. A document was obtained from the bank which outlined the formal objectives and overall structure of the technology division. This is shown in Table 9.4.

According to senior managers, a formal structure was critical to 'enable the full exploitation of technology within the banking sector'. The above structure was primarily concerned with financial control and the delineation of formal reporting arrangements for managers and technical specialists. The document 'covers all projects initiated on behalf of the business divisions and projects initiated by technology to improve service levels or quality of the IS service'. It was intended as a policy statement and was not concerned with the operational (day-to-day) management of technology projects; the methodologies used to manage them; nor the technologies used for software development. Neither was it concerned to identify the competencies and skills for managers and technical specialists in a financial services setting.

Executive management responsibility for expenditure incurred by the technology division was provided by a two tier committee structure:

1. an executive management committee; and
2. a group technology steering committee.

Table 9.4   *Formal objectives and overall structure for the technology division*

Executive management guidance and control	Sound planning and control of systems development must be ensured for the entire organisation. This requires that the department has a formal direct reporting relationship with executive management.
Organisational commitment	Without a clear demonstration of the organisation's commitment, proper resources may never be allocated to the project.
Business management direction	Primary responsibility for the functional success of a new system should be placed with its major beneficiaries. Business management should therefore be in a position to provide clear guidance on project scope and direction to the project team.
Accountability of IS project management	The IS team must be clearly accountable for delivery of the agreed functionality. The organisation structure must allow the team to involve business management in all key decisions affecting a project, to resolve conflicts within the team and gain access to computing resources.

The first committee was responsible for the allocation of financial resources to selected technology projects. The role of the second committee was to assist in the management of the technology division by

- participating in the planning process;
- monitoring the progress of projects;
- ensuring adequate user commitment; and
- resolving conflicting priorities for IS resource where necessary.

The group technology steering committee had a number of responsibilities which included:

- the development of organisation policies for technology;
- to serve as project steering committee for long-range information planning projects;
- to approve initiation of all projects above £1 million budgeted expenditure and above £0.2 million unbudgeted expenditure (technology projects over £5 million require approval from the board of directors);
- to monitor progress of all development projects; and
- to set priorities and settle user disputes.

The technology steering committee was responsible for all the technology projects undertaken by the technology division. The divisional steering committee acted within the policy framework set out by the group technology steering committee. Its key responsibilities included: the agreement of annual technology budgets and quarterly revisions; approval of all significant projects (or budget allocations in the case of smaller grouped activities such as support/maintenance); ensuring that the business was adequately supported by production systems (this included any new business areas or products); prioritising of technology budgeted resources available to the division; regular review and monitoring of all major activities; submissions to the group technology steering committee as required; the resolution of conflicts, issues and problems raised by the project control committees; justification of material variances from group strategic aims; establishing a project control committee to execute and control specific division projects or portions of the budget, and, finally, to ensure adequate business staff were made available to support technology projects. This itemised list of key responsibilities of the divisional steering committee focused primarily on the financial monitoring and control of the bank's technical activities.

Financial control was described as the major senior management responsibility. At a lower level, the project control committee (PCC) was ascribed a less *strategic* and more *operational* role. The PCC was concerned with the approval, review, monitoring and control of technology projects, plans and budgets, and the submission of proposals and progress reports to the divisional technology steering committee. In addition, the PCC was responsible for the overall management and progress of technology projects to ensure that problems were dealt with swiftly. The PCC also signed off and approved all previously agreed milestones throughout the life of a project, and was responsible for the development of competencies and skills of project personnel (including technical specialists). This structure ensured a clear division between the strategic role of senior managers and the operational responsibilities of project managers. Whereas the strategic management of technology was synonymous with financial control, operational management was more concerned with the day-to-day running of technology projects.

But according to one project manager, many of the activities identified as operational were in fact 'strategic in nature'. For example, tasks allocated to project managers and even technical specialists, such as the evaluation of new technologies (e.g. client-server) and their eventual purchase, could influence the strategic direction of future technology purchases. This was evident by examining how legacy systems (e.g. past investments in technology) influenced current technical choices and possibilities. One analyst/programmer suggested that, 'Since senior managers in the business units do not understand the software we are using, we tend to carry out the evaluation and feasibility of software for the projects we work on. I suppose we, as technologists, steer the technology decisions rather than senior managers.'

Building Relationships for Managing Technology Projects

To avoid confusion over roles and responsibilities the bank had created a framework for building relationships between the business units and technology division to improve the management of technology projects (see Figure 9.2). This was euphemistically described by one project manager as, 'a formal attempt at building strong relationships between banking and technology to enhance the exploitation of technology'. The rationale for the structure was to ensure a good return on investment (ROI) from technology projects. In the past this had not always been the case as poor relations between technology and the business had resulted in project failures, low morale and the emergence of a *blame culture*. Senior management now demanded 'tangible' benefits from technology projects, and this would be achieved through a relationship-building exercise.

Such an approach is complementary to the prescriptive information systems literature which stresses the importance of aligning technology projects to business objectives by decentralising technology to line managers (Scott-Morton, 1991). Notwithstanding the debate about the merits of centralisation and decentralisation of technology (Tavakolian, 1991), senior managers at the bank perceived the formal framework as a 'control mechanism' to expose poorly

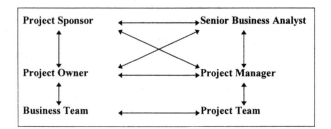

Figure 9.2 *Building relationships for managing technology projects*

defined technology projects; inadequate project management; waste of resources (time and money); and project over-runs. The formal framework developed by the bank was intended to strengthen relationships between six key groups from the business units and technology division. A senior business analyst opined:

> The initiation of technology projects is a haphazard process. It is my job as a senior business analyst to build a relationship with one of the business units. For example, a project sponsor may suggest the development of an information system that will do xyz. As a representative from the technology division, I will advise whether or not this is feasible and affordable. When we have agreed that the project should be funded, we send a proposal to the technology steering committee. Once the funds have been released, a project owner is responsible for overseeing the development of the project with a project manager from the technology division. Each group has a team, and it is up to these teams to develop a fully functional information system which meets all the criteria set out in the original proposal document.

Recognising the knowledge gap between the business managers and technical specialists, senior managers, notably from the business units, embraced the rhetoric of the British Computer Society (Earl and Skyrme, 1992; Palmer and Ottley, 1990), which advocates the development of the hybrid manager role. Hybrid managers, according to Earl (1989, p. 205) are either

- someone with a technical background who has become a manager, or
- a manager put in charge of technology projects.

Whilst the concept of hybrid management is widely embraced in North America and Britain, its theoretical justification and practical viability remain questionable (Currie and Glover, 1999). This is because the knowledge gap which is purported to exist between managers and technical specialists is seemingly created through entry into management, the result of which is a loss of technical competence (assuming of course the person followed the first route suggested by Earl, 1989). Important questions also arise about the likelihood of someone acquiring technical competence by following the second route. For although technical competence is difficult to measure (Bohn, 1994), it is not unreasonable to suggest that six months running a technology project is unlikely to make someone an expert. The role of the senior business analyst was an attempt by the bank to create a *hybrid* manager. One senior business analyst confirmed that, 'Most senior business analysts either have a background in programming or began their careers in trainee management positions. Before coming to the bank I used to work in insurance. The last time I programmed was fifteen years ago in COBOL.'

Although senior business analysts worked for the technology division, their level of technical competency was the subject of many debates by the project team (analyst/programmers), and to a lesser extent by project managers. Analyst/ programmers, many of whom were hired in as contractors, voiced scathing criticisms about the senior business analyst role. According to one senior analyst/programmer:

> I think the role of senior business analyst is futile. First of all, they are not business managers so their knowledge of the business is questionable. Second, their technical skills are almost nil. What usually happens during IS projects is that I am constantly asked to provide technical

advice to the client (business unit). This means that the senior business analyst rarely contributes anything to the discussion.

It emerged that analyst/programmers were critical of management's perception of them as 'purveyors of technical services' (a term used by Finniston, 1980) to the business units. In essence, they felt that people without an in-depth knowledge of technology were 'unable to take effective business decisions'. Political friction was also apparent between project managers and analyst/programmers based upon a disagreement over the competencies and skills needed to run a technology project. It is interesting to compare two statements from a project manager and an analyst/programmer, respectively:

> I have a background in personnel management but I decided to become a project manager because I felt there was likely to be greater job security working in the technology division. In recent years the bank has made nearly 2000 people redundant. I don't think you need a lot of technical knowledge to manage IS because its all about budgeting and controlling the work of others. My main task is to keep the project within budgetary and time constraints (Project manager).

> I don't accept the view that you don't need a technical knowledge to be able to manage the work of technical specialists. I spend most of my day writing code. Since my project manager doesn't know anything about C++, he is unable to assess whether I write good code or rubbish. Most of the time I tell my project manager how long it will take for me to complete a software program. All they seem to do is walk around with GANTT charts and checklists. I consider that I manage my own work (Analyst/programmer).

Further interviews with senior business analysts, project managers, and analyst/programmers suggested that the knowledge gap between managers and technical specialists was not resolved through attempts by the bank to create a formal structure for managing technology projects, nor by the development of new roles such as the *hybrid* senior business analyst. Political tensions and conflicts between the user groups (project sponsors, project owners and business teams) and technology division remained an inherent part of the technology project development process (Knights and Murray, 1994). To a large extent, the organisational structure designed to crystallise roles and responsibilities tended to formalise the divisions between managers and technical specialists (Currie, 1996c). Whilst technical specialists derived power from their status as knowledge workers and their ability to work autonomously (Friedman and Cornford, 1989), project managers continued to promulgate the view that technical competence was not crucial for managing technology projects (Boynton *et al.*, 1992). The business users and senior managers outside the technology division equally shared this view. Definitions of core management competencies and skills were generally those of budgeting and co-ordinating (Fayol, 1949). Technical competency was clustered within the technology division, specifically in the *hands-on* roles of analyst/programmer and database administrator. Respect for project managers from technical specialists was largely based upon the perceived level of technical competence of the former group. However, it was generally agreed that once a person became a manager, his or her *technical edge* (knowledge of the latest technology) would be lost. Very little respect was given to project managers brought into the technology division from the business units.

SUMMARY

This chapter has been concerned with a series of complex issues relating to the management and technical capabilities and skills required for contemporary organisations. As we have seen, 'classical' or traditional models of management continue to inform debates about the type of people needed to manage technology and technical specialists. In the business and management literature, many Anglo-American writers argue the case for the generalist or line manager to be put in charge of technical resources (equipment and people). Yet this view has come under some criticism because it fails to address, or at least provide a practical solution to, the perceived *culture gap* between managers and technical specialists. Having ascertained that a dichotomy exists between the business and technology functions, the chapter examined the concept of the *hybrid manager*. This concept was criticised for offering a narrow and impractical solution to the complex issues surrounding the management of technology and technical specialists.

In concluding this chapter, the words of Martin (1996, p. 3) offer a pessimistic picture of the capabilities and skills in contemporary organisations. Thus, 'Most of today's corporations are structured for an age that is gone. Many employees and managers are cogs in an obsolete machine.' Such a view, however, offers today's managers a challenge which is perhaps to rethink some of present management models with a view to closing the gap between business and technical functions. As we have argued above, it seems that managers and technical specialists will need to develop capabilities and skills which are business and technology sector specific, particularly in so far as many companies now use technology in their product and process design (Argyris, 1991). This is especially the case in the computer software industry. For example, Cusumano and Selby (1995, p. 9), who have made a detailed study of Microsoft, remind us of the importance of hiring people with both business and technical know-how. Thus:

> If the CEO, senior management team and key employees truly understand their technology and markets, seize opportunities as they arise, and make the future follow their vision, then they have a chance to dominate not one but many promising markets. They have a solid basis to create an organisation centred on the right products and markets. They should be able to reorganise as needed, find more outstanding people to help run the company, and prepare for the future.

The difficulty, however, in achieving this goal is that there are too few people with the right capabilities and skills mix in the international labour market. This chapter has attempted to examine a range of issues relating to the IS skill shortage crisis by focusing upon models of managerial work and common assumptions about technical specialists. It has argued that the concept of the hybrid manager, whilst offering an analysis of a problem, is not a solution in itself.

Endnotes

1. A more detailed discussion of management methods and techniques during the twentieth century is given in Chapter 6.
2. The global information society (GIS) is a term used to incorporate: the virtual society; digital and information economy; virtual community; Internet revolution, web workstyle/web lifestyle, etc. (Gates, 1999).
3. The term electronic commerce is used in both the narrow sense of 'doing business electronically', and in the broader sense of developing international 'networks of small businesses, government agencies, large corporations, and independent contractors'. It therefore seems appropriate to adopt the term e-commerce to describe the former activity and Internet commerce to encompass the latter activities. This book will adopt the term Internet commerce as it is concerned with these wider activities.
4. http://www.ibm.com/e-business
5. A distinction should be made between Internet *access* and Internet *use*. The former tends to refer to the number of people who have access to the Internet while the latter refers to people who actually use the Internet. The terms tend to be used interchangeably in surveys and reports, etc. and this may lead to some confusion as statistics/figures are likely to vary.
6. Total global Internet use is estimated to be 147 million people. (These estimates are for regular use of the Internet, not just the number of connections. They have been taken from a variety of worldwide sources and compiled by NUA Internet Surveys, 1998). *Source*: Adapted from *The Times, Interface*, 30 September 1998, p. 13.
7. E-business is a term currently used by IBM.
8. The term Internet commerce will be used to avoid confusion between e-commerce and EDI.
9. The terms Internet commerce and electronic commerce are often confused. In this chapter, the term Internet commerce is used to mean commercial negotiations and transactions conducted over the Internet. These include business-to-business, business-to-consumer and within-business. E-commerce is an established term and is sometimes used more narrowly to include business-

to-business and within-business commerce (e.g. such as the use of EDI channels). However, some literature referred to in this chapter refers to e-commerce in the broader business-to-consumer context.

10. Whilst some people believe that paper-based books/journals/magazines, etc. will not be phased out by the Internet, this section is concerned with the potential for transforming products/services from physical to virtual. It is therefore the responsibility of individual companies to determine whether this process would enhance or undermine their competitive position.

11. At the time of writing, local telephone calls in the United States are free, unlike Europe and the rest of the world. Thus, Internet use in the United States exceeds anywhere else in the world.

12. One of the current and most frustrating aspects of using the Internet to procure goods/services is the poor design of some Web sites, which leave the customer confused and uncertain.

13. The GII represents the worldwide infrastructure that supports the transmission and delivery of electronic content, including the goods and services involved in electronic commerce.

14. http://www.iitf.nist.gov/eleccomm/glo_comm.htm

15. The GII represents the worldwide infrastructure that supports the transmission and delivery of electronic content, including the goods and services involved in electronic commerce. The Internet is a global matrix of interconnected computer networks using the Internet Protocol (IP) to communicate with each other. For simplicity, the term 'Internet' encompasses all such data networks, even though some electronic commerce activities may take place on proprietary networks that are not technically part of the Internet. The term 'on-line service provider' is used to refer to both companies that provide access to the Internet and other on-line services, and companies that create content that is delivered over those networks. *Source*: http://www.iitf.nist.gov/eleccomm/glo_comm.htm

16. The first is the development of the silicon chip and PC back in the 1970s and 1980s, respectively.

17. The concept of competitive advantage has been widely discussed in the literature. In particular, see Porter (1985).

18. Lou Gerstner, Chairman, IBM, *Information Week*, 1–17 March 1998, p. 14.

19. The term *core competency* refers to all those business processes, functions and activities that are deemed critical to a company's performance. For example, whereas IT strategy formulation and planning may be perceived as a core competency, the procurement, maintenance and management of IT hardware (PCs, databases, networks, etc.) may not. Therefore, a company may make a decision to outsource the latter activities to a third party.

20. All the case studies presented here were verified by the company in question as a true reflection of the outsourcing (or insourcing) experience.

21. Best Value is an initiative promoted by the UK Labour government and is designed to replace the previous Conservative government's policy of compulsory competitive tendering (CCT).

22. The typology presents four *ideal types* of IT sourcing. It is unlikely that one type will exist in its pure form in an organisation given that *reality* is not easily captured in an heuristic device. However, the ideal types are a useful way of understanding the phenomena under scrutiny.

23. Technical specialists are defined in a contemporary business and organisational context as IS professionals, IS managers and staff, and even 'techies'. These people usually have a technical background. For example, they have formal qualifications in engineering and/or computing/computer science, and/or they may have a background in working as a programmer, developer, systems analyst or some other technical role.

24. Technical specialists with supervisory responsibilities may be given the title of Project Manager. These people may have a technical background, yet be put in charge of IS projects and the technical specialists working on them. In recent years, people in this position have also been labelled 'Hybrid Managers'. Definitions, labels, roles and responsibilities, however, vary within and between organisations.

25. The culture gap between management and technical specialists is often seen as leading to IS project failure, poor communication, power struggles and other problems which impact upon overall company performance.

26. Large-scale outsourcing deals usually involve a third party taking over much of the IS resource (equipment, software licences, maintenance contracts, etc.). IS staff are also transferred, taking with them their technical knowledge, expertise and skill.

27. A distinction can be made between the peripheral IS labour market where people work on short-term, temporary employment contracts and the permanent IS labour market where people work as IS professionals on a permanent basis. In recent years, the growth of the former, peripheral IS labour market, has been significant, with many IS professionals now wishing to work on lucrative short-term, freelance contracts.

28. There has been a tendency to put non-IS literate managers in charge of IS projects and staff. Whilst this may work in some capacities, evidence shows that IS professionals often disparage the lack of technical awareness demonstrated by some managers, often to the detriment of the project.

29. This may become more apparent over time as businesses reorganise themselves into geographically dispersed networks.

Bibliography

Ackoff, R.L. (1970) *A Concept of Corporate Planning*, Wiley, Chichester.

Ackroyd, S. (1995) On the Structure and Dynamics of Some Small UK-Based Information Technology Firms, *Journal of Management Studies*, **32**(2).

Adler, P.S., McDonald, D.W. and MacDonald, F (1992) Strategic Management of Technical Functions, *Sloan Management Review*, Winter, 19–37.

Aldridge, A., White, M. and Forcht, K. (1997) Security Considerations of Doing Business via the Internet: Cautions to be Considered, *Internet Research: Electronic Networking Applications and Policy*, **7**(1), 9–15.

Allen, T.J. and Scott-Morton, M.S., eds (1994) *Information Technology and the Corporation of the 1990s*, Oxford University Press, Oxford.

Alvesson, M. (1995) *Management of Knowledge-Intensive Companies*, Walter de Gruyter, Berlin.

Angehrn, A. (1997) Designing Mature Internet Business Strategies: The ICDT Model, *European Management Journal*, **15**(4), August, 361–369.

Ansoff, H.I. (1965) *Corporate Strategy*, McGraw-Hill, New York.

Apgar, M. (1998) The Alternative Workplace: Changing Where and How People Work, *Harvard Business Review*, May/June, 121–136.

Applegate, L.M., McFarlan, F.W. and McKenney, J.L. (1996) *Corporate Information Systems Management: Text and Cases*, Irwin, London.

Argyris, C. (1957) *Personality and Organisation*, Harper & Row, New York.

Argyris, C. (1977) Double Loop Learning in Organisations, *Harvard Business Review*, September/October.

Argyris, C. (1991) Teaching Smart People How to Learn, *Harvard Business Review*, May/June.

Armstrong, A. and Hagel, J. III (1997) The Real Value of On-line Communities, *Harvard Business Review*, May/June, 134–141.

Armstrong, P. (1996) The Expunction of Process Expertise from British Management Teaching Syllabi: An Historical Analysis, in: I. Glover and M. Hughes, eds, *The Professional-Managerial Class: Contemporary British Management in the Pursuer Mode*, Gower, Aldershot.

Arunachalam, V. (1995) EDI: An Analysis of Adoption, Uses, Benefits and Barriers, *Journal of Systems Management*, March/April, 60–64.

Attal, J. (1997) Technology Empowers Small Businesses, *Electronic Commerce in Practice*, ICC, London.

Austin, D. (1996) Keeping it Simple, *Banking Technology*, April, 16.

Ba, S., Whinston, A.B. and Zhang, H. (1999) Small Business in the Digital Economy: Digital Company of the Future, Conference *Understanding the Digital Economy: Data Tools and Research*, US Department of Commerce, Washington, DC, 25–26 May.

Barnard, C. (1938) *The Functions of the Executive*, Harvard Business School Press, Cambridge, MA.

Bartram, P. (1992) *Business Reengineering: The Use of Process Redesign and IT to Transform Corporate Performance*, Business Intelligence, London.

Bashein, B.J. and Markus, M.L. (1997) A Credibility Equation for IT Specialists, *Sloan Management Review*, Summer, 35–360.

Beer, M., Eisenstate, R.A. and Spector, B. (1990) Why Change Programs Don't Produce Change, *Harvard Business Review*, 158–166.

Belmonte, R. and Murray, R. (1993) Getting Ready for Strategic Change: Surviving Business Process Redesign, *Information Systems Management*, Summer, 23–29.

Benjamin, R. and Wigand, R. (1995) Electronic Markets and Virtual Value Chains on the Information Superhighway, *Sloan Management Review*, Winter, 62–71.

BIM/CBI (1987) *The Making of Managers. A Report for the British Institute of Management and the Confederation of British Industries into Management Training, Education and Development*, HMSO, London.

Birkinshaw, J. and Fry, N. (1998) Subsidiary Initiatives to Develop New Markets, *Sloan Management Review*, Spring, 51–61.

Blackler, F. (1995) Knowledge, Work and Organizations: An Overview and Interpretation, *Organization Studies*, **16**(6), 16–36.

Bohn, R.E. (1994) Measuring and Managing Technological Knowledge, *Sloan Management Review*, Fall, 61–73.

Boynton, A.C., Jacobs, G.C. and Zmud, R.W. (1992) Whose Responsibility is IT Management?, *Sloan Management Review*, Summer, 32–38.

Brannbach, M. (1997) Is the Internet Changing the Dominant Logic of Marketing?, *European Management Journal*, **15**(6), 698–707.

Brenner, W., Kolbe, L. and Hamm, V. (1997) The Net: Extinction or Renaissance for Intermediaries: An Analysis of Core Competencies in the Book Business, Paper presented at *ECIS*, 19–21 June, Cork, Ireland.

Broh, R.A. (1982) *Managing Quality for Higher Profits*, McGraw-Hill, New York.

Bromwich, M. and Bhimani, A. (1989) *Management Accounting: Evolution not Revolution*, CIMA, London.

Brooke, C. (1995) Analyst Programmer Stereotypes: A Self Fulfilling Prophecy?, *Journal of Information Technology*, **10**, 15–25.

Buck-Lew, M. (1992) To Outsource or Not?, *International Journal of Information Management*, **12**, 3–20.

Burke, G. and Peppard, J. (1995) *Examining Business Process Reengineering*, Kogan Page, London.

Burns, T. and Stalker, G.M. (1961) *The Management of Innovation*, Tavistock Publications, London.

Buxmann, P. and Gebauer, J. (1998) Internet-Based Intermediaries: The Case of the Real Estate Market, *Sixth European Conference on Information Systems*, 4–6 June, Aix-en-Provence, pp. I, 61–74. Euro-Arab Management School, Spain.

Cabinet Office (1999) E-commerce@its.best.uk, A Performance and Innovation Unit Report, September. http://www.cabinet-office.gov.uk/innovation/1999/ecommerce.

Cairncross, F. (1997) *The Death of Distance*, Harvard Business School Press, Boston, MA.

Carley, M. (1981) Analytic Rationality, in: A.G. McGrew and M.J. Wilson, eds, *Decision Making*, Manchester University Press.

Carroll, S. and Gillen, D. (1987) Are the Classical Management Functions Useful in Describing Managerial Work?, *Academy of Management Review*, **12**(1), 38–51.

Champy, J. (1995) *Re-engineering Management*, Harper Collins, New York.

Chandler, A.D. (1962) *Strategy and Structure*, MIT Press, Cambridge, MA.

Chesbrough, H.W. and Teece, D.J. (1996) When is the Virtual Virtuous?, *Harvard Business Review*, January/February, 65–73.

Child, J. (1972) Organisational Structure, Environment and Performance: The Role of Strategic Choice, *Sociology*, **6**(1), 1–22.

Child, J. (1974) What Determines Organisational Performance? The Universals v. The It-All-Depends, *Organisational Dynamics*, Summer, 2–18.

Child, J. (1984) *Organization*, Harper & Row, New York.

Christiaanse, E. and Venkatraman, N. (1998) Monitoring and Influencing as Key Capabilities in Electronic Channels, *Sixth European Conference on Information Systems*, 4–6 June, Aix-en-Provence, pp. I, 233–246. Euro-Arab Management School, Spain.

Cobb, I. (1991) Understanding and Working with JIT, *Management Accounting*, **69**(2), 44–46.

Cockburn, C. and Wilson, T.D. (1996) Business Use of the World Wide Web, *International Journal of Information Management*, **16**(2), 83–102.

Cole-Gomolski, B. (1997) Users Loathe to Share their Know-How, *Computerworld*, **31**(46), 6.

Computer Weekly (1998) Making Waves: Outsourcing Future Trends, 21 May, 48–49.

Consumers' Association (1997) *Consumer Transactions on the Internet: Policy Report*, 2 Marylebone Road, London NW1 4DF.

Conti, R.F. and Warner, M. (1994) Taylorism, Teams and Technology in 'Reengineering' Work Organization, *New Technology, Work and Employment*, **9**(2), 93–102.

Cooper, R.F. (1991) Explicating the Logic of ABC, *Management Accounting*, **68**(10).

Cooper, R. and Kaplan, R. (1991) Profit Priorities from ABC, *Harvard Business Review*, May/June, 130–135.

Costello, G.I. and Tuchen, J.H. (1998) A Comparative Study of Business to Consumer Electronic Commerce Within the Australian Insurance Sector, *Journal of Information Technology*, **13**, 153–167.

Coyne, K.P. and Dye, R. (1998) The Competitive Dynamics of Network-Based Businesses, *Harvard Business Review*, January/February, 99–109.

Crane, D.B. and Bodie, Z. (1996) The Transformation of Banking, *Harvard Business Review*, March/April, 109–117.

Cronin, M., ed. (1996) *The Internet Strategy Handbook*, Harvard Business School Press, Boston, MA.

Crosby, P.B. (1979) *Quality is Free*, McGraw-Hill, New York.

Cross, J. (1995) IT Outsourcing: British Petroleum's Competitive Approach, *Harvard Business Review*, May/June, 94–102.

Currie, W. (1989) The Art of Justifying New Technology to Top Management, *Omega: International Journal of Management Science*, **17**(5), October, 409–418.

Currie, W. (1991) Managing Technology: A Crisis in Management Accounting? *Management Accounting*, February, 24–27.

Currie, W. (1994) The Strategic Management of Large Scale IT Projects in the Financial Services Sector, *New Technology, Work and Employment*, **9**(1), March, 19–29.

Currie, W. (1995a) The IT Strategy Audit: Performance Measurement and Control at a UK Bank, *Managerial Auditing*, **10**(1), 7–16.

Currie, W. (1995b) *Management Strategy for IT*, Pitman, London.

Currie, W. (1996a) Organization Structure and the Use of IT: Preliminary Findings of a Survey in the Private and Public Sectors, *International Journal of Information Management*, **16**(1), 51–64.

Currie, W. (1996b) Outsourcing in the Private and Public Sectors: An Unpredictable IT Strategy, *European Journal of Information Systems*, **16**(1), 226–236.

Currie, W. (1996c) Direct Control or Responsible Autonomy? Two Competing Approaches to the Management of IS Projects, *Creativity and Innovation Management*, **5**(3), 190–203.

Currie, W. (1997) Computerising the Stock Exchange: A Comparison of Two Information Systems, *New Technology, Work and Employment*, **12**(2), 75–90.

Currie, W. (1998) Using Multiple Suppliers to Mitigate the Risks of IT Outsourcing in Two UK Companies: ICI and Wessex Water, *Journal of Information Technology*, **13**, 169–180.

Currie, W. (1999a) Revisiting Management Innovation and Change Programmes: Strategic Vision or Tunnel Vision?, *Omega: The International Journal of Management Science*, forthcoming.

Currie, W. (1999b) Meeting the Challenge of Internet Commerce: Key Issues and Concerns, *Fifth International Conference of the Decision Sciences Institute*, Athens, Greece, 4–7 July.

Currie, W. and Galliers, R.D. (1999) *Rethinking M Information Systems*, Oxford University Press, Oxford.

Currie, W. and Glover, I. (1999) Hybrid Managers: An Example of Tunnel Vision and Regression in Management Research, in: W. Currie and R. Galliers, eds, *Re-thinking Management Information Systems*, Oxford University Press, Oxford.

Currie, W. and Seddon, J. (1992) Managing AMT in a JIT Environment in the UK and Japan, *British Journal of Management*, **3**(3), 123–136.

Currie, W. and Willcocks, L. (1995) Some Recent Empirical Findings on the Cultural, Political and Technical Dimensions of BPR, *Third SISNET Conference*, Institute for Wirtschaftinformatik, Bern Switzerland, 18–20 September.

Currie, W. and Willcocks, L. (1996) The New Branch Columbus Project at Royal Bank of Scotland: The Implementation of Large-Scale Business Process Re-engineering, *Journal of Strategic Information Systems*, **5**, 213–236.

Currie, W. and Willcocks, L. (1997) *In Search of Value-Added IT Outsourcing, Fast Track*, Business Intelligence, London.

Currie, W. and Willcocks, L. (1998a) New Strategies in IT Outsourcing: Major Trends and Global Best Practices, *Business Intelligence*, London.

Currie, W. and Willcocks, L. (1998b) Analysing Four Types of IT Sourcing Decisions in the Context of Scale, Client/Supplier Interdependency and Risk Mitigation, *Information Systems Journal*, **8**, 119–143.

Currie, W. and Willcocks, L. (1998c) Managing Large-Scale IT Outsourcing Contracts: The Case of British Aerospace Plc, Paper presented at UKAIS, Lincoln, 15–17 April.

Currie, W. and Yoshikawa, T. (1995) The Evolving Role of IT: A Case Study of Ten Japanese Companies, *Technology Management: Strategies & Applications for Practitioners*, **2**, 216–227.

Cusumano, M.A. and Selby, R.W. (1995) *Microsoft Secrets*, Harper Collins Business, London.

Davenport, H. (1993a) *Process Innovation: Reengineering Work Through Information Technology*, Harvard Business Press, Boston, MA.

Davenport, H. (1993b) Book Review of *Reengineering the Corporation*, *Sloan Management Review*, Fall, 103–104.

Davenport, T.H. (1994) Saving its Soul, *Harvard Business Review*, March/April, 119–131.

Davenport, T.H. (1996) Why Re-engineering Failed: The Fad that Forgot People, *Fast Company*, January, 70–74.

Davenport, T.H., De Long, D.W. and Beers, M.C. (1998) Successful Knowledge Management Projects, *Sloan Management Review*, Winter, 43–57.

Davenport, T. and Stoddart, D. (1994) Reengineering: Business Change of Mythic Proportions?, *MIS Quarterly*, **18**(2), 121–127.

David, P.A. (1999) Digital Technology and the Productivity Paradox: After Ten Years What Has Been Learned?, Conference *Understanding the Digital Economy: Data Tools and Research*, US Department of Commerce, Washington, DC, 25–26 May.

Deighton, J. (1996) The Future of Interactive Marketing, *Harvard Business Review*, November/December, 151–162.

Deming, W.E. (1982) Improvement of Quality and Productivity Through Action by Management, *National Productivity Review*, Winter, 12–22.

Drucker, P. (1946) *Concept of the Corporation*, John Day, New York.

Drucker, P. (1969) *The Age of Discontinuity: Guidelines for Our Changing Society*, Harper & Row, New York.

Drucker, P. (1985) *Innovation and Entrepreneurship*, Butterworth-Heinemann, London.

Drucker, P. (1988) The Coming of the New Organisation, *Harvard Business Review*, January/February, 45–53.

Drucker, P. (1990) The Emerging Theory of Manufacturing, *Harvard Business Review*, **90**(3), May/June, 94–102.

Drucker, P. (1993) *Post-Capitalist Society*, Butterworth-Heinemann, London.

DTI (1984a) IT Skills Shortages Committee. *First Report: The Human Factor—Supply Side*, HMSO, London.

DTI (1984b) IT Skills Shortages Committee. *Second Report: Changing Technology—Changing Skills*, HMSO, London.

DTI (1999a) *Promoting Electronic Commerce: Consultation on Draft Legislation and the Government's Response to the Trade and Industry Committee's Report*, HMSO, London.

DTI (1999b) *Our Competitive Future: Building the Knowledge Driven Economy*, CM4176, HMSO, London.

Earl, M. (1989) *Management Strategies for Information Technology*, Prentice-Hall, London.

Earl, M. (1994) The New and the Old of Business Process Redesign, *Journal of Information Systems*, **3**(1), 5–22.

Earl, M.J. and Feeny, D.F. (1994) Is Your CIO Adding Value?, *Sloan Management Review*, Spring, 11–20.

Earl, M. and Khan, B. (1994) How New is Business Process Redesign?, *European Management Journal*, **12**(1), 20–30.

Earl, M.J. and Skyrme, D.J. (1992) Hybrid Managers—What Do We Know About Them?, *Journal of Information Systems*, **2**, 169–187.

Economist (1999) Business and the Internet, Survey, 26 June to 2 July.

Edmondson, J. (1997) Creating a Profit in the Digital Age, in: International Chamber of Commerce, *Electronic Commerce in Practice*, International Systems and Communications Ltd, London, pp. 76–80.

Eisenhardt, K. and Brown, S. (1998) Time Pacing: Competing in Markets That Won't Stand Still, *Harvard Business Review*, March/April, 59–69.

EITO (1997) *ActivMedia*, ROMTEC in European Information Technology Observatory.

Electronic Commerce Resource Centre (1996) quoted by Charles Steinfield, *Electronic Commerce: An Introduction to the Special Issue*, Michigan State University.

EURIM (1997) Briefing 15, *Electronic Commerce and the Law*, Eurim, Sidcup, Kent, UK, 1–7 May.

European Commission (1998) *Report on the Communication from the Commission to the Council, the European Parliament, the Economic and Social Committee and the Committee of the Regions on a European Initiative in Electronic Commerce* (COM (97) 0157–C4–0297/97), April, Brussels.

Evans, P.B. and Wurster, T.S. (1997) Strategy and the New Economics of Information, *Harvard Business Review*, September/October, 71–82.

Evans, R. (1994) Should IT Stay or Should it Go?, *Management Today*, November, 66–71.

Fayol, H. (1949) *General and Industrial Management*, translated by C. Storrs, Pitman, London.

Federal Trade Commission (1997) *Public Workshop on Consumer Privacy on the Global Information Infrastructure*, Federal Trade Commission, Washington, DC.

Feeny, D., Earl, M. and Edwards, B. (1989) *IS Arrangements to Suit Complex Organizations 2. Integrating the Efforts of Users and Specialists*, RDP 89/5, Templeton College, Oxford.

Feher, A. and Towell, E. (1997) Business Use of the Internet, *Internet Research: Electronic Networking Applications and Policy*, **7**(3), 195–200.

Financial Times (1994) Computers in Finance Survey, 15 November.

Financial Times (1999) Online Revolution Set to Overthrow Many Established Practices, 19 July, 8.

Finniston, M. (1980) *Engineering Our Future*, HMSO, London.

Fiol, C.M. and Lyles, M.A. (1985) Organisational Learning, *Academy of Management Review*, October.

Fitzgerald, G. and Willcocks, L. (1994) The Outsourcing of Information Technology: Contracts and the Client/Vendor Relationship, *British Academy of Management Conference*, pp. 143–156.

Folt, M. (1996) Doing Business on the Information Highway, *Internet Research: Electronic Networking Applications and Policy*, **6**(2/3), 79–81.

Forrester, T. (1980) *The Micro-Electronics Revolution*, Blackwell, Oxford.

Forrester, T. (1985) *The Information Technology Revolution*, Oxford University Press, Oxford.

Forrester Research (1997a) *Sizing Intercompany Commerce*, Report by Erwin, Blane *et al.*, Forrester Research, MA.

Forrester Research (1997b) *Valuing On-line Audiences*, by Chris Channon *et al.*, Cambridge, MA.

Forrester Research (1999) *Survey on Internet Commerce*, Cambridge, MA.
    http://www.ipomonitor.com/services/example-sheet.html.

Friedman, A. and Cornford, D. (1989) *Computer Systems Development*, Wiley, Chichester.

Galliers, R. (1994) Information Technology and Organisational Change: Where Does BPR Fit In? Paper at the *Information Technology and Organisational Change: The Changing Role of IT and Business Conference*, Nijenrode University, Breukelen, The Netherlands, 28–29 April.

Galliers, R.D. and Swan, J. (1999) Information Systems and Strategic Change: A Critical Review of Business Process Re-engineering, in: W. Currie and B. Galliers, eds, *Re-thinking MIS: An Interdisciplinary Perspective*, Oxford University Press, Oxford.

Gantt, H. (1919) *Organising for Work*, Harcourt, Brace & Hove, New York.

Gartner Group (1999) *Survey Results: The Real Cost of E-Commerce Sites*, Stamford, CT.

Garvin, D.A. (1993) Building the Learning Organisation, *Harvard Business Review*, July/August, 78–91.

Gates, B. (1999) *Business@the Speed of Thought*, Penguin, Harmondsworth.

Gellman, R. (1996) Disintermediation and the Internet, *Government Information Quarterly*, **13**(1), 1–8.

Gerwin, D. (1982) Do's and Don'ts of Computerised Manufacturing, *Harvard Business Review*, March/April, 107–116.

Ghosh, S. (1998) Making Business Sense of the Internet, *Harvard Business Review*, March-April, 126–135.

Gilbert, J.P. (1989) The State of JIT Implementation and Development in the USA, *International Journal of Production Research*, **28**(6), 1099–1109.

Glazer, R. (1991) Marketing in an Information Intensive Environment: Strategic Implications of Knowledge as an Asset, *Journal of Marketing*, **15**(55), 1–19.

Glover, I. and Hughes, M. (1996) *The Professional–Managerial Class*, Avebury, Aldershot.

Granger, M.J. and Schroder, D.L. (1996) Integrating the Internet into the Business Environment, *Internet Research: Electronic Networking Applications and Policy*, **6**(2/3), 85–89.

Granick, D. (1961) *The European Executive*, Weidenfeld & Nicolson, London.

Grant, (1996) In: M. Cronin, ed. *The Internet Strategy Handbook*, Harvard Business School Press, Boston, MA.

Gray, M. (1996) *Web Growth Survey*. On-line at http://www.mit.edu:8001/people/mkgray/net/web-growth-summary/html.

Gray, P. (1996) The Global Information Infrastructure: From the Internet Toward Worldwide Commerce, *Information Systems Management*, Summer, 7–14.

Greenstein, S. (1999) Framing Empirical Research on the Evolving Structure of Commercial Internet Markets, Conference *Understanding the Digital Economy: Data Tools and Research*, US Department of Commerce, Washington, DC, 25–26 May.

Grint, K. (1993) *Reengineering History: An Analysis of Business Process Reengineering*, Management Research Paper 93/20, Templeton College, Oxford.

Grint, K. and Willcocks, L. (1995) Business Process Reengineering in Theory and Practice: Business Paradise Regained?, *New Technology Work and Employment*, Autumn.

Grint, K., Case, P. and Willcocks, L. (1995) Business Process Reeengineering: The Politics and Technology of Forgetting, *Proceedings of the IFIP WG 8.2 Conference Information Technology and Changes in Organisational Work*, University of Cambridge, 7–9 December.

Guthrie, R. and Austin, L.D. (1996) Competitive Implications of the Internet, *Information Systems Management*, Summer, 90–91.

Hagel, J. and Armstrong, A.G. (1997) *Net Gain: Expanding Markets Through Virtual Communities*, Harvard Business School Press, Boston, MA.

Hales, C. (1986) What Do Managers Do? A Critical Review of the Evidence, *Journal of Management Studies*, **23**(1), 88–113.

Hall, R.W. (1983) *Zero Inventories*, Dow-Jones-Irwin, Homewood, IL.

Hall, G., Rosenthal, J. and Wade, J. (1993) How to Make Reengineering Really Work, *Harvard Business Review*, November/December, 119–131.

Haltiwanger, J. and Jarmin, R.S. (1999) Measuring the Digital Economy, Conference *Understanding the Digital Economy: Data Tools and Research*, US Department of Commerce, Washington, DC, 25–26 May.

Hamel, G. and Prahalad, C. (1994) *Competing for the Future*, Harvard Business Press, Boston, MA.

Hammer, M. (1990) Reengineering Work: Don't Automate, Obliterate, *Harvard Business Review*, November/December, 104–112.

Hammer, M. (1996) *Beyond Reengineering: How the Process Centred Organisation is Changing Our Work and Our Lives*, Harper Business, New York.

Hammer, M. and Champy, J. (1993) *Reengineering the Corporation: A Manifesto for Business Revolution*, Nicholas Brearley Publishing, London.

Hammer, M. and Stanton, S. (1994) No Need for Excuses, *Financial Times*, 5 October, p. 20.

Hammer, M. and Stanton, S. (1995) *The Reengineering Revolution*, Harper Collins, New York.

Harrison, D.B. and Pratt, M.D. (1993) A Methodology for Reengineering Business Processes, *Planning Review*, March/April, 6–11.

Harrison, F. (1979) Towards a General Model of Management, *Journal of General Management*, **5**(2), 33–41.

Harvey, D. (1995) *Reengineering: The Critical Success Factors*, Business Intelligence, London.

Hayes, R.H. and Abernathy, W.J. (1980) Managing Our Way to Economic Decline, *Harvard Business Review*, July/August, 67–77.

Hayes, R.H. and Jaikumar, R. (1988) Manufacturing's Crisis: New Technologies, Obsolete Organisations, *Harvard Business Review*, September/October.

Hayes, R.H. and Wheelright, S.C. (1984) *Restoring our Competitive Edge: Competing Through Manufacturing*, Wiley, Chichester.

Hejndorf, C. (1998) *The Western European Forecast for Internet Usage and Commerce*, International Data Corporation, USA.

Henderson, J.C. (1990) Plugging into Strategic Partnerships: The Critical IS Correction, *Sloan Management Review*, Spring, 7−18.

Henderson, J.C. and Venkatraman, N. (1994) Strategic Alignment: A Model for Organizational Transformation via Information Technology, in: T.J. Allen and M.S. Scott-Morton, eds, *Information Technology and the Corporation of the 1990s*, Oxford University Press, Oxford.

Hertzberg, F. (1966) *Work and the Nature of Man*, World Publishing, New York.

Heygate, R. (1993) Immoderate Redesign, *The McKinsey Quarterly*, **1**, 73−87.

Hibbard, J. and Carrillo, K.M. (1998) Knowledge Revolution, *Information Week*, **5**(663), 49−54.

Hill, L.A. (1992) *Becoming a Manager*, Harvard Business School Press, Cambridge, MA.

Hirsh, W. and Bevan, S. (1988) *What Makes a Manager?*, Report No. 144, Institute of Manpower Studies, Brighton.

Hirst, P. (1988) The Politics of Industrial Policy, in: P. Hirst and J. Zeitlin, eds, *Reversing Industrial Decline?*, Berg Press, London.

Hirst, P. and Zeitlin, J., eds (1988) *Reversing Industrial Decline?*, Berg Press, London.

HMSO (1987) *The Making of Managers*, HMSO, London.

HMSO (1993) *Realising Our Potential: A Strategy for Science, Engineering and Technology*, HMSO, London.

HMSO (1994) *Competitiveness: Helping Business to Win*, HMSO, London.

HMSO (1998) *Our Competitive Future: Building the Knowledge Driven Economy*, HMSO, London.

Holway, R. (1998) *Software and Computing Services Industry in Europe: Markets and Strategies, 1998−2002*, PAC Gmbh, Munich.

Hori, S (1993) Fixing Japan's White Collar Economy: A Personal View, *Harvard Business Review*, November/December, 157−172.

Huber, R.L. (1993) How Continental Bank Outsourced its Crown Jewels, *Harvard Business Review*, January/February, 121−129.

Iansiti, M. and MacCormack, A. (1997) Developing Products on Internet Time, *Harvard Business Review*, September/October, 108−132.

IMRG (1998) *Electronic Commerce in Europe: An Action Plan for the Marketplace*, IMRG Ltd, London.

Information Week (1998) How to Click with an ISP, 82−89.

Inkpen, A.C. (1996) Creating Knowledge Through Collaboration, *California Management Review*, **39**(1), Fall, 123−140.

Inman, R.A. and Mehra, S. (1990) The Transferability of Just-In-Time Concepts to American Small Businesses, *Interfaces*, **20**(20), 30−37.

Input (1997) Quoted in US Department of Commerce (1999).

International Data Corporation (1998a) Press Releases. http://www.idc.com/em1.htm.

International Data Corporation (1998b) Internet Commerce Revenues in Western Europe to Reach $30 Million by 2001. http://www.idc.com/f/HNR/225.htm.

International Data Corporation (1998c) The Global Market Forecast for Internet Usage and Commerce. http://www.idc.com/f/HNR/225.htm.

International Data Corporation (1998d) *European Outsourcing Markets and Trends, 1995−2001*, IDC, London.

Ishikawa, K. (1985) *What is Total Quality Control? The Japanese Way*, translated by David Lu, Prentice-Hall International, London.

Ives, B. and Jarpenpaa, S.L. (1996) Will the Internet Revolutionise Business Education and Research?, *Sloan Management Review*, Spring, 33−41.

Ives, B. and Learmonth, G. (1984) The Information System as a Competitive Weapon, *Communications of the ACM*, **27**(12), 1193−1201.

Janson, R. (1993) How Reengineering Transforms Organizations to Satisfy Customers, *National Productivity Review*, Winter, 45–53.

Jeans, M. and Morrow, M. (1989) The Practicalities of Using ABC, *Management Accounting*, November, 42–43.

Johannsson, H., McHugh, P., Pendlebury, A. and Wheeler, W. (1993) *Business Process Reengineering: Breakpoint Strategies for Market Dominance*, Wiley, Chichester.

Judd, S. (1993) Hybrid Managers in Information Technology, in R. Ennals and P. Molyneux, eds, *Managing Information Technology*, Springer-Verlag, Berlin.

Jupiter Communications (1998) On-line advertising report.

Juran, J.M. (1986) The Quality Trilogy, *Quality Progress*, August, 19–24.

Kalakota, R. and Whinston, A.B. (1996) *Frontiers of Electronic Commerce*, Addison Wesley, Harlow, UK.

Kalakota, R. and Whinston, A.B. (1997) *Electronic Commerce: A Manager's Guide*, Addison Wesley, Harlow, UK.

Kantrow, A.M (1980) The Strategy-Technology Connection, *Harvard Business Review*, July/August, 6–21.

Kaplan, R. (1984) Yesterday's Accounting Undermines Production, *Harvard Business Review*, July/August, 95–101.

Kaplan, R. (1985) Accounting Lag: The Obsolescence of Cost Accounting Systems, in: K. Clark, R. Hayes and C. Lorenze, eds, *Technology and Productivity: The Uneasy Alliance*, Harvard Business School Press, Boston, MA, pp. 195–226.

Kaplan, R. (1986) Must CIM be Justified by Faith Alone?, *Harvard Business Review*, March/April, 87–95.

Kavanagh, J. (1994) Business Process Re-engineering, ABC of Computing, *Financial Times*, 26 April.

Keen, P.G.W. (1981) Information Systems and Organisational Change, *Communications of the ACM*, **24**, 24–33.

Kehoe, B. (1995) Internet and the Implications of the Information Superhighway for Business, *Journal of Systems Management*, May/June, 16–65.

Klein, M. (1994) Reengineering Methodologies and Tools, *Information Systems Management*, Spring, 31–35.

Kling, R. and Lamb, R. (1999) IT and Organizational Change in the Digital Economies: A Socio-Technical Approach, Conference *Understanding the Digital Economy: Data Tools and Research*, US Department of Commerce, Washington, DC, 25–26 May.

Knights, D. and Murray, F. (1994) *Managers Divided*, Wiley, Chichester.

Kotha, S. (1998) Competing on the Internet: The Case of Amazon.com, *European Management Journal*, **16**(2), 212–222.

Kotter, J. (1982) *The General Managers*, The Free Press, New York.

Kumar, R. and Cooke, C.W. (1996) Educating Senior Management on the Strategic Benefits of Electronic Data Interchange, *Journal of Systems Management*, March/April, 42–62.

Kurbel, K. and Teuteberg, F. (1998) The Current State of Business Internet Use: Results from an Empirical Survey of German Companies, *Sixth European Conference on Information Systems*, 4–6 June, Aix-en-Provence, pp. II, 543–556. Euro-Arab Management School, Spain.

Lacity, M. and Hirschheim, R. (1993a) The Information Systems Outsourcing Bandwagon, *Sloan Management Review*, Fall, 73–93.

Lacity, M. and Hirschhiem, R. (1993b) *Information Systems Outsourcing*, Wiley, Chichester.

Lacity, M.C. and Willcocks, L.P. (1998) An Empirical Investigation of Information Technology Sourcing Practices: Lessons from Experience, *MIS Quarterly*, September, 363–408.

Lacity, M., Willcocks, L. and Feeny, D. (1995) IT Outsourcing: Maximise Flexibility and Control, *Harvard Business Review*, May/June, 84–93.

Lacity, M., Willcocks, L. and Feeny, D. (1996) The Value of Selective Sourcing, *Sloan Management Review*, **37**, Spring, 13–25.

Lacovou, C.L., Benbasat, I. and Dexter, A.S. (1995) Electronic Data Interchange and Small Organizations Adoption and Impact of Technology, *MIS Quarterly*, December, 465–484.

Lankford, W.M. and Riggs, W.E. (1996) Electronic Data Interchange: Where Are We Today?, *Journal of Systems Management*, March/April, 58–62.

Lansing State Journal (1995) People Still Like To Go Shopping, 26 December, 5B.

Lawrence, P. (1995) *Through a Glass Darkly: Towards a Characterisation of British Management*, Loughborough University, Loughborough.

Lerner, J. (1999) Small Business, Innovation and Public Policy in the Information Technology Industry, Conference *Understanding the Digital Economy: Data Tools and Research*, US Department of Commerce, Washington, DC, 25–26 May.

Levitt, B. and March, J.G. (1988) Organisational Learning, *American Review of Sociology*, **14**.

Likert, R. (1961) *New Patterns of Management*, McGraw-Hill, New York.

Lindblom, C. E. (1959) The Science of Muddling Through, *Public Administration*, **19**, 79–88.

Locke, R. (1996a) *The Collapse of the American Management Mystique*, Oxford University Press, Oxford.

Locke, R. (1996b) The Limits of America's Pax Oceonomica: Germany and Japan after World War II, in: I. Glover and M. Hughes, eds, *The Professional-Managerial Class: Contemporary British Management in the Pursuer Mode*, Gower, Aldershot.

Loh, L. and Venkatraman, N. (1992) Determinants of Information Technology Outsourcing: A Cross-sectoral Analysis, *Journal of Management Information Systems*, **9**(1), 7–24.

Luthans, F., Hodgetts, M. and Rosenkrantz, S.A. (1988) *Real Managers*, Ballinger, Cambridge, MA.

Lymer, A., Johnson, R. and Baldwin, A. (1997) The Internet and the Small Business: A Study of Impacts, Paper presented at *ECIS*, 19–21 June, Cork, Ireland.

Maddox, K. (1997) Information Still Killer App on the Internet, *Advertising Age*, 6 October.

Maloff, J.H. (1996) Measuring the Value of the Internet for Business, in: M. Cronin, ed., *The Internet Strategy Handbook*, Harvard Business School Press, Boston, MA.

Mangham, I. and Silver, M. (1986) *Management Training—Context and Practices*, School of Management, University of Bath.

Manpower Services Commission (1985a) *The Impact of New Technology of Skills in Manufacturing and Services*, Moorfoot, Sheffield.

Manpower Services Commission (1985b) *A Challenge to Complacency: Changing Attitudes to Training*, Moorfoot, Sheffield.

Manpower Services Commission (1987) *The Making of Managers: A Report on Management Education in the USA, West Germany, France, Japan and the UK*, NEDO, London.

March, J.G. and Simon, H.A. (1958) *Organization*, Wiley, New York.

Martin, J. (1996) *Cybercorp—The New Business Revolution*, Amercom, American Management Association, New York.

Maslow, A.H. (1970) *Motivation and Personality*, Harper & Row, New York.

Mayo, E. (1949) *The Social Problems of An Industrial Civilisation*, Routledge, London.

McFarlan, F,W. (1984) New Electronics Systems Can Add Value to Your Product and Throw Your Competition Off Balance, *Harvard Business Review*, May/June, 98–103.

McFarlan, W. and Nolan, R. (1995) How to Manage an Outsourcing Alliance, *Sloan Management Review*, **36**(2), Winter, 9–23.

Meall, L. (1996) Are You Being Served?, *Accountancy*, March, 65–66.

Mills, D.Q. and Friesen, B. (1992) The Learning Organisation, *European Management Journal*, **10**, 146–156.

Mintzberg, H. (1973) *The Nature of Managerial Work*, Harper & Row, New York.

Mitchell, V. and Fitzgerald, G. (1998) The IT Outsourcing Market Place: Vendors and their Selection, *Journal of Information Technology*, **12**, 223–237.

Moad, J. (1993) Does Reengineering Really Work?, *Datamation*, 1 August, 22–28.

Morone, J.G. (1993) Technology and Competitive Advantage—The Role of General Management, *Research-Technology Management*, 6–25.

Morris, D. and Brandon, J. (1993) *Reengineering Your Business*, McGraw-Hill, London.

Mumford, E. (1972) *Job Satisfaction: A Study of Computer Specialists*, Longman, London.

Mumford, E. (1987) Using Reality in Management Development, *Management Education and Development*, **18**(3), 223–243.

Mumford, E. (1999) Routinisation, Re-engineering, and Socio-technical Design: Changing Ideas on the Organisation of Work, in: W. Currie and B. Galliers, eds, *Re-thinking MIS: An Interdisciplinary Perspective*, Oxford University Press, Oxford.

Network News (1998) UK Suffering E-Commerce Blindness, 3 June, VNU Business Publications, London, 45 pp.

Nonaka, I. (1991) The Knowledge-Creating Company, *Harvard Business Review*, November/December, 96–104.

Nonaka, I. and Takeuchi, H. (1995) *The Knowledge Creating Company*, Oxford University Press, Oxford.

NTIA (1995) *Privacy and the NII: Safeguarding Telecommunications-Related Information*, National Telecommunications and Information Administration.

Nua Internet Surveys (1998) *Banks Are In The Dark*, Nua Ltd, New York.

Nystrom, P.C. and Starbuck, W.H. (1981) *Handbook of Organizational Design*, Vol, 1, Oxford University Press, Oxford.

Oakland, J.S. (1995) *Total Quality Management: Text with Cases*, Butterworth-Heinemann, Oxford.

Orlikowski, W.J. (1999) The Truth Is Not Out There: An Enacted View of the 'Digital Economy', Conference *Understanding the Digital Economy: Data Tools and Research*, US Department of Commerce, Washington, DC, 25–26 May.

OTR Group (1998) Article entitled Always Read the Small Print by T. Harrington, *Computing*, 12 March, 52–54.

Palmer, C. and Ottley, S. (1990) *From Potential to Reality: Hybrids—Critical Force in the Application of Information Technology in the 1990s*, A Report by the BCS Task Group in Hybrids, British Computer Society.

Pascal, R., and Athos, A. (1981) *The Art of Japanese Management*, Penguin, Harmondsworth.

Peppard, J. (1993) *IT Strategy for Business*, Pitman, London.

Pitt, L., Berton, P. and Watson, R.T. (1996) From Surfer to Buyer on the WWW: What Marketing Managers Might Want to Know, *Journal of General Management*, **22**(1), Autumn, 1–13.

Poon, S. and Swatman, P.M.C. (1997) Emerging Issues on Small Business Use of the Internet: 23 Australian Case Studies, *ECIS*, 19–21 June, Cork, Ireland.

Porter, M. (1980) *Competitive Strategy*, The Free Press, New York.

Porter, M. (1985) *Competitive Advantage: Creating and Sustaining Superior Performance*, The Free Press, New York.

Porter, M. and Millar, V. (1985) How Information Gives You a Competitive Advantage, *Harvard Business Review*, July/August, 149–160.

Prahalad, C. and Hamel, G. (1990) The Core Competencies of the Corporation, *Harvard Business Review*, **68**(3), 79–91.

Price Waterhouse (1998) *Technology Forecast 1998*, Report by T. Retter and M. Calynuik, July.

Quelch, J.A. and Klein, L.R. (1996) The Internet and International Marketing, *Sloan Management Review*, Spring, 60–75.

Quinn, J.B. and Hilmer, F.G. (1994) Strategic Outsourcing, *Sloan Management Review*, Summer, 43–55.

Rao, A., Carr, L.P., Dambolena, I., Kopp, R.J., Martin, J., Rafii, F. and Schlesinger, P.F. (1996) *Total Quality Management*, Wiley, Chichester.

Rayport, J.F. and Sviokla, J.J. (1995) Exploiting the Virtual Value Chain, *Harvard Business Review*, November/December, 75–85.

Reynolds, J. (1997) The Internet as a Strategic Resource: Evidence from the European Retail Sector, in: L. Willcocks, D. Feeny and G. Islei, eds, *Managing IT as a Strategic Resource*, McGraw-Hill, New York.

Rockart, J.F. (1988) The Line Takes the Leadership—IS Management in a Wired Society, *Sloan Management Review*, Summer, 57–64.

Rockness, H. and Zmud, R.W. (1989) *Information Technology Management: Evolving Managerial Roles*, Financial Executives Research Foundation, Morristown, NJ.

Rose, G., Khoo, H. and Straub, D. (1999) Current Technological Impediments to Business-to-Consumer Electronic Commerce, *Communications of the Association for Information Systems*, **1**, Article 16, June, 1–52.

Rowe, C. and Herbert, B. (1990) IT in the Boardroom: The Growth of Computer Awareness Among Chief Executives, *Journal of General Management*, **15**(4), 32–44.

Sauer, C. (1993) *Why Information Systems Fail*, Alfred Waller, Henley.

Sauer, C. (1999) Deciding the Future for IS Failures: Not the Choice You Might Think: in W. Currie and B. Galliers, eds, *Re-thinking MIS: An Interdisciplinary Perspective*, Oxford University Press, Oxford.

Saunders, C., Gebelt, M. and Hu, Q. (1997) Achieving Success in Information Systems Outsourcing, *California Management Review*, **39**(2), Winter, 63–79.

Saxenian, A. (1999) *Regional Advantage: Culture and Competition in Silicon Valley and Route 128*, Harvard University Business Press, Boston, MA.

Scarbrough, H. (1999) The Management of Knowledge Workers, in: W. Currie and B. Galliers, eds, *Re-thinking MIS: An Interdisciplinary Perspective*, Oxford University Press, Oxford.

Schein, E. (1994) The Role of the CEO in the Management of Change: The Case of Information Technology, in: T.J. Allen and M.S. Scott-Morton, eds, *Information Technology and the Corporation of the 1990s*, Oxford University Press, Oxford, pp. 325–345.

Schonberger, R. (1982) *Japanese Manufacturing Techniques: Nine Hidden Lessons in Simplicity*, The Free Press, New York.

Schonberger, R. (1986) *World Class Manufacturing*. The Free Press, New York.

Schonberger, R. (1990) *Building a Chain of Customers*, Hutchinson Books, New York.

Scott-Morton, M.S., ed. (1991) *The Corporation of the 1990s*, Oxford University Press, Oxford.

Senge, P. M. (1990a) The Leader's New Work: Building Learning Organisations, *Sloan Management Review*, **32**, 7–23.

Senge, P.M. (1990b) *The Fifth Discipline: The Art and Practice of the Learning Organisation*, Doubleday, New York.

Shank, M.E. (1985) Critical Success Factor Analysis as a Methodology for MIS Planning, *MIS Quarterly*, **9**(2), 121–129.

Shingo, S. (1989) *A Study of the Toyota Production System*, Productivity Press, Cambridge, MA.

Simon, H. (1960) *Administrative Behaviour: A Study of Decision Making Processes in Administrative Organizations*, Macmillan, London.

Skyrme, D. (1996) The Hybrid Manager, in: M. Earl, ed., *Information Management*, Oxford University Press, Oxford.

Sloan, A.P. (1963) *My Years With General Motors*, Doubleday Books, New York.

Smith, M.D., Bailey, J. and Brynjolfsson, E. (1999) Understanding Digital Markets: Review and Assessment, Conference *Understanding the Digital Economy: Data Tools and Research*, US Department of Commerce, Washington, DC, 25–26 May.

Smith, P. (1985) The Stages in a Manager's Job, in: V. Hammond, ed., *Current Research in Management*, Pinter, London.

Smits, S.J., McLean, E.R. and Tanner, J.R. (1993) Managing High-Achieving Information Systems Professionals, *Journal of Management Information Systems*, **9**(4), 103–120.

Sorge, A. and Warner, M. (1986) *Comparative Factory Management: An Anglo-German Comparison of Manufacturing, Management and Manpower*, Gower, Aldershot.

Spar, D. and Bussgang, J.J. (1996) The Net, *Harvard Business Review*, May/June, 125–141.

Spinardi, G., Graham, I. and Williams, R. (1996) EDI and Business Network Redesign: Why the Two Don't Go Together, *New Technology, Work and Employment*, **11**(1), 16–27.

Stata, R. (1989) Organizational Learning—The Key to Management Innovation, *Sloan Management Review*, Spring, 63–74.

Steinfield, C., Kraut, R. and Plummer, A. (1995) The Impact of Electronic Commerce on Buyer–Seller Relationships, *Journal of Computer Mediated Communication*, **1**(3).

Stewart, R. (1961) *The Reality of Management*, Pan Management, London.

Stone, W.A. (1997) Electronic Commerce, *Internal Auditor*, December, 28–34.

Swan, J. *et al.* (1999) Knowledge Management: The Next Fad to Forget People, *7th European Conference on Information Systems*, Copenhagen, 23–25 June, Vol. II, pp. 663–678.

Swatman, P.M.C. and Swatman, P.A. (1992) EDI Systems Integration: A Definition and Literature Survey, *The Information Society*, **8**(3), Summer, 169–205.

Takac, P.F. (1994) Outsourcing: A Key to Controlling Escalating IT Costs?, *International Journal of Technology Management*, **9**(2), 139–155.

Tavakolian, H. (1991) The Organization of IT Functions in the 1990s: A Managerial Perspective, *Journal of Management Development*, **10**(2), 31–37.

Taylor, F.W. (1911) *Principles of Scientific Management*, Harper, New York.

Taylor-Cummings, A. (1997) Bridging the User-IS Gap: Successful Integration Arrangements for Systems Involving Significant Organisational Change, in: L. Willcocks, D. Feeny and G. Islei, eds, *Managing Information Technology as a Strategic Resource*, McGraw-Hill, Maidenhead.

Terdiman, R. (1996) reported in I. Schmerken and K. Goldman, Outsourcing Megadeals: Drive the New IT Economy, *Wall Street & Technology*, **14**(4), April, 36–41.

The Times (1998) Corporate Profile: ICI, *The Times* Newspaper, London, p. 43.

TradeWave Corporation (1996) *Electronic Commerce and the Internet: Building a New Paradigm for Business*—A White Paper.

Trist, E. and Bamforth, K. (1951) Some Social and Psychological Consequences of the Long Wall Method of Coal Getting, *Human Relations*, **4**, 3–38.

Trist, E., Higgins, G., Murrary, H. and Pollack A. (1963) *Organizational Choice*, Tavistock, London.

US Department of Commerce (1999) *The Emerging Digital Economy*, June. http://www.ecommerce.gov.

US Government (1997) *Privacy and the National Information Infrastructure: Principles for Providing and Using Personal Information*, Government Printing Office, Washington.

Vedin, B.A., ed. (1994) *Management of Change and Innovation*, Dartmouth, Aldershot.

Venkatraman, N. (1997) Beyond Outsourcing: Managing the IT Resources as a Value Center, *Sloan Management Review*, Spring, 51–64.

Voss, C.A. and Robinson, S.J. (1987) Applications of JIT Manufacturing Techniques in the United Kingdom, *International Journal of Operations and Production Management*, **7**(4), 46–52.

Watson, G. (1995) *Business Systems Engineering*, Wiley, New York.

Weber, M. (1947) *The Theory of Social and Economic Organisation*, Free Press, Glenview, IL.

Willcocks, L. (1995a) A Survey of Current BPR Practice, in: D. Harvey, ed., *Reengineering: The Critical Success Factors*, Business Intelligence, London.

Willcocks, L. (1995b) False Promise or Delivering the Goods? Recent Findings on the Economics and Impact of Business Process Reengineering, *Proceedings of the Second European Conference in IT Evaluation*, Henley Management College, Henley, United Kingdom, July.

Willcocks, L., ed. (1996) *Investing in Information Systems: Evaluation and Management*, Chapman & Hall, London.

Willcocks, L. and Choi, C.J. (1995) Co-operative Partnership and 'Total' IT Outsourcing: From Contractual Obligation to Strategic Alliance?, *European Management Journal*, **13**(1), 67–78.

Willcocks, L. and Currie, W. (1996) Information Technology and Business Process Reengineering: Emerging Issues in Major Projects, *European Work and Organizational Psychologist*, Special issue, **5**(3), 325–350.

Willcocks, L. and Feeny, D. (1995) IT Outsourcing: The Strategic Implications, *Long Range Planning*, **28**, 59–70.

Willcocks, L. and Harrow, J. (1992) *Rediscovering Public Services Management*, McGraw-Hill, Maidenhead.

Willcocks, L. and Smith, G. (1995) IT-Enabled Business Process Reengineering: Human and Organizational Dimensions, *Journal of Strategic Information Systems*, **4**(3).

Woodwood, J. (1958) *Management and Technology*, HMSO, London.

Wu, B. (1992) *Manufacturing Systems Design and Analysis*, Chapman & Hall, London.

Wu, B., Seddon, J.J.M. and Currie, W.L. (1992) Computer-aided Dynamic Maintenance for a JIT Environment, *International Journal of Production Engineers*, **30**(11), 2683–2696.

Yankee Group (1998) *The Outsourcing Fundamentals Look Good: A Yankee Group Forecast*. http.www.yankeegroup.com/abstract/3q96abs/MSv.6n.22.html.

Yeates, D., ed. (1991) *Project Management for Information Systems*, Pitman, London.

Zipkin, P.H. (1991) Does Manufacturing Need a JIT Revolution?, *Harvard Business Review*, January/February, 40–50.

Zmud, R.W., Boynton, A.C. and Jacobs, G.C. (1987) An Examination of Managerial Strategies for Increasing Information Technology, *Proceedings of the Eighth International Conference on Information Systems*.

Zwass, V. (1998) *Foundations of Information Systems*, Irwin, Boston.

Index